# 797,885 Books

are available to read at

# Forgotten Books

www.ForgottenBooks.com

Forgotten Books' App
Available for mobile, tablet & eReader

ISBN 978-1-333-00953-3
PIBN 10449642

This book is a reproduction of an important historical work. Forgotten Books uses state-of-the-art technology to digitally reconstruct the work, preserving the original format whilst repairing imperfections present in the aged copy. In rare cases, an imperfection in the original, such as a blemish or missing page, may be replicated in our edition. We do, however, repair the vast majority of imperfections successfully; any imperfections that remain are intentionally left to preserve the state of such historical works.

Forgotten Books is a registered trademark of FB &c Ltd.
Copyright © 2017 FB &c Ltd.
FB &c Ltd, Dalton House, 60 Windsor Avenue, London, SW19 2RR.
Company number 08720141. Registered in England and Wales.

For support please visit www.forgottenbooks.com

# 1 MONTH OF FREE READING

## at
## www.ForgottenBooks.com

---

By purchasing this book you are eligible for one month membership to ForgottenBooks.com, giving you unlimited access to our entire collection of over 700,000 titles via our web site and mobile apps.

To claim your free month visit: www.forgottenbooks.com/free449642

\* Offer is valid for 45 days from date of purchase. Terms and conditions apply.

English
Français
Deutsche
Italiano
Español
Português

# www.forgottenbooks.com

**Mythology** Photography **Fiction**
Fishing Christianity **Art** Cooking
Essays Buddhism Freemasonry
Medicine **Biology** Music **Ancient Egypt** Evolution Carpentry Physics
Dance Geology **Mathematics** Fitness
Shakespeare **Folklore** Yoga Marketing
**Confidence** Immortality Biographies
Poetry **Psychology** Witchcraft
Electronics Chemistry History **Law**
Accounting **Philosophy** Anthropology
Alchemy Drama Quantum Mechanics
Atheism Sexual Health **Ancient History**
**Entrepreneurship** Languages Sport
Paleontology Needlework Islam
**Metaphysics** Investment Archaeology
Parenting Statistics Criminology
**Motivational**

# PROCEEDINGS

OF THE

## FIRST ANNUAL MEETING

OF THE

# NATIONAL BOARD OF TRADE, *U.S.*

HELD IN CINCINNATI,

DECEMBER, 1868.

BOSTON:
1869.
J. H. EASTBURN'S PRESS.

Econ 6680.75

*1869, May 29.
Gift of
the Boston Board of Trade.*

---

Entered according to Act of Congress, in the year one thousand, eight hundred and sixty-nine, by HAMILTON A. HILL, in the Clerk's Office of the District Court of Massachusetts.

---

# TABLE OF CONTENTS.

|  | PAGE. |
|---|---|
| INTRODUCTORY NOTE, | v |
| CONSTITUTION OF THE NATIONAL BOARD OF TRADE, | vi |
| BY-LAWS, | xii |
| OFFICERS FOR 1869, | xiii |
| LIST OF MEMBERS, | xv |

PROCEEDINGS OF THE ANNUAL MEETING:

FIRST DAY:
| Opening Exercises, | 1 |
|---|---|
| Mr. Gano's Address, | 1 |
| List of Delegates, | 2 |
| Annual Report of the Executive Council, | 4 |
| Election of Officers, | 9 |
| Mr. Fraley's Address, | 15 |
| Order of Business, | 17 |
| Committee on Admissions, | 19 |

SECOND DAY:
| Admission of New Members, | 21 |
|---|---|
| Debate on Civil Service Reform, | 26 |
| Debate on Cash Sales of Produce, | 29 |
| Committee on American Commerce, | 49 |
| Debate on International Maritime Law, | 49 |
| Debate on Telegraphic Reform, | 62 |
| Committee on Telegraphic Reform, | 67 |

THIRD DAY:
| Admission of New Members, | 69 |
|---|---|
| Debate on Currency and Finance, | 74 |

FOURTH DAY:
| Debate on Currency and Finance, | 124 |
|---|---|
| Committee on Currency and Finance, | 163 |
| Mr. Walbridge's Speech on Railroad Interests, | 164 |

FIFTH DAY:
| Report on American Commerce, | 177 |
|---|---|
| Debate on American Commerce, | 204 |
| Resolutions on Currency and Finance, | 214 |
| Resolution on the Telegraphic Service, | 224 |
| Debate on the Telegraphic Service, | 225 |
| Resolutions on Pacific Railroads, | 238 |
| Debate on Pacific Railroads, | 239 |
| Debate on Direct Importations, | 256 |
| Debate on the Improvement of the Mississippi, | 260 |

## CONTENTS.

PROCEEDINGS OF THE ANNUAL MEETING:
 SIXTH DAY:

|   |   |
|---|---|
| Mr. Monroe's Speech on Internal Improvements, | 281 |
| Resolutions on the Erie Canal, | 304 |
| Resolutions of Thanks, | 307 |
| Debate on the Passes of the Mississippi, | 311 |
| Committee on Virginia Water Communication, | 317 |
| Debate on the Copper Tariff, | 319 |
| Mr. Fraley's Resolutions on Finance, | 325 |
| Resolution on the Alluvial Lands of the Mississippi, | 329 |
| Resolution on Civil Service Reform, | 335 |
| The President's Closing Address, | 336 |
| Adjournment, | 337 |

APPENDIX:

|   |   |
|---|---|
| RECEPTION AT PIKE'S MUSIC HALL, | 341 |
| MUNICIPAL BANQUET, | 347 |
| INDEX, | 363 |

# INTRODUCTORY NOTE.

A WORD of explanation is perhaps due to the constituent bodies, for the delay which has taken place in the appearance of this volume. The size of the book, however, will itself indicate in some measure the labor involved in carefully editing it, and carrying it through the press.

The proceedings of the National Board at Cincinnati were reported by Mr. BENN PITMAN, the well-known phonographer of that city; and, except as relates to some of the points of order discussed from time to time, the aim has been to give them with almost literal exactness.

The important questions which came under consideration, have, since the adjournment, been kept prominently before the country, by the debates in Congress and by the utterances of the press. Upon most of them, no definite legislative action has yet been taken; but it is believed that the views expressed by the National Board, represent fairly the general commercial sentiment of the country in reference to them, and hence there is reason to anticipate that they will in due time be accepted at Washington.

A Committee has been appointed by Congress, to make careful enquiry during the recess, into the causes which have led to the present lamentable decline in the ocean commerce of the country. A correct knowledge of these causes, is indispensable to the discovery and application of the proper means of relief; and it is hoped that the investigation in the present instance will lead to a full understanding of the remedies, and to their prompt use by Congress, so far as they may lie within its scope and sphere.

To the great regret of the business men of the United States, Mr. JENCKES's great measure for promoting Civil Service Reform has not yet become a law. Additional and impressive illustrations have recently been furnished to the nation, of the urgent necessity which exists for the passage of some such Bill as has been presented on this subject, in order to secure the highest degree of efficiency and purity in the administration of public affairs; and there is reason to hope that at the next session a decided step may be taken in this direction.

On pp. 223, 224, will be found the text of the Bill to promote the public credit, which passed both branches of the Fortieth Congress, but which failed to receive the Executive approval. The two sections of which it is comprised, furnish an interesting parallel to the action of the National Board, and of the Boston Commercial Convention, held ten months previously, on the financial questions of the day. The first of these, declaratory of the purpose of the Government to pay in coin or its equivalent, all the obligations of the United States not bearing interest, and all the interest bearing obligations of the United States, except those payable by specific enactment in other currency than gold or silver, has been adopted with a few modifications, making it no less satisfactory, by the Forty-first Congress, and is now a law. The second, relating to the validity of coin contracts, was regarded as having been covered by the decision of the Supreme Court of the United States, in the case of *Bronson* v. *Rodes*, in which it was laid down that " express contracts for the payment of coin dollars can only be satisfied by the payment of coin dollars, and are not debts which may be satisfied by the tender of United States notes." Congress judged that a law upon this subject is now unnecessary; and these contracts which have hitherto been supposed to rest for their security upon the honor of those entering into them, are now understood to be valid in law, and will undoubtedly be enforced by the courts.

The principle involved in the resolution adopted by the National Board, (p. 224,) relating to the returns required from the National Banks, has likewise received the sanction of Congress.

It is gratifying to notice that no action has been taken in Washington upon any of the questions discussed by the merchants of the country convened at Boston, Philadelphia and Cincinnati, decidedly contrary to the conclusions reached at these meetings; although in reference to some of them, there has been a failure thus far to act at all. There is no doubt that members of Congress are disposed to recognize this organization as one of the principal exponents of opinion in the country, on financial and commercial questions; and this being so, it will be the aim of the membership in the future, as it has been in the past, to deliberate carefully and candidly upon all the subjects which come before them, and to make such recommendations as they may decide to make, with a proper sense of their responsibility and with a due regard to all the interests of our widely extended and now happily united republic.

H. A. H.

BOSTON, April 14, 1869.

# CONSTITUTION

OF THE

# NATIONAL BOARD OF TRADE,

ADOPTED AT PHILADELPHIA, JUNE 5, 1868.

### DECLARATION.

In order to promote the efficiency and extend the usefulness of the various Boards of Trade, Chambers of Commerce, and other chartered bodies, organized for general commercial purposes, in the United States; in order to secure unity and harmony of action in reference to commercial usages, customs, and laws; and espec'a'ly, in order to secure the proper consideration of questions pertaining to the financial, commercial and industrial interests of the country at large, this Association on this fifth day of June, 1868, is hereby formed by delegates, now in session in the city of Philadelphia, representing the following named commercial organizations, to wit:

| | |
|---|---|
| Albany Board of Trade, | New York Produce Exchange, |
| Baltimore Board of Trade, | New York Chamber of Commerce, |
| Boston Board of Trade, | Oswego Board of Trade, |
| Boston Corn Exchange, | Peoria Merchants' Exchange, |
| Buffalo Board of Trade, | Philadelphia Board of Trade, |
| Charleston Board of Trade, | Philadelphia Commercial Exchange, |
| Chicago Board of Trade, | Pittsburgh Board of Trade, |
| Cincinnati Chamber of Commerce, | Portland Board of Trade, |
| Cleveland Board of Trade, | Providence Board of Trade, |
| Denver Board of Trade, | Richmond Chamber of Commerce, |
| Detroit Board of Trade, | St. Louis Board of Trade, |
| Dubuque Produce Exchange, | St. Louis Union Merchants' Exch., |
| Louisville Board of Trade, | St. Paul Chamber of Commerce, |
| Milwaukie Chamber of Commerce, | Toledo Board of Trade, |
| Newark Board of Trade, | Troy Board of Trade. |
| New Orleans Chamber of Com., | Wilmington, (Del.) Board of Trade, |

And the following Constitution is adopted:

### ARTICLE I.

SECTION 1. This Association shall be designated the NATIONAL BOARD OF TRADE.

### ARTICLE II.

SECTION. 1. Every local Board of Trade, Chamber of Commerce, or other body organized for general commercial, and not for special or private purposes, and duly chartered under State or National laws, shall be entitled to membership in this Association, on the approval of two-thirds of the bodies represented at any meeting of the Association, and shall be accorded the following representation: Each such association having fifty members who have the right to vote therein, shall be entitled to one delegate; having one hundred members, two delegates; having three hundred members, three delegates; having five hundred members, four delegates; and for each additional five hundred members, one additional delegate.

SEC. 2. Delegates shall be selected by the local organizations in such manner and for such term of not less than one year, as each may see fit. At each meeting of the Board they shall present credentials under seal from the Secretaries of their respective constituencies; these credentials shall certify the number of members authorized to vote then connected with the body which is claiming representation, and which may present or may have a copy of its charter on file in this Board.

### ARTICLE III.

SECTION 1. Each delegate shall be entitled to one vote in person, but no voting by proxy shall be allowed. All votes, except for election of officers, shall be *viva voce*. Any delegate may demand a division of the house, and on the demand of three or more delegates, a call of the yeas and nays shall be had, the result of the same to be duly recorded.

### ARTICLE IV.

SECTION 1. The administration of the affairs of this Board shall be vested in a President and fourteen Vice-Presidents, who shall be elected at the annual meeting by ballot on a majority of all the votes cast, and who shall serve until their successors are chosen.

Their election shall be the first business in order. They shall be constituted and known as an Executive Council, and five of their number shall be a quorum for the transaction of business. In the absence or disability of the President, a Vice-President, to be designated by his associates, shall serve.

SEC. 2. It shall be the duty of the Executive Council immediately after their election to select a Secretary and a Treasurer, (neither of whom shall be of their own number,) who shall hold office for such time, and who shall receive such compensation as the Council may determine.

SEC. 3. The offices of the Secretary and the Treasurer may be located at such places as the Council shall determine.

SEC. 4. Special meetings of the Council shall be held on the call of seven members thereof, at such place as they may designate, on twenty days' notice to be given by the Secretary.

SEC. 5. In case of the removal, resignation, or death of any member of the Council, his place for the unexpired term, shall be promptly filled by the constituent association of which he was a member.

ARTICLE V.

SECTION 1. It shall be the duty of the Executive Council:
1st. To provide for full and accurate records of the proceedings of the Board and of its own meetings.
2nd. To submit to each annual meeting a report of the doings of the Board and of its own official acts, as well as a statement of what new or unfinished business may require attention.
3rd. To make full statement concerning the finances of the Board to the annual meetings, and to other meetings, when called on to do so.
4th. To apportion to each constituent body, its assessment for the expenses of the Board, as provided elsewhere.
5th. To make such recommendations as it may deem to be necessary for the welfare and to promote the objects of the Board.

SEC. 2. The Secretary shall conduct the official correspondence, and shall make and have charge of the records of the Board and of the Executive Council.

SEC. 3. The Treasurer shall give such security as the Executive Council may require, receive and account for all moneys belonging to the Board, and collect assessments and fines, but he shall pay out money and dispose of the property of the Board only on a warrant of the Secretary, countersigned by the President.

## ARTICLE VI.

SECTION 1. A meeting of the National Board of Trade shall be held on the first Wednesday in December of each year, at such place as shall have been determined upon at a previous meeting, on the majority vote of all the constituent bodies represented.

SEC. 2. Special meetings may be held on the call of eight members of the Executive Council, at such place as they may designate.

SEC. 3. The attendance of forty delegates shall constitute a quorum.

SEC. 4. Notice of the annual or other meetings shall be served by the Secretary on each constituent body at least thirty days before the time appointed for assembling. The notice shall state the objects of the meeting, and the questions to be considered.

SEC. 5. A meeting of the Executive Council shall be held on the day preceding the day of any meeting of the Board and at such other times as may be provided in its By-Laws.

## ARTICLE VII.

SECTION 1. The expenses of the Board shall be provided for by an assessment to be made by the Executive Council on each constituent body, according to the ratio of its officially reported membership.

## ARTICLE VIII.

SECTION 1. Questions or resolutions, except those which involve points of order, or refer to matters of courtesy, can be submitted only by the constituent bodies of the Board; and when any constituent body shall desire to present a subject for the consideration of the Board, it shall do so in a written paper to be placed in the hands of the Secretary at least forty days previous to the annual or special meeting at which it is to be considered : *Provided, however,* That any subject not thus submitted may be considered and acted upon by a vote of two-thirds of the delegates present.

### ARTICLE IX.

SECTION 1. Any constituent body charged with a violation of the laws of this Board may, after formal complaint thereof in writing, on a vote of two-thirds of all the delegates of the other bodies represented herein, be expelled; but it shall not be exempted from the payment of assessments levied for the year current.

SEC. 2. Any constituent body may withdraw from membership in the Board on submitting a formal request to that effect at an annual meeting, and on full payment of all dues.

### ARTICLE X.

SECTION 1. This Constitution may be amended at an annual meeting, on a vote of two-thirds of the delegates present; notice of the proposed amendment having been first submitted to the Secretary by a constituent body, at least forty days previous to the meeting at which the same is to be considered, and transmitted by the Secretary in circular copies to each constituent body at least thirty days before said meeting.

### ARTICLE XI.

SECTION 1. This meeting of delegates, called in accordance with the plan of preliminary organization adopted by the Commercial Convention held in Boston on the fifth day of February last, shall be regarded as the first meeting of the National Board of Trade, and is hereby empowered to choose officers, to serve until their successors shall be elected, and to act upon all papers and resolutions laid before it, the same to be considered as having been submitted in the form and manner required by this Constitution.

# BY-LAWS.

No. 1. A vote of two-thirds of the delegates present shall be necessary to carry the approval of the Board upon any proposition which may appear, or which may be placed upon the official programme.

No. 2. The annual assessment laid by the Executive Council shall be considered as due at the beginning of the year; and no constituent body shall be represented at any meeting of the Board, unless its assessment then due shall have been paid.

No. 3. The Executive Council shall recommend at each annual meeting the place at which it judges it to be expedient that the next annual meeting shall be held.

# OFFICERS FOR 1869.

### PRESIDENT.

FREDERICK FRALEY, *Philadelphia*.

### VICE-PRESIDENTS.

| | |
|---|---|
| ROBERT R. KIRKLAND, | *Baltimore.* |
| JAMES C. CONVERSE, | *Boston.* |
| GEORGE S. HAZARD, | *Buffalo.* |
| WILLIAM L. TRENHOLM, | *Charleston.* |
| WILEY M. EGAN, | *Chicago.* |
| JOHN A. GANO, | *Cincinnati.* |
| GEORGE F. BAGLEY, | *Detroit.* |
| J. J. PORTER, | *Louisville.* |
| WILLIAM M. BRIGHAM, | *Milwaukie.* |
| GEORGE A. FOSDICK, | *New Orleans* |
| GEORGE H. THURSTON, | *Pittsburgh.* |
| JOHN B. BROWN, | *Portland.* |
| JAMES R. BRANCH, | *Richmond.* |
| E. O. STANARD, | *St. Louis.* |

### SECRETARY and TREASURER.

HAMILTON A. HILL, *Boston*.

# MEMBERS OF THE NATIONAL BOARD OF TRADE.

| NAMES. | Date of Organization. | Date of Incorporation. | Reported Membership, January, 1869. | President, 1869. | Secretary, 1869. |
|---|---|---|---|---|---|
| Albany Board of Trade | 1847 | 1864 | 307 | ...... | W. Lacy. |
| Baltimore Board of Trade | 1849 | 1852 | 200 | A. Schumacher | G. U. Porter. |
| Baltimore Corn and Flour Exchange | 1855 | 1855 | 512 | P. P. Pendleton | W. F. Wheatley. |
| Boston Board of Trade | 1854 | 1854 | 680 | A. H. Rice | H. A. Hill. |
| Boston Corn Exchange | 1855 | 1868 | 270 | E. H. Sampson | E. Kemble. |
| Buffalo Board of Trade | 1844 | 1857 | 400 | S. S. Guthrie | W. Thurstone. |
| Cairo Chamber of Commerce | 1865 | 1865 | 70 | G. D. Williamson | L. Mathews. |
| Charleston Board of Trade | 1866 | 1866 | 160 | W. L. Trenholm | H. Baer. |
| Chicago Board of Trade | 1848 | 1859 | 1207 | J. M. Richards | C. Randolph. |
| Cincinnati Chamber of Commerce | 1839 | 1850 | 1292 | J. A. Gano | G. McLaughlin. |
| Cleveland Board of Trade | 1847 | 1866 | 212 | G. W. Gardner | J. C. Sage. |
| Denver Board of Trade | 1867 | .. | 80 | W. M. Clayton | R. W. Woodbury. |
| Detroit Board of Trade | 1856 | 1863 | 244 | C. A. Sheldon | R. Haddock. |
| Dubuque Board of Trade | 1868 | 1868 | 100 | W. Westphal | T. L. Bordman. |
| Galveston Chamber of Commerce | 1865 | 1866 | 50 | T. H. McMahan | S. A. Edgerley. |
| Louisville Board of Trade | 1862 | 1862 | 535 | J. J. Porter | C. H. Clarke. |
| Memphis Chamber of Commerce | 1860 | 1860 | 300 | W. H. Cherry | S. Ridgely. |
| Milwaukie Chamber of Commerce | 1858 | 1868 | 344 | E. Sanderson | W. J. Langson. |
| Newark Board of Trade | 1868 | 1869 | 216 | W. H. McClave | G. N. Abeel. |
| New Orleans Chamber of Commerce | 1834 | 1834 | 150 | A. Moulton | A. C. Waugh. |
| New York Chamber of Commerce | 1768 | 1770 | 845 | W. E. Dodge | G. Wilson. |
| New York Produce Exchange | 1843 | 1862 | 1935 | E. Hincken | R. S. Holt. |
| Norfolk Board of Trade | 1858 | 1868 | 100 | W. Lamb | J. H. Hendren. |
| Oswego Board of Trade | 1849 | 1868 | 125 | C. Ames | H. C. Stillman. |
| Peoria Merchants Exchange | .. | 1864 | .. | ...... | D. McKinney. |
| Philadelphia Board of Trade | 1833 | 1838 | 1433 | J. Welsh | A. J. Perkins. |
| Philadelphia Commercial Exchange | 1853 | 1863 | 500 | J. H. Michener | G. R. Tisdale. |
| Pittsburgh Board of Trade | 1854 | 1854 | 300 | G. H. Thurston | T. Wickersham, Pro tem. |
| Portland Board of Trade | 1853 | 1854 | 270 | J. H. Perley | M. N. Rich. |
| Providence Board of Trade | 1868 | 1868 | 340 | A. D. Smith | F. P. Little. |
| Richmond Chamber of Commerce | 1867 | 1868 | 302 | D. J. Burr | P. G. Coghlan. |
| St. Louis Board of Trade | 1866 | 1866 | 413 | L. R. Shryock | W. B. Baker. |
| St. Louis Union Merchants Exchange | 1862 | 1863 | 1250 | G. P. Plant | G. H. Morgan. |
| St. Paul Chamber of Commerce | 1867 | 1867 | 122 | J. C. Burbank | J. D. Ludden. |
| Toledo Board of Trade | 1849 | 1867 | 300 | F. J. King | C. Colton. |
| Troy Board of Trade | 1863 | 1868 | 401 | P. E. Toles | J. F. Calder. |
| Wilmington Board of Trade | 1867 | 1869 | 176 | E. Betts | G. W. Stone. |

NOTE.—There may be a few mistakes in the above statement; as the Secretary has found it difficult to obtain from the constituent bodies, the information necessary to make it complete and absolutely correct. It is believed to be the first attempt to give a list of the commercial bodies of the United States, with their officers and membership; the latter, according to the above, amounts, in the total, to 16,140.

# NATIONAL BOARD OF TRADE.

## FIRST DAY.

WEDNESDAY, DECEMBER 2, 1868.

THE National Board of Trade assembled in the Council Chamber in the city of Cincinnati, to hold its first Annual Meeting, on Wednesday, the second of December, 1868.

The chair was taken at half-past eleven o'clock, by Mr. FREDERICK FRALEY, the President of the Board, who called the meeting to order, and announced that a quorum was present.

Mr. GANO: From my official position, the agreeable duty devolves upon me of tendering to the National Board of Trade, the salutations of the Cincinnati Chamber of Commerce, and of expressing the gratification which its members experience, in common with our citizens generally, in having our city honored by its selection as the place for the first regular session of the Board.

Allow me, gentlemen, to extend to your organization, our best wishes for a successful meeting, and to yourselves, individually, a cordial welcome.

We hope to have you feel at home among us, and that you will not hesitate to ask at the hands of our Chamber of Commerce, whatever may contribute to the furtherance of your important work, or to the promotion of your personal comfort and welfare.

Members of our body will place themselves at your disposal during your hours of intermission, and we shall all hope, although your sojourn with us is appointed for an inclement season of the year, that nevertheless you may not leave us with unfavorable impressions as to our interest in your work, or with feelings of disappointment as to the merits and attractions of this, practically, the first-born city of the Ordinance of 1787, constituting the Northwest Territory.

Prayer was then offered by the Rev. W. A. SNIVELY, of Christ Church, Cincinnati.

The Secretary, Mr. HAMILTON A. HILL, read from the credentials which had been handed in, the names of the delegates in attendance, as follows:

#### Board of Trade, Albany.
Henry T. Buell, Samuel Wilbor, Jr.

#### Board of Trade, Baltimore.
Robert R. Kirkland, Francis B. Loney.

#### Board of Trade, Boston.
Geo. O. Carpenter, Charles G. Nazro,
Jas. C. Converse, Joseph S. Ropes.

#### Corn Exchange, Boston.
Avery Plumer, Eugene H. Sampson.

#### Board of Trade, Buffalo.
Solomon S. Guthrie, George S. Hazard,
Edward B. Smith.

#### Board of Trade, Charleston.
Henry Cobia, W. L. Trenholm,

#### Board of Trade, Chicago.
Wiley M. Egan, Ira Y. Munn,
George M. How, Charles Randolph,
V. A. Turpin.

#### Chamber of Commerce, Cincinnati.
Thomas R. Biggs, John A. Gano,
George F. Davis, L. R. Hull,
N. G. Nettleton.

#### Board of Trade, Cleveland.
J. C. Sage, Thomas Walton.

#### Board of Trade, Detroit.
George F. Bagley, Thomas McGraw.

#### Board of Trade, Louisville.
A. O. Brannin, J. J. Porter,
Charles Cobb, F. S. J. Ronald.

#### Chamber of Commerce, Milwaukie.
Wm. M. Brigham, Edward D. Holton,
Charles F. Ilsley.

# LIST OF DELEGATES.

**Board of Trade, Newark.**
Thomas W. Dawson, George Peters.

**Produce Exchange, New York.**
John H. Boynton, William H. Harris,
Edward Hincken.

**Chamber of Commerce, New York.**
William E. Dodge, Jas. S. T. Stranahan,
Samuel B. Ruggles, Hiram Walbridge.

**Board of Trade, Oswego.**
A. P. Grant.

**Board of Trade, Philadelphia.**
George N. Allen, James C. Hand,
Frederick Fraley, John P. Wetherill,
Henry Winsor.

**Commercial Exchange, Philadelphia.**
George L. Buzby, S. E. Malone,
C. J. Hoffman, John H. Michener.

**Board of Trade, Pittsburgh.**
Felix R. Brunot, George H. Thurston.

**Board of Trade, Portland.**
John B. Brown, Benjamin T. Manson.

**Chamber of Commerce, Richmond.**
James R. Branch, Charles S. Carrington,
Lewis D. Crenshaw.

**Board of Trade, St. Louis.**
Clinton B. Fisk, Adolphus Meier,
L. R. Shryock.

**Union Merchants Exchange, St. Louis.**
Thomas Allen, E. O. Stanard,
A. Kreikhaus, W. Taussig.

**Chamber of Commerce, St. Paul.**
E. F. Drake, James W. Taylor.

**Board of Trade, Toledo.**
George W. Davis, F. J. King.

**Board of Trade, Wilmington.**
James Bradford, Howard M. Jenkins.

The Secretary read the Report of the Executive Council :

The Constitution of the National Board of Trade makes it the duty of the Executive Council to submit at each annual meeting of the Board, a report of what has been done during the year, and of what unfinished business still requires attention.

It is almost six months to a day since the representatives of thirty-two Boards of Trade and other commercial bodies in the United States, assembled in the city of Philadelphia for the purpose of organizing this National Board. What was then done, we all remember. Articles of association, after careful consideration and full discussion, were adopted; officers were chosen, and the machinery of the Board was set in motion. The result of that meeting has been in the main fully approved by the respective bodies in whose behalf the action was taken, and has been warmly commended by the public at large, so far as the proceedings have been made known and have been understood. It would be strange, however, if the work performed by us, somewhat in haste, and without any precedent in our own country for our guidance, had proved to be altogether complete and satisfactory. Changes in the Constitution of the Board have already been notified by some of the membership, to be acted upon at the present meeting; and others, doubtless, will be proposed from year to year. These changes, so far, relate only to details, and do not contemplate any essential modification of the general plan upon which the association is based; nor is there any evidence that this plan, in its outline and prominent features, can be improved upon. Our Constitution, as it stands, is calculated to secure for the Board broad nationality; carefully selected representation; full and fair discussions, and impartial action. It guards against everything special, sectional or political. It aims to bring thoughtful and practical men together once a year, or oftener if necessary, to deliberate as business men, and as American business men, upon the financial and industrial capabilities and exigencies of the nation. These leading characteristics of our organization, no one, we may be sure, will desire to change.

The Philadelphia meeting was convened, as has been said, for the particular purpose of bringing the Board into existence, and it did not afford opportunity for the examination of many questions of a general commercial character. Positive action, however, was had in favor of a few important measures, (1) the reduction of the tax on whiskey to fifty cents a gallon, (2) direct importations to inland cities, (3) the cental measurement of all the products of the soil, (4) the free and unobstructed navigation, through its entire length, of the Mississippi river. Memorials were duly addressed to Congress on each of these subjects; but no legislation followed, except in reference to the tax on whiskey, which was reduced to the point indicated by the judgment of this Board. The encouragement of direct importations to the interior appears on the official programme of our present proceedings, at the instance of the St. Louis Board of Trade; also, the free navigation of the Mississippi, by the notification of the same body. The cental measurement of grain does not appear upon our programme; and it is for the Board to determine whether any, and what further, action is desirable. A bill (756) introduced by the Hon. JOHN V. L. PRUYN, is now pending in the House of Representatives, covering, substantially, the recommendations of the Boston Convention, which were confirmed at Philadelphia, on this subject. The proposition of the Cincinnati Chamber of Commerce, for a general system of cental measurement, will come up in the same connection.

Other questions came up at the Philadelphia meeting, which were referred to the Executive Council; these were:

1st. *The resumption of specie payments.* The report of the Business Committee recommended the Council to bring this question in such a way before the constituent bodies, that our representatives at Washington will be given to understand "that the country wants a currency based on something that is substantial." There was not time before the adjournment of Congress, to fully carry out this suggestion; but, as is known, no financial legislation was consummated at the late session, and we may now give such expression of opinion as we may judge to be expedient, in this regard, for the consideration of members at the approaching session. In view of the importance of this subject, it will, perhaps, be presented by the Council in a special report.

2d. *The Shipping Interest.* The Business Committee expressed the desire, also, that the Council would place this before Congress in such a manner that it might know that "we want the concession of every privilege necessary to enable our friends on the seaboard, to go again into the building of ships." The magnitude of this question, and the importance of a full knowledge of all the statistics relating to it, have seemed to render it desirable that it should be presented in a special paper.

3d. *The improvement of all the outlets of the valley of the Mississippi.* This will come up for the consideration of the Board at this meeting, in connection with the resolutions proposed by the Louisville Board of Trade, on the best means of uniting the Mississippi valley with the Atlantic seaboard.

4th. *The Pacific Railroad, Kansas Branch.* This, also, will be considered at the present time, at the instance of the St. Louis Board of Trade, and will probably lead to definite action in favor of a well defined and truly national Pacific railroad system, comprehending the wants of the entire country, and designed to secure for the United States the full advantages of its position for controlling the trade of the Pacific Ocean.

5th. *The regulation of the Civil Service of the United States.* The Hon. Mr. JENCKES's bill on this measure, and his able speech in its advocacy, have been widely circulated through the country, and have received the commendations of the press more promptly, more generally, and more unqualifiedly than is often accorded to a proposition for a wide-sweeping reform. The details of the bill are probably understood by the delegates. They contemplate competitive examination for positions of public trust and duty; appointments in view of personal character and capability, and no removals from office simply for political reasons. They have received the approval of some of the constituent bodies, and it is recommended that the Board give its sanction and support to them, as being well adapted to secure efficiency in the various departments of our National government, especially those having in charge the administration of the finances and the collection of the revenue.

6th. *The Incorporation of the National Board of Trade.* The Council was instructed to make application to Congress for a charter for the Board, and a memorial was sent to Washington accordingly. Congress took no action on the subject, and it is recommended that the Executive Council of the coming year be directed to renew the request.

At its first meeting, the Executive Council elected Mr. HAMILTON A. HILL, Secretary and Treasurer, and located the offices of the Board in the city of Boston.

This is the third occasion during the present year, when the representatives of the commercial associations have been convened to take counsel together in reference to the great material concerns of the nation; and two other commercial conventions have been held, more restricted in the attendance upon them, but of considerable local importance. We meet for the first time, however, as a purely deliberative body, and not as a popular assembly. In commenting upon the meeting at Portland last summer, the "Commercial Bulletin" of Boston, used this language:

"We thus have another illustration of the entire capability of our business men to discuss, and to decide upon, great questions of commercial policy; indeed, we can not recall a single resolution passed at the conventions of merchants, which, within three years past, have been held at Detroit, Boston, Philadelphia and Portland, respectively, which, so far as subsequent events have had opportunity to show, has not been eminently sound, wise and worthy of adoption on the part of Congress."

From the regular meetings of this Board, certainly, results no less satisfactory may be anticipated. We have no questions of organization, or methods of procedure, to divide and perplex our attention. We are, it is hoped, as individuals, in no undue haste to depart from this city, until the responsible work which has been delegated to us here, has been carefully and faithfully performed. And we are prepared, doubtless, to consider every question in its broadest relations, and in its bearings upon the public good. The merchants, the manufacturers, and the active business men of the nation, are our constituency; and the local commercial bodies vest the authority and influence which they possess as the exponents of commercial opinion, in our organization. Let us, therefore, with patience, with impartiality, and with patriotism, devote ourselves to the duties before us, in the interest of every section of our common country, and of every branch of its varied industry.

Cincinnati, December 2, 1868.

The Secretary also presented his report as Treasurer, for the year ending December 1, 1868, showing the receipts of the Board, since the sixth of June, to have been $4,288.00; and the expenditures for the same period, $3,536.28; and leaving a balance in the Treasury of $751.72. The account had been audited and certified to as correct, by three members of the Executive Council.

A DELEGATE: Would it be in order to move to accept the reports at this time? If so, I would make that motion.

The PRESIDENT: Our Constitution provides that the first business in order shall be the election of officers. I do not understand that the reading of reports is business; voting upon them would be business. If a motion were made, a vote would be necessary, and to take a vote at this time, would be in violation of the Constitution.

Mr. HINCKEN: There is a proposition to amend the Constitution, which would affect the officers we are about to vote for; would it not be well to suspend part of the election till we know the sense of the meeting upon that point?

The PRESIDENT: We have no power to do anything until we are regularly organized. We have a Constitution which must remain in force until it is amended in the regular way.

Mr. KIRKLAND: As there are gentlemen here who have submitted their credentials to this body, it occurs to me that they should have the right to vote on this question, and on others brought before us; I would ask if it is in order to apply for membership.

The PRESIDENT: No, sir; the admission of new members is not now in order. It requires the concurrence of two-thirds of the existing members of the body to admit them. I think it advisable to steer the ship in strict accordance with the rules.

A DELEGATE: I move that the rules be suspended, and that the gentlemen who have presented their credentials, be received by an unanimous vote.

The PRESIDENT: We have not the power to do that until we are regularly organized. As the Executive Council goes out of office, it seemed proper that their annual report should first be submitted. The business now in order, is the election of officers. Afterwards, the admission of new members, in the way prescribed by the Constitution, can be carried out. I must, therefore, insist upon it, unless my decision be overruled by an appeal, that the only order of business at the present time, is to proceed to the election of officers. After that has been accomplished, all the business of the Board will be subject to the action of the body, in conformity with the rules and regulations of the House of Representatives of the Congress of the United States, in so far as they may apply; and by adhering to those principles, I think we shall be able to get along and transact our business in order, taking up every question as it arises, and giving to it its proper attention. I will appoint Mr. NAZRO, of Boston, and Mr. RANDOLPH, of Chicago, to be the tellers of the election. Pending the election, I will vacate the Chair, and request Mr. GANO to preside and receive the report of the tellers.

Mr. GANO then took the chair.

Mr. ROPES: I understand the first section of Article 2, not as stating that any new body coming in with proper credentials shall be admitted, but that it shall be entitled to membership. It has the same right to membership as those bodies which appeared at the last meeting. Every such body, presenting proper credentials, is *ipso facto* a member of this body, without any vote whatever, on the approval of two-thirds of the members of the Board. This two-thirds consent, I submit, is not an act of business, but an act of organization, or recognition of membership. I would also submit, that it is very difficult for us to select officers without any general understanding among so many; and it was my intention to move the appointment of a Committee of Nomination, consisting of one from each body, to present a list of officers for the approval of the Board.

The CHAIRMAN : My judgment is that every other body than those which participated in the formation of this Constitution must be admitted by a vote of two-thirds of the members; and further, that the proper time for such admission, is after the election of officers. Personally, I should desire that every local board should participate in this election, but I feel myself controlled by what I believe to be the plain provisions of the Constitution in this matter. I will, of course, receive and entertain any appeal from that decision with great respect, and throw myself entirely upon the judgment of this body as to the result. I think we should be guided by the Constitution, and proceed strictly in the line of our duty.

The suggestion of Mr. ROPES seems to bear upon its face a great deal of good, practical sense. Yet it seems to me that the admission of new members to this Board is a matter of business, and should therefore come after the election of officers.

Mr. KIRKLAND : I would appeal from the decision of the Chair.

The CHAIRMAN : The gentleman from Baltimore has appealed from the decision of the Chair; the question then will be, shall the decision of the Chair stand as the opinion of the Board?

On being submitted to vote, the Chair was sustained.

Mr. RANDOLPH : I now move that we proceed to the election of a President; and I beg to nominate the Hon. FREDERICK FRALEY, of Philadelphia.

The motion being seconded and put to vote, it was carried unanimously.

A delegate moved that Mr. NAZRO be requested to cast a ballot as the unanimous vote of the Board for Mr. FRALEY, as President.

The CHAIRMAN: It was decided in Philadelphia that that should not be done.

Mr. RANDOLPH: I move that we proceed with the ballot.

Mr. THURSTON: I move that the nomination be closed.

Mr. SHRYOCK: I desire that the nomination should not be closed till other names have been put in nomination. I think the Western people are entitled occasionally to representation in this body, and I should like to put in nomination, a gentleman from the West.

Mr. THURSTON: I withdraw the motion.

Mr. SHRYOCK: I desire to put in nomination Mr. JOHN A. GANO, of the Cincinnati Chamber.

The CHAIRMAN: I beg to say to the gentleman, that I consider it my duty to decline. Personally I prefer the nomination of Mr. FRALEY, and shall give my influence for his election.

Mr. ROPES: While the ballots for President are being counted, I beg to move that a Committee be appointed, consisting of one person from each body in this Association, that the choice of such person be made by the Association itself, and that this Committee nominate a list of Vice-Presidents for the Board to vote upon.

Mr. HOFFMAN: I move to amend that each State present its own candidate; that the delegates from each State be at liberty to place in nomination, one from each of the fourteen or more States represented.

Mr. ROPES: I suggest that one person be appointed by each body represented here, to constitute a Nominating Committee.

The CHAIRMAN: Mr. HOFFMAN proposes as an amendment to Mr. ROPES's motion, that each State, through the respective delegations, present a name to be balloted for as Vice-President.

The delegates having deposited their ballots, Mr. NAZRO announced the whole number of votes cast for President, to be 65; necessary to a choice, 33; Mr. FRALEY received 59 votes, and Mr. GANO 6.

The result was received with cheers.

The CHAIRMAN: Mr. FRALEY, gentlemen, is your President for the coming year.

The question is now before us on the motion as amended.

On a vote being taken, it was declared carried.

Mr. HOFFMAN: I suggest that we now proceed to the nomination of Vice-Presidents; also, that when the delegates are prepared to cast their ballots, the Secretary call the roll as each delegate deposits his ballot.

On motion, a recess of ten minutes was taken for consultation.

The time having expired, the delegates resumed their seats.

The Secretary proceeded to call the States, when the following names were put in nomination:

| | | |
|---|---|---|
| New York, | GEO. S. HAZARD, | Buffalo. |
| Maryland, | ROBT. R. KIRKLAND, | Baltimore. |
| Massachusetts, | JAS. C. CONVERSE, | Boston. |
| South Carolina, | W. L. TRENHOLM, | Charleston. |
| Illinois, | W. M. EGAN, | Chicago. |
| Ohio, | JOHN A. GANO, | Cincinnati. |
| Michigan, | GEO. F. BAGLEY, | Detroit. |
| Kentucky, | J. J. PORTER, | Louisville. |
| Wisconsin, | W. M. BRIGHAM, | Milwaukie. |
| New Jersey, | JOSEPH P. BRADLEY, | Newark. |
| Pennsylvania, | GEO. H. THURSTON, | Pittsburgh. |
| Maine, | JOHN B. BROWN, | Portland. |
| Virginia, | JAMES R. BRANCH, | Richmond. |
| Missouri, | E. O. STANARD, | St. Louis. |
| Minnesota and Iowa, | E. F. DRAKE, | St. Paul. |
| Delaware, | JOSHUA T. HEALD, | Wilmington. |

MR. DAVIS, of Toledo : I would ask if all these gentlemen proposed for Vice-Presidents were members of the old Board, or does the list include names which have not as yet, been regularly admitted?

A DELEGATE: Is it necessary that candidates for Vice-President must be already admitted as delegates?

The CHAIRMAN : It is necessary.

The name of Mr. BRADLEY, for New Jersey, was withdrawn, and Mr. THOS. W. DAWSON'S was substituted in its place. The name of Mr. HEALD, of Delaware, was withdrawn, and Mr. JAMES BRADFORD'S was substituted.

Mr. ALLEN, of St. Louis: We have no one from the South. New Orleans was represented in the Philadelphia Convention. That great section of country is entirely unrepresented here. Would it be in order, Mr. Chairman, to make nominations from that section of the country?

The CHAIRMAN: The action of the Convention must depend on the course taken on the motion of Mr. HOFFMAN. Such nominations are not now in order.

Mr. ALLEN: Would it be in order to move that nominations be made from that section of the country? I ask that I have unanimous consent to nominate Mr. GEO. A. FOSDICK.

Mr. BAGLEY: Is he a delegate to this meeting?

The CHAIRMAN: He is a delegate for the remainder of the year.

The motion being seconded and submitted to vote, it was agreed to.

Mr. SHRYOCK: Would it be in order to put in nomination a gentleman from Mobile, Mr. GEO. M. STEWART?

The CHAIRMAN: Mobile is not in the organization.

The Board proceeded to ballot for Vice-Presidents.

The Secretary read the following:

"OFFICE OF THE PACIFIC AND ATLANTIC TELEGRAPH COMPANY OF THE U. S.,
Pittsburgh, November 30, 1868.

Hon. FREDERICK FRALEY,
    *President of the National Board of Trade,*

    Dear Sir,—

Permit me to tender, through you, to the officers and delegates of the National Board of Trade, the free use of the lines of the Pacific and Atlantic Telegraph Company of the U. S., during its sessions in Cincinnati. I am also authorized by J. B. STEARNS, Esq., President of the Franklin Telegraph Line, whose lines connect with those of the Pacific and Atlantic Telegraph Company, to include the use of the lines of that Company, in this tender of telegraphic facilities.

The presentation of the badge of membership, will frank all messages to points reached by our lines.

Officers of the Company will be found at No. 60 West Third Street, at the Burnet House, Spencer House, Walnut Street House, and Merchant's Exchange.

        Most respectfully,
            GEO. H. THURSTON,
  *President of the Pacific and Atlantic Telegraph Company of the U. S.*"

Mr. SHRYOCK: I move that the thanks of the Board be tendered to the Company for this courtesy.

Unanimously carried.

The CHAIRMAN: I will take occasion now to say that our citizens, members of the Chamber of Commerce and the City Council have provided a modest entertainment, or rather a series of them. The programme is presented in some very formidable looking envelopes. I hope none will suppose there are national bonds in them; but I trust that our municipal hospitalities will be appreciated as highly as the bonds would be.

This evening there will be a reception, in the way of a promenade concert, at Pike's Music Hall. It is expected that all will be ready to assemble by eight o'clock, when the Committees appointed to attend the various delegates, will escort them there. If any one should unfortunately be overlooked, his card will entitle him to admission; but we hope to see all there promptly at the hour named.

I would also state that S. S. L'HOMMEDIEU, Esq., President of the Hamilton and Dayton Railroad, has tendered the delegates a ride to Toledo and back, and will be happy to extend the offer to all delegates who can accept.

It was moved that the thanks of the Association be tendered to S. S. L'HOMMEDIEU, Esq.; seconded, and unanimously carried.

Mr. NAZRO: I have to announce as the result of the ballot, that the whole number of votes cast is 66; necessary to a choice, 34;

| | | | | | |
|---|---|---|---|---|---|
| Mr. CONVERSE, | has | 63 | Mr. FOSDICK, | has | 48 |
| " STANARD, | " | 62 | " TRENHOLM, | " | 48 |
| " BRIGHAM, | " | 60 | " THURSTON, | " | 47 |
| " EGAN, | " | 60 | " DRAKE, | " | 46 |
| " GANO, | " | 59 | " THOMAS, | " | 17 |
| " HAZARD, | " | 58 | " BRADFORD, | " | 10 |
| " BRANCH, | " | 55 | " BOYNTON, | " | 2 |
| " PORTER, | " | 55 | " SCHUMACHER, | " | 1 |
| " BROWN, | " | 55 | " CARPENTER, | " | 1 |
| " BAGLEY, | " | 53 | " ARMSTRONG, | " | 1 |
| " KIRKLAND, | " | 49 | " E. F. TRAIT, | " | 1 |

The Constitution requires that the Vice-Presidents shall be elected on a majority of all the votes, fifteen gentlemen have a majority of all the votes.

Mr. HOFFMAN: Would not the fourteen highest have the majority of all the votes, and would they not be duly elected?

A DELEGATE: The name of E. F. TRAIT is evidently intended for Mr. DRAKE.

Mr. RANDOLPH: Then it would be in the nature of a tie.

Mr. HOFFMAN: You would not vote for the two having the tie; they cannot both be elected.

The CHAIRMAN: The fourteen having received the greater number of votes will be declared elected.

Mr. TAYLOR: Under the circumstances, should we not proceed to another election?

The CHAIRMAN: It is the decision of the Chair that the fourteen names, read by Mr. NAZRO as having the highest numbers, have been elected Vice-Presidents of this Association. We will take no further action unless there is an appeal.

Mr. RANDOLPH: It is not a fair and honest expression of this Board of Trade in regard to the two persons who have so near, if not a tie vote; I think we ought to make the trial over again.

Mr. DAVIS, of Toledo: I appeal from the decision of the Chair.

A vote was then taken, but the Chair being unable to determine whether his decision was sustained, the Yeas and Nays were called, with the following result: Yeas 33; Nays 23.

The following gentlemen were then declared to be duly elected as Vice-Presidents:

| Messrs. CONVERSE, | Messrs. PORTER, |
|---|---|
| STANARD, | BROWN, |
| BRIGHAM, | BAGLEY, |
| EGAN, | KIRKLAND, |
| GANO, | FOSDICK, |
| HAZARD, | TRENHOLM, |
| BRANCH, | THURSTON. |

Mr. GANO: Gentlemen, I have now the honor to introduce to you your President, Mr. FREDERICK FRALEY, of Philadelphia. His presidency has been eminently satisfactory, and as you have been pleased with his rulings heretofore, I am sure you will be equally so in the future.

Whereupon Mr. FRALEY ascended the platform and said,—

For this renewed mark of your confidence, and for the honor conferred upon me by this election, I tender you my cordial thanks. It has been my good fortune to be associated upon three different occasions with a majority of the gentlemen that constitute the present National Board of Trade. The recollection of the intercourse that took place between us upon those occasions is green and vigorous, and will endure as long as consciousness remains with me.

In the good providence of God we have been permitted again to assemble to consult together upon great objects of national interest; upon matters that affect the constitution and the welfare of society at large; upon matters upon which the great business interests of this country must turn; and if we are as happy upon this occasion, and as fortunate in coming to unanimous resolutions as we have been heretofore, we shall repair to our homes with a conviction that we have done some good in the world, and have presented for the consideration of those who are to legislate those objects into national life and national power, counsels which may be received as the counsels of mature wisdom and consideration from those who are familiar with the subjects so treated. I will not detain you long by any formal speech. You are men of business, and we have come here for business purposes. It should be our aim to attend diligently to the questions that will be properly presented to our consideration; to treat fairly those that may be in a constitutional manner presented for our action; and by courtesy, forbearance and willingness to receive the opinions of others, however they may differ from our own, arrive at results at last which shall be the deliberately expressed opinion of this body of men, and, as so deliberately expressed, entitled to public confidence.

We are here in the midst of the hospitalities of a hospitable city; but we must recollect that amid all the hospitalities that may be tendered to us, and amid our acceptance of them, there should be a consciousness on our part that these hospitalities are to be received in strict subordination to the fulfilment of the duties that have been confided to us while here, and that we shall not suffer pleasure to interfere with business. (Applause.)

I shall endeavor, gentlemen, to the extent of my ability, in occupying this chair, to carry on your deliberations with ease and simplicity, to facilitate a decision upon the questions that may be presented, without a resort to very complicated or technical rules. And in so far as the preservation of order may depend upon me, I shall rely upon the support, upon the confidence and upon the intelligence of the individual gentlemen who compose this body, satisfied that that support will always be given when the decisions of the Chair are entitled to it.

I must impress upon you, gentlemen, that I labor under a difficulty of vision which considerably impairs my ability as a presiding officer, and I must, therefore, ask a strict adherence to the practice which has obtained in the recent commercial conventions of the country, that gentlemen rising to address the Chair will give their name and the locality from whence they come, so that they may be recognized and properly announced, and that those gentlemen who are so kind as to attend here to report our proceedings, may give to each delegate the credit he is entitled to for the remarks that he makes and for the questions which he may present for the consideration of the body.

With these remarks, gentlemen, this Convention is now organized for business; and I hope that it will be blessed with harmony, and with results that shall be felt not only here, but throughout the world.

Mr. GANO: I am glad of the opportunity of saying a few words suggested by the remark of the President, that we should subordinate the matter of entertainment to that of business. That has, so far as our own delegation from Cincinnati is concerned, been admitted from the start. Our city government has, however, insisted, against our protest, in tendering a dinner; they have provided that it shall take place on Friday evening, being apprehensive that if they defer it till Saturday, the Convention will have adjourned. I would say here, that it is our particular desire that this body should not hasten through with its important work; and we earnestly hope that any hospitalities that may be tendered will not in any way interfere with the regular business of the Convention. (Applause.)

The PRESIDENT: For the purpose of disposing of matters which were considered of importance, the Executive Council at their meeting last evening agreed to present to this body, after its regular organization, a plan for proceeding; and, with your permission, the Secretary will now read it. I commend it to your consideration for the reason that the first in order which it presents is the question of the admission of new members to this body; it being considered on the part of the Executive Council that in view of the stringent provisions of the Constitution, delegates coming from bodies described in the Constitution and properly entitled to be represented here, should have the earliest possible chance of admission permitted by the Constitution.

The Secretary read the Order of Business as designated by the Executive Council:

The Executive Council respectfully recommend to the Board the adoption of the following Order of Business at the present annual meeting:

1st. The call of the roll.

2nd. The reading of the reports of the Executive Council and the Treasurer.

3rd. The Election of Officers.

4th. The reception of papers from associations seeking admission to membership, to be referred to a Committee on Credentials, which shall have leave to sit during the sessions of the Board.

5th. The consideration of the topics referred to in the report of the Council.

6th. The consideration of the subjects on the official programme, and in the order in which they there appear.

The PRESIDENT: If there is no objection, that will be the order.

Mr. TAYLOR: I would inquire with respect to the admission of new members, if on presenting their credentials doubts should be raised, whether the Board will proceed to the next order of business, or whether such application will be received. It seems to me eminently proper whenever a delegation appears in the presence of the body, seeking admission, that their admission should be entertained.

The PRESIDENT: The credentials of delegates seeking admission will be referred to the Committee on Credentials, which will continue in existence during the sessions of the body; and if after to-day any new membership be applied for, the credentials of such associations will be referred immediately to the Committee, who will report upon them as speedily as possible.

Mr. ALLEN, of Philadelphia: I would ask whether a resolution would be in order. It refers to our business, not to credentials.

The PRESIDENT: It may be read for information.

Mr. ALLEN: That no delegate shall speak more than twice upon the same subject, and not more than fifteen minutes at one time, except by the consent of a majority of the delegates present.

The PRESIDENT: I think that would not be in order at the present time.

Mr. STANARD: I move to amend by inserting ten instead of fifteen minutes.

The PRESIDENT: That proposition is not before the body; it is as to the order of business.

Mr. RANDOLPH : It seems to me we may get at the proposition of Mr. ALLEN, after we move to adopt the report of the Executive Council.

The PRESIDENT : The question now before the house, is the adoption of the order of business, as recommended by the Executive Council. Mr. ALLEN proposes to amend that by limitation of the time of speech.

A DELEGATE : I move to separate the questions.

The PRESIDENT : The question is on the adoption of the amendment.

Mr. MONROE : There will come before this Board some propositions of great importance, which cannot be presented in ten or fifteen minutes; nor can the delegates be sufficiently interested in them in that time, unless they have already considered them and know their importance. It seems to me that if the party presenting such propositions shall be limited to ten or fifteen minutes, it will place it within the power of those who have not considered the matter, to prevent discussion; whereas, if fully presented, they would like to hear it thoroughly discussed. I think the limitation is too short. There ought, I think, to be a limitation, but time enough should be given to allow the house to see into the character of the proposition to be discussed, before they determine whether they will hear anything more upon the subject. I prefer that the time should be increased to thirty minutes. As to the number of times for speaking, I think it should not be oftener than twice. But I would like to see the proposition divided. I move an amendment to thirty minutes.

The PRESIDENT : The question is on the amendment to the amendment, extending the time from fifteen to thirty minutes.

Mr. RANDOLPH : If fifteen minutes are allowed for a delegate to open his speech, and he cannot convince the Board that it is a matter of interest, it is time he should stop; he should not be allowed to talk for an hour before we can determine whether it is of interest.

Mr. STANARD : Most of us can tell about what we know in twenty minutes, and I believe it is the desire of these gentlemen here, that we shall not be bored by long speeches. I think that the merchants who are here can express themselves intelligibly upon a subject in ten minutes, and then with another ten minutes allowed, I think the sixty-five delegates here can tell what was intended; but if we give permission to speak for thirty minutes, and then allow another thirty, we shall be in session till the first of January.

Mr. ROPES: I entirely agree, sir, that it would prolong our session indefinitely to allow each speaker thirty minutes twice over. We have many subjects before us, and they need as much time as the good nature of the Board will give to them. I object to limiting any man to speaking only twice. There are gentlemen here who are more competent to discuss commercial questions than for instance I am, and I would gladly give up my time and privilege to them; on the other hand, there are some things which we could explain in one or two minutes, that could not perhaps be done if we had not the privilege of speaking. If you cut a man off from speaking more than twice, you may cut yourselves off from much valuable information. It would be best, I think, to shorten the time, with the privilege of continuing by unanimous consent; and then give each person the privilege of speaking afterwards. The great majority of subjects before us I should not want to speak upon; but there are also subjects upon which I might be glad to speak three or four times, if I only spoke five minutes at a time. Cannot we have five minutes, and be allowed to speak three times?

Mr. FISK: I think the best proposition is to speak ten minutes and twice.

The proposition of Mr. ROPES was withdrawn, and a vote was taken upon the amendment:

That no delegate shall speak more than twice upon the same subject, nor more than ten minutes at each time, except by the consent of a majority of the delegates then present.

Carried.

A vote was then taken upon the whole, which was also agreed to.

The PRESIDENT: The first business in order will be the consideration of the application for new memberships. How shall the Committee on Credentials be appointed?

SEVERAL DELEGATES: By the Chair.

Carried.

The PRESIDENT: The Committee will consist of the following delegates:—

CHARLES RANDOLPH, Chicago,
CHARLES G. NAZRO, Boston, ROBT. R. KIRKLAND, Baltimore,
GEORGE W. DAVIS, Toledo, JAMES R. BRANCH, Richmond.

Mr. RANDOLPH : Before we adjourn, I move that during the session of this Board in this city, there be held at least two sessions a day. We have voted now to meet at 9 o'clock; let us have another session in the afternoon or evening, and let it be announced now, as many of us desire to get away on Friday evening or Saturday morning at furthest.

Agreed to,

The Board then adjourned to meet on Thursday morning at 9 o'clock.

# SECOND DAY.

### THURSDAY, DECEMBER 3, 1868.

The National Board of Trade met pursuant to adjournment.

The President, Mr. FRALEY, in the chair.

Prayer was offered by the Rev. J. L. ROBINSON.

On motion, the reading of the Journal was dispensed with.

The President read a communication from Mr. GEO. T. WILLIAMS, Superintendent of the Western Union Telegraph Company, tendering to the members of the Board the free use of the wires of the Company, during their sessions. The President stated that the communication had been left at his room in the hotel on the preceding day, which had delayed its presentation till now.

Communications were also read from the School Board, inviting the members to visit the Public Schools; also from the Young Men's Christian Association, tendering the use of its library and reading rooms. Thanks were returned for these courtesies.

On motion of Mr. WETHERILL, the vote of yesterday by which the Board decided to meet daily at nine o'clock, and to hold two sessions, was reconsidered; and it was determined to assemble at ten o'clock in the forenoon, and to remain in session during the pleasure of the Board.

The PRESIDENT: Is the Committee on the admission of new members prepared to report?

Mr. RANDOLPH: The Committee reports favorably on the admission of the Corn and Flour Exchange, of Baltimore; and it cordially recommends the reception of its delegates, Messrs. ISRAEL M. PARR, W. S. YOUNG, WILLIAM CRICHTON and HENRY DUVALL, whose credentials are entirely satisfactory.

The PRESIDENT: The question is on the proposition reported by the Committee, that the Corn and Flour Exchange, of Baltimore, be admitted to the Board, and the delegates accredited thereby be permitted to take their seats.

Mr. KIRKLAND: I move that the recommendation be adopted by the National Board of Trade.

The motion was seconded, and the Secretary called the roll of Boards, which resulted in an unanimous vote in the affirmative.

The PRESIDENT: I have the pleasure of announcing that the admission of this Association is unanimously carried, and tender to its delegates on behalf of the National Board of Trade, a cordial welcome.

Mr. RANDOLPH: The credentials just reported upon are the only ones that are in every respect regular and in accordance with the Constitution. The next are from the Board of Trade of Dubuque, Iowa. Messrs. THOS. M. MONROE and LEWIS A. THOMAS are the accredited delegates. Since the Philadelphia meeting in June, the Dubuque Produce Exchange has been merged into the Board of Trade. The last session of the Iowa Legislature did not grant charters for Boards of Trade. The preamble and articles of association under which they have organized, have been presented, and the original is filed for record in the Recorder's Office of the city of Dubuque. The paper presented is clearly a copy of the original charter. We therefore conclude that so far as that is concerned this Board is entirely regular and entitled to membership. The only point on which there is any irregularity, is in the absence of the seal upon their credentials. As our Constitution is so explicit in this regard, we have felt obliged to report the facts as they are, leaving the Board to determine what action shall be taken. The gentlemen advise us that at present they have no seal, but are about to procure one.

The PRESIDENT: Does the Committee submit any resolution.

Mr. RANDOLPH: No, sir.

Mr. KIRKLAND: The absence of a seal is really unimportant; the making of a scroll seal with a pen would have answered the purpose. In view of this fact I think we should consider the document a legal instrument entitling the delegates to admission.

Discussion ensued on the requirements of the Constitution in reference to a seal; and on a call of the roll of the constituent bodies, the Dubuque Board was admitted by an unanimous vote.

The PRESIDENT: All the Boards having voted aye, the delegates of this body are welcomed to their seats.

Mr. RANDOLPH: The Committee have next to report upon the Memphis Chamber of Commerce. Four delegates are accredited, Messrs. BARKER, CHALMERS, TREZEVANT and TOPP. These delegates have agreed that Mr. BARKER shall act as reporter, and that the three other gentlemen shall represent that body if admitted. The gentlemen present a copy of their annual report, which shows them to be a live organization, associated, as most other similar Western organizations are, for the general transaction of business, and for the especial promotion of trade in Memphis. The report does not contain a copy of the charter. The credentials are duly signed, and represent that the body has over three hundred voting members. In the absence of a copy of the charter, the gentlemen have this morning handed us a copy of the laws of Tennessee, containing their charter, and they present that as temporarily fulfilling the requirements of our Constitution. This paper makes their application, in our judgment, complete, and we therefore recommend that the Memphis Chamber of Commerce be recognized as a member of this Board, and that the three gentlemen named be admitted to seats.

The PRESIDENT: The question is on the admission of the body to membership.

The roll of Boards being called, the motion was unanimously adopted.

The PRESIDENT: The admission of the body is unanimously agreed to, and the three gentlemen will take their seats as delegates.

Mr. RANDOLPH: The Committee would next report upon the application of the Springfield (Ohio) Board of Trade. The gentlemen whose names are mentioned in these credentials, did not appear before the Committee; we have, therefore, no report to make, except upon the paper itself, which is merely an ordinary certificate of membership in the Springfield Board of Trade, with an interlineation that the gentlemen are members of that body, and delegates to the Convention at Cincinnati; dated 24th November, 1868. There is no seal, and the Committee have no evidence that the organization is a chartered one, nor do they know anything of the number of its members, or whether it is established for general or private purposes. The Committee are therefore compelled to report unfavorably to the admission of the Springfield Board of Trade or its delegates.

Mr. VOORHEES, of Springfield, asked permission to be heard. Agreed to.

Mr. VOORHEES: The President of our Board, whose name is affixed, and myself, were appointed delegates to attend this Convention. Not having a copy of the Constitution of this body, not being acquainted with its organization, and not knowing the requisites necessary to become members of the Association, we brought with us a certificate, recognized as valid by the laws of Ohio. When bodies of this kind are recognized, it is necessary that they leave with the Auditor their charter, certifying their existence, and by that instrument being so deposited, the Board becomes legalized by the laws of the State. We brought with us a certificate of such deposit, and I sent it up to the clerk yesterday, but afterwards wishing to examine it, I retook it, and it has disappeared, but whether from my pocket or in some other way, I do not know. I showed it to Mr. GANO, who recollects the circumstance, and that it was the certificate of the Auditor of Clark County, in which county Springfield is situated, stating that the charter of our Board of Trade had been filed and was recorded. I deemed this a sufficient authority that we were a regularly constituted Board of Trade, and the certificate which had been read, I thought was authority that the delegates were regularly appointed to represent the body in this Board.

Mr. GANO: I can verify what the gentleman has said in regard to the certificate. It was on file here, but he withdrew it for some purpose, and it has disappeared. If the papers presented are not in order, I would like, if possible, to make an exception in favor of this Board. I move that the Springfield Board of Trade be admitted to membership, and that the report of the Committee be amended to that effect, provided the credentials of the delegates are correct.

The motion was seconded.

The PRESIDENT: I do not consider the proposal to be in order.

Mr. WETHERILL: I move to refer this matter back to the Committee for re-consideration.

Mr. RANDOLPH: Do I understand that any instructions are given.

The PRESIDENT: No, sir.

The motion was put and carried.

Mr. RANDOLPH : The Committee have in hand two other credentials which they are not yet ready to report upon. Mr. R. P. GLENN, from Atlanta, Ga., a very important position in the South, and one which the Board would be glad to have represented, has presented himself. Mr. GLENN comes from the Commercial Exchange, of Atlanta, but he does not know positively that it is a chartered institution; nor is he able to state the number of its members, though, he says it is a large and vigorous body. The Committee have concluded, upon Mr. GLENN's statement, which they fully credit, that while they can not report in favor of admission to membership, they will recommend that Mr. GLENN be allowed the courtesies of the floor; and they suggest that he request his Association to comply with the terms of our Constitution, so that its delegates may in due time be admitted to this body.

Mr. DAVIS, of Cincinnati: I wish to ask whether that would involve freedom to deliberate in the meetings, without the privilege of voting; if not, I would move an amendment to that effect.

The PRESIDENT: The resolution as amended, is before the body, that the gentleman from Atlanta be admitted to a seat in the Board with the privilege of participating in our discussions, but without the right of voting.

Carried.

The PRESIDENT : The Board will now listen to a brief supplementary report from the Executive Council.

The Secretary read the following : —

The Executive Council was instructed at Philadelphia, to prepare By-laws for the consideration of the Board. The Council has not as yet been able to decide upon these in full; but it is unanimous in recommending to the Board the adoption of the following, which will make a two-thirds vote necessary to carry the judgment of the Board in favor of any subject presented before it. As the action of the Board is not legislative, but recommendatory simply; the delegates will appreciate the value of the provision now suggested :

By-law No. 1. A vote of two-thirds of the delegates present shall be necessary to carry the approval of the Board upon any proposition which may appear, or which may be placed, upon the official programme.

The By-law as reported, was adopted.

The PRESIDENT: The next business, according to the order of procedure agreed to yesterday, is in relation to Mr. JENCKES's Civil Service bill, referred to in the report of the Executive Council.

Mr. WETHERILL: I beg to introduce a resolution indorsing the bill of Mr. JENCKES, and asking the Executive Council to memorialize Congress, urging its passage. I consider this one of the most important bills ever presented to Congress. By its enactment we shall secure what we all want, good and efficient officials, men of character and integrity, fitted to carry out the laws and to administer the different departments of the Government in the interest of the whole country. As I understand the bill, it creates a new department called the department of the Civil Service, comprising a commission of four persons with the Vice-President at its head. Every officer appointed by the President, must come before this commission to be examined. The selection of officers will thus be made to depend upon their qualification and fitness for office, instead of upon political influence. I therefore offer the following:—

*Resolved*, That we heartily indorse the bill now before Congress, offered by Mr. JENCKES, of Rhode Island, entitled An Act to regulate the Civil Service of the United States, and to promote the efficiency thereof; and that we desire the Executive Council to memorialize Congress, urging the great importance of the measure, and asking for its passage.

Mr. TURPIN: It seems to me that the plan proposed will simply take the appointing power from persons who are responsible, and commit it to a set of men who are irresponsible. I prefer that responsible officers of the Government shall retain the appointing power, that the people may hold them to account for the selection of proper persons. For this reason I shall vote against the resolution.

Mr. DRAKE: I am not familiar with all the details of the bill, but with its general principles I am pretty well acquainted, and of these I approve. But I move to insert that we indorse the general features of the bill. I think we should be cautious in acting in a semi-political matter, not to commit ourselves too fully to the details of a bill, which on a full examination, we might not entirely accept.

Mr. WETHERILL: The bill is now before Congress. It has been sent to the Committee on Retrenchment, who have examined it carefully and have reported in its favor. What we want to do is to urge its passage. Everybody is satisfied that we ought to have better men in office, and the only way to obtain them is to ascertain by examination who is, or is not fit. The commission proposed would establish its rules and receive applications from candidates, irrespective of politics; they would examine these candidates, and guided by their respective merits, would seek in every instance, to give the office to the best man. It seems clear to me that this Board should indorse such a bill as this. The simple indorsement of its general features would be an intimation that the National Board of Trade is dissatisfied with some specific features of the bill.

Mr. RANDOLPH : I hope the amendment of the gentleman from St. Paul will prevail. I disagree with Mr. WETHERILL in this regard. I think that this Board cannot afford to utter its opinions in behalf of a bill, of which it does not know the full details. The bill is not before us, and I do not see why we should commit ourselves to everything which it contains. It is its general features that we wish to indorse, and nothing else, otherwise we shall be committing ourselves to something which we may not fully approve, and hereafter may find that we have been wasting our time and expressing opinions upon matters which we did not understand.

Mr. HINCKEN : I rise to say that I think this is a question which does not concern us as merchants. I was sent here to confer with members of this Board upon matters of commercial importance. The delegates from New York were not supposed to be instructed on matters which relate to the general Government. The idea in organizing this Board was that we should confer on subjects purely commercial, and I do not see that the appointment of civil officers has anything to do with any commercial project. I move that the whole subject be laid on the table.

Mr. WETHERILL called for the Yeas and Nays, and they were ordered.

The PRESIDENT : The question is on laying Mr. WETHERILL's resolution on the table.

The resolution was tabled, by the following vote :

Yeas : Messrs.—

| | | | |
|---|---|---|---|
| Allen, (Thomas,) | Branch, | Chalmers, | Dawson, |
| Bagley, | Brannin, | Cobia, | Duvall, |
| Biggs, | Brown, | Crichton, | Gano, |
| Boynton, | Brunot, | Davis, (Geo. F.,) | Grant, |
| Bradford, | Carrington, | Davis, (Geo. W.,) | Guthrie, |

| | | | |
|---|---|---|---|
| Harris, | Kreikhaus, | Peters, | Stranahan, |
| Hazard, | Loney, | Plumer, | Thomas, |
| Hincken, | Manson, | Porter, | Thurston, |
| Holton, | McGraw, | Ronald, | Topp, |
| How, | Monroe, | Sage, | Trezevant, |
| Hull, | Munn, | Sampson, | Turpin, |
| Jenkins, | Nettleton, | Shryock, | Wilbor, |
| King, | Parr, | Stanard, | Young,—52. |

Nays: Messrs.—

| | | | |
|---|---|---|---|
| Allen, (Geo. N.,) | Converse, | Hoffman, | Randolph, |
| Brigham, | Drake, | Ilsley, | Ropes, |
| Buell, | Egan, | Malone, | Taussig, |
| Buzby, | Fisk, | Meier, | Taylor, |
| Carpenter, | Fraley, | Michener, | Wetherill, |
| Cobb, | Hand, | Nazro, | Winsor—24. |

The PRESIDENT: The resolution to lay upon the table is agreed to. The next business in order is the recommendation of the Executive Council to renew our application to Congress for a charter of incorporation.

Mr. HOFFMAN: I move that the Executive Council be instructed to renew its application to Congress for a charter of incorporation.

Agreed to.

Mr. BAGLEY: I have a communication from the Detroit Board of Trade in regard to the copper interests of our State, and I ask that it may be referred to the Executive Council.

Carried.

Mr. BRANNIN: I have a communication from the Louisville Board of Trade on the subject of repairing the levees of the Mississippi and Arkansas rivers, for which I ask a reference to the Executive Council.

Mr. FISK: I second the motion for a reference.

Mr. HINCKEN: I suggest that this proposition is already embraced in the subject of the navigation of the Mississippi, and should go to the Committee who may have that subject in charge.

The PRESIDENT: The motion is to refer the matter to the Executive Council.

Carried.

Mr. CHALMERS: I desire to ask if resolutions having reference to the improvement of the Mississippi are in order.

The PRESIDENT: No, sir. The business now in order is the first proposition on the official programme, and comes from the Chicago Board of Trade in reference to cash sales of produce.

There is a communication before me inviting the Board to an excursion on the Steamer "America," from Mr. THOMAS SHERLOCK.

Mr. KIRKLAND: I move that the thanks of the Board be presented to the Company, and that the invitation be respectfully declined.

The PRESIDENT: The recommendation of the Chicago Board of Trade in reference to cash sales of produce is now in order.

The Secretary read the following preamble and resolutions:

WHEREAS, The custom prevails in most cities at the seaboard of selling produce, provisions and other property, nominally for cash, but in reality upon a credit to the purchaser of from five to fifteen days; and

WHEREAS, The Western or interior consignor of such property has been in many cases obliged to suffer loss by credits so given by his consignee to irresponsible parties, and at other times has been obliged to pay largely for guarantee by his consignee of such sales on credit; and

WHEREAS, It is demonstrated by the experience of those cities where the custom alluded to does not prevail, and where capital is less abundant than at the East, that it is not necessary to grant such credits, but that property can be paid for on delivery of control of it, as well as at a later day; therefore

*Resolved*, That it is the opinion of the National Board of Trade, that all sales of grain, flour, provisions and other similar property consigned for sale on owner's account to commission merchants, should be sold for cash on delivery.

*Resolved*, That this Board recommends to local organizations associated with it, the adoption of such regulations touching the sale of and payment for property as will conform to the spirit of the foregoing resolutions.

The PRESIDENT: The first of these resolutions is before the Board.

Mr. RANDOLPH: I move its adoption.

The motion was seconded.

Mr. HOFFMAN : I object to the passage of these resolutions because they are local, and this body therefore has no right to take action upon them. Another objection is, that if they were passed it would be utterly impossible to carry them out. We, in the East, would certainly be very glad if we could make all our sales for cash on delivery, but the gentlemen who consign to us from the West must remember that when Eastern merchants sell upon credit it is more for the advantage of the Western merchants than if they adopted the strictly cash system. We, as sellers, are always guaranteers, and we never charge an extra price for the guaranty. If the resolutions were to be passed they would be a nullity, because no house would miss an opportunity of making a sale on credit when it could obtain a price in a dull market which it could not otherwise obtain. I move to lay the resolution upon the table.

Mr. DRAKE : I hope the gentleman will withdraw his motion. I did not propose saying anything upon this subject, until the gentleman who has just taken his seat, made these remarks. Upon this particular subject the Chamber of Commerce that I represent, feels a deep interest. Our State is a large grain-exporting State; we shall probably export, this year, ten millions of bushels of wheat. That wheat finds itself ultimately in a New York, or Philadelphia, or Baltimore market. We have felt the evils and inconveniences of the present system practiced there. As I understand it, it is the custom for commission houses in many of the eastern cities, to sell nominally for cash, but practically, upon a ten or fifteen days' credit, which, in effect, makes the Western consignor furnish the capital for men dealing in New York. The flour and bread dealers in New York may carry on a business of hundreds of thousands of dollars without one dollar of capital. They make the Western man, shipping the property, practically furnish the capital for their trade. That is not the greatest evil. Another evil arises. I may say that I speak feelingly, because I have practical experience of what I say. I made a consignment to a commission merchant in the East, who sold a part of the consignment for cash, and part upon a credit of fifteen days. He charged three per cent. for guaranteeing the fifteen days' credit, and took his guarantee money out of the cash sales. He himself, and the party to whom he sold the produce, both failed, and I have not, to this day, realized a dollar out of the transaction. Now, the gentleman tells us that this is to be a nullity. I believe no such thing. If the Western Boards of Trade adopt this system, and demand that their sales shall be for cash, they will find plenty of commission men who will make sales for cash. I hope that this thing will be considered.

It is almost a national evil at present, and my constituency desire and demand that a reform shall take place.

Mr. STANARD: I would be very glad, sir, if we should be able all over this country, in all our great markets, to sell our products for cash. I mean cash when the property is delivered. Chicago has set us an example. I believe that Chicago is the safest place to do business in in this country; and simply for the reason that they hold on to their property until they get their money. They started right, and it has been easy, apparently, to go on in that way. It is evident to every merchant who is in the habit of doing business, that if I owe the gentleman at my right a thousand dollars, and pay him to-day, the day that the transaction is made, and if he owes the gentleman at his right a thousand dollars, he can pay it that day, just as well, and better, than if I paid my debt ten days after it came due. It would, perhaps, be very difficult to do this at first, but if we could only educate our people in the older States, where their habits have been formed, up to this point, it would be just as practicable as it is in Chicago, and it would take no more money to do the business. But the question arises here: Can we educate the people up to this point in Philadelphia, and New York and St. Louis? I say St. Louis, for we need education as much there as in any other city I know of. I am fearful that we can not do it, and that the resolutions which have been offered here, if passed, would have very little effect in the great cities of the Union. But, although there is that difficulty, I believe there is no great fear of loss to the consignor if he will only make such arrangements with the consignee in Philadelphia and New York and Boston as he is able to make. There are plenty of good houses in all these cities, who make guarantee sales and charge no extra rate for doing it. There is a law in Missouri, by which a commission merchant is made not responsible, but, practically, the commission merchants there are responsible. Any man can go to St. Louis and get a guarantee that the sales made for the account of the party in the country shall be guaranteed to him without any charge for the guarantee; without any thing but the regular two and a half per cent. If the man in the country does not make this arrangement, it is his own fault. There is no shipper in the West who can not go to any of the great marts of the country and get his sales guaranteed, if he will only ask for it. If any house refuses to do this, the only way for us to do is to ship to no house that will not guarantee sales for two and a half per cent., without any extra charge. I will ask what the commission merchant is for, if it is not to be supposed that he knows the man he is selling to? I have paid two and a half per cent. in New York and Boston as much for this purpose as any other. The man I consign to there, is on the ground. He is supposed to know to whom he is selling. I expect him to know. I don't believe it would be practicable for the Board to try to regulate this in exchanges where they have habits and customs older than we are. It is a matter that we, as consignors, must regulate for ourselves.

Mr. MUNN: I am pleased with the remarks of our friend from Minnesota, because they are just and true. I am partially pleased with the remarks of our friend from St. Louis, although his conclusions are not such as I should arrive at. The first objection that meets us, from the arguments and statements made, is that this plan can not be carried into effect. Now, sir, in my eventful life I have seen greater obstacles than this overcome, when men of as good sense and judgment as we who sit here to-day, have thought them insurmountable. I honestly believe that all we want is the right sort of action, and this measure can be carried through effectually, and to the advantage of all parties. Go back to 1861, when, by a financial convulsion, nine or ten millions of circulation were struck out of existence. What did the West do? Did they say, "We will take your currency from Pennsylvania, from New York, and from New England?" No, sir. They said, "We will have the gold for our products," and the gold came. Until the country became in a measure settled, you could not buy the wheat, flour, corn and pork, unless you paid for it in gold, or a bill of exchange that went for gold. It is just so with this proposition. Our friend from St. Louis says that he would not ship to a commission merchant without a guarantee of sales. Neither would I. We know that if the merchant to whom we consign our property gets the cash on delivery, he will sell it for us as cheerfully at one and a half per cent. as he will when he guarantees it for two and a half per cent. This system has been adopted by us in Chicago, where we have less money than they have in the large and wealthy cities of the East, and we find no difficulty in carrying it into effect. Adopt that system in New York, Philadelphia and Boston, and the merchants there will get the greater proportion of all consignments. When the producers of the West know that these men sell for cash and cash only, they will send their consignments to them. Once adopted, and it will be just as easy for purchasers to pay the cash on delivery, as to get fifteen days to do it in. We of the West are tenacious upon this point, because we believe it to be for our interest. We believe that business can thus be done more easily, and that the result to all parties will be much more satisfactory.

Mr. PORTER: As a delegate from the Southwest, I approve entirely of the position of the gentlemen from St. Paul and from Chicago. All that has been said in the argument on this question, as applied to grain, applies with quite as much force to the great staple of the South — cotton.

The gentleman from St. Paul says that by this system of doing business upon the Eastern seaboard, the West is compelled to furnish the capital with which the speculators of the seaboard operate. This is entirely true with regard to cotton. If the merchant or the planter in the South makes a shipment to the seaboard, his property is sold by the commission merchant, and is not delivered for ten days. If there is no special arrangement, the purchaser will, as a general thing, reject a large part of the property as not coming up to the sample by which he bought. If the property should happen to advance in the interim, he accepts every bale; so that, by this system, you place the whole power within that ten days, in the hands of the purchaser, the seller getting no benefit whatever from any advance that may take place. Certainly, if the people upon the seaboard have not money enough to do their own speculating with, they ought not to rely upon that of the impoverished South or of our friends in the Northwest.

Mr. HINCKEN: This resolution is harmless, for it only calls upon us to *recommend* the adoption of cash sales. We can do that; but I want to correct one or two opinions I have heard. If the gentlemen were conversant with the trade of New York they would know that there is a great difference between the price of cotton sold on the docks, and of cotton sold in store, which covers the charges and the additional accommodation it gives the shipper. Cotton is sold at ten days, not at ten days' credit; but if I buy a hundred bales of cotton, I am entitled to ten days to make my arrangements for freighting it and receiving it. But if I receive the cotton to-day, you will expect my check to-morrow. I speak, now, of those who export, only. I may make a contract for cotton, so much cash to be paid for it next week. This matter is altogether a question of contract made at the time of sale. If I purchase a thousand barrels of flour I may take a week to pay for it; but if I take that flour to-day, ordinarily I pay for it to-morrow. These principles cover the export trade. The difference in price between cotton sold on the dock and in store is one and a quarter cents per pound. The time given is not regarded as credit on the sales, but for freighting and receiving it.

Mr. PARR: The object of this resolution is not to legislate for the advantage of any local Board, but to get the expression of the National

Board. I should like to see a resolution adopted to the effect that the products of the soil ought to be sold everywhere for cash. I desire to correct the gentleman from St. Paul in regard to the city of Baltimore. The products of the soil are there sold for cash. Consignors from the West who send grain or flour to Baltimore may have it sold for cash if they say so. Cash sale there means cash on delivery. If credit is given it is at the risk of the commission merchant himself. I think it very proper that the opinion of this Board should be expressed in favor of exclusively cash sales of grain and flour, and the products of the soil.

Mr. BUZBY: I have felt that this debate ought not to cease until some who transact business in the Eastern cities can be heard. I know, by my own personal experience, and I think that all the gentlemen about me, that have been engaged in the commission business, know to their cost, that in the accommodations they afford to Western men they are continually out of pocket. They have lost very large sums, about which they never say anything; and the virtuous diffidence which prevents them from telling their consignors in the West, is now the cause why we must submit to an attack for not doing our business in a proper manner. Habitually we carry thousands of barrels of flour and other commodities for these Western men. If the market falls, and we, with drafts matured which we are bound to pay, venture upon that declining market and sell for cash, which they insist on receiving, at the sacrifice of one or two dollars a barrel, then we are charged with being reckless, and slaughtering the property of the West, and yet in coming upon that market and selling for cash, we would exactly comply with what these Western men demand at our hands. Let us understand this. Are they willing that by way of bringing about these cash sales we shall under all circumstances go upon the market and sell for what the property will bring? I have all my life had the strongest desire to do business in that way, but I never have been able to do it, because I never could find the Western consignor that would be satisfied with the result. I could not permit this debate to conclude without stating to the gentlemen what would happen if they want this to be done. This applies more especially to the local trade of the cities, which is the best part of the business.

Mr RANDOLPH: I am surprised, and more than surprised, that an objection to this resolution should come from the East. I have understood, always, from gentlemen doing a large business, especially in the produce way, that they would be very glad to have a system similar to this, but that one man in a city could not do it. They have said, "If we insist upon cash, our neighbors giving a little credit will get more for the property than we can, and we shall lose our business." It is true, as Mr. BUZBY says, that it frequently occurs in the large cities of the East that there is an accumulation of property which purchasers for consumption or export do not immediately want, and which the capital of commission merchants or bankers must " carry." That is no more true of Eastern than of Western merchants. We have held, for several years, in Chicago, on our own capital, twice what Philadelphia ever held in produce. This property is brought there for country account, and sold for cash. It is held on Chicago capital until it is shipped. More than half of it is held on Chicago capital until after it reaches the Eastern cities. It is paid for with Chicago capital to the farmer, consumes from three to ten days in getting to Chicago, and is held there from ten to forty days, during the season of open navigation. It is sent East, and the majority of it is drawn on at as many days as will run it into the Eastern cities. This, perhaps, may not apply to flour, but it does apply to the bulk of the grain. We hold this produce of the soil at our expense, longer than the Eastern cities hold it at their expense. We know that in Philadelphia, merchants establish it as the rule and not as the exception, that their established market price is based on cash. If a good man wants credit, and is entitled to it, let it be given upon their own responsibility, and let him be charged interest for it, but let the rule be cash. Prominent merchants say that it can be done, and we know from experience that it can, and how well it works with us.

Mr. HINCKEN has alluded to the custom in New York in produce and cotton, that the purchases for export are understood to be paid for on delivery. It is not so represented. Again and again it has occurred, when sales of produce have been made to exporters, that prior to the time the bills matured, according to the understanding of the trade, the property was on its way to Europe, and the pay also. In reply to the arguments of gentlemen from the East, I would say, that we hold that the great bulk of the expenses of guarantee, whether paid directly or not, are really paid by the seller. If my friend HOFFMAN has a thousand barrels of flour for sale, (and he guarantees his correspondent against loss) and he makes the sale to a party, giving him ten days credit, it is because he feels that the party is entitled to credit, and that there is no risk; but if another man comes along who wants the flour, and Mr. HOFFMAN does not consider him safe, he will not sell it to him, if he is a conscientious man, as I know him to be. But if the rule is that sales of produce are for cash, and cash only, it is no question whether this man or that is a good man; if he takes the flour he pays the money. This arrangement will relieve gentlemen in the East from taking this responsibility.

It may occur that when risks are taken, no guarantee is charged. The gentleman from St. Louis says he does not pay guarantee charges. It reminds me of the story of the man who sailed a merchant's vessel. On returning from a voyage, a brother captain chanced to tell him that he always charged a suit of clothes in his expenses. Our captain undertook to do this, but the claim was objected to as not customary, and it was not allowed. When next he met his friend and related his experience, he was enlightened: "Make your charge," was the reply, "put it on something, but don't call it a suit of clothes." He did so in future, and got his extra pay. So in the cases where they do not charge for guarantee, the consignor has to pay for it in some way or other. If no guarantee is charged, the party is sure to sell it where there is no risk.

These resolutions are submitted by the Chicago Board of Trade as recommendatory only. We ask that this Board shall initiate some measures that may result in securing this recommendation. I am surprised and amazed that gentlemen from Philadelphia or New York should come here and say that this recommendation cannot be carried out because of the existence of old rules and methods. If it is desirable, as some of them have admitted, will they not help us to obtain it?

Mr. HAZARD: I can see no objection to the resolutions, and I hope they will pass. I almost wish this Board had the power to compel every association represented here to adopt these measures. It is necessary that we should approach the cash system as nearly as possible. In Buffalo we have approached it, but still we have not got into it thoroughly. I should wish to see all sorts of produce sold for cash. I wish that every Board of Trade would adopt this as a principle. I can recollect the time, when in the city of New York, they could not deliver a canal-boat load of corn unless it was measured out in half-bushels. It was thought almost impossible to change that, but it was finally done, and I can see no reason now why the credit system should not be likewise abolished, and the system of selling for cash adopted thoroughly.

Mr. JENKINS: Of course there are in this Board a great many interests. I am not sure that it would be entirely proper for the Board to take action upon these resolutions, to pass them or to vote them down. It seems to me that it is a matter which only concerns the producers in the Southwest, and the commission merchants who sell at the seaboard. If these gentlemen would get together and agree upon some plan among themselves in regard to their transactions I think that would be the proper plan of action; and except so far as this refers to the general subject of selling everything for cash, and having no credits in anything, it seems to me that this Convention as a body, should have very little to do with it.

Mr. KIRKLAND: This preamble sets out with a proposition, that generally not only meets my views, but those of the Board who have sent me here partially to represent them.

Whilst in some instances this usage of claiming five, ten or fifteen days' credit, on cash sales, has prevailed of late in Baltimore, it never did or does apply, to the general business of that city. The products of the soil, such as flour, wheat, corn, rye, oats, tobacco, &c., are there sold for *cash*, and this pernicious system, or usage of credit, on cash sales, never has been recognized. In passing these resolutions, I apprehend that this Board does not take the position, that a man shall not under any circumstances, sell on a credit. It is not competent to prevent a special bargain, under which credit sales can be made, when so agreed upon, between buyer and seller; but they do mean to say, that cash sales, mean *cash*, and that when you send your merchandise to Eastern cities, with instructions, that it shall be sold for *cash*, and the consignee presumes to sell it on ten or fifteen days credit, the consignee, so receiving, and selling the merchandise, shall pay for it. A business experience of thirty years has given me some knowledge of selling on credit, and I am happy to say that if any gentleman of the West, of good local standing, and entitled to credit, desires it from me, I would give ten, fifteen, sixty days, or even more, on merchandise that we import, and I do not apprehend that in passing this resolution this Board intends to prohibit such a transaction.

I hope therefore, this Board will pass this resolution, and urge upon all local organizations, component parts of this body, to take action, and not only adopt the resolution but add to it, that every and all sales of all merchandise for cash means *cash on delivery*, and that no usage that anywhere prevails to the contrary, shall be recognized. It has been said such action could not be enforced, but in all well-regulated Boards, I can see no difficulty. In our own Board, any member who openly and defiantly refuses to be governed by its constitution, by-laws, and regulations, would be expelled and dishonored, and I presume it is the same in all well-regulated commercial communities; I therefore hope, that the local Boards will take such action under this resolution as will abolish, wherever it prevails, this pernicious usage.

Mr. BRIGHAM : I feel that the West has a large interest in this question, and that it should be settled, and settled definitely, for all time. The idea that in the East they cannot pay the cash for actual sales when they have more money than we have, is to me a little ridiculous. I cannot understand it. In Baltimore they sell for cash; we, in Milwaukie, sell for cash, and we find no embarrassment, except that sometimes we take a check, and if we are not fast, and get it certified, we may slip up in that respect. I have known of instances where we have certified, and slipped up then. So that with all our diligence in doing a cash trade, there are disappointment and loss enough at the best. My experience in selling produce in the city of Milwaukie is, that the man who ships it to me makes more money by taking the market prices the day it arrives, than he does at any other time. Sometimes he will lose, but he will as often gain as lose; and I think that if the delegates from Chicago, or from any of our Western Boards, will give their experience in this matter, it will be universally in favor of selling produce for cash on delivery, whenever it arrives in the market. I certainly hope that this resolution will pass.

Mr. BRANCH : If I could be satisfied that practical good would result from the passage of these resolutions, I would most heartily vote for them ; but I say; respectfully, that I think it is important for us, just starting out on a treacherous sea, not very well assured that we have a strong, staunch ship, that we should be exceedingly cautious to avoid the breakers, and not attempt to do things which are impossible, or pass resolutions that will not result in any practical good. I take it for granted that the delegates from New York, Philadelphia, Boston and Baltimore, have fully canvassed this question, and I am sure that the consignee is as anxious to sell for cash as the consignor, if not more so. I take it that every consignment that comes from the West is followed by a draft that pretty nearly covers its prime cost, and though that produce may sometimes remain in the warehouse many days, the draft is paid, while yet the produce is in the warehouse of the consignee. Though I regard it of vital interest to the Eastern commission merchants that sales should be made for cash, yet they are not, simply because it is, practically, impossible. But I make this distinction. You can make cash sales for export, but you cannot make them for home consumption. The difficulty at the East is that the people of New England and along the Atlantic shore are so essentially a manufacturing people, that they do not raise enough to eat, and the East, therefore, becomes a great consuming market. The merchants who come to Boston, New York, Philadelphia and Baltimore, come there to get in their supplies to send out into the country, and they must have time. Cotton or grain which is bought throughout the West for cash, when sent to Liverpool or London,— the great commercial centres of the world — is sold for ninety days' credit, which you are obliged to give, and this in a city where you can borrow money at from one and a half to two per cent. per annum. The same difficulty exists along our Atlantic seaboard. If produce were sold for export there would be no difficulty in selling for cash. I say therefore, while I have the utmost respect for anything emanating from my worthy friends in Chicago, I submit that the proposed resolutions are not practicable, and on this ground I should hesitate to vote for them.

Mr. HOFFMAN : This cash principle has been tried in single associations all over the country; and if you pass these resolutions they will not last, as I said before, for a single day. The gentlemen in Chicago do not always sell their flour for cash. I know parties there who deal in flour very extensively, who have told me so more than once. We have to be governed by circumstances, and the very men who offer these resolutions may be the first to break them. The iron men say that they sell for cash and for cash only, but if an iron man meets a customer who wants his iron but cannot pay for it for thirty days, if he is trustworthy the iron dealer will make his sale rather than lose his chance. My chief objection to the resolutions is that they will never be carried out. Resolutions of this kind have been passed by local Boards, but they have rarely held good for a single day. Besides this is a local matter and should not, I think, be acted upon by the National Board of Trade.

Mr. HOLTON : This question I regard as much broader than some of the views which have been taken of it. It is a question of shortening credits. It is a question of contracts between merchants, which must continue to excite attention, and which well deserves to be discussed. Gentlemen here from all parts of the country know how advantageous it has been to shorten mercantile credits. When I was a boy going to Boston from New Hampshire, the merchants there were accustomed to give us twelve months' credit, and I regard it as one of the misfortunes of my life that I was thus early initiated into the practice of long credits. This charge of two and a half per cent. for commission and guarantee is a serious question as applied to the millions of bushels of grain that go out from Lake Michigan, and the credit given amounts to fifteen days' interest on the sales of Western produce, and this amounts in the year to hundreds of thousands of dollars. But it is not merely to the disadvantage of the merchant that we must look; we want to take back to the *producer* the very last mill to which he is entitled, and this can only be done by establishing the system of cash sales. The young man starting in business must have the fairest and best field for the exercise of his energies. He must cut down his two and a half per cent. commission to one per cent., and it becomes us as mercantile men in this National Board of Trade to help to reduce these expenses to the lowest possible point. These resolutions are but recommendatory, as are all our measures, but I wish to see this go forth as the conclusion of the business men here assembled. We want commercial transactions completed with all the rapidity compatible with fair dealing and security, and we want to see the last mill paid to those who are the producers, and these results I believe will be furthered by the adoption of these resolutions.

Mr. PARR : Being a resident in Baltimore, and somewhat familiar with the custom of the trade there, I rise to correct some statements that have been made with respect to the sales of flour consigned to Baltimore from the West. If the receiver or consignee chooses to give credit to the purchaser, it is at his own risk. The rule at the Baltimore Corn and Flour Exchange is, that sales shall be for cash. I have been in the grain trade for nearly thirty years, and for twenty-six years I have been a receiver of grain; and though I have, on occasions, sold upon credit, I have returned my account of sales to the consignor without his knowing there was any credit in the case. But the rule, the unvariable rule, I may say, with every one there, is to sell for cash. In the flour trade too, the rule is cash, and whenever there is an exception, it is at the risk of the seller.

Mr. HAZARD : It may be urged in favor of the adoption of these resolutions, that cash sales would make an uniform price, and that in giving ten or fifteen days' credit, the purchaser has to pay more for the produce, and thus a fictitious price is given, which being quoted at the West from Baltimore or New York, causes grain to be reported at four or five cents per bushel more than it is actually worth for cash. I would say, however, that these resolutions are not exactly what we want, and I would hardly like to be put upon the record at this stage of our proceedings as for or against them. The real essence of the matter is, that the Chicago Board of Trade does not want to be charged for this guarantee, and at the same time its members are not willing that the responsibility, after the produce leaves the hands of the consignor, should fall upon them. This I take it, is the matter in a nutshell. They don't care whether the Eastern commission merchants sell for cash, and get cash positively into their hands, or whether they sell it on ten, fifteen or twenty days' credit, so that the consignee pays the cash, and the Western merchant gets it without paying for guarantee. I believe it would be an excellent thing if the principle of cash sales for produce were made universal all over the country.

I think the matter of sufficient importance to have it referred to a Committee of five, representing the various interests, East and West. I think this Committee would be able to make such a report as would tend to correct the evils complained of. I propose, therefore, that such a Committee be appointed to report to-morrow morning.

Mr. GUTHRIE : I have listened with considerable interest to this discussion, and I am more and more convinced that these resolutions now before the Convention, should pass. My seventeen years' experience has convinced me that cash on delivery is possible, and that we should adopt the principle. The gentleman who says it is not possible, is mistaken; because Chicago has set us the example. There can be no question about the possibility of it.

The first resolution is that the sentiment of this Board should be expressed for the payment of property in cash upon delivery; and then it is expected that we pass a resolution recommending every Board associated with us to carry it into action at once. In 1857, in 1859, and last fall, when there was such an excitement in regard to the financial interests of our country, there was no question on the part of any one who sold property, that he should have payment on delivery. Property was not sold on time; this was so with us, as I know from my own experience. In New York, Philadelphia and Boston they sell their property on a few days' time; but let them take action that they will have cash on delivery, and I believe it would be found to be practicable. It depends more upon the seller, than upon the buyer. There may be exceptions, but there is one general rule laid down in the resolution, namely, that when a man sells property, it shall be paid for on delivery. The Chicago Board does not intend so much that the two and a half per cent. shall be saved, as that the property shall be paid for on delivery.

Mr. RONALD : These resolutions, it has been said, are impracticable; but if we do not make the attempt, we shall never succeed. In my experience, so far as it has been attempted, it has been successful. I am engaged in the tobacco trade, in a business amounting to from five to eight millions yearly, and we sell for cash on the day, and on no other terms. If a man comes into my warehouse, and makes a contract, he pays for the tobacco; if he does not take it away, he pays for it as soon as he gets control of it. I never have to wait an hour for the money after the purchase is effected.

We sell from five to eight million dollars a year, all cash, and to tell us that it cannot be done in cities that have ten dollars to our one, is idle. If I send this tobacco to New York, they send back cash in ten days; but these resolutions say that if the sale is for cash, it shall be cash. There is no attempt to prevent parties from selling for credit. It seems important, however, that when cash is stipulated, *it shall be cash;* and if this were understood, there would be fewer failures. The Chicago trade and the Dubuque trade conclusively prove that cash sales are practicable.

The motion to refer was then withdrawn.

Mr. PLUMER: I have listened to this discussion with much interest, and trust that I have profited thereby. I think every reflecting mind must be convinced that after all, whatever resolutions we may pass here as a National Board of Trade, when we go home we shall do business in the same way as we have been accustomed to; we shall conduct our business in whatever way we may think will be conducive to our own interest, no matter what may be passed here with regard to cash sales and guarantee. Why, people in Chicago do business in a way that does not differ materially from our way in the East. A man may buy his flour in Chicago, pay a sight draft for it, and the draft when matured may be paid; or it may not; and what do you call that? Who loses, if the draft is dishonored on its presentation? Does not the commission merchant who sells the flour? So we at the East take the risk. We sell the property, and guarantee our sales for two and a half per cent. commission. I have sold a great deal on commission, and have lost a great deal on sales; I sold the property to what I considered good parties, and for the best interest of my shipper, but after all I have made losses, and have invariably pocketed those losses, as I expect to do to the end of the chapter.

I do not object to these resolutions, except on this ground, that I want this National Board of Trade to be a power in the nation, and I do not wish to come here and spend time in passing resolutions which will be utterly inoperative when we get home. When I return home I shall be met with, " You have been to Cincinnati?" " Yes." " And you have passed resolutions that you will sell all your flour for cash; now let me see you do it." Is it judicious for us to pass resolutions that will be utterly inoperative and of no avail?

Mr. WILBOR: I think there is no doubt that the sentiment of every one on this floor is in favor of cash payments; but how can these be secured? It seems to me that this question of cash sales depends very much upon how you construe the word cash. In

Albany, if we sell a car load of grain to-day, the purchaser expects to pay for it to-morrow. If the purchaser is short, and perfectly good, financially, we may extend the time a little, perhaps to six days; or sometimes on a cargo of flour or grain we give the jobber as much as fifteen days; then the jobber gives the country dealer thirty, perhaps fifty days' credit; the country dealer sells to the consumer, and gives him thirty days. All these are the customs of the trade, and in every instance it is considered a cash sale. The Board of Trade of Chicago wishes to change this order of things, to get at the root of the matter, and to compel the consumer to pay the cash when he buys an article, and to teach the dealer and the jobber that instead of having thirty or sixty days' time, they too must buy with cash. This, I fear, is an utter impossibility. I agree with the spirit of the resolutions, and shall vote for them, though I fear they cannot be carried into effect.

A vote was then taken upon the first resolution; the Chair being unable to decide, the Yeas and Nays were called, with the following result: —

Yeas: Messrs.—

| | | | |
|---|---|---|---|
| Bagley, | Drake, | King, | Randolph, |
| Biggs, | Duvall, | Kirkland, | Ronald, |
| Bradford, | Egan, | Kreikhaus, | Sage, |
| Branch, | Fisk, | Loney, | Smith, |
| Brannin, | Fraley, | McGraw, | Stanard, |
| Brigham, | Gano, | Meier, | Taussig, |
| Brunot, | Grant, | Michener, | Taylor, |
| Buell, | Guthrie, | Monroe, | Thomas, |
| Carrington, | Hazard, | Munn, | Thurston, |
| Cobb, | Holton, | Nettleton, | Turpin, |
| Crichton, | How, | Parr, | Wetherill, |
| Davis, (Geo. W.,) | Hull, | Peters, | Wilbor, |
| Dawson, | Ilsley, | Porter, | Young—52. |

Nays: Messrs.—

| | | | |
|---|---|---|---|
| Allen, (Geo. N.,) | Chalmers, | Jenkins, | Sampson, |
| Allen, (Thomas,) | Converse, | Malone, | Shryock, |
| Boynton, | Hand, | Manson, | Stranahan, |
| Brown, | Harris, | Nazro, | Topp, |
| Buzby, | Hincken, | Plumer, | Trezevant, |
| Carpenter, | Hoffman, | Ropes, | Winsor—24. |

The President announced the whole number of votes cast to be 76; in favor of the resolution 52, against it 24.

The first resolution was therefore declared to be carried.

The second was adopted by the following vote; for, 44, against, 7.

On motion of Mr. RANDOLPH, the preamble was adopted as a whole.

Mr. TREZEVANT: I desire, by courtesy of the house, to be allowed to offer a resolution to be submitted to the Executive Council.

Permission being granted, Mr. TREZEVANT read the following:—

WHEREAS, Railroads are the most influential and powerful agents to develop a country, by inviting population, building factories, machine shops and founderies, and creating constantly increasing demand for iron in all its varied and ever-changing forms; therefore,

*Resolved,* That it is the manifest interest of both government and people that the construction of railroads should be encouraged by the former, and this can be best done by permitting railroad iron to be imported duty free.

Referred to the Executive Council.

Mr. WETHERILL: I beg leave to offer the following:—

WHEREAS, The provision in the National Bank Act, requiring the banks to make a statement of their condition on the first Monday of each quarter, oftentimes compels them, on a certain day of April and October, periods when money is most active, to call in loans in order to place their affairs in a conservative condition, thereby holding out a temptation to speculators to produce an artificial stringency; and whereas, this has been the case on such an extended scale, that the recurrence of the April and October statements has become a source of much uneasiness in the money market, and of regular periodical disturbance to business; therefore,

*Resolved,* That this Board memorialize Congress to so modify the National Bank Act as to require the National Banks to make statements of their condition, not upon any fixed or invariable date, but at periods not less than four times each year, to be determined from time to time by the Comptroller, and always antecedent to the date of notification, and of the required return.

It was moved and seconded that this be referred to the Executive Council.

Mr. RANDOLPH: It strikes me that we are running along rather loosely. I understand that no resolutions of this kind can be introduced at all. Article VIII of the Constitution says, " Questions or resolutions, except those which involve points of order, or refer to matters of courtesy, can be submitted only by the constituent bodies of the Board. . . . . *Provided, however*, that any subject not thus submitted may be considered and acted upon by a vote of two-thirds of the delegates present." Here are several propositions to refer various matters to the Executive Council; is it expected that they will be brought back here for discussion at this session of the Board? If so, they might as well be introduced at once. But before attempting to introduce them, let us see whether two-thirds of the delegates are willing to entertain them. Considerable business is being blocked out by these resolutions, and I am therefore opposed to receiving them, except by a two-thirds vote; and that after the business in order is disposed of.

The PRESIDENT: It seems that the question is ruled by this proviso of the eighth Article,—"That any subject not thus submitted may be considered and acted upon by a vote of two-thirds of the delegates present." It occurs to the Chair that under this provision of the Constitution, upon such a motion as has been made, it would be first right to take the question upon considering it, and then if two-thirds of the delegates present agree to consider it, it might either be taken up and acted upon by the Board at such time as it may appropriate for that purpose, or be referred to the Council. I therefore rule that such propositions shall be submitted in this form: Shall they be considered? and upon the concurrence of two-thirds of the delegates present, they are open for consideration, and action by the Board.

Mr. WETHERILL: I desire that that resolution should be referred. I want the action of the Executive Council upon it.

Mr. HINCKEN: We have for the regular business of this Board questions that have been submitted by constituent bodies for forty days: these questions have been considered and discussed in our local bodies, and if they are thrust aside, and a precedent allowed for new matter to be introduced, nothing will be done. The regular business should be first disposed of.

Mr. STANARD: By what authority is this business referred to the Executive Council? If such matters are coming up here, why not create a Special Committee for the purpose? If they are referred to the Executive Council they will have to be brought in here again; and I think the Council has enough work without this extra labor.

Mr. RANDOLPH: I hope the Chair will rule that the entertainment of these matters is out of order until the regular business, as prescribed by the Council and approved by the Board, has been gone through with.

The PRESIDENT: The question is on the reception of the resolution of the gentleman from Philadelphia, and it will require the concurrence of two-thirds of the members to receive it.

Mr. WETHERILL: The gentleman from Memphis offered a resolution without objection, therefore I offered one which I consider of equal importance; and inasmuch as this Board indicated its wish in regard to the former, I think it would be no more than right that it should do the same thing for mine. If it had objected to the resolution of the gentleman from Memphis, I should not have offered mine.

Mr. NAZRO: I desire to make a motion to lay the resolution offered by the gentleman from Philadelphia, upon the table, as preliminary to another motion, that all the resolutions which have been referred to the Council, and which are out of order, may be recalled.

Carried.

Mr. NAZRO: I now move that the votes by which the several resolutions passed this morning were referred to the Council, be reconsidered.

Carried. These resolutions were then laid on the table.

The PRESIDENT: The subject next in the order of business, is the recommendation of the St. Louis Board of Trade, on the resumption of specie payments.

Mr. MEIER: I move the adoption of the resolution as it stands:

We recommend a declaration in favor of an early return to specie payments, and of the adoption by the National Government of measures efficient for that purpose.

The PRESIDENT: That amounts only to a recommendation, unaccompanied by a resolution. We hoped that the St. Louis Board of Trade would present a distinct resolution expressive of its views upon this subject, so as to bring this matter fairly before the house. If the gentleman has no such resolution, perhaps another delegate will offer one.

Mr. MEIER: I move that the consideration of this proposition be postponed, to enable the delegates of the St. Louis Board of Trade to present a resolution embodying their views.

Mr. TURPIN: I would suggest to the gentleman from St. Louis to add, "and that it be made the special order for to-morrow morning at the opening of the session."

Mr. KIRKLAND: I move that it be the first business in order to-morrow, after the completion of the unfinished business pending at the time of adjournment.

Carried.

Mr. BRUNOT: I desire to correct what I deem to be a little misapprehension; that the paper presented by Mr. BAGLEY, of Detroit was also to be laid upon the table with the resolution of the gentleman from Memphis. I think there is a slight error, if that is the understanding, because in the one case there was a resolution, which has now been laid upon the table, and the other was a communication to this Board, offered by Mr. BAGLEY, from the body he represents, and which was very properly referred to the Executive Council. That reference has not been laid upon the table.

The PRESIDENT: It has been laid upon the table, but may be recalled upon the concurrence of two-thirds of the delegates present.

The next question is that of American Shipping; propositions have been submitted by the New York Produce Exchange and the Boston Board of Trade.

The Secretary read the recommendation from the New York Produce Exchange:—

The New York Produce Exchange having a deep interest in the prosperity of the commerce of the country, and feeling that the United States flag *can* be restored to its position of supremacy on the ocean, proposes the subject of the restoration of the United States flag to the ocean from which it was driven by rebellion, and from which it is kept by want of proper legislation.

Also a resolution proposed by the Boston Board of Trade:—

*Resolved*, That the National Board of Trade respectfully and earnestly urges on the Congress of the United States the enactment of such measures of relief to the foreign and domestic commerce of the United States as shall enable us to compete with the commerce of other nations on the ocean, and thereby permit the promoters of our merchant marine to regain for our country her proud position on the high seas, from which she has been driven by the late war of rebellion.

Mr. HINCKEN: On arriving here we find that the subject embodied in the proposition of the New York Produce Exchange has been so much more carefully discussed, and the matter examined so much more thoroughly by the Boston Board of Trade, that we prefer that their resolution should be put in place of ours.

The present condition of American shipping is pretty well understood. It is well known that most of the carrying trade of the United States is at present done in foreign vessels. The decline in our tonnage has been about 1,500,000 tons. In the month of December last there left the port of New York alone thirty-eight foreign steamers, carrying from 90,000 to 95,000 tons, and these steamers also returned to us with merchandise, showing that we have to pay for freightage of 1,500,000 tons to foreign capitalists. The proposition of the ship-owners of New York, if this Convention go so far as to indorse it, is for the ship-owner to be allowed to buy his ships where he can buy them the cheapest: that is, that he may be able to go to England, the same as France or the North German Confederation, buy steamers on the Clyde and sail them under the American flag. The present state of our law is such that a vessel must be built in the United States to enjoy the privileges of the American flag; she must be built and manned by Americans, or two-thirds of her seamen must be American. The practical working of this is, that in consequence of the lower price at which tonnage can be built on the other side of the Atlantic, we are forced to buy and sail under a foreign flag. A great deal of our tonnage, much more than is generally considered, is registered under the British flag, not to avoid the perils of the waters, but because tonnage which has been purchased for commercial purposes can be more advantageously sailed under a foreign than under our own flag. A foreign government reaps the advantages of this arrangement; and foreign governments put in their men. All we want is that we may purchase our ships where we can buy them the cheapest; that is the simple proposition of the Produce Exchange of New York.

As this is a matter of much importance, and may create much discussion, I should prefer that it be referred to a Committee. We think we can put forth such facts as will justify this Board in adopting this resolution, and we should not adopt any resolution, unless supported by facts; and as the presentation of these facts will take up much time, I think it must go to a Committee to have justice done it.

Mr. WETHERILL: This is an extremely important matter, and I should much regret if this resolution should pass without some report from a Committee, so that it may be printed and scattered broad-cast throughout the country. I move that it be referred to a Committee of seven, of which the gentleman who offered the resolution shall be Chairman.

Carried.

The Chair appointed the following gentlemen to constitute the Committee:

EDWARD HINCKEN, New York,
CHAS. G. NAZRO, Boston,           HENRY WINSOR, Philadelphia,
JOHN B. BROWN, Portland,          J. R. BRANCH, Richmond,
W. M. EGAN, Chicago,              E. O. STANARD, St. Louis.

Mr. CARPENTER: I move that the resolution of the Boston Board of Trade upon the same subject, be referred to the Committee of seven.

Agreed to.

The PRESIDENT: The next business in order is the recommendation of the Baltimore Board of Trade on International Maritime Law.

The Secretary read the following action of the Baltimore Board of Trade:—

WHEREAS, This Board, in response to a communication from the Birmingham Chamber of Commerce, February 9, 1867, did unanimously adopt the resolution: "That, in their opinion, the declaration of the principles by the Congress of Paris, in 1865, falls short of the demands of civilization, the requirements of commerce, and the growing desire to lessen the calamity of war, in not extending to private property of belligerents on the ocean, the freedom from seizure proclaimed for that of neutrals;" therefore be it

"*Resolved*, That this Board present* to the National Board of Trade, to assemble in the city of Cincinnati, in December next, the above important commercial and national subject, and that its delegates be instructed to urge prompt and energetic measures by the National Board of Trade, for the accomplishment of so desirable an end, through national and executive action."

Mr. KIRKLAND : This question is not a new one. One of the most distinguished sons of Pennsylvania, BENJAMIN FRANKLIN, as early as 1785, in the then infancy of our country, advocated these principles, and made a treaty with Prussia at the Hague in that year, to that effect. In 1856, that distinguished citizen of New York, Mr. MARCY, as Secretary of State, enunciated the same doctrine, refusing to have this country represented in the convention of Paris to abolish privateering, unless the principle of exemption from seizure of private property on the high seas, not contraband of war, was included. In Bremen, in December, 1858, a meeting was held on the same subject, which being brought before the Baltimore Board of Trade, was referred to their Committee on Commerce, who made a report that fully expresses the opinions of our Board, and succinctly covers the whole subject. I beg leave to quote:

"That the subject has had their full attention, involving as it does principles of equal importance to the American merchant and ship-owner as to their present advocates in Europe. The United States may indeed claim for one of her noblest sons, the illustrious BENJAMIN FRANKLIN, the merit of having been among the first to advance the doctrine that private property should be held inviolate in war, when on the high seas; the treaty concluded by him with the King of Prussia, at the Hague, in the year 1785, containing a provision to that effect.

"This sentiment, that the peaceful mariner, engaged in the pursuit of lawful commerce, ought not to be molested, though not vindicated in subsequent treaties, has steadily been gaining friends, and has received in more recent times a most able exposition at the hands of Gov. MARCY, late Secretary of State, in his justly celebrated note addressed to the Minister of France, on the 28th of July, 1856.

"Your Committee could not add to the incontrovertible arguments used by that great statesman, nor could they express their own views more clearly than by quoting his letter to a committee of our citizens in answer to their invitation to a public dinner, in which he says : 'The recognition of the principle referred to — the immunity of all private property on the high seas in time of war — I am confident would prove a blessing to the world. The extreme limits of belligerent rights have been gradually contracted as civilization has advanced, and the spirit of the age calls for a mitigation of the rigors of war. The beneficent principle proposed by this government, exempting property upon the ocean from pillage, to the same extent that it is now exempted upon land, by the usage of modern warfare, has been received with favor by all enlightened nations, and the way seems to be already prepared for its introduction into the code of international maritime law.' Apart from all consideration of justice and humanity, self interest manifestly points to the same line of policy; the interests of nations have become so interwoven, and attained such vast dimensions that any serious damage to the commerce of one nation is felt by all. Though we trust that this country will not be obliged to take an active part in future European wars; the apprehension that its neutrality would not be preserved, cannot fail to prove injurious, and even mere rumors of impending conflicts among the powers in Europe must always damage our business.

"The mitigation of the evils of war, by placing private property out of the pale of hostile arrays, is so clearly in the interest of all nations, that the ultimate recognition of this principle cannot be doubtful; public opinion must eventually overcome all opposition, and enforce its universal adoption. In furtherance of that object, and as an expression of the sentiments of the Board, your Committee would offer the following resolutions:

"*Resolved*, That this Board has witnessed with deep interest the efforts now making in Europe for the introduction of a code of international law which shall abolish privateering, and at the same time interdict the seizure of persons and private property by public armed vessels; articles contraband of war only excepted.

"*Resolved*, That it behooves the Government of the United States to take an active part in bringing about these changes, equally demanded by the march of civilization and the true interests of our people, and to take such measures for the promotion of that object as in its wisdom may seem best calculated to secure its early success."

Again in 1866, our Board had its attention called to this most important subject, by a visit from a distinguished gentleman holding the position of President of the Board of Trade and Mayor of the city of Birmingham, England. Our Board reiterated its views, and promised coöperation, and hence have presented to this National Board this question for its action and approval, and that through its influence and its local Boards, our government may be induced at this auspicious moment when liberal views prevail and treaties are being made, and when that most irritating question with Great Britain, growing out of this very question of privateering, and seizure of private property on the high seas, is about being happily settled, to bring the question through our ministers at the courts of the great powers of the world, and have incorporated in the law of nations, that privateering shall be deemed *piracy*, and that private property shall be exempt from seizure on the seas, the great highway of nations, upon which all peaceful mariners may sail without fear of molestation or danger. In the infancy of our country, privateering was found an useful and important arm of a defensive warfare, and the Baltimore Clippers, fitted out from the port of Baltimore, particularly in the war of 1812, performed as important a part, as probably those from any other part of the country; but now that we have reached, as a nation, the strength of vigorous manhood, and are not likely to be subjects of attack, we can dispense with this barbarous service; why in a war between this country and England, should Brazil, who derives her principle supply of bread from us and sells us a very large portion of her coffee in return, be punished because we are at war with another power? why China? why France? It has been said that our privateers were to be considered the same as our volunteers on land; but I apprehend that in no civilized country can a volunteer company go out, commissioned with full license, to rob, burn and destroy private property, and appropriate to their own use and benefit, all they may deem worth saving from destruction.

Commerce is the handmaid of Christianity and civilization; war is destructive to both, and whilst war may at times be a necessary evil to be resorted to, to save national life or principles, its evils have been from time to time mitigated, and the spirit of the age now calls for the adoption of the principles referred to by all civilized people; and I hope and trust this Board will adopt them, and urge all local Boards to adopt them, and send them to their representatives in Congress, so that from all parts of our great country there may come this pressure to induce Congress to take action by such legislation as may be necessary, to authorize the Secretary of State, by treaty or otherwise, as they in their wisdom may devise, to make these beneficent principles the Universal Law of Nations.

Mr. TREZEVANT: I fear my views may be unpopular with some of the members of this Board; but, at the same time, feeling constrained to give a reason for the vote that I shall give, to justify myself, I rise to take exception to the proposition.

I am opposed to the abolition of privateering. I think that the history of our country during the war in which we accomplished our independence, shows most conclusively that this was a most important element in our strife; and I call the attention of gentlemen to the fact that the resolutions from New York and Boston, recently under consideration, pointed out to this body that we are not able to compete with foreign nations in the building of vessels. If we adopt resolutions of this kind, and war should occur, we tie our own hands. If we are unable to compete with England in the building of vessels, and have to call upon Congress to give us the liberty of buying vessels from abroad, in time of war we would be at the mercy of those nations whose ships surpass our own in tonnage and capacity; and it is contrary to the nature of a republican government to maintain a large standing army, or a large navy. The late war has shown it to be true that we do not need a great standing army. Soldiers spring up from all sides when they are called upon by their country; and though trained to the peaceful pursuits of life, they quickly develop capacities for war, and thus relieve us of the expense of keeping a large standing army. But if we tie our hands, as here proposed, I say we shall be at the mercy of nations who are superior to us, as France and England unquestionably are, in time of war. We commercial men are for peace, and we should preserve it as long as possible; but when war does come, the commercial men are as ready to make sacrifices for the government as any class of people. If we permit the nations of Europe to have more war vessels than ourselves, to blockade our ports and shut us up, we must starve like rats; and what good would it be to announce that property shall be free when it gets upon the high seas, if we are thus shut up?

I maintain that the privateer is precisely like the volunteer soldier; he is a soldier that is called upon in time of need; a soldier that costs the government nothing in time of peace, but when war comes, is ready to strike for the flag of his country. The doctrine held by Mr. PIERCE, when President of the United States, and by Mr. MARCY, was that the government would not give up the right of privateering, for the reason that it did not desire to keep a large navy; and inasmuch as we want the merchant service in time of war to help the government to protect our flag, I am opposed to abolishing that which I regard as the great strength of a republican government.

Mr. TAYLOR: As I recollect the negotiation to which reference has been made, the argument of the gentleman from Memphis has force and application. It was proposed to the United States, then having a feeble navy, to relinquish the right of volunteer warfare upon the ocean. Our government held this language to the powers of Europe, that then, as now, had powerful maritime armaments: " We will not entertain the question of the abolition of privateering, unless you, with your present advantages in case of war, shall relinquish any right to confiscate, or seize, or destroy private property upon the seas, which the law of nations forbids to hostile forces upon land." The proposition to abolish privateering was coupled by Mr. MARCY, and by his superior, with that fundamental and broad condition.

If I understand the Baltimore proposition, it has reference more particularly to this, that there should be the same regard for the rights of neutrals on the sea, which the law of nations has established upon land. But that negotiation occurred before the great civil war, through which we have successfully passed, and which has placed us in a very different relation to this subject.

The restraint which we desired to impose upon the great maritime powers of Europe was rejected, and then, in our great hour of trial, privateers were equipped in English ports, in violation of the law of nations and of the law of England, and more than that, those privateers, ranging the broad seas thus by the sufferance of Great Britain, were recognized as men-of-war in English colonies and ports, and thus was fastened indelibly upon the English government the obligation to respond in damages for every dollar of American property which was destroyed by the Alabama or the Shenandoah. However I might regard this proposition under other circumstances, and I remember I regarded it with great favor when presented by Mr. MARCY, I think now is not the time to bring it forward, as a sort of cloak and cover, and in some degree, an apology for these English depredations. Let this proposition be withheld. Let us stand and enforce the reclamations to which I have alluded, and until the Alabama claims are settled and discharged to the satisfaction of every American citizen, I say let the law of privateering, the present maritime usage of nations, remain. When England has done her duty, and before the whole world, has made restitution, then we will go back to the law of Mr. MARCY, and establish the broad principles that should govern the nations.

Mr. DAVIS, of Cincinnati: When Mr. FIELD, representative from the Birmingham Chamber of Commerce, was here to lay this matter in person before the Boards of Trade and Chambers of Commerce of this country, the facts, as given by Mr. TAYLOR, were stated in our conversations with Mr. FIELD, and were well understood; and when that gentleman was informed that while the Alabama claims were still unsettled, it was a very unfavorable time to ask our people to do what we were so willing to do in 1855; that our people were not willing to give up the right to seize the property of belligerents; and that, in view of the new state of things introduced by the rebellion, it would not be a proper time to do it; Mr. FIELD confessed that his work was merely to prepare the minds of the people of the United States to entertain the subject after the Alabama claims were settled, and that it would not be expected of the people of the United States, angered as they were at the improper conduct of the British government, neither would they be asked to give this up at the present time.

Mr. ROPES : In reference to what has been said, I would first remark that the passage of the resolutions contemplated by this Board at the present time, would not, I conceive, interfere with the peculiar position of our government towards Great Britain. They would not compromise our government in any way, but merely announce what we conceive to be the right principles to regulate this question. And, in the second place, I am free to say that I think in this Board we are not to ask what is the expediency of the principles that we are to decide upon, but what is right. If the principle is right, let us take that principle and announce it in all its fullness, and leave it to our government to use it or refuse it, and compel Great Britain to a speedy settlement of our demands upon her.

In regard to the argument of the gentleman from Memphis, it seems to me that it cuts both ways. He says we have no large navy, we are not in the habit of keeping up a large standing army and navy, and I entirely agree with him. I believe the smaller our army and navy, compatible with safety, the better.

But, Sir, we were suddenly called upon, a few years ago, to enter upon a great struggle. Did we commission a single privateer? The gentleman says that on the sea a privateer would take the place of a volunteer on land. Did our government give to any such a roving commission, like the infatuated rebels, in order to destroy commerce? Our vessels went out with an honest and honorable commission for the time being; sometimes they were chartered, sometimes purchased, but always commissioned as *vessels of war;* and in that capacity they did the work of putting down the rebellion; and they will do it again when called upon. The same tactics may be employed again, if any power likes to go to war with us. I am not expecting a war between any European power and our nation; but if a war comes, there are our ships, and they can be commissioned in a short time and sent to sea under the government flag. And that is the only proper and respectable way in which we can employ them.

There was, it is true, a certain government that used privateers recently, but they came, nearly all, to a most inglorious end. It had one or two government ships, which did some mischief, but its privateers were the most shabby failures that were ever heard of in history.

We stand upon the broad ground that the more private enterprise we have, and the more ships we have, the better able our government will be to enter promptly into war with any nation, by commissioning private ships.

It has been said by the gentleman from Memphis, that if we relinquish the principle of privateering, we discourage our mercantile marine. He says, truly, our shipping interest is falling off. It is true that we have almost lost our commerce at sea, and our merchant service would gain nothing by the example which the gentleman would set before them. Privateers get their letters of marque and go on their own plundering expeditions, destroying property or seizing it for their own gain.

Mr. TREZEVANT: Do they not sail under the flag of the government.

Mr. ROPES: They do carry the flag of the government, but they don't carry any pennant of a government commander, they have no officer appointed by a government, they are strictly and entirely private property. They are privateers. They go on the ocean as a speculation, with their own armament, and with their own men, often sailing on shares, like whalers, or like fishermen on the Banks. And so they go about, making all the mischief they can, destroying all the property they can, and plundering all they can, to enrich themselves at the expense of the helpless and harmless subjects of the opposing power. It is high time that all this should come to an end.

I maintain that the progress of the present age is not towards barbarism, but towards civilization. I say war is essentially barbarous. If you please, it is a necessary barbarism. It is a horror which we ought to avoid in every possible instance, and this was done lately, until we were called fools and cowards, in our endeavors to avoid that civil war into which we were finally plunged. I hope we shall entertain the principle that war is an evil, to be deprecated and guarded against; and far be it from us to do anything that would promote war for the sake of the pitiful spoils that might be gained by the plunder of innocent men. When we are fighting, we want to do the enemy all the harm we can, we have a right to take his forts, to attack him on his own ground, but we should always respect private property as much as possible. We have a right to checkmate him as a foe, but to single out poor private citizens, and rob them of their little property, on the high seas or anywhere else, is a shame and a disgrace to any civilized nation.

I take it on the broad ground of Christianity, civilization and decency. The time is come, I think, for every Board of Commerce to speak out on this subject, and I hope that we may view it in this light. There are points, I am aware, that may be urged in its favor. It may appear, sometimes, that the destruction of private property may accomplish important ends, or that the assassination of a General or a President may accomplish very important ends; but does the enemy do it? Does any one believe that the assassination of the late President of the United States was sanctioned by any honorable man who was opposed to him in lawful warfare?

When Philip the Second of Macedon was murdered, and when the Prince of Orange was assassinated by a fanatical Jesuit, did not all Europe set up a cry of horror? And is it not pitiful for us to attempt to carry on, or to sanction anywhere, such a mode of warfare?

Shortly after the visit of the gentleman from Birmingham, (Mr. FIELD) the Boston Board of Trade passed unanimously a series of resolutions, which I hold in my hand, and as they convey my own impressions on the subject, I will read them:

"WHEREAS, War, in all its forms, is repugnant to the spirit of Christianity and to the genius of civilization, and is opposed to the development of industry, as well as to the mental and moral progress of society; and

"WHEREAS, The success of every effort tending to mitigate its horrors, and to diminish the motives and temptations to its prosecution, is greatly to be desired, and in every way promoted and encouraged; and

"WHEREAS, The Government of the United States has already given repeated evidence of its desire to mitigate to the utmost these evils, particularly those of maritime warfare, by proposing to abolish, not only privateering, but all warfare on, or seizure of private property at sea, whether of belligerents or of neutrals, and whether by national armed ships or otherwise; therefore

"*Resolved*, That this Board heartily approves and. indorses the principle of immunity of all private property (except when contraband of war) on the high seas, and pledges itself to coöperate heartily with the efforts of enlightened statesmen and philanthropists in all parts of the world to obtain its practical and permanent recognition by our own and all other nations."

Mr. NAZRO: I concur with all that my colleague has said, and can add nothing to it, except a single suggestion. I have always considered privateering as simply legalized piracy; and usually, I believe, Sir, it results in unlegalized piracy; for generally those men who will go on the high seas and take to stealing, in a legal manner, the property of private citizens, simply because their nation is at war with the country to which those citizens belong, would take the private property and take the lives of those men illegally, if they were not deterred from doing it by the fear that their own lives were in danger of being forfeited.

One argument has been used that needs a reply, and that is in regard to the smallness of our navy, — that we do not want a large navy. Take the nations of Great Britain and France, with their powerful navies, let war break out suddenly, and they can sweep the ocean. And what is the result? What was the result in our late rebellion? The very disgraceful sight which we now exhibit to the world, of a great portion of our commerce swept from the ocean, and placed under a foreign flag! If these resolutions had been in force, and private property respected, there would have been no necessity for private owners to put their vessels under foreign flags.

There are various reasons for demanding this; there are reasons of a public nature, in regard to the character of our marine; and reasons of a far higher nature, called for by the religion we profess, and by the common humanity which we hold, that we should abolish every such relic of barbarism. I hope, as this country rises in power, and eventually takes front rank, as we suppose we shall, among the nations, that we shall always stand upon high and noble principles; that we shall not be afraid to take high, moral ground in reference to every question of this nature; that we shall not, either for private interests, or because of any fear that Great Britain may make better terms on the claims of the Alabama, lower our standing. Let us take our position, and demand redress of Great Britain, or any other nation, that dare infringe upon our rights; but let us not do it as a matter of expediency; let us not wait till this Alabama question is settled, but reiterate the principles held by a majority of the nation, that privateering is piracy. Then let us settle our claims upon the justice of those claims, and not upon any consideration of expediency.

Mr. WINSOR: As I do not wish to be considered an immoral or irreligious man, I will give some reasons for the views I hold. I do not understand these resolutions to be levelled so much against privateering as against the capture of private property on the ocean. There is a difference between property on the ocean and on the land; and a reason why one should be respected, and the other not. Property on the land, consisting of the homes of men, where they have their wives and children, should ever be respected; but on the ocean there are no women and children; men go as sailors for their own private interests, and if they do not want to put their property in peril, they should keep it at home. That is one reason why property should not be respected on the ocean as on the land.

Such resolutions, and the passage of an act carrying out those resolutions, would tend to produce war instead of preventing it. I hold that it is a shameful thing that we should respect property and not respect human lives. It is proposed that private property shall be respected in all cases; but I hold the reverse of that, that we should spare the lives and let the property go.

There is no such thing as international law. There can be no law without penalty. What is called international law, is nothing but certain rules and regulations, and strong nations break through them whenever it is to their interest to do so. There is, I assert, no nation that would observe this law in an extremity.

Mr. CRICHTON: I am surprised to hear in this Board, composed of merchants, representing the commercial interests of the country, a dissenting voice to the truly Christian and humane resolution proposed by the Baltimore Board of Trade, and presented here by the delegation from that body, the "Suppression of Privateering and the immunity of private property, not contraband of war, on the high seas, in time of war."

In all civilized nations, commerce has ever been the pioneer of Christianity and humanity, and the hand-maid of peace; through the world, commerce has opened up the pathway to the missionary, civilizing and bringing the "waste places of the earth" under the benign teachings of Christianity; and shall it be said that this intelligent body refuses to recommend and uphold so Christian a proposition? Such a recommendation would be at this time especially fitting on the part of this country, with her wounds not yet healed from the recent civil war, and when privateering in all the horrors of "licensed piracy" is still fresh in our memories. Who does not recollect how the loyal heart swelled with indignation as report after report came to our shores of the devastations of private property by the Alabama; or of the seizure of that steamer, and the murder of part of her crew, while on her trip from New York to Portland, in very sight of land?

This proposition would come therefore from this country, at such a moment, with great magnanimity.

The gentleman from St. Paul would not yield one iota of the right of privateering while the claims upon England, for destruction of property by the Alabama were still pending and unsettled, and while the naval power of that country was so great as to be a standing menace to the world. He would, by the spirit of his remarks, enforce the law of retaliation, instead of, as a man of commerce, and consequently, by all his interests, a man of peace; unfortunately, we from the seaboard, know something more of the devastations and horrors of privateering than our friends from the valley of the Mississippi.

Sir, the decrease of tonnage of the United States, during the war, was over one and one half millions of tons, by the destruction of vessels by privateers.

But we, at this day, in view of the very facts he recites, while we are sufferers, and with the recollections of those sufferings, still fresh in our memories, from the evils and cruelties of privateering practised by the enemy during the recent war, should deem it an act of the highest magnanimity to announce to the world our detestation of privateering.

It has been well said that the spirit of the age calls for a mitigation of the rigors of war, and hence the abolishment of standing armies and navies is now widely agitated in England.

That able statesman and philanthropist, JOHN BRIGHT, in a speech recently made by him in England, said,—

"There is no necessity whatever for those fleets, at your cost, traversing every ocean as they do now. I do not know whether it is a dream, or a vision, or a foresight of the reality that sometimes passes across my mind,—I like to dwell upon it, that the time will come when the maritime nations of Europe and the United States may see that these fleets are of no use :—they are, merely menaces offered from one country to another,—and when navies as a great instrument of war and aggression shall no longer be upheld."

These sentiments shadow forth the views of the age. Shall we, as a mercantile body, ignore such sentiments? I trust not; it would be one of the highest and holiest aspirations of this Board to send forth to the world that this country, as a Christian nation, demands the abolishment of that cruel and barbarous system of warfare.

Mr. TREZEVANT : I move to amend the resolution, to read thus:

"That in our opinion, the declaration of the principles by the Congress of Paris, in 1865, falls short of the demands of civilization, the requirements of commerce, and the growing desire to lessen the calamity of war, in not extending to private property of belligerents on the ocean and on the land, the freedom from seizure, proclaimed for that of neutrals."

Commerce is called the "healthful and beautiful daughter of peace;" truly is it so called. This is a Convention of business men,— men who, of all classes of citizens, in all ages of the world, have been advocates for the progress of peace and civilization. I see nothing objectionable in the resolution, if the principle be right that private property should be exempt at any time from seizure and destruction by belligerents. But I should regret very much if it were not amended so as to include the exemption from destruction of private property on land as well as on the high seas.

The gentleman from Boston has spoken of the ravages and depredations of the Alabama. I could take him down south, Sir, and show him depredations upon our quiet land, and the destruction of our homesteads, houses and barns, which it was not at all necessary to commit, any more than the destruction of property on the high seas. War is an evil; and when I hear gentlemen speak in justification of it, I always conclude that right makes might, and whenever war breaks out, might makes law.

I do not intend to oppose the resolution. It is in the progress of refinement, peace and humanity. But I heartily wish that my friends from Baltimore had incorporated the one idea I have thrown out, that private property on the land should as religiously be exempted from destruction as private property upon the seas.

Mr. KIRKLAND: I will accept the preamble and resolution of the gentleman from Boston, substantially as read by him, making one or two unimportant additions. They embody admirably the views of the Baltimore Board of Trade. They now stand thus:

WHEREAS, War, in all its forms, is repugnant to the spirit of Christianity and to the genius of civilization, and is opposed to the development of industry as well as to the mental and moral progress of society; and

WHEREAS, The success of every effort tending to mitigate its horrors and to diminish the motives and temptations to its prosecution, is greatly to be desired, and in every way promoted and encouraged; and

WHEREAS, The Government of the United States has already given repeated evidence of its desire to mitigate to the utmost these evils, particularly those of maritime warfare, by proposing to abolish not only privateering, but all warfare on or seizure of private property at sea, whether of belligerents or of neutrals, and whether by national armed ships or otherwise; therefore

*Resolved*, That this Board heartily approves and indorses the principle of immunity of all private property (excepting when contraband of war) on the high seas, and pledges itself to coöperate heartily with the efforts of enlightened statesmen and philanthropists in all parts of the world, to obtain its practical and permanent recognition by our own and all other nations; and it would respectfully urge upon Congress, legislation to this desirable end.

*Resolved*, That all local organizations, component parts of this Board, are hereby requested to take action for the furtherance of this object.

The first resolution was then voted upon, with the following result: Yeas, 50; Nays, 6.

The second resolution received, Yeas, 46; Nays, 3.

The preamble was carried by, Yeas, 44; Nays, none; and the whole were declared to have been adopted.

Mr. RANDOLPH: I move to postpone the order of business now before the house, for the purpose of offering a resolution to take from the table the communication from the Detroit Board of Trade, submitted by. Mr. BAGLEY.

Mr. HINCKEN: This communication from the Detroit Board of Trade, is addressed to the National Board of Trade, and I am in favor of receiving it, but I am opposed to its taking any precedence of other business.

The PRESIDENT: That would not be the effect of the motion; it would not give it any preference.

The question is upon postponing the order of business for the purpose suggested by Mr. RANDOLPH; it requires the concurrence of two-thirds of the delegates present.

Agreed to.

Mr. BAGLEY: In presenting this communication from the Detroit Board of Trade, I do not wish to occupy the time of this body in attempting to show its importance; but will move that this Board refer it to the Executive Council.

Agreed to.

Mr. RONALD: I move that the resolution offered by my colleague, with respect to the Mississippi levees, take the same course; it came from the Louisville Board of Trade.

Mr. BRANNIN: We offered it in ample time, but by some mishap of our Secretary, or of myself, who offered it, it got misplaced, and was not presented in time to come up in the regular order of business. I would like to have it referred to the Executive Council.

The PRESIDENT: The question is as to withdrawing from the table, for reference, the communication from the Louisville Board of Trade in relation to repairing the levees of the Mississippi river.

Unanimously agreed to.

The PRESIDENT: The order of business will now be resumed. The next subject in order, is the recommendation of the St. Louis Board of Trade in reference to telegraphic reform, as follows:

We recommend a declaration in favor of the adoption by the general government, of measures to cheapen and extend telegraphic communication between the different points of the country, by making it a part of its postal system.

Mr. SHRYOCK: This is a question which emanated from the St. Louis Board of Trade, and comes in the form of a recommendation. It is a subject that will, I think, take a very wide latitude in debate, and that it may be properly initiated, the St. Louis Board of Trade have thought proper to draw up for presentation to this body, the following preamble and resolution:

WHEREAS, The experience of European governments, where the telegraphic system has been worked for years, and where its benefits have been enjoyed by a much larger number of the people in all the various walks of life, and at a cost of not over one-third the rates paid by the people of this country; and

WHEREAS, The Board of Trade of St. Louis are satisfied that the work of telegraphing could and should be performed in the United States as cheaply as in any country in the world; and, believing that the blessings of telegraph communication between the several sections of our wide domain could be better and more fully brought within the reach of all classes at very small cost; therefore,

*Resolved*, That we recommend to Congress to buy all the present lines of telegraph, or construct others in sufficient numbers as shall be found necessary to do the business of the country, unite the same to the postal system, to be under the same control, making it a part and parcel of the same service, in order that the rates for telegraphic messages can be so reduced as to make the maximum rate for a message of ten words twenty cents for five hundred miles, and in like ratio for service performed for any greater distance.

It is a matter of very great importance, and I am not fully prepared to give it that consideration, or to argue the question as fully as its merits and importance demand. There is, however, a gentleman who is fully prepared to give us all the statistics of the system as it is now worked in Europe, and who will very clearly present the advantages that will accrue from its adoption in this country. If the Board will extend to him the courtesy of presenting this matter to them. I am satisfied that he can give us all the necessary light upon the subject, and in the most concise and well digested form. The gentleman to whom I refer, is Mr. HUBBARD, and I will without detaining you longer, move that Mr. HUBBARD be invited to address the National Board of Trade on this subject.

The PRESIDENT: That can only be done by the unanimous consent of the Board.

Mr. BRUNOT: I hope that consent will not be given; not that I doubt that the gentleman who it is proposed shall address us, would be able to give us a great deal of information, but it establishes a precedent which is, I think, an unwise and a dangerous one for us to adopt. On the ground recommended, every gentleman from any part of the country might come here with his special project, though it be a project of national importance, of which he is the advocate, and might ask to take a position upon this floor in advocacy of its adoption. I do not think it is best to open the door by establishing such a precedent as that now asked for; and I hope that all the questions that come before us will be confined in their discussion to members of this body.

Mr. WETHERILL: I desire to address the Board on the propriety of permitting Mr. HUBBARD to present this matter of telegraphic reform before this National Board of Trade.

The PRESIDENT: That is not in order.

Mr. WETHERILL: I will endeavor to confine my remarks to the resolution now before the body.

The question as to the feasibility of the government controlling the telegraph lines of the country, and uniting them with the postal system, is an important one, and should receive that due consideration which its importance demands. The plan which the resolution now under consideration proposes is, as I understand it, similar to that which is now before Congress in the form of an act to establish the postal telegraph system, prepared by Mr. HUBBARD. As that gentleman is in this city, and is thoroughly posted in the workings of the present system, and the advantages to be derived by the proposed change, I had hoped that an opportunity would have been granted by this body for his being heard. His plan, if I am correctly informed, is this: the Postmaster-General is to be authorized to receive bids from any telegraph company, for the transmission of messages received and delivered through the post-offices throughout the country, at a rate not exceeding twenty-five cents for any message of not over twenty words, for any distance not exceeding five hundred miles; said messages to be received as letters are now received, without extra expense. All messages to be stamped or written on stamped paper. In case there should be no bidders for the contract, then a new company shall be incorporated, with restrictions as to the price and details of the work to be done, in accordance with the proposals asked for in the contract. The advantages to be derived from this system are obvious. It will, from the increased number of messages sent, greatly cheapen the cost of transmission. At present the system is under the control (with the exception of a line of twenty-five hundred miles) of one company. This company, with an original capital of about five millions of dollars, has been so largely increased, that its present capital reaches nearly forty millions of dollars; and with about one hundred thousand miles of wire, controls the entire telegraph business of the country. The rates charged by this company are very much higher than they should be, and from the vast importance to the mercantile community of the work performed, it is not right that it should be under the control of so gigantic a monopoly. The rates are also variable, and are not governed by any apparent rule. Thus, I am informed, for a message sent from this city to New Orleans, the charge would be two dollars and fifty cents, while if the message is reversed, that is from New Orleans to this city, the rate charged would be two dollars and seventy-five cents. This want of uniformity is improper; it is an outrage upon the business men of the country, and they should therefore indorse the proposed change, and ask Congress to adopt the remedy. It is confidently believed that if the entire matter were placed under the charge of the postal department, the officials and the officers of that department could be advantageously used, and through the facilities thereby obtained, greatly increase its use and cheapen its cost. The penny postage in England, years ago, was considered impracticable; time has shown the reverse of this. It is now confidently believed that the present system of telegraphing can be so modified and cheapened, that a like result may be secured. The government, with the appliances at its command, can do much towards the accomplishment of this desirable result, and in my opinion, the good work thus commenced, should be fully indorsed by this body.

The chief objections to the movement, are these: it is asserted that the important elements of the system, security, secrecy and despatch, cannot be secured to the people through corrupt officials, who by party politics, control the departments. To this I reply that this objection holds good to the postal system; yet we hear of no complaints, for that system is conducted to the entire satisfaction of the community. We listen, I fear, with an attentive ear, to much that is said of the corruption of officials of the government, yet we care to do but little to remedy the evil. The civil service bill of Mr. JENCKES, would, if adopted, go far towards the desired result. If merit were the standard to be reached, and all applicants were compelled to come up to the mark, objections like these would be removed. No, the government can do the work; the postal department can be made just as secure, just as reliant, just as speedy, as the monopoly now working the lines; and to this may be added, that the department will, from the necessity of the case, be bound to furnish to the public, telegraphic messages at a low rate, while the main object of the monopoly is to declare large dividends to their stockholders.

Mr. JENKINS: I conceive the subject now presented, to be one of very great importance. I think it would be a very good way to get at its merits, to refer it to a Committee similar to that on American shipping. I therefore move that the preamble and resolutions now before the Board, be referred to a special Committee of seven, with instructions to report to-morrow.

Mr. DRAKE: I hope this motion will not prevail. A number of important questions are yet to be presented, and if this is referred to a Committee, we shall not have time to get back a report in time for action. This question of telegraphic communication, is one of the most practical questions that will come before us, and it is important that an expression of this Board should go forth in favor of cheapening and extending telegraphic communication all over this country. I speak feelingly on this subject, as I come from a remote point, where the tax on telegraphing is so heavy, as, for instance, from St. Paul to New Orleans, that messages are only sent in cases of the greatest emergency. We therefore feel more interest in this subject than other cities may do who are nearer together. A bill is now pending before Congress on this subject, and hence the importance of our speaking, in order to strengthen the friends of this measure. The bill to which I refer, proposes that the government shall by contract let out the transmission of telegraphic communications throughout the United States, and establishes an office in each place where a post-office now exists, and provides that charges shall be graduated upon some uniform scale. It is proposed that each telegraphic communication shall have placed upon it a postage letter stamp, in order that the government shall by that means keep up its revenue, as it is supposed the extended use of the telegraph would correspondingly decrease the number of letters transmitted by mail. In attaining this end, it would be unjust for the government to step in and take the business out of the hands of the private companies already established, whose capital is invested in the enterprize, and thus to ruin their business. It is thought that they should have an opportunity to make their present capital and facilities available by becoming themselves carriers for the government. An important end gained by the proposed arrangement, would be, that it would take from the government the construction and maintenance of telegraphic lines, as all experience has shown that similar work can be better done and maintained by private enterprise than by the government. It is estimated by those conversant with the subject, that messages could be delivered at the rate of twenty-five cents for ten words, at the most remote parts of our country. Telegraphing can be, and ought to be made cheaper. The present lines represent many millions of capital, and are managed in the selfish interest of the directors and managers. We know that telegraphic lines can be constructed at one hundred dollars per mile, and that such an investment of capital would enable a line to transmit messages at twenty-five cents each and make a profit, and thus relieve the commercial interests of our country from the incubus that now presses upon it.

Mr. JENKINS : I am in favor of some general postal telegraph system. I am satisfied that it is necessary, that it is practicable, and that whatever course this Board may take, it is coming very soon. I should be very glad if this Committee would give a very decided expression of its opinion in favor of some general system, without any reference to Mr. A. or Mr. B.'s bill that may be presented to Congress. I think the Committee should not commit itself to any particular bill.

Mr. ALLEN, of Philadelphia : I hope that this resolution will be referred to a Committee. I was in hope that a short and distinct resolution would have been presented here. The one under discussion does not satisfy me.

The motion on referring the resolution to a Committee, was then put and carried.

The Chair, by request, appointed the Committee, consisting of—

H. M. JENKINS, Wilmington,
L. R. SHRYOCK, St. Louis,    E. F. DRAKE, St. Paul,
GEO. O. CARPENTER, Boston,    JOHN T. TREZEVANT, Memphis,
J. S. T. STRANAHAN, New York,    F. R. BRUNOT, Pittsburgh.

The President read a communication from CHAS. F. WILSTACH, Esq., Mayor of Cincinnati, on behalf of the city government, inviting the delegates to a dinner to be given at Pike's Music Hall on the following evening, at half-past six.

Mr. WETHERILL: I move that this invitation be accepted, and that a Committee of two be appointed to return suitable acknowledgments.

Carried.

Messrs. WETHERILL and BAGLEY were appointed the Committee.

The Board then adjourned.

FRIDAY, DECEMBER 4, 1868.

The National Board of Trade met pursuant to adjournment.

The President in the chair.

The PRESIDENT: The inclemency of the weather seems to have prevented the arrival of the clergyman who was to have officiated; we shall, therefore, have to dispense with the usual religious services.

On motion, the reading of the Journal was dispensed with.

The PRESIDENT: I have received a telegraphic dispatch from Mobile, accrediting Messrs. STEWART, SMITH and WALKER as delegates to the National Board of Trade.

Mr. MONROE: I move to refer the application to the Committee on Admissions.

Carried.

The PRESIDENT: The next business in order is the report of the Committee on Admissions.

I would suggest, in view of the vast importance of the subject we are to consider this morning, after the report of the Committee on Admissions has been received, that to enable us to hear from all sections of the country upon the resumption of specie payments, the delegates from the St. Louis Board of Trade, by whom the resolutions on this subject have been introduced to our notice, shall open the debate, and shall first say every thing they desire; and that then the different organizations represented here shall be called as they stand upon the roll, so that members from each of the delegations may discuss the question. I presume that one, and perhaps more, from each of the larger delegations, are prepared to give their views and the views which, as they believe, prevail among their constituents upon this matter. If this course meets with your approbation, I shall pursue it in ruling this discussion.

Mr. RANDOLPH: I beg to report further from the Committee on Credentials. The first application is from the Board of Trade of Norfolk, Virginia.

The credentials of Mr. HUGHES were read, together with a certificate of the charter from the Clerk of the Court.

Mr. RANDOLPH: The Committee have concluded upon the representation made to them of the facts, that the Board is clearly entitled to be a member of this organization. It seems to be chartered, and it is an old and important body and the Committee therefore recommend its admission to membership. The credentials of Mr. HUGHES are straightforward, and perhaps he ought to be received, but as they are not under seal, the Committee suggest that if Mr. HUGHES be not admitted as a delegate, he should be allowed the courtesies of the floor, with the right of speaking but not of voting, and that the Norfolk Board be admitted to membership.

Mr. STANARD: I move that the Norfolk Board of Trade be admitted as a member of this Board.

The roll of Boards having been called, the motion was carried.

Mr. NAZRO: I move that the delegate be admitted to the privilege of the floor, without the right of voting.

The motion, after some discussion on giving full privileges to the delegate, was agreed to.

Mr. RANDOLPH: The next credentials are those of Mr. VOORHEES, of Springfield, which were referred back to the Committee. This gentleman appeared before us and made the statement that the Springfield Board of Trade has been organized under the laws of Ohio. It has a charter or paper necessary to make it a corporate body, which paper has been deposited with the proper State official, and a certificate to that effect was brought here and handed to the Secretary. It was afterwards withdrawn by Mr. VOORHEES and lost. We have, consequently, no documents in regard to this Board now before us. Mr. VOORHEES is not clear as to what are the terms of its organization; he understands it to be an association of merchants and manufacturers for general commercial purposes, but we have no certain knowledge that it would come within the rules required by our Constitution. The Committee, therefore, after carefully considering the subject, have concluded to report unfavorably to the admission of the Springfield Board, but as gentlemen have come here in good faith to represent it, we recommend that they be allowed the courtesies of the floor, hoping that at the next session they may present credentials which will satisfactorily admit their Board to membership with us.

Mr. HOFFMAN : I move that the delegates from Springfield be admitted to seats on the floor, without permission to speak.

The motion was seconded.

Mr. GUTHRIE : Is that intended to modify the action of the Board with regard to Mr. HUGHES?

The PRESIDENT : No, Sir.

Mr. MUNN : It strikes me that the recommendation of the Committee is not very consistent. They have asked us to refuse to admit the Board of Trade of Springfield, and yet they recommend that its members be received by us.

Mr. RANDOLPH : Allow me to correct the gentleman. We don't pretend to decide that the Board is not entitled to membership, only that we have not sufficient evidence that it is.

Mr. DAVIS, of Cincinnati : We have evidence that the charter of the Springfield Board of Trade has been on our files. Mr. GANO yesterday testified to that fact, but it seems to have been withdrawn and lost.

Mr. RANDOLPH : Allow me to make another correction. The paper referred to was not a charter. It was merely a certificate that a charter is on file.

Mr. DAVIS : I accept the correction. I am of opinion that though we cannot admit these gentlemen to vote, they should be permitted to speak freely on all questions which may be brought before the Board. I move to amend to that effect.

The amendment prevailed, and the resolution as amended was carried.

Mr. RANDOLPH : The Committee have now to report in regard to the Council Bluffs Board of Trade. Mr. JOHNSON, the delegate, is not certain that the body is incorporated, but has no doubt of it. He did not know that it was necessary that he should present evidence of this. The Committee recommend that he be entitled to the courtesy of the floor, with the right to speak, but that the Board be not entitled to membership.

Mr. HOFFMAN : I move that the latter portion of the recommendation referring to the "right to speak," be stricken out.

The amendment was put and carried.

The PRESIDENT : The question is on the resolution as amended.

Carried.

Mr. RANDOLPH : The Chamber of Commerce of Galveston, Texas, is the next body seeking admission. There are no delegates present. The Secretary writes under date of November 6th, desiring admission, and sending the necessary documents. The Committee recommend that the body be admitted a member of the National Board of Trade.

The roll of Boards being called, the recommendation was unanimously adopted.

Mr. RANDOLPH : The next application is from the Cairo Chamber of Commerce. The application is duly sealed with the corporate seal; 'Mr. RAUM, the President, is the delegate. We recommend that the body be admitted to membership. Everything is regular but the production of a copy of their charter, which I know, personally, they possess. We therefore also recommend the reception of the delegate.

Mr. HINCKEN : I shall vote no, for the reason that the charter is not presented. We do not know what that charter may contain. It may contain clauses which have led to the rejection of other bodies.

Mr. HOFFMAN : For the same reason as has been given by the gentleman from New York, the Philadelphia Board of Trade will vote no.

The roll of Boards being called, the Cairo Chamber of Commerce was admitted by a vote of 23 Ayes to 6 Nays.

Mr. RANDOLPH : The Committee have to report in regard to the Mobile Board of Trade, having received another application by telegraph, Messrs. STEWART, SMITH and WALKER, delegates; we recommend that the body be admitted to membership.

Mr. HINCKEN : I hope we shall pursue the same course as was adopted with respect to Philadelphia and New York. No one would welcome the delegation more heartily than I would, but we know nothing of their Constitution. We are proposing to admit this organization without proof. Let us exact from them all the proof required by our Constitution. We must admit all, or confine our admission to Chambers of Commerce and Boards of Trade, which comply with the terms of the Constitution. Mercantile Libraries might apply for admission, and instead of merchants we might have this hall filled with men who are not merchants.

On the roll of Boards being called, 7 were for the admission; against it, 22.

Mr. HOLTON: I rise to a question of privilege. I beg to offer the excuses of my colleague, Mr. W. M. BRIGHAM, for his absence. He has been sick during the session, hardly able to occupy his seat, and has therefore thought it best to return home.

The PRESIDENT: The question is, shall Mr. BRIGHAM be excused.

Carried.

Mr. HINCKEN: The Committee on American Shipping, to whom was confided this important subject, have met together and have agreed upon a report which we think will be accepted by the Convention.

The documents upon which this report is founded, are too extensive, and would take too much time to read; but the Committee would like the privilege of selecting from those documents, certain statistical facts, upon which their report is based, and of sending these forth to the world, to show upon what ground the Board has been asked to act.

We have come here prepared to ask for a total change in the revenue laws of the United States, so far as ships are concerned. There is no prohibitory tariff in terms, no prohibitory act on anything but ships. Any other article consumed or used in the United States, can be imported on the payment of certain duties. The man who would own American ships, must have his vessels built in the United States.

When we came to ask this Board to indorse a plan which proposes to annihilate the long-settled policy of the Government, and to adopt a policy more in accordance with the advance of the age, we felt that we should meet with opposition, not because the policy is wrong, but because it is entirely new, so far as ships are concerned. We come here and ask for the privilege of buying our ships wherever we can buy them the cheapest; paying for them the same duties you pay on other articles, and we bring abundant evidence to show that what we ask for, ought to be granted.

If the Board will give us permission to print our report, it will save a good deal of time at this stage of the discussion.

What we ask is that we shall be permitted to purchase ships in a foreign market, and pay an *ad valorem* duty on those ships; and also that the American ship-builder shall be protected by such duty, fixed, or *ad valorem*, as shall protect him from the competition of foreign ship-builders. This is the general substance of the report; the details would occupy the entire page of a modern newspaper.

Mr. KIRKLAND: I move that the report and resolutions be printed to-day, and laid to-morrow morning before the house, and that action be taken upon them after the unfinished business is disposed of.

The PRESIDENT: Having been referred yesterday, this has lost its place in the order of precedence.

A vote was then taken on the motion to print, which was agreed to.

Mr. HINCKEN: We should like every delegate in the Board, and every man in the United States to know the facts upon which we base our report. We do not come here to smuggle anything through. This effort is almost our last hope; we come here for the purpose of asking for free trade in ships. We wish to compete with England and France, and to buy our ships as they do, in the cheapest market; and we wish the American ship-builder to be protected. We wish to pay a duty on ships, and to be relieved from competition with foreign builders; we ask for a remission of duties on the materials used.

The PRESIDENT: The report will be printed, and will come up in order at the close of the present order of business.

The next business is the report of the Committee on Postal Telegraph.

Mr. JENKINS: The Committee to whom was referred the subject of a general postal telegraph system, have instructed me to report to this Board, the following resolution, with the recommendation that it be adopted: —

*Resolved*, That the National Board of Trade recommend the adoption by the general government of measures to cheapen and extend telegraphic communication between the different points of the country, by making it a part of the postal system.

It might be proper to add that the Committee was not willing to recommend any particular bill, or any specific means by which the proposition could be carried into effect, but contented itself with the language, substantially, of the St. Louis Board of Trade, as found in the official programme.

The PRESIDENT: That will be in order after the shipping question.

Mr. WETHERILL: I have to report that the Committee appointed to wait on his Honor the Mayor of Cincinnati, and to thank him for his kindness in extending to us the hospitality of the city, and in inviting us to partake of a banquet, have performed that duty, and we informed his Honor we shall with pleasure accept his invitation.

The PRESIDENT: The next business in order is the resumption of specie payments.

Mr. MEIER: I have to offer the following resolution, in behalf of the St. Louis Board of Trade:—

*Resolved,* That this Board deem it most desirable that Congress should, by legal enactment, declare its purpose to restore the currency of the nation to a specie basis, and to redeem the unpaid and depreciated promises of the Government by resuming specie payments at the National Treasury at the earliest practicable period.

And for the furtherance of this object, this Board recommend the adoption of the following measures:

1. The passage of an act, by the present Congress, legalizing all gold contracts which may be entered into from and after the passage of said act.

2. The passage of an act, by the present Congress, providing for the resumption of specie payments and the redemption of legal tender notes at the National Treasury, on the 4th day of July, 1870, by means of the withdrawal and destruction of one hundred millions of dollars of the present legal-tender circulation, in equal instalments, during the months of April, May, June, July, August, September and October, 1869, and February, March, April, May and June, 1870, and part, or the whole of the above amount shall, if the exigencies of the Government require it, be raised by the issue and sale of five-twenty bonds.

It has been remarked, that it was astonishing that St. Louis should move in this matter, that this proposition should not have come from the East; but we claim that the principles of a good currency have been upheld by our people; they were upheld by Mr. BENTON; and we claim that a city doing a large business on sound principles has some right to make such a motion, some interest in it.

The Committee thought it would be wise to fix some date for the resumption of specie payments, and not leave it optional. If the day is known, preparations will be made in anticipation of the change, and matters be arranged accordingly.

The reduction of our currency becomes necessary, to enable the Government to pay. The currency circulation of the country, in round numbers, is nearly three hundred million dollars, the legal-tenders about three hundred and sixty million dollars, making a total of six hundred and sixty million dollars, without counting the precious metals, which, of course, are excluded from circulation as long as Government paper money is a legal tender.

The effect that a resumption of specie payments would have upon the bonds held in Europe, would be very beneficial; the moment it is found that we intend to pay our obligations in specie, the bonds will appreciate in value. There is no fear of their being sent here, but on the contrary, more money would be invested in them. We want for our home and foreign commerce, the money that is acknowledged as such before the world. It will not do for us to have a special currency, unknown out of this country. The present system is attended with great inconvenience, loss and uncertainty to business men who have dealings with foreign countries; and, therefore, we think that this Board will desire that as soon as possible, we should resume specie payments. We thought that nineteen months hence would give ample time to prepare for the resumption.

Mr. WETHERILL: Would an amendment be in order?

The PRESIDENT: I am desirous to relieve the discussion of this question from all embarrassment. I think the resolutions submitted by the St. Louis Board of Trade, open fairly a field for the full discussion of every proposition that may be contemplated; as members speak upon the subject, they can present their views; and when the discussion has reached a certain point, every Board having had an opportunity of participating in the debate, according to the order suggested this morning, amendments to these resolutions could be made, considered and disposed of seriatim.

Perhaps the Board is not satisfied with the suggestion of this morning. With the view of testing the sense of the body, I ask if the delegates will consent to the order of proceeding which was proposed?

Unanimously adopted.

The President accordingly called first for an expression of opinion from the Albany Board of Trade.

Mr. BUELL: The Albany Board of Trade desire to return to specie payments; but, without offering any special suggestions, are ready to sustain any practical measures to that end.

Baltimore Board of Trade. Mr. LONEY: I think that every one will agree to the first resolution introduced by the St. Louis Board of Trade; that all contracts made in gold should be settled with gold, and that a law should be passed by Congress to that effect. That does not admit of discussion.

The next proposition, fixing a day for the resumption of specie payments, I cannot agree with. I think the resumption of specie payments will be a matter of trade, fixed by the value of gold, the value of which must be reduced to the par value of greenbacks, or rather the greenbacks must be raised to the full value of coin, instead of the Government pursuing the policy, as proposed by the St. Louis Board of Trade, of increasing the bonded debt of the country by borrowing the money upon five-twenty bonds. That will tend to increase the bonded debt, and to depreciate the value of the United States bonds. I think the main thing towards a resumption of specie payments, will be to show the capitalists of Europe that we mean to pay our debt; and the proposition to use the public money received for customs, (which was originally pledged in payment of the interest of the public debt,) for the payment of the principal, would show the world that we have begun to pay the debt. In view of that idea, I have drawn up a preamble and resolution, which I will read:

WHEREAS, The receipts from duties on imports were pledged to the payment of the interest on the public debt, and whereas it is the opinion of this Board that all excess of such receipts should be appropriated to the reduction of said debt; therefore, be it

*Resolved,* That the Board recommend to Congress the passage of a law forbidding the sale of any gold in the United States Treasury for legal-tender notes or other currency, and requiring the Secretary of the Treasury, from time to time, to dispose of the surplus coin actually on hand, for six per cent. gold interest-bearing bonds of the United States, to the highest bidder, and that all bonds so purchased shall be immediately cancelled.

I have another proposition which I desire to submit. The idea is to reduce the bonded debt of the country. Under this proposition, the Secretary of the Treasury will have fifty million dollars to one hundred million dollars of surplus coin, which when invested in United States bonds, will serve to cancel those bonds. The proposition, also, has in view the buying of United States bonds, with paper money, making a compromise between those who desire the bonds of the United States to be paid in coin, and those who would have them paid in currency. The Secretary of the Treasury would come into open market and buy up these bonds, reducing the debt some twenty million dollars or thirty million dollars per annum, which sum would go as a sinking fund in payment of the debt.

The preamble and resolution I will read:

WHEREAS, There has recently been a great pressure in the money market, caused partly by natural, and, more particularly, by artificial means, which has had the effect of damaging the business of the country, upsetting values, and causing great depreciation in the value of the products of the land; and,

WHEREAS, The banking basis of the country being legal-tender notes, which according to law, can not be increased, while the various bonds and other securities thrown on the market, which have to be floated or carried, are increasing rapidly; and,

WHEREAS, A continuance of the system of keeping the legal-tender notes at a fixed amount, while the securities and general business of the country is largely increasing, must eventually produce ruinous consequences and render the community liable at all times to great loss by sudden contractions of the currency by the locking-up process, so successfully practiced by combinations of large speculators; and,

WHEREAS, It is the duty of the United States Government to reduce its interest-bearing debt, and at the same time render every facility to the industrial interests of the country necessary to develop our great and boundless resources; therefore, be it

*Resolved*, That this Board recommend to Congress the passage of a law to the following effect, viz.:

Requiring the Secretary of the Treasury to buy up the six per cent. gold-interest-bearing bonds of the United States, at the following prices, whenever he can do so during the times specified, viz.:

In the year 1869, at one hundred and ten dollars for one hundred dollars par. In the year 1870, at one hundred and twelve dollars for one hundred dollars par. In the year 1871, at one hundred and fourteen dollars for one hundred dollars par. In the year 1872, at one hundred and sixteen dollars for one hundred dollars par. And all bonds so purchased to be cancelled at once.

In order to give the Secretary of the Treasury the means to purchase the bonds, legal-tender notes may be issued to the extent of one hundred and twenty-five millions of dollars annually for the four years specified, but only to be issued as the Secretary of the Treasury can buy the bonds at the prices stated, and not to be issued for any other purpose whatever, and all the bonds so purchased to be at once cancelled.

Now the value of gold is fixed. United States bonds in Europe selling at seventy-five cents in gold, would be one hundred and ten cents in this country; therefore, one hundred dollars at the price of gold is one hundred and thirty-five dollars; or a bushel of wheat selling there at seventy-five cents in gold, would be one dollar and ten cents on this side of the water. What we want is to put up the credit of the Government, so that in Europe our five-twenty bonds will bring one hundred cents instead of standing, as they now do, lower than English consols at three per cent. And the best thing to put up the credit of the Government, is to show a disposition to pay the debt. I think the whole internal revenue receipts of the Government, and all the receipts from customs should be applied to the payment of the debt, and then it will be understood in Europe that we intend to pay it.

Mr. KIRKLAND: I have had no consultation with my colleagues upon this subject, but we are instructed by our constituents to submit any views of our own which we may deem of importance, and to coöperate with this Board in whatever will best accomplish this desirable result. They look upon this question as a most important one; and they hope that the conclusion that may be arrived at by this Board, will meet the sanction of Congress and become the law of the land.

The preamble to the resolutions submitted by the Chamber of Commerce of St. Louis, meets my approbation, as I hope it does that of every member of this Board; I also approve of the first resolution.

Having heard the views now presented in the second resolution for the first time, I am not prepared either to condemn or to accept them. I have my own views upon the subject, which I will briefly present, and afterwards submit a resolution.

The idea of the credit of the Government being high, while our currency is depreciated, is preposterous. The Government has one currency for itself and another for the people. You have to take for your corn and pork a piece of paper which fluctuates from hour to hour, while the Government demands gold from us in payment of duties on imports, thus forcing us to be purchasers of gold.

The first step towards a resumption of specie payments will be for the Government to withdraw gradually the greenback circulation by receiving it as duty on imports. The duties on imports amount to about one hundred and fifty million dollars per annum; and my idea is, that if the Government should say that ten per cent. of the duties on imports will be receivable in legal tenders on the first of April next, and ten per cent. additional quarterly, by the end of the year forty per cent. of the import duty would be paid in greenbacks, which should then be cancelled, thus withdrawing from circulation sixty million dollars; at the end of the second year, an additional sixty million dollars would be withdrawn; so that in the course of two and a half years from the time of duties being receivable in legal tenders, I would reduce the currency to the amount of one hundred and fifty million dollars. To meet this, I would authorize Congress to charter National Banks in sections of the country now needing them, to the extent of one hundred and fifty million dollars, issuing to them five per cent. bonds as a basis for their circulation; these bonds to be purchased with greenbacks, which shall go into the Treasury to be destroyed. That would absorb another one hundred and fifty million dollars. I would also compel the National Banks from time to time, say quarterly, to substitute gold for greenbacks as their reserve, until all the reserves of the banks, held at the places appointed for the resumption of their currency, should be in coin.

The amount of fractional currency might be reduced in a similar manner; you might make your postal dues receivable in silver if you choose. In that way, with a certain point fixed not too far off, nor yet too near, without trouble and without panic, the country would find its currency and its credit gradually floating up, until in the sure and natural course of business, specie payments could be resumed.

My views may be crude and ill digested, but it strikes me that some such plan, if authorized by law, would accomplish the desired result; and I have drawn up a resolution, which I think covers the point:

*Resolved,* That in the opinion of this Board, the Government, as the first step towards the resumption of specie payments, may receive, on the 1st of April proximo, ten per cent. of the duties on imports, in legal-tenders, and thereafter quarterly, ten per cent. additional, until the whole amount is receivable in legal-tenders, such notes, when received, to be cancelled.

*Resolved,* Further, That Congress authorize an increase of National Banks to the extent of one hundred and fifty millions of dollars ($150,000,000), and that five per cent. bonds shall be issued for legal-tenders, to such parties as wish to avail of the privilege; said legal-tenders, when received, to be cancelled by the Secretary of the Treasury. Further, That all National Banks, on the 1st of April proximo, shall hold ten per cent. of their reserves in gold, and thereafter quarterly, ten per cent. additional, until their whole reserve shall be held in gold, when their circulation shall, when presented, be redeemed in gold.

## Baltimore Corn and Flour Exchange. Mr. PARR:

We are not ready, at this stage, definitely to present our views upon this subject.

Boston Board of Trade. Mr. ROPES : It would be impossible, in ten minutes, to give even an outline of all that might be said on this subject. Every one of us probably has a separate scheme for bringing about the restoration of the currency to a specie basis. I have mine, which, on the whole, I deem preferable to any other, but I am ready to sustain any scheme based on right principles. There are certain great principles which underlie this subject, and to these I wish chiefly to call your attention.

In the first place, one of the most important duties of a government is to maintain a sound, correct, uniform standard of value. The debasement of this value has always been recognized, both in sacred and profane history, as the greatest of crimes. This standard is now, and has been for years, utterly ignored, falsified and debased among us, and our Government has not only taken no steps to remedy the evil, but has stopped, by authority, all the steps which had begun to be taken.

Secondly, it cannot be denied that a debt payable on demand ought to be discharged at the first moment compatible with the means of the borrower. What would you think of me, Sir, if I should, in distress, incur such an obligation from you, and when my credit was restored, utterly refuse payment? Yet such is the position of our Government. It issued its notes payable on demand in time of war, and when the war ceased and it could have borrowed money in any amount, it soon utterly refused to allow any part of these notes to be redeemed. It stands, to-day, before the world, a dishonored debtor.

Thirdly, there must always be a certain equilibrium between the money of the country and the other property it represents. Each of us has usually a certain amount in his pocket, and in the bank, and so it is with the people generally. The aggregate amount of this money varies but little, growing, of course, with the wealth of the community, but always corresponding closely to the exchangeable amount of that wealth. If this amount is greatly increased, the people being on the whole no richer, they cannot hold it at its former value, and, if irredeemable, it must depreciate. Now before the war, this amount was some five hundred million dollars, and now it is at least one billion dollars. The result is obvious. There never can be specie resumption while this continues. It is simply impossible.

From this we see at once that there can never be two currencies in common use, except when their mutual value is definitely fixed. The cheapest one, which is a legal tender, will always supplant the other, until it is itself brought up to par, or redeemed at a discount, as was done in Russia.

We see, also, that it is impossible, under such circumstances, to resume suddenly. It is like the equilibrium of physical forces. You may run up a mountain at full speed and fall dead on the way; or you may walk slowly, but steadily, up, and arrive at the summit none the worse. So in Chicago, millions of tons of houses were quietly lifted upward by the screw, while the inhabitants at their work hardly noticed what was going on.

It is plain then that we can not resume safely until the volume of paper currency is no greater than the people are able and willing to hold at specie value, and until its purchasing power is equal to that of the same amount of specie. But how shall this be brought about?

It is obvious that neither banks nor merchants will do anything toward it beyond what the law may render necessary. Every man looks out for himself, and when the Government enforces action they will take it and not before. It is essential, then, that all should have fair warning to prepare for specie payments, and that the necessary process of funding the currency should be at once commenced. The Government should authoritatively announce that specie payments shall be resumed as soon as possible, and should begin at once to withdraw the legal-tender currency from circulation. While I heartily indorse the general statement of this subject by the St. Louis Board of Trade, I am unwilling to commit myself to the positive and unvarying withdrawal of one hundred millions in a specified time. A period of panic may come when no currency can be spared, and, at other times, the process might go on even more rapidly.

Now, I believe that this object may be accomplished more easily and safely *by the voluntary action of the people themselves.* Is it not a clear matter of right and justice, that a man holding these unredeemed promises of the Government, should have the privilege of exchanging them for bonds bearing interest? Now, if this were done, and the notes cancelled, and it was clearly understood that the Government would continue the process until the restoration of the currency was accomplished, I am confident that the mere offer of a five per cent. five-twenty bond, in exchange for greenbacks, would so raise our credit abroad as to turn the exchanges in our favor and bring in gold to swell our specie reserves. This would not certainly distress the individuals who voluntarily made the exchange. Would it distress the banks by a too rapid withdrawal of greenbacks? This does not seem probable. At least three-fourths of the legal-tender notes are now held by the people outside of the banks. Now, the banks hold a large amount of bonds which they can sell for greenbacks, if their supply runs short. They also hold some six hundred million dollars of claims on the people, and they can easily call in enough of these for the same purpose, without distressing their debtors. And we must remember that any pressure sufficient to reduce five per cent. bonds below par would at once stop the process of conversion.

It has been said that if we do this we shall lose the interest on the amount of greenbacks exchanged for bonds. Well, supposing we have to exchange three hundred million dollars (which is not at all probable,) we pay fifteen million dollars more interest. And is this a high price to pay to redeem the honor of a great nation, while we spend so much larger amounts in mere political speculations? But the Government would gain far more in taxes by the development of industry and wealth which would at once follow the restoration of the currency to a sound basis. Capital, now withheld from productive industry for fear of depreciation hereafter, would at once be released, invested in ships, factories, and active enterprises of all sorts, and the gain to the Treasury would offset this paltry loss an hundred fold.

Mr. President, with many thanks for the indulgence of the Board, I beg to offer the following resolutions :

*Resolved*, That this Board deems it most desirable that the Congress of the United States should authoritatively declare its purpose to restore the currency of the nation to a specie basis without unnecessary delay, and to redeem the unpaid and depreciated promises of the Government by resuming specie payments at the National Treasury at the earliest practicable moment, not less than one nor more than two years distant.

*Resolved*, That in the opinion of this Board, it is a duty demanded of the Government, alike by expediency and by honesty, to make immediate provision for the steady but gradual withdrawal of its legal-tender notes, not by an arbitrary and compulsory contraction, but by allowing all holders of such notes to exchange them at all times for bonds bearing interest, at such rate or rates as will secure their prompt conversion, without seriously disturbing our commerce and industry.

Mr. NAZRO : I suppose it is admitted by all, that no country can expect prosperity for any length of time, when its citizens are not on a footing of equality with those of other countries, or when they are, as far as their financial status is concerned, in an abnormal condition. We are in that state now. We have no circulating medium which is recognized by the other nations of the world. But it seems to me that the difficulties of this question are more seeming than real, and that the great thing we require for the resumption of specie payments is *confidence.* My colleague has stated that should the legal-tenders be called in, probably not more than three hundred million dollars would be presented for redemption. I think he has stated this much too high. I do not think that one hundred million dollars would be presented for gold redemption, provided they were brought up to a specie standard. All that specie is really required for in this country is to settle our foreign debt, and when confidence is restored, that will be a very small amount. You could not prevail upon our merchants to take gold in preference to greenbacks, if they were of equivalent value, which they would be if the latter were brought to a specie standard. It has been so in former times, and will be so again; but we cannot return to that position until we have reëstablished confidence. Let it be known that our Government is as good as its word; that in no extremity will it make a promise to the ear and break it to the hope. Let it be known that having implored its citizens, in order to save its life, to accept its promises, and these were accepted in the shape of bonds, — and when the exigency having passed, it thinks it can make better terms, let it be known that it will do that which is strictly and legally demanded in the contract. When we shall find the Government, both by our own citizens and by those of other nations, recognized as intending to deal with every one who comes in contact with it in strict justice, we shall find also more money flowing into the Treasury than we want; our bonds will be sought for and we shall have no difficulty in resuming specie payments. I think we might resume in six months, if we had that confidence in the Government which we ought to have.

Various schemes have been suggested here, but I am not at present prepared to discuss them in detail. I desire, however, to say one word in reference to a suggestion offered by the gentleman from Baltimore; he said that the banks should keep a certain proportion of their capital, say ten per cent., as a reserve, in specie. I do not object to that proposition so far as the specie comes into the hands of the bankers, but I object to the principle that banks shall be forced under any and all circumstances to go into the market and buy specie at twenty to forty per cent. premium to enable them to keep it on hand. If that is the intention of the resolution, it would not receive my approbation.

There was another proposition submitted by the Baltimore delegation, in regard to the chartering of new banks to the extent of one hundred and twenty-five million dollars. That, Sir, after some deliberation, strikes me very favorably, provided that the new banks shall purchase the bonds of the Government with legal-tenders, which legal-tenders shall be cancelled and withdrawn from circulation. I do not object to the volume of currency now in circulation, because I think the requirements of the country may demand it; but this gradual reduction of the circulation will be beneficial to our industrial interests. I think, Sir, we shall have to come down to a specie basis, and while I would not advise an arbitrary contraction, which might possibly frighten the community by the temporary inconvenience it would occasion, I would attempt it by a sliding scale, by which I think it could be attained. The practical conclusion of the varied schemes that have been devised, is the plain, simple fact, that we *must* resume specie payments. But we are not to forget, as far as the banks are concerned, that they are mere agents between the Government and the people, and that they will regulate their affairs accordingly as mercantile and financial affairs outside of them are regulated. There is no necessary antagonism between the banks and the people; what is the interest of the people is the interest of the banks. If the Government will announce that at a stated time, say in two years, — but fixing the time — it will resume specie payments, then every man and every bank in the country will regulate his or its business with that prospect distinctly in view. But I want a definite period fixed for this resumption, and I believe it may be attained in such a way that we shall in the end hardly know that we have ever been without it.

I have somewhat hastily prepared a couple of resolutions, which I now beg leave to submit:

*Resolved*, That, as a preliminary measure to enable the Government and the country to resume specie payments, it is necessary that confidence in the intention of the Government to deal in entire good faith in the payment of its debts, should be fully established in the minds of our own citizens and those of foreign nations.

*Resolved*, That the National Board of Trade respectfully urges upon Congress the passage of a declaratory act, that all the bonds issued by the Government shall be paid in coin when not expressed to the contrary, and that such bonds shall not be subject to taxation.

**Boston Corn Exchange.** Mr. PLUMER: In the main, I concur with my friend Mr. ROPES, who has so acceptably presented his views here. I desire to mention three propositions, which I am decidedly in favor of.

The first is the resolution offered by Mr. DAVIS, of Toledo, at the last Convention, requiring the banks to keep their specie received from the Government, till the whole amount of their reserve is in gold. My colleague, Mr. NAZRO, has said that the interest of the banks is identical with that of the community; but I do not want them to continue to hold the position which they now occupy, and saying they will be ready to resume specie payments when the Government is ready. It is well known that the banks are making money faster than any other commercial or industrial interest, and I think that they should be compelled to afford what aid they can in the attainment of the object before us. If an act shall be passed, declaring the intention of the Government to resume specie payments, I believe we shall have all the talent and brains of the directors and managers of these banks throughout the nation, taxed to the utmost to hasten this much-wished-for result.

A second proposition I am in favor of is, the legalization of gold contracts; and another is, the fixing of a certain day by Congress, when resumption shall take place.

Buffalo Board of Trade. Mr. HAZARD: I wish to be excused for a while, but will reserve the privilege of offering a few remarks on this question by and by.

Charleston Board of Trade. Mr. COBIA: As far as Charleston is concerned, we have only to say that the sooner a return to specie payments is reached, the better. We have no suggestion to make as to the manner or the time of resumption.

Chicago Board of Trade. Mr. EGAN: I do not desire to speak now, but reserve my right to offer a few suggestions.

Mr. RANDOLPH: I did not intend to say one word on the question now under discussion, but in the progress of the debate, some principles have been advanced, which induce me to say a few words. I do not propose to offer any suggestions as to the means by which this most desirable result, — specie payments — may be secured. I presume that every one here has a distinct and a different idea as to the means by which it may be attained. For myself, I do not believe that we ought to mark out a definite programme or indicate to Congress all the details of the road it shall travel in its journey towards a specie currency. I think we should be content to enunciate certain leading principles, without going into particulars. The gentleman from Baltimore said that to the first proposition of the St. Louis Board, he thought there would be no objection, and I believe almost every delegate on the floor thus far, has indorsed it, namely, legalizing gold contracts. For myself, I never will vote for that, because I consider that it involves a partial repudiation of our circulating medium; we cannot legalize gold contracts, and maintain uniformity in our circulating medium. It will be to the interest of every importer in New York, Boston, Philadelphia and Baltimore, to insist that his goods shall not be sold for currency, but only for gold. They will hold that the contracts of the whole country are to be payable in gold. I believe, if such a law were passed, that instead of raising the price of greenbacks, it would work exactly the reverse. While for a loan of gold, I hold that a party should be obliged to pay gold; I look upon it as a matter of merchandise, but I never will vote for a proposition that shall make two kinds of money in the community. Let us raise the legal-tenders to the gold standard, but not undertake to make two classes of currency. I beg to submit the following resolution:

*Resolved*, That it is the opinion of this Board that the true policy to be pursued by the Government, in any attempt to bring the financial affairs of this country to a specie basis, is a strict adherence to national integrity, and this can not be done by the entertainment of suggestions looking to any partial repudiation of its obligations.

Mr. TURPIN: My colleague has remarked upon the first of the St. Louis resolutions so conclusively, and in so clear a manner, that I have nothing to add. I fully agree with all he has said upon the disadvantages of having two kinds of circulating medium. As to the desirability of specie payments, I presume there is no diversity of opinion. It is not a debatable question; but as to the means for its attainment and the proper time for it, there is a wide difference of views; and it is probable that on these details I shall differ as widely from the gentleman who has just preceded me, as any other delegate on this floor. To me it seems preposterous to talk about resumption of specie payments, when the credit of the Government is some twenty-five per cent. below the credit of other governments in the great money centres. We see the bonds of the Government of the United States, the six per cent. bonds, selling in London at twenty-five per cent. below the three per cent. bonds of the British Government.

Mr. ROPES: I must beg to correct that statement.

The PRESIDENT: The gentleman must not be interrupted.

Mr. TURPIN: The British consols are selling at ninety-four, while the bonds of the United States are quoted at seventy-four, both in London. Why should this state of things exist? Are the great capitalists of the world afraid that this Government will not stand? I think not. That question is settled, if not for all time, at least for this generation. But here is the difficulty; with a high rate of taxation,—as high as it is possible to enforce successfully — the Government of the United States is hardly able to hold its own. The expenses, and the interest on the debt, absorb its whole income. Some months we may gain a little perhaps, and then for some months we lose; but on the whole it is about even. That state of affairs must necessarily be destructive to the credit of the Government. It is a condition of things similar to that of a man who lives precisely up to his income, using all his means and energies in order that he may continue to exist. The moneyed men of the world want to be assured that we can pay, not only the interest, but the *principal*. They dread the effect of possible financial convulsions, and more especially of political convulsions upon the credit of this country. A foreign war with any respectable European power, would, at this time, be almost fatal to our credit, for we are so strained now, that we cannot bear any more.

If we adopt such means as will reduce the expenses of this Government below its income, and give the world assurance that we have the ability and the willingness to pay, we shall have made considerable progress towards the realization of specie payments. I venture to suggest, — what may be somewhat unpopular — that this Government should, in the first place, reduce its running expenses to the lowest possible point. I believe a reduction may be made to the extent of about one-third of the present expenses. Taking our annual expenditure at three hundred million dollars, — I use round numbers — I believe it may be reduced thirty-three and one-third per cent.; that is, by reducing our interest and our expenses, we may bring it down to two hundred million dollars per annum. This would give us one hundred million dollars per annum, to apply on the principal of the debt, and that amount, Sir, I would apply in taking up bonds, rather than in taking up currency.

The question of interest, I approach with some hesitation. It has been a fruitful topic of discussion in politics, which I despise, and it has become somewhat contaminated. It is not worth while to enter into an argument to prove the justice of paying off the six per cent. bonds in paper. I would suggest three per cent. in gold, and gold redemption bonds to be given to the creditors of the Government for greenbacks, and I would take these greenbacks and pay the six per cent. bonds. The proposition of the gentleman from Boston is, that we are already paying as much interest as we can. If you issue more bonds, you will still further depreciate our credit in the markets of the world. I do not see how it is possible to attain to a par credit anywhere except we do so right at home, and not here while we are increasing our debt rather than diminishing it. This, then, is my plan, to repair the credit of the Government by reducing its indebtedness, and by the reduction of its expenses and interest; and as soon as the bonds of the Government reach par, we have accomplished resumption, without any effort on our part; it comes naturally and inevitably by the improvement of our credit. We have had two illustrations of the effects of contraction, when the Secretary of the Treasury was contracting the currency at the rate of four million dollars a month. We found the whole trading community of the country embarrassed, and Congress had to prevent that officer of the Government from carrying out his plans any further. This showed that we have no redundancy of the circulating medium. It was to my mind conclusive; but if further proof were needed, we had it in the recent occurrences in New York, where by locking up the comparatively contemptible sum of fifteen million dollars, the whole country was shaken from centre to circumference; clearly showing that the interests of the commercial world will not at this time bear a reduction in its circulating medium.

We have always been taught to believe that New England is patient, hopeful, toiling steadily and continuously for great ends by slow and gradual progress; but yet we are asked here, by men from the heart of New England, to jump from a condition of monetary demoralization right into specie resumption at once. We must approach this by degrees, if we would avoid the consequences we have experienced in former times. Many of us remember the terrible times following the disasters of 1837. It is probably in the memory of every one present, what took place in 1857, and we of Illinois and Wisconsin remember particularly the consequences following on the destruction of our banks in 1861, when corn had become so reduced in price by the destruction of confidence and the locking up of the circulating medium, that,— as I actually saw myself — it was burnt for fuel.

It is my firm conviction, Mr. President, that such a rapid contraction of the currency, as would result from the plan proposed, would give us a worse condition of affairs than we had in 1837, 1857, or 1861. We must take this "walk up the mountain," that has been referred to by the gentleman from Boston, but I would advise that we move slowly, patiently and carefully, lest we stumble and fall; for if we make the attempt and fall, our condition will be far worse than if the attempt had not been made

The Board took a recess of an hour for lunch.

On its reassembling, the Committee on Credentials obtained leave to make a report.

Mr. RANDOLPH : I have to announce from the Committee on Admissions, that the delegates from the Minneapolis Board of Trade have presented their credentials, and I might add, in the best form of any yet submitted to the Committee. The delegates are Messrs. PRICE and MENDENHALL. These gentlemen say that their Board is incorporated under the laws of Minnesota. We have nothing but their word for this fact, but inasmuch as we have refused to admit other organizations without a copy of their charter, the Committee recommend that these gentlemen be admitted to the right of the floor without the privilege of voting, but that the admission of the body be postponed in the absence of a copy of its charter.

Carried.

The PRESIDENT : The gentlemen are received to the privilege of the floor, without the right of voting. The discussion on finance will now be resumed.

Mr. MUNN : I approach this subject with a great deal of diffidence, because I consider it one of the most vital to the business prosperity and even to the perpetuity of our nation. We are to-day a bankrupt nation; at least a suspended one,— applying the best term to it that you can. We are in the condition of a man who does not pay his liabilities. We should examine, then, as far as in us lies, into the condition of our suspended Government, and make the best arrangements for the payment of its bills that we possibly can. I say here at the outset, that I do care everything that the Government keeps its pledges and obligations inviolate, paying as it has the ability, to the utmost farthing, and not one cent more. While this is the duty of the Government, its honor not less than its ultimate credit depends upon keeping all its obligations perfectly inviolate and to the end. A suspended business man will examine into his assets, and the creditors will enquire as to the prospect of ultimate payment before they assent to his proposed terms. So with the general Government. The people believe that the Government is able to pay its debts, that its credit may be made still better than it now is, and that it can take up all its liabilities. I am one of those who believe this. In arriving at that point, as my colleague has said, the first thing is retrenchment, retrenchment in every department; and this must come, not only in our commercial circles, but in city governments, in State legislation, and in the general Government, and let us hope that it may be voluntary retrenchment.

The Government must retrench its various departments, and then it must diminish its interest. At present the debt bears six per cent. interest in gold, without any drawback, and that is more interest than any government in the world, standing as our Government now does, is compelled to pay. If these obligations are binding upon the Government in law and in equity, keep them; but if they are not, then reduce the rate. The effect of this high rate of interest reaches all classes of the community; the merchant, the manufacturer, the business man of every description; all are bound to pay a rate of interest approximating to that paid by the Government, and perhaps a little higher, and this amounts to about eleven per cent. In order to equal the interest received from the Government, a man cannot afford to loan his money to a merchant or manufacturer at less than eleven per cent. per annum. Now this is much too high for the present condition and general prosperity of our country. I am not one of those whose chairs and lounges are stuffed with the spoils of the Government, and who desire and demand that my bonds shall be paid in gold. I might be, if I thought the Government bound in law and justice to do it; but when I read the Act of Congress, and the debates and resolutions relating to the five-twenty bonds, the only construction I can put upon them is, that the Government is neither legally nor morally bound to pay in gold unless it chooses to do so. With this conviction forcing itself upon me, and believing that our interest upon the debt is too high, I am one of those who say, " make a new loan at a lower rate of interest, one more in consonance with that paid by other nations of the world." Those who have our bonds at a high rate of interest, ought to be paid in the currency which the people are obliged to receive for their debts, let whatever consequences follow. I believe it to be just to the people, and have no fears for the result. It is argued that the agents of the Government have said that these bonds would be paid in gold, and that this is a binding pledge. Mr. President, no legal authority of any country or state, has ever yet dared to go beyond the legislative enactment, and to say that the opinion or dictum of one of its executive officers is law. When such a decision is declared binding, we shall be under a despotism and not under a republican government. I am not in favor of a contraction of the currency. The currency was contracted at the rate of four millions a month, and at that time did gold get lower? Not at all. If you force contraction before the country is ready for it, you will destroy the vital industries that support our country and that pay the interest of its debt. Besides, here are important projects before this Board for the development of our country. I would have gentlemen bear in mind that if you force a speedy resumption of specie payments, all your projects for internal improvements will be laid upon the shelf. I think we should go slow and sure. Some gentlemen seem to think that it is only necessary to declare that on a certain day specie payments shall be resumed, to bring it about. I think this will have to be left to the business interests of the country, and only when the people are ready for it, be it one year or five, can it be secured with true advantage.

Mr. HOW: I do not intend to make a speech; it is somewhat out of my line. I am in favor of the Government returning to specie payments as soon as it can, but I am not prepared to say how this shall be done. My financial creed is very concise; I can state it in very few words. The Government should retrench in every possible way; and should use its surplus funds in retiring its interest paying bonds. In that way you will appreciate the bonds, and you will come to a specie basis sooner than by any other way.

I would only further say that I indorse the views advanced by Mr. RANDOLPH in regard to gold contracts; his ideas accord with mine exactly, and I propose, when the time comes, to vote on that project as he suggests.

Cincinnati Chamber of Commerce. Mr. DAVIS: I have never ventured to discuss so important and so elaborate a question as the finances of the country in any public manner, and approach it with a diffidence becoming so important a subject.

That resumption of specie payments is important, — as has been well said — none can doubt or deny; we all desire it. I agree with the resolution from the St. Louis Board of Trade, that it is very desirable that Congress shall proceed at once to adopt measures for that purpose. But the question is, what shall these measures be? And there is where we may all differ. The *how* is the question. I doubt whether any of the elaborate theories on the subject are practicable, because they all proceed upon the supposition that we have the ability to do it at once; the only thing needed being confidence on the part of the holders of the Government obligations. But is this true? It seems to me that we are in the condition of a suspended merchant. His assets having been examined, they are found to be ample in every respect; he has huge resources and fair prospects in the future, but in the immediate present he has not the means to pay his obligations. How will he pay them? By an extension of credit on the part of his creditors, by their taking his paper to be paid at such time as he may be able to pay it in full. These United States having declared as a fact, or at least presumed that they could not pay their debts in specie, have given their paper, and moreover have by law given their obligations an actual value, which no merchant has the power to do with his own paper.

As no merchant can pay his debts in such case at once, without forcing his assets, neither can the Government pay their obligations at once, without injury to their debtors, by forcing their assets into the market at a large discount, and without acting in bad faith by disturbing the value of property which has conformed itself to the currency as settled by Act of Congress. We must satisfy the holders of our obligations that we have the wherewith to pay our debts, or a resumption would only be transient, and the permanent attainment of our desires placed far in the future. Having transformed our currency bonds into gold-bearing interest bonds, and these having largely gone abroad, how can we, in this state of the case, withstand the drain of specie which would unavoidably occur, to pay, not only this interest, but our foreign debt, which would require gold; while now the day of payment is being unfortunately postponed by paying in gold-bearing interest obligations. If our present rate of extravagance continues, we shall never reach the goal of our hopes. If in our peculiarly American way we could do it by a series of resolutions, — which is about all that is involved in the theories most in vogue — we might say,

WHEREAS, The resumption of specie payments is very desirable; therefore,

*Resolved*, That the people of the United States, during the next three years, shall live very economically; and that the Government shall retrench its expenses in every manner possible,

*Resolved*, That for the next three years we will have good wheat and corn crops, also large cotton and sugar crops, and by every avenue of legitimate commerce, will endeavor to increase our assets, so as to pay our debts.

Then, if we can make our resolves, *acts*, the thing will be accomplished. We could resume specie payments in this way, without disturbing the commerce of the country enough to be aware of it. But we must earn the money by work, hard labor, honest trade, and habits of economy, just as any merchant would be expected to do in like circumstances; or if he were a farmer, by a faithful tilling of the ground, and increasing his crop of cereals for home and foreign market; or if a miner, by bringing forth the treasures of coal and iron, gold, silver and copper, from the exhaustless deposits of our hills and valleys. What country on the face of the earth has such a wealth of resources? If we could only be sure of such crops of corn and wheat from the great northwest as we had during the first two years of our late struggle, almost supplying the lack of cotton export, and keeping up the balance of trade in our favor; if with these we could for the three years next ensuing, have such cotton crops, and as large a production of sugar and molasses as this year's result has given us, we could resume specie payments, with a good hope of continuance.

But we cannot pay our debts without an equal value to pay them with. We may resolve to do this, that, and the other, but, Sir, until we get the means, it cannot be done. I would be glad to do it, to be relieved from our position of dishonor before the world, but in this case it is "better to bear the ills we have, than to fly to others we know not of." Our experience recalls many an instance of a merchant, presuming upon the value of his assets and the confidence of his creditors, resuming too soon, only to fall back into irremediable bankruptcy, insolvent and disheartened.

With these remarks I will give my plan for reaching the position we so much desire. I would have the Government hold the matter of the currency with a strong arm, right where it is. Let Congress refrain from adopting any laws looking to any inflation of the currency. It should not permit in any way, an increase of the circulating medium, except in coin. While a sure but steady contraction will be constantly going on by the process of absorption in the regular channels of trade, going along the lines of our great Pacific Railroad, through the Territories, constantly expanding their area of settlement by immigration throughout the South, moving the great crops of the country, and permeating constantly, the ever increasing ramifications of trade and commerce, it will cause a contraction at the great money centres, that will soon be felt, and cause a cry for relief. This was recently seen in New York, and the Secretary of the Treasury was called upon for assistance. With the banking capital of the country in the hands of the Government, and the maximum of stock having been taken, we shall be free from the fluctuations of banking capital, which the usual increase of business calls out in the different States, and by a strict adherence to the present volume of currency, the Government paying its obligations by taking up its paper only as it may be able to do so, we believe the values of the country will in a short time be brought up to the value of coin in the present circulating medium, without any other mode of contraction. If this shall be known as the policy of the Government, business will conform itself to it, and the present uncertainty and fear of a violent contraction of the currency avoided. As the business of the country absorbs the currency, urgent calls will be made to increase it, by increasing the circulation, but if these can be resisted, it will gradually reduce values by the system of averages, (if I might use such an expression) until the standard of coin value shall be attained.

Mr. GANO : If I can reserve the right to present a proposition after the discussion has gone round the circle, I shall be glad.

Detroit Board of Trade. Mr. McGRAW : I beg to offer the following resolution :

*Resolved,* That it is not expedient for the Government to attempt the resumption of the payment of its indebtedness in gold, till such time as it has accumulated sufficient gold in its Treasury to enable it to resume successfully the payment of all its indebtedness in specie as it matures, and when the Government is in such a position, the people and the banks of the country will be ready to respond in like manner.

Mr. BAGLEY : I beg to submit the following :

*Resolved,* That it is the duty of the Government to return to specie payments at the earliest moment practicable, and we believe the retrenchment of expenses in all its departments, and the preventing by severe penalties of the officers and citizens of the country from defrauding the Government of its just revenue, will tend rapidly towards that end, and restore confidence in the United States securities, both at home and abroad.

Louisville Board of Trade. Mr. RONALD : We are all in favor of resuming specie payments as soon as it can be practically done, but we differ in details as to how it can be accomplished, whether to work down or up to it; whether to reduce the currency to a specie standard, or to develop the resources of the country to the amount of currency at present in circulation. I am in favor of both plans; of reducing the currency gradually, and of bringing the resources of the country up to the present amount of currency. I am opposed to fixing any day for the resumption of specie payments, because that must depend upon so many things which we cannot now foresee. The Secretary of the Treasury, whose special business it is to give this subject the most careful consideration, has recommended that specie payments should be resumed; but with all his information, which must be very great, he does not suggest any particular time. He merely says that it ought to be done at the earliest practicable period.

We talk about returning to specie payments, with a paper circulation, *per capita*, of twenty dollars, and of fixing a time when we will do it. I do not say that the circulation *per capita* is too great, it depends so much on the amount of property there is in the country; how the people live, whether poorly or extravagantly; and how much money is wanted and used. But it is notorious that on two occasions we have suspended specie payments with a paper circulation of less than seven dollars *per capita*. I do not see how we can fix a day for resumption with nearly twenty dollars of paper currency to each person. We must develop the wealth of the country, to make our own markets in which to buy, to export and not import, to produce as far as possible, every thing we need, and if possible, buy nothing from abroad. We produce many things which the world must have. Flour, pork, cotton, the world wants and is bound to have, but our prices for these articles have risen so high, that we scarcely export any of them. We want our currency reduced so that the produce we have to offer to foreigners, shall bring gold and silver into the country. Notwithstanding the difference of twenty-five to thirty per cent. between currency and coin, our exports are less than the imports. As long as that state of things lasts, the idea that specie resumption is possible, is simply preposterous. We have to work and increase the productive resources of the country till they are so abundant and so cheap that we can export to all the markets of the world. The Egyptian and the Indian cotton, of which we have heard so much of late years, was not known till our prices for cotton ran up so high that the nations were driven to seek elsewhere for their supply. When our cotton prices go down, we shall again have control of the markets of the world.

Our currency is at a discount, and therefore we cannot enter into the commercial exchanges of the world on a fair and equitable principle. What we want is to bring our currency up to the coin standard of the world. It does not matter whether we use paper or gold for our circulating medium, provided our paper is worth as much as gold. But there will be no resumption and there is no safety for us unless we retrench in all the relations of life; and the Government and the people must alike do this. We must lessen the importation of silks and jewelry and other extravagances. We shall have to do as our fathers did; we must work harder, spend less, buy less and sell more; and if the people do this, the Government will have to follow the example. The people can control the Government; they made it and they own it, and it will be the part of wisdom for them to insist that it greatly lessen its expenditures. As long as the present extravagant ideas obtain in the Government and among the people, it is nonsense to talk of the resumption of specie payments.

One great impediment to resumption is the existence of the National Banks. Gentlemen say we must curtail the circulation of greenbacks till they are worth as much as gold. This National Bank paper is redeemable in legal-tenders; if we take all the legal-tenders away by contracting the currency, where are the Banks to get the circulation with which to redeem their paper? It would be a good idea, as Government holds the bonds for the redemption of the National Bank currency, for the Government to issue a sufficient number of legal-tenders to absorb and take up all the Bank circulation, to pay them all off, and to supply their place with Government legal-tenders. That would not increase the paper circulation a dollar; the Government owns these bonds which are pledged for currency redemption and have paid for the circulation which they are pledged to secure. They are pledged for the redemption of the National Bank currency; it is a substitution of Bank paper for that of the Government, though without interest; but everybody would prefer a direct obligation from the Government. As long as the Government pays the interest it does on bonds, all the surplus capital will go into the Government bonds of the country. The Government is paying six per cent. in gold, without taxation, which makes it nine or ten per cent. in currency; — higher than any man can pay for money with which to do business.

There is no violation of the public faith in paying off the five-twenties in legal-tender notes. I believe that on the plain face of the paper it is provided that they shall be so paid. The chairman of the Committee upon whose recommendation Congress acted, announced that that was the understanding. The difference in the reading of the five-twenty and the other bonds issued, clearly indicates that Congress and everybody recognized that the former were to be paid in legal-tenders.

Mr. BRANNIN: I see by the remarks of several gentlemen who have preceded me, that they are disposed to postpone far into the future, the resumption by the Government of specie payments. In my judgment, that plan is dangerous to the Government and to the people. An indefinite postponement of resumption will, in my opinion, continue to increase the complication of the finances of the

Government and the demoralization of the people now being brought about and continued in a large degree by an irredeemable and inflated circulation. We all know the monetary demoralization existing all over the country. At Washington we have what are called "whiskey rings," and "railroad rings," asking for subsidies from the Government in amounts that are perfectly frightful. In Wall street, New York, are the "gold rings," the "stock rings" and "money corners." This speculation or gambling is largely superinduced by an inflated currency. A circulation with a view to handle the products of the country and promote trade, of legitimate currency, is a good thing, but when you issue it without regard to a law of limit, with no foundations for its redemption, and spread it broadcast over the land, its results are fearful both to the Government and to the people. It induces wild and extravagant speculation, enhances values far beyond a safe limit, turns aside the great natural laws of trade that should control the prices of the products of the country, (the law of supply and demand,) and supplies illegitimate influences in their stead. Before the war we had a circulation not exceeding one-third of the present issue of paper money, which was sufficient to move and control the products of the country and enough for all legitimate purposes. We had then a currency of some intrinsic value and which was convertible into gold and silver. The trade was healthy and not subject to the quick and enormous revolutions that now prevail. Then, Sir, a merchant, a manufacturer, or a general tradesman could at the commencement of a season of business make some calculations ahead of his operations, with a fair degree of certainty that if prudent and discreet, he would be compensated for his year's labor. Now we have a circulation of three hundred and fifty-six millions of greenbacks, and some two hundred and eighty millions of National Bank paper; in the aggregate, six hundred and thirty-six millions of circulation. Such is the increasing mania for speculation, and such the demoralization of the people and even the heads of the Government, that no prudent man, no matter how wise he is, can pursue a legitimate business with the fair promise of reward. It is said, Sir, that the history of trade for the past few years has demonstrated the fact that the more prudent a merchant is, the less reward he gains. And I am not certain but it is true. The fact is, the cities and even the country is full of a set of speculating adventurers. Wall street, New York, is lined with them. One goes into a banker's office with his few hundreds or thousands and places it up as a margin in a gold stock speculation, for example, and in a few days, sometimes in a few hours, all is lost in the maelstrom of destruction. I might go on, Sir, and enlarge upon the fearful results of a continued and irredeemable currency.

As to a resumption of specie payments, that is a question of the deepest import. In my opinion, the fate of our country for weal or for woe, in a large measure depends upon its early solution. The present circulation of greenbacks, as I have said, is three hundred and fifty-six millions. Now, the question is, how much of this circulation can you with safety to the trade of the country, retire in the next eighteen months or two years, and upon what basis can you retire it. I am aware that the question is a difficult one, and it is hard to find a solution, but in my humble opinion, it can be done, and I think, successfully.

First, By an economical administration of the Government, and an administration of its affairs under its Constitution. The Freedman's Bureau should be closed, which is not only costing the people millions of dollars annually, but is tending to the continuation of the estrangement between the North and the South, and more than this, is adding to the demoralization of the colored population, the laboring class of the South, and thus is retarding the solution of the labor question in the cotton and sugar districts, a section which if fully developed will prove better than all the gold mines to contribute to the financial strength of this great country. The Southern country, from 1820 up to the time of our unhappy civil war, increased in population, production and exports to an extent which would compare favorably with the advancement of the great Northwest.

Secondly, By the encouragement of commerce and industry, and the development of the nation's resources to the fullest and broadest extent. Among the most essential of these at the present is, to give aid and assistance to the Southern people, to rebuild their broken levees, destroyed during the war. Resolutions adopted by the Louisville Board of Trade in reference to this matter, I shall present at the proper time, and I think this Board will have the sound judgment to regard them favorably, and to assist in bringing the production of cotton back to its old status of four to five million bales annually.

In the third place, I would require the legal-tender notes to be retired by degrees, consistent with the safety of the trade of the country, by the issue of five per cent. gold-bearing bonds. Fix the time for resumption, say two years hence, and in my opinion, before the time elapsed, our bonds in Europe would attain a very close approximation to par.

In the fourth place, I would issue in the place of the legal-tender notes, National Bank currency, equal to the wants of the country, but the circulation not to exceed in any event, four hundred millions, and permit the creation of National Banks in the West and South, so as to make something like a fair distribution of the currency, and require the National Banks to keep instead of their present legal-tender reserve, gold and silver as a reserve.

These, Mr. President, are some of my views, though very imperfectly presented, on this great and vital question. And I trust, Sir, we shall soon commence the process of resumption and move forward by proper legislation and the development of the resources of the country, in such a way as will make resumption not an experiment but a success and a reality. I wish to see the day come when if the merchant, the mechanic, or the tradesman holds a dollar in paper, he can present it at the counter of the Bank or to the Government that issues it, and receive a gold or silver dollar for it, — which is the only legal-tender recognized under the Constitution of our country. Then, Sir, will we have sure and perfect peace, and a healthy and well regulated trade, and not until then. And I trust this National Board of Trade will speak on this subject with such a decided vote as will awaken Congress to action and proper legislation for the attainment of the end so much desired.

There is one point in the resolutions of the St. Louis Board of Trade, to which I have not alluded; that is the resolution recommending a distinction between gold and currency contracts. I cannot give my approval to this measure. It would, in my opinion, result in a further depreciation of the currency and would operate as a great drawback to resumption. It would be contravening a great principle to which the Government should adhere, and would create by its own legislation a distinction in value between its issue and gold, thus increasing the demand for gold, and, in that ratio, lessening the value of the circulating currency and retarding the resumption of specie payments.

### Memphis Chamber of Commerce: Mr. CHALMERS:

I cannot understand how gentlemen can favor a resumption of specie payments and at the same time be opposed to legalizing gold contracts. This is the very element of resumption. This is the first blow we can strike, the first step we can take towards the resumption of specie payments. We may pay our contracts in gold in the future, but we may not be able to promise to pay our contracts for the past in gold.

The success of the South, referred to by the gentleman from Louisville, is in itself the very best answer to the position of those gentlemen who are not in favor of legalizing gold contracts at this time. It is the difference between cash and credit. The people of the South had no credit; but they went to work, practiced economy, paid what they could, and have made their crops, and they are now full-handed, or will be at the close of this season. And the people of the United States are in the same situation. They have no credit abroad; they have as little credit as the Southern planters had at the commencement of the season; who by economy were enabled to make their crops.

Suppose the people agree that for the future the basis of their contracts shall be gold, and that all debts that they have contracted which are not otherwise provided for, shall be paid in gold. But we must first bring ourselves to a gold basis; we must avoid all this inflation of the currency. How is it now? Gold is the standard of value; notwithstanding the legislation of Congress, and in spite of acts of Parliament. England once endeavored to depreciate the currency, but the genuine shilling stood for just as much after the adulteration as before; and the Goverment that undertakes to prescribe something as a circulating medium, and to give value to that which has no value in itself, will fail, as it always has done. Here is a species of currency which the Government says is a dollar, and it says you shall take it as a dollar; but the very moment you do this, you place in the hands of bad men all the rights of honest and good men. These legal tender notes are made receivable dollar for dollar, for old contracts as well as for new; that was the position in the country at the time the law was passed; and I grant you that the circumstances which surrounded the nation justified it; the time justified the suspension of the writ of *habeas corpus*, and like measures not in accordance with our preconceived notions, for the life of the nation was involved; therefore, men submitted to it. But when it is no longer necessary to suspend the writ of *habeas corpus*, it is no longer necessary for the Government to force me to take that for a dollar which is not a dollar.

The resolution of the St. Louis Board solves the whole question. If a contract is made, it shall go into the Courts and be recovered in gold; then everything will come upon a gold basis. When you sell your corn, rice, or tobacco, you bargain for so many dollars in gold; and if you don't take gold you take its equivalent.

The gentleman from Boston who made me believe yesterday I was a barbarian, has said truly that the two currencies may go together; but the ruling currency will always determine the value. There were two currencies before the war, before the legal-tender; a gold and a paper currency; and the bankers of the country maintained that they had a right to issue two dollars in paper for every dollar they had in gold. They did it by establishing confidence in the community, that when they presented their notes they would obtain the gold. If you make gold the standard value of this paper currency, all the bankers will be thrown upon their wits and ingenuity to bring their money up to par value; and any bank that cannot do this, will have its currency below par standard.

Mr. RANDOLPH: I understand this discussion is to determine what is the duty of the Government in coming to a specie basis, a basis for paying its notes in coin; the argument of the gentleman seems to me to be entirely in the line of repudiation,— that we shall establish another kind of currency. I think he is out of order.

The PRESIDENT: I think the gentleman is perfectly in order.

Mr. CHALMERS: I think I am a very unfortunate man; in the first place a pirate, and in the next place a repudiator. I certainly do not aspire to either character. I maintain, Sir, that the very first step towards a resumption of specie payments is, to bring our transactions to a gold basis. Do not trade on an inflated currency. Let the contracts of the country be made upon a gold basis; and if there are any banks who think they can bring their paper up to gold, we will take their currency; but until they do that, we are opposed to receiving it. I maintain that a law passed by Congress, giving men the right to contract for gold payment, and compelling the party to pay gold, is the first step that is to be taken. When we have done that, we shall no longer be at the mercy of stock gamblers. The one currency or the other will be an article of merchandise; if not the paper, then the gold. Shall we take gold, which is the universal standard, and let that be the standard of all our values? I think we had better come to the plain gold standard at once.

As to the question of repudiation, I do not think, Sir, that it will result in repudiation. We may not be able now to pay these debts; like the people of the South who could not pretend to pay their past debts, but have paid cash for the few things they wanted to enable them to make this year's crop, the people of the United States may not be able to pay in gold for their past debts, but they may be able to pay gold for everything in the future; and pay these debts as soon as they are able to. We pay gold for everything we get abroad, and yet the English can pay us in greenbacks; they can compel us to receive greenbacks when we expected to get gold. Even though gold is expressed in the contracts, some Courts have decided that we are still obliged to receive greenbacks. Our country is thus placed at the mercy of other countries, and the honest man is placed at the mercy of the dishonest man.

I differ with the gentleman from Chicago, in the opinion that this Board ought not to go into details. You are the very men who should. If you resolve that the Government should return to a specie basis as fast as possible, you only give expression to that which every man believes. But you are above the ordinary mechanic, the planter, and others; you stand here as the representatives of the trade of the country; you are monied men, the men who make contracts, and you are superior in this respect to Congress. Upon questions involving money, upon financial subjects, there is no body that can be assembled in this country, whose opinions ought to take precedence of those of the National Board of Trade; and any details that can be pointed out by this body ought to have great weight with Congress.

Every one who has studied the subject at all, knows that it has been announced that no legislation can give value to that which has intrinsically no value.

The Government of this country in its late "unfortunate unpleasantness;"—indeed we upon both sides,—undertook to make money out of that which was not money, and we absolutely coined the patriotism of our people when we did it.

Upon the subject of repudiation, it would not be proper in me to discuss the views presented by Mr. MUNN, from Chicago, on one side, and Mr. RANDOLPH on the other, as to exactly how much ought to be paid on these bonds. Mr. MUNN says they ought not to give full value, and Mr. RANDOLPH says they should; I will let the gentlemen fight it out and settle it between themselves.

I ask this Board to come to this proposition:

*Resolved*, That the best interests of the country demand a return to specie payments at as early a day as practicable, and that, in the opinion of this Board, the best method of accomplishing this object is the passage of a law making it lawful to make contracts payable in gold, and enacting that such contracts shall not be discharged in legal-tender notes, and that from and after a certain date all new contracts, where it is not otherwise provided, shall be deemed payable in gold.

When we do that, we shall bring ourselves to the real standard. The confidence of the country is wanting in the National Bank currency. When a man is called upon to tell what a dollar is, he is not able to say; you cannot tell what it represents, because gold is worth so much to-day and so much to-morrow. If the banks have the capacity, they will have a certain amount of gold in their vaults, and get the confidence of the people. But we must first take away that law, that is now a fraud upon the people, which says we shall take as a dollar, that which is not a dollar, and must declare that men may contract for gold, and compel payments to be made in gold.

Mr. TREZEVANT : I am not a financier, therefore shall not attempt to enter into details as to how, or at what stated period, specie payments may be resumed. I apprehend there is no doubt on the part of this body, as to the propriety of the earliest possible resumption; the simple question is as to the means of reaching it.

I regard the solution of this question as depending upon the degree of credit and confidence that may be given to the Government; and that credit and that confidence will depend upon its resources. These, it is admitted, are wonderful and rapidly increasing. Leaving gentlemen from other portions of the Union to speak of the wealth and power of these portions, I shall confine my remarks to my knowledge of the resources of the Southern States of the Union — the States formerly known as slave States, and lying, generally, on a line south of the Ohio River. The time allotted to debate, is so limited, that nothing but a synopsis of what I would like to say, can be presented now.

We generally judge of the future by the past; and I presume the wisdom learned from such comparison, is the safest and surest guide to right conclusions. Let me state some few facts touching the production of two or three of the great exports of the Union.

In 1860, the Southern States produced five million one hundred and ninety-six thousand bales of cotton; four hundred and thirty million pounds of tobacco; and three hundred and two thousand hogsheads of sugar, of one thousand pounds each. All of us know that the two former constitute the great articles of national export. I have stated that *all* the tobacco was raised in the South. I will modify this by saying that seven-eighths were raised there.

The cotton crop was by far the largest ever raised in the Union; and it brought the enormous sum of at least two hundred and fifty million dollars. Nearly one million bales were consumed in the United States, leaving more than four million bales for export, worth two hundred million dollars. The tobacco was worth at least twenty million dollars, and the sugar fifteen million dollars. These simple facts show the wonderful resources of the Southern States. Since this time, these States have been suffering from the ravages of war; and their sufferings have not yet ended. For the past three years we have been struggling with trials and poverty in all their exacting forms; and have been living on "shorter commons" than we ever thought would be our lot. Our people felt that with them it was "root, hog, or die," (if I may use a vulgarism) and they went to "rooting." The result is, that for a country so devastated, we have accomplished wonders; such wonders as strikingly manifest the vast and varied resources of that glorious land of the magnolia and jessamine. We are still poor, Sir; still sadly in need of many of the comforts of life; but we all feel there is a better day coming.

The cotton crop of 1866–'67, was upwards of two million four hundred thousand bales, worth at least two hundred million dollars; and the crop of this year will not be short of two million bales, which will be worth two hundred million dollars more. This, Sir, is a marvellous exhibit of resources and wealth; and it presents the question,— " Can a government with such resources, be long without the credit necessary for a return to specie payments?" Some of my friends seem particularly anxious to prove that the South is utterly ruined beyond redemption, and object even to the entertaining of any pleasant hope for the future, which these facts give us. I am not one of these. I think it an extremely difficult job to "ruin" such a country as the South, if we can have quiet and justice. The crop of this year, and the bankrupt law, will lift such an amount of debt from the shoulders of our people, that the next crop — that of 1869 — will place them nearer out of debt than they have been in a quarter of a century. From this time forth, our people will raise their own food, their own corn, wheat, potatoes, etc.; and then their cotton and tobacco will enter still more largely than ever before, into the export wealth of the country. The cotton crop of this year will bring as much cash as the largest crop ever did; for, in that largest crop year, we spent millions for food, which we will hereafter raise at home. More than this. In former years, the cotton planter *owned* his tobacco, but really *paid* for it in the expenses necessarily attendant not only upon feeding the laborer, but also in feeding, clothing, doctoring, etc., both the laborer and his unproductive family. In the Northern States, the farmer pays for the labor of his hired man, but the support of that man's family is not a part of his contract. This is now the case with us; and we hire our "help," as is done in the North. In this way, Sir, we shall be at less expense than in former years, though our labor will never be as efficient as formerly. Hence we shall expend less of what we make; and as we do not expect ever to have to buy food again, the value of our export wealth must be greater. In reviewing these simple facts, I am again induced to say that if resources give a country credit, these vast, and annually increasing staples of export wealth, must surely soon give our country such a credit as will enable it to resume specie payments at an early day. As to the particular period and manner of doing this, I am willing to leave that to abler minds. My only wish was to prove that our vast resources would soon give us the credit needed for resumption.

Mr. TOPP: I do not rise to make a speech, but as my colleague has urged it upon me to say a few words, I will offer a resolution, if in order:

*Resolved*, That, in the present embarrassed condition of the country, it is unwise and inexpedient to attempt the resumption of specie payments or to name a time for resumption.

That such efforts, if attempted, would result in commercial embarrassment, disaster and wide-spread ruin.

That the best way to resume payments will be to adhere with scrupulous fidelity to our obligations, retrench the expenditures of Government, develop our resources, and thereby restore the country to prosperity.

## Milwaukie Chamber of Commerce. Mr. HOLTON:

I think that the gentleman from Memphis must have directed his remarks to me, when he referred to the necessity of retrenchment in our domestic circles, and talked so bravely of the curtailment of ribbons, and the shortening of trails; for, if I remember aright, I used language before the Boston Convention, in the discussion of this very question, demanding the "curtailment of ribbons, and the shortening of trails," as one of the ways by which we could get back to specie payments. If he thinks I have not done my duty in this respect, I must refer him to my wife, and I fear she may say that I am a hard-hearted husband, for having so practically carried out the doctrine of my own preaching.

I am glad, Sir, that a voice of cheering encouragement comes to us from the South. The gentleman from Memphis says that "root, hog, or die" has become the watchword of the South. I thank him for that text. The genius of Industry speaks, and in homely but expressive phrase, says "root, hog, or die!" That, Sir, is my doctrine, and we see the admirable results of its application in the South, when nearly two hundred and fifty million dollars worth of cotton is reported by the gentleman, as the product of that section of our country for the last year; and yet, Sir, we stand here and talk of the nation's bankruptcy, when the teeming abundance of the nation's industry is pouring in upon us on all hands! The nation's present wealth, and its undeveloped resources, are alike boundless and inexhaustible.

I am, Sir, in favor of the earliest moment for the resumption of specie payments. The present time has been compared by my friend Mr. TURPIN, of Chicago, with that of 1837, but the cases are by no means parallel. Who does not know the viciousness of the banking system of that time, when the States, impelled by a mistaken idea of properly supplying the vacuum occasioned by the demise of the United States Bank, created numberless local banks, without due regard to safety, so that the proper limit of one hundred and fifty million dollars was expanded to three hundred million dollars of their miserable paper currency, with altogether too large a proportion of their assets for its redemption in paper towns and balloon schemes. Our position to-day is a very different one. The banks are sound, and individual credit was never better. *It is only the Government that has defaulted; and she is abundantly able to pay.*

We are told further, that this vast country, the United States of America, is to-day in the position of a merchant debtor, unable to pay his debts, and that not until our debts are paid, can we resume specie payments. Now I hold that our Federal Government will most easily take up its four hundred million dollars in circulation. The Government owes nothing to-day but this four hundred million dollars. It has the run, at its own option, of fifteen years, more or less, before its bonds begin to fall due. And the resources of the country may be so husbanded as to quickly make its credit par on the street. The Government can do this, just as the prudent man, in like, but limited circumstances, with an abundance of assets in his hand, could do it. As business men, we find fault with the individual who, having means in hand, suffers his credit to be below par. And if he does not quickly change his plan, he is thrown beyond the pale of commercial confidence. The Government has got to stand or fall, by the same rule of judgment.

The Government has one hundred million dollars of gold in the Treasury. Let her buy another one hundred million dollars, and all the wealth of the country would be pledged for the payment of the nation's indebtedness. With such an amount of specie, and with such a resource of credit, will you tell me that resumption is impossible?

As to the precise method and ways which it may be desirable for the Government to take, or this body to recommend, I am not prepared to state. I shall listen with patience to everything that may be advanced here. I am satisfied to present my general ideas, leaving it to the Committee on Finance to recommend any details, should they so determine.

I beg to offer the following preamble and resolution:

WHEREAS, During the period of war, the Government found it necessary to suspend specie payments not only on its own account, but, by issuing a large amount of paper currency, and legalizing the same, compelled suspension on the part of the people; and

WHEREAS, Now that the war has ended, and the products of the soil have been abundantly favored of heaven, and from the same divine source the public health has in all our land been preserved, so that the natural capacity of industry was never greater; and

WHEREAS, We are at peace with all the world; and

WHEREAS, The national ability has been abundantly demonstrated by the national revenue of four hundred millions in one year, without serious abridgment of the ordinary comforts of the people; and

WHEREAS, It is a well settled axiom, derived from the history of all commercial nations, in all periods, that there is no safe basis for the transaction of domestic and foreign trade, except upon the precious metals as the proper measure of the value of such surplus wealth, as the individual, or, as the nation may have to dispose of; therefore,

*Resolved*, That it is the duty of the Government, in such way and in such manner as, in the wisdom of the financial officers of the Government, it can best be done, to resume the payment of its indebtedness in specie, and to establish the constitutional provision that coin shall be the legal money of the country.

New York Produce Exchange. Mr. HINCKEN: The New York Produce Exchange makes no other suggestion regarding the resumption of specie payments, than to express its belief that it should occur as soon as the country will permit; and it believes that this period will be hastened by a rigid adherence to the rules of economy in all matters pertaining to the Government; that its expenditures should be limited to actual necessities, and that all extraordinary calls upon its credit should be stopped. And it further believes that the subject spoken of by other delegations, the payment of contracts in gold, should be legalized.

It is the custom in New York, and I believe in most of the seaboard cities, to sell all articles of import for gold. The importer must base his calculations on what is the price of gold; and we therefore believe that the Government should at once legalize that kind of contract which is daily made in New York and elsewhere. Our freights are paid in gold, imports also; and but one house, so far, has dared to violate the contract. That house received a verdict of the Courts in its favor, but public opinion was so strong, that it voluntarily came back and paid the amount claimed by the original contract; it paid gold, though the Courts had decided that it should pay paper. That was brought about by public opinion; but we wish it to be put beyond the power of any man who has made a contract for gold to come and say, "There's the paper."

### New York Chamber of Commerce. Mr. STRANAHAN:

I shall not occupy more than a minute of time in answering the call made upon the Chamber of Commerce of New York. Our views on this question are highly practical. We do not believe in any of the patent processes which have been urged in favor of the resumption of specie payments We think that the true course to pursue will be to travel the old turnpike road directly to the object in view. We would have the Government husband its resources in the common business way. We would have the banks of the country do the same; and we would ask the people of the country to do the same. We would further suggest that no one of these shall live upon or be a burden to the other; but that each should perform its own labor.

I will only add, Sir, that we are strenuous as to time. We would give every suggestion, and every plan that has been proposed, for one single Act of Congress; and we would have that fix the time, simply and irrevocably for resumption. That done, in our humble opinion the work of resumption will be half accomplished.

### Newark Board of Trade. Mr. DAWSON: 
The Newark Board of Trade will most heartily adopt a portion of the resolution suggested by the St. Louis Board of Trade, as far as legalizing the sale of gold as merchandise; but we rest upon the broad axiom that any attempt by Government to legislate into existence a resumption of specie payments will end in a miserable farce. We claim that Government should take the same stand that would be taken by any intelligent merchant, who found himself in an embarrassed position; he would seek to find out what his resources are, and what he is able to do; he would adopt a close, careful, economical administration of his affairs, cutting off all useless expenditure, by these means reducing his expenses, and shortly he would find himself abundantly able to pay his debts.

Mr. PETERS : We have three hundred and fifty million dollars of greenbacks, but it is not proposed to redeem this amount of money at the present time, we have not got the gold ; and it is not possible to pay one promissory note by another. Our friends in the South, who have raised this large amount of cotton, and almost without anything to do it with, should have a chance of sharing with us in the use of the national currency. They have little or none ; owing to the fact that when it was issued, they were out in the cold. Having scarcely any currency, they cannot buy exchange ; and when they wish to remit to the North, they are often driven to obtain post office orders for the amount.

To prepare for the resumption of specie payments, the Government should direct that from the first of January next, the National Banks should reserve their specie, so that a resumption of specie payments may be ensured at a period not later than five years from this date. As long as we send sixty-eight million dollars in gold out of the country in a single year, it will not be possible to resume specie payments ; but the measure I suggest would be an important step towards the end we have in view.

Norfolk Board of Trade. Mr. HUGHES : I have been highly edified by the exceedingly able discussions to which I have listened. With many of the opinions I have heard expressed, I most cordially agree ; but I have also heard many from which I dissent. I am one of those who think that the time has not yet arrived for a return to specie payments, and my chief reason is that the foreign trade of the country is not in a condition to admit of any step looking immediately to that result.

The surest way to a resumption of specie payments lies through the restoration of the industrial interests of the country, especially the agricultural, and more particularly those which are connected with the exportable products of the country. For a long time, probably since the commencement of the late war, our exports of agricultural productions have not been commensurate with our imports ; and the deficiency has been supplied, first by our large annual exports of gold, and secondly by a large sale of the bonds of the United States. This source of income, however, will henceforth be discontinued ; we cannot expect to sell any considerable amount of bonds in years immediately at hand. The export of specie is still going on, while, as has recently been remarked, the imports have not diminished, but have rather increased of late ; it seems to me, therefore, that we cannot expect to arrive at a condition of things in which it would be safe to return to specie payments, until the foreign trade of the country is placed upon a better basis; and the best means of accomplishing that, is by developing and encouraging the production of those agricultural staples, which were so seriously checked during the late war.

The gentleman who last addressed the Board, incidentally touched upon one important suggestion, and that is, that the portion of the Union from which I come is in great need of currency. It is in need, not merely of banking capital, but of currency; and if any measure can be adopted by which banking capital and currency can be furnished us in an amount proportionate to that possessed by other portions of the Union, our agriculture will be placed on a more prosperous basis, our industry will revive, and a stimulus will be given to the production of those staples, which enter so largely into foreign commerce.

I believe that the country is now just in that condition in which any measure affecting the currency, instead of being revolutionary, should be conservative. In my opinion, the building up of the great lines of improvement which are projected, increasing the means of transportation by which our products can be carried from the West to the seaboard, and the opening up of communication from this city to the Pacific Ocean, would give a powerful stimulus to the productions of the continent; and any further issuing of Government bonds or currency to promote these improvements, so far from having a tendency to defer, would be in the direction of specie payments.

Oswego Board of Trade. MR. GRANT: We are in favor of a resumption of specie payments as soon as it can be accomplished on a safe and permanent basis. Our intercourse with Canada has opened a large commerce; and it may be a matter of surprise to some here, to learn that in paying duties, we are the fifth among the ports of the United States. This last year, the amount of duties paid at Oswego was something like one million two hundred thousand dollars; our purchases consist of barley, wheat, and other productions of the soil, but more especially lumber, which comes in there in large quantities. In consequence, we use a vast amount of gold; and we are inclined to come back to that basis as early as possible, that we may be relieved of the burden which we now suffer in paying the difference between currency and gold, which we must do, in order to carry on our transactions with our northern neighbors. But we do not ask this, unless it will advance the interests of the entire country. We want a constitutional currency, that shall be equal in all parts of the land; and when that can be had safely, we will be content.

Philadelphia Commercial Exchange. MR. HOFFMAN: Now that so much has been said upon this subject, there is very little left for me to say. I would like to remark, however, that I am in favor of Congress passing an act to legalize specie contracts.

But I am opposed to the idea of compelling bankers to hold their gold. It will have the effect that we know would result with grain, if a certain number of individuals chose to hold their stock of grain. Gold is an article of merchandise; and you will be taking so much gold from the market, as an article of sale. You take at the present time from seven hundred thousand dollars to eight hundred thousand dollars a day, which is required to pay duties, and the difference between our imports and exports; now, if this amount is paid away every day, and the banks have a large quantity in reserve, and the United States holds its gold, what have I to do when I want to pay gold? Why, I must pay a price commensurate with the diminished quantity of gold in the market. I have known the day when it was exceedingly difficult to get gold in Philadelphia, when you could not find it in the market; the same has occurred in Baltimore, and occurs often in New York, where they have to pay more for it in consequence of the difficulty of obtaining it at the particular hour when it is wanted.

You will be compelling people to pay more for the gold they need, just as they would have to pay more for produce if it was held back. If we have but one hundred thousand barrels of flour, and I hold fifty thousand barrels, leaving only fifty thousand for sale, and if there is a large demand for the article, the parties offering these fifty thousand for sale, will get more than if the whole quantity was offered. I favor the idea, that when a contract is made, the party making shall be held by it; that when a man says he will pay in gold, he should be made to pay in gold. I am in favor of returning to specie payments as early as possible, but I do not want Congress to specify any particular day.

Mr. BUZBY: We have heard so much splendid rhetoric about our national integrity, and about the capacity of the United States to raise any amount of money, whether represented in gold or in other commodities, for the almost instantaneous discharge of our debts, that these statements, acting upon the enthusiasm and the excitable minds of our people, would lead them to suppose that the thing could be done in an instant of time; that we have but to bring the matter before Congress, and they by a process of legerdemain, will, at a single touch, evoke the masses of specie requisite to redeem the indebtedness of the country. I should like to do that. It sounds well. The larger the story, the greater our faith; but, under the sunlight of truth, these imaginings must be dispelled, and we must come down to the sober fact.

Now, what is the fact about it? That the United States cannot now pay its debts in gold, is shown by the premium on gold. We have had all sorts of expedients recommended by those who favor an early return to specie payments; one in particular, to prevent gold going away from us; it is recommended that banks should withhold all the specie paid to them in the shape of interest on the national bonds. The Secretary of the Treasury hoards all his surplus gold, as far as he can, and when he finds the premium rising, he puts a little on the market to quiet the excitement; and by that act shows that the public indebtedness requires all his manipulation to keep the premium within reasonable bounds. Are there not indications in this, that the country possesses no immediate capacity for the return to specie payments? Can we see in it any evidence that it will be good sense on the part of this Board, to recommend Congress to fix a day on which resumption shall occur? We might as well attempt to legislate in this body, or in the national legislature, that a child should grow two inches in a year. The thing might occur, and it might not; but if it did, it would not be by virtue of our legislation.

Gentlemen want a short cut to resumption. There are two ways, which I will name.

Suppose the Government should say to the people, "You want us to resume specie payments, and we are disposed to meet you in the matter; but with our immense debt we find a difficulty in the way. In order to enable us to do it, we must issue a bond, say a three sixty-five, which is a favorite figure with some parties, which you must accept in lieu of the obligations now falling due; or we will pay you for the five-twenties in greenbacks." The Government might submit a compulsory proposition of that kind; you shall either be paid in greenbacks, or take the three sixty-five bonds. By this means, the amount of interest being lessened, the Government would find its ability to pay in specie increased, and so far as it went, the thing would be on the way towards accomplishment; in proportion to the lessening of interest, could payments be made in gold.

There is also another way, and that is to scale down all existing debts on a certain day, so that a debt paid in specie upon a sudden resumption would, by this scaling process, be made as light to the debtor as the payment of the debt in paper currency would have been.

But that would involve great difficulty; and it would lead to the cry of repudiation. Neither plan is submitted for the consideration of gentlemen present.

There is another mode, which I prefer, and which has had the support and approval of the body which I here represent. In January, 1867, a preamble and the following resolutions were submitted to the Commercial Exchange of Philadelphia and adopted:

*Resolved*, That the resumption of specie payments can only be permanently effected when full crops, successful industry, and restored political harmony, shall cause gold to flow hither and remain with us.

*Resolved*, That premature resumption will prove a curse and not a blessing.

We stood unanimously on that ground two years ago, and we stand there to-day, as far as I know.

Now, why is this matter to be forced? The entire population of the country are satisfied and content to use this greenback money; and I have never been able to respect the feeling which has led to the continual vilification of the greenback, by so many people, ever since it was issued. I see in the use of that instrumentality the salvation of my country; and I know very well, Sir, that those who decry it most are well satisfied to receive it in trade; they buy and sell with it, and they get all they can for it. And the six hundred million dollars of paper currency are backed by sixteen billion dollars worth of property in the United States; and what currency in the world is better secured than that? You talk of its being irredeemable; but we redeem it every day.

I am not in favor of so manipulating this specie resumption as to make our country directly subservient to foreign influences. I want to see a little financial independence, as well as a little political independence. I am not willing that the instructions I am to receive as to whether our currency is to be in paper or in gold shall come from the foreign trade of the country, whether represented by our own citizens or by foreign residents here. I am sorry that much of the inspiration we receive is from foreign sources. I for one, am content with the greenback. It represents what it is worth on its face. I believe gold is a commodity; and it makes an important difference in our conclusions as to how we regard that.

Gentlemen seem afraid that we may have a superabundant supply of the machinery of commerce; they are afraid of too much circulating medium. It is possible that a wealthy operator, a great speculator, a man of gigantic means, would be well satisfied that other people should not by any action of the Government be put a little more on a level with himself.

What was the state of things in all the countries of Europe prior to the discovery of the gold mines of America, and the consequently more abundant use of this medium of commercial exchange? I had occasion to read a very instructive and valuable work recently, and I will take the liberty of giving an extract from it here, because I think it very interesting and directly relevant.

The article treats on the effect of volume of money on prices. To the masses of this people the argument has been used with telling effect that they have paid tremendously for every thing they consumed, because there has been so much paper money in circulation; and this has gone very far to create an unnecessary prejudice in their minds.

I will read from COLWELL's Ways and Means of Payment, p. 500:

"It appears from the careful investigations of ARTHUR YOUNG, that the whole average advance of prices did not exceed two hundred and eighty per cent. from the fifteenth to the nineteenth century, or to the year 1810; that is, less than in the proportion of one to three. In that same period, the increase of the precious metals was one to eleven. HUMBOLDT estimates the receipts from American mines, up to the year 1500, at not over two hundred and fifty thousand dollars yearly, but as having grown to nearly forty million dollars in 1810, that is, as one to one hundred and sixty. In the period from the fifteenth to the sixteenth century, general prices were enhanced twenty-four per cent., while the whole stock of money had increased three hundred and eighty per cent. In the seventeenth century prices advanced eighty per cent., while the stock of coin increased eight hundred and seventy-five per cent. In the next, or eighteenth century, prices rose to one hundred and ninety per cent., while the stock of money was increased one thousand one hundred and twenty per cent. So little do general prices appear by this statement, to obey any influence arising from the increased stock of money, that it seems doubtful if we should allow any portion of the actual advance to go to that account. In fact, we shall not go far wrong if we attribute the whole rise in prices to that increased activity in all kinds of business, which increases demand. So far as the quantity of money is an element of prices, it seems to be one of the least influential; and it can not be one of those causes to which great and sudden fluctuations of prices are ever due."

That disposes of one great question which has been agitating our minds. For it must be remembered that paper money was growing in use and volume the whole time; yet the rise in price of a bushel of wheat in Spain in one hundred and ten years, varied only in the relation of thirty-seven and two-tenths to forty-two. Therefore, I hope we shall cease to be alarmed by the existence of a large quantity of money, as increasing prices and oppressing the poor. If it does not swell the price of the necessaries of life, it certainly renders possible the vast improvements that are needed; it makes your Union Pacific Railway, and all the other railways, possible, which I think they would not be without paper currency.

I will not consent to the legalizing of gold contracts. I agree with the gentleman from Chicago that the legal-tender currency is good enough for all; and I do not see why covert advances should be made, as a wedge, to make difficulty; I look upon it as a cunning device for that effect. Since paper money has been the great circulating medium of the world, gold has become essentially a commodity. Gentlemen imagine that when specie payments are resumed, this will cease to be the case. Suppose the Bank of England draws upon us for a few millions of dollars; the banks immediately feel the loss of the specie, and begin to contract their loans; money rises to one and a half to two and a half a month; at once you find the price of money has risen, but it is merely an imaginary difficulty, and not one in fact.

I beg to offer the following resolution:

*Resolved*, That the National Board of Trade witnesses with pleasure the gradual restoration of amicable political relations throughout the entire country, and the consequent revival of industry and increase of wealth, and sees in them the sure foundation for the resumption of specie payments at no distant day, without the interference of disturbing, premature and injurious legislation.

Philadelphia Board of Trade. Mr. HAND: The points of the whole matter have been so thoroughly covered, that I shall simply state that I am in favor of the early resumption of specie payments. And I believe if Congress would pass an Act fixing a day not later than the first of January, 1871, it would be accomplished as easily and with as little disturbance to the business and commercial circles of our country as at any later period. If the Government would pass such an Act, it would sound the note of warning for banks and individuals to prepare for the new order of things; extravagance would necessarily be checked, if it did not disappear, and values would undoubtedly shrink. We cannot go on with this inflated currency; the great masses of the people cannot stand it. We must bear in mind that the laboring classes are not much better off, indeed perhaps, they are worse off than they were before the expansion of the currency; and again, there is a larger portion of our population who are living on a limited income, which at present barely suffices to enable them to live, in consequence of the high price of every necessary of life.

I think that the shrinkage in values should be borne by those who have had the advantage of the inflation; and that we should not postpone resumption to a later day than January 1st, 1871.

Mr. ALLEN: As I think that every part of the ground has already been covered, I will simply say that I give a hearty concurrence to the St. Louis resolutions. I think they are right in fixing the day, so that we may all look forward to it, and be preparing for it.

I offer the following resolution:

*Resolved,* That the payment of interest on deposits by the National Banks, should, in the opinion of this Board, be prohibited by law.

Mr. WINSOR: We all desire to return to specie, but we differ very much as to the means by which it shall be best brought about. The truth is, I imagine, that we are not willing to pay the price for it. There are two ways by which we can return to a specie basis. One is by contracting the currency so as to make it more and more valuable, until it shall become as valuable as specie itself. This currency of ours follows the law of all merchandise; if you increase the quantity, you diminish the value, and *vice versa.* Or, again, you may, by increasing its quantity, diminish its value, until it will require one thousand dollars to buy a barrel of flour, and until finally you cannot buy anything with it at all, and you may come to specie payments in that way.

We cannot return to specie payments without some difficulty; and we must not shrink from that difficulty. It is a mistake to fix any time; but we should strive to devise some plan which the people can see will result in success, and then they will accept it. What we want is to pay the debt in this paper money; and when all men see that it is appreciating in value, that it is as good as gold, or moving in that direction, they will begin to believe in it, and they will help the matter on. Any plan, therefore, that is proposed by this National Board of Trade, should be so plain that everybody can understand it; there should be nothing elaborate about it, but everything perfectly simple and straightforward.

Mr. WETHERILL: I have listened with much attention to the remarks made upon this important question, and as the entire day has been consumed in receiving the plans and entertaining the propositions of nearly every delegation that has as yet been called, I will be brief in the remarks I have to make. At this late hour I do not conceive it to be my duty to present any new plan. So varied are we in our ideas upon the subject, — each delegation it seems to me, having a plan of its own, which doubtless it conceives to be the best — would it not, I would suggest, be wiser for the few delegations yet to follow in the argument, to so concentrate, sift and examine the whole subject, that we may be enabled to form a conclusion, which shall be the united opinion of this body. The two extremes have been represented here to-day, and all the varied intermediate grades. On the one side we have extreme contraction. My friend from Milwaukie is ready for immediate and prompt measures for the withdrawal of greenbacks. I cannot agree with him either as to the wisdom or the expediency of requiring the merchants and manufacturers of this country to submit to a contraction at once of thirty-three per cent. of their products. Nor do I agree on the other hand, with my friend from Cincinnati, who, judging from his remarks, takes the other extreme of the question. He is willing to let matters go on for a while as at present. In eloquent language he has alluded to the resources of this country; he has spoken of its mighty products, of its vast mineral wealth and of its rich lands, teeming with abundant crops; each and all combining to make our country the most productive in the world. And while upon this question, I am reminded of the boy who whistled so well, and when asked how he did it, his reply was, "it whistles itself." Vast as our advantages are, mighty as are our resources, I do not believe we can slide into specie payments as easily as the boy did in his accomplishment.

Retrenchment and economy have also been alluded to as essential requisites to obtain the wished for result. To this I cordially assent, but I also add, that you might preach economy forever, and yet the merchant or manufacturer who is prosperous and successful, will be liberal to himself and those about him. To make him economical, he must feel by the contraction of currency the pinch that necessarily follows, and it will produce the result desired more certainly and more effectually, than any amount of sermons upon the subject.

I rejoice to hear the encouraging statements of the gentleman from Memphis. Every member of this body must be assured from his remarks, that the South is emerging from her depression, and the people accepting the situation, are being aroused from their despondency. If I heard correctly, that gentleman stated that in cotton alone the South will show next year, with a fair crop, a surplus of two hundred millions of dollars. If this is so, I ask you, gentlemen of the Northwest, with a wheat crop this year of two hundred millions of bushels, and a corn crop of one thousand millions of bushels added thereto, the other products of your soil swelling up the vast sum to many millions more, all showing a surplus profit of more than double the amount named by the gentleman from Memphis, will you not in the face of these grand results, cheerfully come forward, and by contraction, offer but a tithe of your profits, in order that a part of this houseless, homeless currency of ours may be cancelled. I think it evident that a majority of this body favor the proposition that the best way to accomplish resumption, is by contraction; yet but few of us are willing to fix a day upon which we should resume. I listened with great pleasure to the forcible remarks of the gentleman from Boston. His views were clear and practical, but when speaking of contraction he illustrated it by a man with a high mountain before him, which he must climb; the man could not ascend it on a run, or he would fall exhausted, but he must do it by a careful, cautious, prudent walk. This illustration was to the point; he did not tell us, however, upon what day he would reach the top. The speaker was not positive himself, how long the ascent would take, and closed without naming a day for resumption. The distinguished gentleman from New York, who was in his remarks, terse, close, and to the point, led me to believe that by the wisdom of that delegation, we might possibly arrive at the proper time when we should commence this important work; but here, too, I was disappointed. I honestly believe that if we want our influence in this matter felt in Congress, we must not be satisfied with a vague and general resolution, that the Government is expected to resume. From a body like this, representing fourteen thousand merchants in our land, Congress will expect better things. And I believe, from the information we have to-day gathered from the representatives of the merchants of the land, men of all others most interested, men whose success depends upon its speedy settlement, men who know that if left to drift on without check, a fearful future is in store for us; with all this in view, can we not say to Congress that, in our opinion, we can resume upon a given day, and be confident enough in our own judgment to name it.

Mr. GANO : I move that the resolutions on finance, as far as they are presented to-day, be printed.

Carried.

Pittsburgh Board of Trade. Mr. BRUNOT: The delegates from Pittsburgh had decided that their voices should not be heard upon this subject, believing that so many abler minds would have given the result of their attention to it, that the Board would readily reach a conclusion, not only in regard to the importance of early resumption, but also in regard to the means by which this would be best accomplished. But, Sir, in listening to the discussion, I have become satisfied that any settlement of details, in the time this body can command, is not possible. A man engaged in ordinary business may have such a perfect comprehension of the nature of his engagements, and of the amount of the resources with which he may meet them, that he may fix some day, even during a time of embarrassment, when he will liquidate his obligations. He determines to make so much here, to save so much there, and by this or that expedient, to strive to gain his point. But for some other person to name the day of settlement, who has no control over the resources or the personal efforts of the principal, would be useless, as a measure by which either to hasten the desired event, or to secure its accomplishment.

So it seems to me that in reference to the Government, we cannot wisely and properly urge Congress to any specific enactment as to the date of resumption, unless we have a knowledge of all the details by which the desired end is to be reached. There is one point which is absolutely essential to a proper understanding of this question, and which must be settled before Congress can fix upon a date; whence and how shall we get the specie? Congress has the regulation of the revenue laws of the country, and upon these laws will depend, very greatly, whether we can hold gold enough in 1870, to resume or not.

If we expect to resume specie payments, we must have the specie with which to redeem our notes. The gentleman from Memphis has told us that nearly all our gold comes from England; on the contrary, I think nearly all our gold goes to England. The United States Government collects for duties, in round numbers, one hundred and fifty million dollars in gold, and pays out one hundred and twenty million dollars. Gold must be had with which to pay the duties; and the interest paid by the Government, together with the sales of the surplus received for duties, meets that demand. I do not believe that gold is being hoarded, when it will command ten per cent. premium, much less when it stands at thirty-five per cent. For what other purpose then, is it required? Manifestly to pay for the imported products of countries in which our greenbacks have but little value, and no circulation. They must have gold, or its equivalent, to carry from us in payment for their productions supplied to us. They take some bonds and a little grain, but they prefer gold; and until the demand for this purpose is lessened, the aggregate amount of gold in the United States will continue to decrease. Now, Sir, the very first step towards resumption, it seems to me, should be the enactment of such laws as would supply the specie for resumption, by keeping it in the country. Instead of contracting the currency, expand the gold by such modifications of the revenue laws as will lessen the amount of importations to be paid for in gold. I submit that this Board, having no control over, and no premonition of the action Congress may take in regard to the revenue laws, upon which so much of the ability to resume, depends, can hardly designate a day for resumption. I am in favor of the resolution of the gentleman from Boston; and failing in that, shall favor the resolution of the gentleman from Milwaukie (Mr. HOLTON.) But let us not name a day for resumption. If, as is probable, Congress shall immediately set to work for the accomplishment of an early resumption, so far as legislation may do this, and if it shall see proper to fix a day, let us resolve that this Board, and the constituent boards, so far as we may rightly pledge them, will heartily sustain such laws as Congress shall make.

Mr. President, permit me to dissent from an expression used by a gentleman upon this floor, who ventured to characterize the United States as a "bankrupt nation." A bankrupt nation! If this, Sir, is a bankrupt nation, then no nation upon the face of the earth is solvent. When we listen to the eloquent gentleman from Memphis, as he describes the capabilities of the South, and as he adverts to the wonderful fact that in the very time of their poverty the people there have, this year, a surplus of two hundred million dollars, and are preparing to accept cheerfully, their share of the public burdens; when we hear the Northwest proudly boasting of its marvellous wealth of breadstuffs; when California tells us of her mines; when the advocates of Pacific Railroads depict the grandeur of the Territories which lie between the Pacific coast and ourselves; and when we remember that in our own Middle and Eastern States we have a wealth-producing capacity in mines, manufactures, agriculture and commerce, equal to all the rest combined, we know that the nation cannot be or become bankrupt. Nor am I willing to admit that the present state of suspension is even "disgraceful." It is simply a condition of affairs agreed upon, or at least accepted, between the people and the Government, at a time when it was for their mutual interest to do so. As between our Government and ourselves the arrangement was perfectly legitimate. Other people had nothing to do with it; we have never asked them to take our suspended paper, and if they have chosen to take it, they have no business to call names. The state of suspension, as it exists, is not "disgraceful," it is merely inconvenient and inexpedient, and therefore both the Government and the people desire to return to specie payments. It helps nothing, to denounce unduly, either our

Government or ourselves. It does harm. If every man would cease to predict disaster, and in quiet confidence would continue to add his share to the grand aggregate of national wealth, the ability to resume, and the event of resumption, would soon be reached. Let the members of this Board, and the constituencies they represent, realize that we are not a bankrupt nation; that we are not a disgraced nation; that we never intend to be either; that every national obligation will be fully met; and that specie payments, being desirable, will come.

The Board adjourned to meet on Saturday, December 5th, at ten o'clock, A. M.

# FOURTH DAY.

### SATURDAY, DECEMBER 5, 1868.

The Board met pursuant to adjournment.
The President in the chair.
Prayer was offered by the Rev. W. T. MOORE.
The reading of the Journal was dispensed with.

The PRESIDENT: On behalf of the Executive Council, I beg to report that they have passed a resolution recommending that the next session of this Board be held in the city of Richmond, Virginia.

In reference to the proposition from the Detroit Board of Trade, on the subject of copper, the Executive Council recommend that the resolution relative thereto be placed at the foot of the programme now before us; and that the proposition from the Louisville Board of Trade in regard to the levees of the river Mississippi follow next to it.

Mr. BRUNOT: I move the acceptance and adoption of the supplementary report of the Executive Council, in regard to the papers which have been referred to.

Carried.

The PRESIDENT: The next business is in respect to the New Orleans Board of Trade, which has accredited a delegate to this body.

The SECRETARY: Mr. WM. M. BURWELL has presented himself as a delegate from the New Orleans Board of Trade.

The credentials of Mr. BURWELL having been read, and declared to be in due order, that gentleman was requested by the President to take his seat as a delegate.

The PRESIDENT: When we adjourned yesterday, the Pittsburgh delegates were entitled to the floor on the resumption of specie payments.

Pittsburgh Board of Trade. Mr. THURSTON: Our Board does not desire to add anything to the further discussion of the subject.

The PRESIDENT: I suppose that in my position as delegate from the Board of Trade of Philadelphia, I should have spoken at the time the delegates from that body were entitled to the floor, but I was deterred from doing so by considerations relative to the occupancy of this chair. I think it is hardly fair to the other delegates that I should withhold at the proper time and place, the opinions which I might submit for the resumption of specie payments.

I would ask your indulgence, therefore, to permit me to present them now, in order that they may take the course that the propositions of the other delegates have taken.

Mr. GANO will have the kindness to take the chair.

Mr. GANO having taken the chair, Mr. FRALEY continued:

Gentlemen of the National Board of Trade:—What I have to say upon this subject will be very brief. I will preface it by reading the resolution which I have to submit:

*Resolved*, That the National Board of Trade recommend to the Congress of the United States to provide by law for the resumption of specie payments on and after the first Monday in July, A. D. 1870, on the following basis:

1. That no further sales of gold shall be made by or under the authority of the Government of the United States.

2. That on and after the first Monday of March, 1869, the legal-tender notes of the United States and the notes of the National Banks shall be receivable for duties on imports, in the following sums and proportions: For the said month of March, five per cent., and for every month thereafter, an increment of five per cent. until, by such increments, the whole amount of duties on imports may be thus payable.

3. That the legal-tender notes of the United States so received for duties shall forthwith be cancelled and destroyed.

4. That the notes of the National Banks so received for duties, shall be forthwith redeemed by the several banks issuing the same, in legal-tender notes of the United States in six per cent. five-twenty bonds of the United States, or in coin; and on such redemption being made, the United States legal-tender notes so received shall be cancelled and destroyed, and the said bonds shall be cancelled, declared paid, and not reissued.

5. That if on the first Monday in May, in 1870, there shall not be in the Treasury of the United States, in coin actually belonging to the United States, a sum equal to one-third of the whole amount

of the legal-tender notes of the United States then outstanding, the Secretary of the Treasury shall be authorized to sell for coin or legal-tender notes, such an amount of five per cent. ten-forty bonds of the United States, of which both interest and principal shall be payable in gold, as will supply any deficiency of said one-third coin.

6. That in case such one-third of the amount of the legal-tender notes of the United States as may then, or at any time thereafter, be in circulation, shall be insufficient to redeem the same in coin when presented, the Secretary of the Treasury shall, in like manner, sell five per cent. ten-forty bonds, for coin, or for the legal-tender notes of the United States, in such amounts as shall be required to redeem such legal-tender notes of the United States as may be presented for payment.

7. That in case any of the said five per cent. ten-forty bonds shall be sold for legal-tender notes of the United States, such legal-tender notes so received in payment therefor, shall be forthwith cancelled and destroyed.

8. That on and after the said first Monday in July, A. D. 1870, the legal-tender notes of the United States shall be redeemable in the gold coin of the United States, at the places where the same have been made payable.

In support of this proposition, I have to say that I concur entirely with my friend, Mr. NAZRO, of Boston, in considering that this is a question more of confidence than anything else. I suppose that if the people of the United States had a sufficient degree of confidence in the ability of their own public officers to effect a speedy resumption, that resumption would take place in six weeks.

I believe that the greater part of the difficulty under which we are now laboring, has arisen from what was a necessity at the time of its adoption, but has grown, in the course of events, to be a great evil — the distinction made by the General Government in the medium in which it would receive payment for duties on imports, and in which it would receive any other payments due to the United States. I believe if circumstances had then so favored the credit of the Government that the legal-tender notes of the United States might have been made receivable for duties on imports, that at the present time the sole difference between the legal-tender notes of the United States and gold would not have exceeded ten or twelve per cent., that percentage being, in my judgment, sufficient, with a well-established currency receivable for all the purposes of the Government, to obtain gold enough to settle for those importations of this country which we would be unable to pay for by the sale of our products for exportation. I think that the moment we can relieve the market of the United States from a daily call for an average sum of about five hundred thousand dollars in gold for the payment of duties on imports, we shall settle the question as to the relative position of our currency with gold, and then the only demand for gold will be to settle what is usually called the balance of trade. I believe that a certain amount of contraction is necessary now to bring about this result, and that the relations between the currency of the country and gold should be gradually established and should be spread over such a moderate extent of time as will not cause a panic, a crisis, or a crash in the community.

The Board will perceive that in the first place I propose that the stock of gold received for the payment of duties on imports shall not be interfered with or reduced by any sales made under authority of the Government of the United States. That, I think, will have a tendency to accumulate a little more gold in the Treasury of the United States than would under the present circumstances be obtained, and will be one of the measures of contraction.

Secondly, that in the receipt and cancellation of the legal-tenders in the way that I have proposed, there will be a moderate, steady and safe measure of contraction, not pressing on the community in any harsh way, and gradually freeing us from the embarrassing position in which we have been placed by the distinction made in the payment of duties on imports and the other payments of revenue to the country. I think that in regard to the receipt of currency for duties, the notes of the National Banks should be placed upon precisely the same footing as the legal-tender notes of the United States, for this reason: that if we were to confine the payment of duties solely to the legal-tender notes, we should have existing in another form, not so extensive in its operation, but still of the same kind, what we have now in regard to the distinction between gold and currency.

Thirdly, I propose that the contraction shall, by this process, operate upon the legal-tender notes of the United States, where I think it in the first place properly belongs; and secondly, that it shall, in a modified form, operate to contract, if necessary, the circulation of the National Banks, compelling them, in proportion to the notes which may be received of their several issues, to redeem those notes, either in United States legal-tender notes or coin, or in the six per cent. bonds of the United States, upon which they now rest for circulation.

If a bank find it more convenient to reduce its circulation by giving up such portions of its bonds as the circulation so redeemed would represent, there is, of course, no strain or stress upon them.

I propose, further, to adopt in regard to the redemption of the notes of the United States, the principle, which I think is perfectly well established in political economy and banking, that a basis of one-third in specie is at all times sufficient to redeem the circulating notes of the banks, and equally efficient it would be in redeeming the circulating notes of the Government.

Gentlemen of the Board of Trade will perceive that I separate, in this view of the case, the redemption of notes from the redemption of deposits. I do not propose in any way to disturb the redemption of deposits, or the amount of reserve which is now required to be held by the banks.

So far as the operation of this system would go, it would only require that they should redeem for the United States, the notes which have been so received for duties in the legal-tender notes of the United States, leaving them to the payment of their deposits, agreeably to the ordinary course of trade, and according to the contract that they have made with their depositors.

I think that under this system of moderate contraction, under this system of calling upon the banks, periodically, monthly, to redeem in the way I have suggested, such portions of their circulation as might be paid for duties, they would be admonished to hold such an amount of protecting reserve, as would prevent them from extending and enlarging their discount lines, to the prejudice of the community, in the way of prices, and to the great delay of the resumption of specie payments. I have named the first Monday in July, 1870, as the time when the resumption shall take place, for the reason that I believe that is a period of the year when the country is comparatively in a state of financial rest; before the great crops of the country have been gathered from the fields; before these crops are pressing upon the market, and calling for the withdrawal of the circulation from the seaboard cities; a time when there would be, in the mercantile expression of the subject, but little pressure for money — and I think that resumption should, if possible, take place at that period of the year. The first of January, or toward the first of January, of any year, is a period, generally, of considerable pecuniary pressure.

We have seen, recently, whether we attribute it to natural or to artificial causes, that during the month of November there was required, as was alleged on the part of those representing the banks, a necessity for curtailing discounts, in order that currency might be provided to be remitted to the South and West, for the payment of the great products of the country, that were then coming to market. Therefore I have adopted as my basis, the first Monday of July, 1870, and I think, by the operations of the plan I have suggested, that on the first Monday in May, 1870, it will be found that, by this process of contraction, there will be in the Treasury of the United States at least one-third of the whole amount of the legal-tender notes of the United States, then outstanding, in coin. But to provide for any deficiency, I suggest that the Secretary of the Treasury shall be authorized to sell five per cent. ten-forty gold bonds to such an amount, as will either put into the Treasury of the United States a sufficient sum in coin to represent one-third, or will reduce the circulation of the legal-tender notes of the United States to such an extent, that the relations between the coin in the Treasury and the currency of the United States outstanding, shall be in this proportion. And it will be seen that in order fully to protect the redemption of the notes in that form, I authorize the Secretary of the Treasury, from time to time, as may be needed, to sell the five per cent. bonds for coin and for the legal-tender notes, to preserve these proportions; and if he sells the five per cent. ten-forty bonds, and receives in payment for them the circulating legal-tender notes, that these legal-tender notes shall be immediately cancelled and withdrawn, so that the Government of the United States shall not have imposed upon it, by the process, a double debt — an increase of the debt rather than a diminution of it. And then I finally conclude, by directing the positive redemption of every legal-tender note of the United States in coin, when it is presented at the place where the Government made it payable.

[The allotted ten minutes having expired, leave to proceed was unanimously granted.]

I have but one more word to say. By reference to the official statement of the public debt of the United States, as recently as I have it in my possession, and the quarterly statements of the banks of the United States, I find this, — that there are seven hundred million dollars of legal-tender notes, and National Bank notes of the United States, in existence; that the banks of the United States, and the Treasury of the United States, together, hold about one hundred and seventy-five million dollars of the seven hundred million dollars, that the remainder, in round numbers five hundred million dollars, are in the hands of the people of the United States, and are used by them for the purpose of effecting the purchases of commodities produced by the United States, or in which the people of the United States deal. These notes are used to that extent, I think, because of the present price of those commodities, and as we gradually circumscribe this circulation, this amount of paper money which is in the hands of the people of the United States, I think that we shall find that the price of commodities will gradually shrink, until, by the extent of the contraction that I have proposed, they shall be brought ultimately to represent the true specie standard.

I am not one of those who believe that the difference at the present time between gold and currency is thirty-five per cent., and that by returning to specie payments we shall have a reduction of thirty-five per cent. in the price of labor and in the price of commodities; but I expect, gentlemen, that the result will be substantially this: that when we effect a return to specie payments, the crops of the country being as good as the average, there will be no panic, no crisis, no strife; and the price of labor, of commodities and of property, may possibly shrink from ten per cent. to fifteen per cent.

That, I believe, is the whole present extent of the depreciation of our currency; and I think that, if we can, by a moderate process, relieve ourselves of about one-fifth of the paper money now in circulation in the United States, by the process I have suggested, or by any process similar in its operation to that, we shall have effected the great result for which we have come together, upon the subject of specie payments; and that by the first Monday in July, 1870, we shall see them fully, practically and efficiently restored. (Applause.)

The President resumed his position in the chair.

Cairo Chamber of Commerce. Mr. RAUM: I have listened, Sir, with a great deal of earnest attention to the discussion of this question. It may be known to some of you, perhaps, that I shall be called upon in another sphere to act authoritatively upon this great and important subject. I have the more earnestly listened to what has been said here, because I have been led to believe that the action which will be the result of the deliberations of this Board of Trade, will very materially influence the action of Congress. There is one point in respect to this great question of the resumption of specie payments, upon which there seems to be an unanimous concurrence, and that is, that the Government of the United States at this time, is not able to resume specie payments. I consider then, that there are two questions which may properly be discussed — the one our ability to pay, the other the mode in which payment is to be made. If the Government was able to resume specie payments to-day, there would be no great difficulty I presume in determining the method by which we should accomplish that very desirable end; but it seems to be the concurrent opinion of the great body of the people — the thinking men of this country — that the Government is not at this time able to resume specie payments.

I find a very diversified opinion in respect to the question of the volume of the currency. I hear upon one hand the statement that the volume of the currency is not too great, while I hear upon the other hand that the volume of the currency is too great. It seems to me evident that there is a disparity between the volume of the currency of paper money, both of national and bank issues; that there is a discrepancy between the paper money of the country and the coin of the country; that in the present want of absolute confidence in the Government and the banks, a resumption of specie payments cannot be brought about.

Now the proposition coming from St. Louis, within a period of twelve months to withdraw from the circulation of the country one hundred millions of legal-tenders, it seems to me, if carried out, would result in wide-spread disaster. That is my opinion, and although I have no great experience in financial matters, yet I believe it is the opinion of the great body of thinking men of the country. As has been remarked on this floor, in the progress of this debate, the banks hold only about one-fourth of the legal-tenders of the country. Where are you to gather up ten millions of dollars per month? Suppose you gather it by taxation, you get it from the great mass of the people of the country, and, instead of paying it out, instead of redistributing the money, you at once destroy it. It is withdrawn from the volume of currency, by which the business of the country is to be transacted. Now, we have seen, within the past few weeks, the effect that the withdrawal of some fifteen millions has had upon the business of the country. It was heralded abroad, and a wide-spread panic in the city of New York was the consequence.

It would seem that there is no excess of paper money in New York, that great centre of commerce, of trade, of capital, and that the immediate withdrawal of fifteen millions of money would have such a stringent effect upon the money market, that a great panic would ensue at once. It was only by the exercise of what many considered an unlawful authority upon the part of the Secretary of the Treasury, that this panic was prevented from having a very disastrous effect upon the finance of the country. What then would be the effect of a steady withdrawal, absolutely ten millions a month, from the currency of the country? The shrinkage in values would be so tremendous, and the contraction of all the business of the country would be so great, that I feel satisfied panic and destruction would be the inevitable consequences resulting from it.

The gentlemen representing the Board from Memphis, favored one of the propositions from St. Louis, as urged upon the consideration of the Board, the propriety of adopting a measure which looks first, to legalizing gold contracts, and secondly, at a fixed period to be named in the law, providing that all contracts shall be payable in gold. This plan, I presume, as a whole, looks to the withdrawal of this hundred millions of currency, with a view of enabling the Government to resume specie payments.

But, Sir, an adoption of this proposition is virtually a repeal of the Legal-Tender Act, and thus nearly two hundred million dollars of notes, which would necessarily be outstanding at the time of the adoption of that measure, would be absolutely valueless. They would be of no use in the payment of debt. The only thing for which they could be used, would be merely the payment of taxes due the United States. With my present view of the case, I would entirely oppose the adoption of a measure looking to the enforcement of the payment of all contracts in coin, until there has been an absolute resumption of specie payments.

I listened with great attention to the last resolutions introduced before this body, and I regard them with a great deal of favor, as far as I have been able to give them attention. They do not contemplate the removal from legal-tenders of the value which necessarily attaches to them, as a means of transacting business. They enlarge their sphere of usefulness, and is it not to be presumed that when you do this you will appreciate their value? Now whether the rapid withdrawal of such a large amount of legal-tenders as is proposed even by these resolutions, would have a deleterious effect upon the finances of the country, is a question that I am not prepared to answer. The withdrawal for the first month would be seven hundred and fifty thousand dollars, estimating the monthly receipts in gold at five hundred million dollars; the withdrawal of the second month would be one and a half millions; of the third month would be two and a quarter millions; of the fourth month, three millions; of the fifth month, three and three-quarter millions; of the sixth, four and a half millions, and so on; increasing monthly at the rate of three-quarters of a million dollars, so that at the end of fourteen months a very large volume of the currency would be swept away.

I say I can not express an opinion as to the result which this contraction would have. Some such measure, it seems to me, must be resorted to; either the volume of the currency must be reduced, or the volume of the coin increased.

I concur in the opinion expressed by the gentleman from Milwaukie, when he stated to this Board, as his opinion, that the people of the country were able to resume specie payments as soon as the Government resumed. I think there is no question about that. I think the banks of the country can resume to-day, if the Government will resume specie payments. There is one thing I have often thought of, in connection with this question; if we are to resume, we must begin the work; we must commence climbing, if we expect to get to the top of the mountain. We never can expect to resume specie payments except by some act of Congress. There is no question that a paper money which floats in the hands of the people, for which they cannot receive coin at the country banks, or of the Government issuing it, must necessarily be depreciating.

There is one point, Mr. President, to which I wish to call the attention of the Board, and it is mainly for that purpose I desire to have the floor on this occasion, because I do not suppose I am able to throw any light on the question of finance, or of specie payments, and it is this: the idea has been thrown out by more gentlemen than one, but Mr. ROPES, the gentleman from Boston, who addressed the house so learnedly yesterday, indicated that the imports must be reduced, that the course of trade must be changed, so that the efflux of gold may decrease.

The gentleman who indicated his intention of aiding in this great work, may perhaps be brave enough to make the attempt, but the measure recommended, cutting off the bonnet strings and shortening the skirts of our wives and daughters, is, I am satisfied, a course that the great body of Americans will not be disposed to follow. If this question of the balance of trade is to turn in favor of the United States, it must be by legislation.

It struck me, after giving the matter some little attention, that there is a defect lying at the foundation of our system of importing foreign goods, and I will indicate it to the Board for their consideration; and it is this, the policy of encouraging the piling up upon the edge of our markets of vast quantities of imported goods, held by the manufacturers of foreign goods, and which may be rapidly thrown upon the market, or if they fail to find a ready market at a remunerative price, may be withdrawn without expense, except for insurance and storage. We buy largely from foreign countries, and I undertake to say that the amount of goods which at the end of each month, lie piled up on the edge of the market, may be so regulated by law, as that those who bring goods to this country, will do so at their peril. It is found that at the end of every month, there are forty-five to fifty million dollars worth of goods ready to be thrown upon the market; they are not bound to pay the duties on them; the goods may remain in the Custom House for six or twelve months, and the only penalty is the mere payment of storage and insurance. Now, Sir, I believe that this Board of Trade should consider that question, and should weigh the subject well, not merely in the interest of importers of goods, but in the interest of the whole country, for the purpose of preventing that great flow of coin from the United States. Whenever a man imports goods to the United States, he should be required to pay the duties on these goods, within thirty days from the time they land at the port. Let him import goods at his peril, if he is a speculator. In the case of the legitimate merchant who deals partially in imported goods, and to a certain extent in goods manufactured in this country, he does his legitimate business, he brings his goods in for consumption; those goods are in the warehouses, and are withdrawn as the necessities require. But is it not the observation and experience of the great body of business men of this country, that the manufacturers in Europe get up what they call American lines of goods, shipping them here to the factors for the sale of these goods, and which, from time to time are thrown upon the market through the medium of auctioneers; and that these goods are sold, not in the interest of the American, but in the interest of the foreign importers? Let these foreign importers import at their peril. Let us say to them, that if you import goods to be sold in the United States, you shall pay the import duty on such goods at the expiration of thirty days, and you shall not have a repayment if you see fit to re-export.

When we come to consider the great efflux of gold from this country, it is startling. This year the exportation of gold coin will reach the enormous sum of eighty million dollars. Look back at the statistics of the country during the past twenty-two years. We have exported nearly twelve hundred millions of gold coin from the United States, to pay for rags which have been worn by our people. And more than that, so great has been the balance of trade against us, that we have exported to the foreign bankers and business men, nearly two thousand million of dollars during the past twenty-two years. Let us legislate in the interest of our own country, and prevent this frightful outpouring of coin.

The products of the mines of this country reach, at the present time, seventy-five million dollars or eighty million dollars per year, and yet every dollar of that coin goes out for the purpose of buying articles which we could just as well do without; the silks, and the satins, and the diamonds, and all the fine jewelry that bedeck the bosoms of our beautiful women; and the fine wines, but not such wines as we drank last night at what was termed a supper, but which was indeed a banquet.

Suppose that instead of pouring out our gold into the commerce of Europe, we should adopt some legislation preventing the importation of foreign goods, thus retaining the gold and silver we produce in our own country. You can see at a glance that all this difficulty of returning to specie payments would be solved at once. The great idea is to keep our gold coin. Let us hoard our gold; let us hoard it for five years, and you have the enormous sum of four hundred million dollars of gold coin to be added to the two hundred and fifty million dollars already in the country. With six hundred and fifty millions of silver and gold coin, do we not all know that a resumption would be brought about without any difficulty at all?

Instead of turning your attention solely to the reduction of the great volume of paper money, I invite your attention to a careful consideration of the subject of increasing the gold and silver coin of the country. But we have a golden future before us. We are reaching out with our arms to the Pacific; I believe that, during the ensuing year, the great Pacific Railroad will be constructed. May we not hope that the construction of that and similar lines, which are clamoring for construction, and which will ask Congress for aid at the ensuing session; may we not hope that this will be the commencement of a revolution in the trade of this country? May we not expect that the trade of the whole world will be revolutionized, and that the United States will be the country for carrying on the trade of the entire East.

The trade of China alone, under American influence, has been increased during the past two years, (to January last,) from eighty to more than three hundred million dollars per annum. The trade of India, which may remain for a long time in the hands of Great Britain, amounts to about five hundred millions per annum for imports and exports. That trade, though, is capable of indefinite extension. Think of that great industrial people, who number five hundred millions of souls, with whom, by a recent treaty, we have the closest relations. Think when they open their gates to the commerce of the United States, what the trade of this country necessarily will be, when we induce them to build railroads and telegraphs, and adopt other American ideas and improvements.

Is it not probable that we may increase the exports to five hundred million dollars, perhaps to the enormous amount of one billion dollars per annum in the next decade? I look forward to, and I believe many of us will live to see the day when the foreign trade of the United States, in exports alone, will have reached the enormous sum of one thousand millions per annum.

Portland Board of Trade. Mr. BROWN : Coming from the far off East, from a State which, in all probability, suffered as much as any from the unfortunate misunderstanding we had with our friends in the South, I can say that in the State of Maine, in the interest I have the honor to represent here, the people are willing and they intend to sustain the proposition offered here by the gentleman from St. Louis.

We believe, Sir, in the ability of the United States to pay their debts, to pay them according to the letter, and according to the understanding; and according, also, to the moral obligations which we believe were entered into when the debt was contracted; and we mean to come up and do our humble part in putting the credit of the country where it should be.

We have listened to Massachusetts to learn the views of her people; we have been to the great city of New York, the money centre of the United States, and soon to be the money centre of the world; and what do we hear there? That they mean to stand up and sustain the credit of this nation. The great State of Pennsylvania through our honored President, has announced its determination to sustain the credit of the nation. Coming further south to Baltimore, we have heard the same; and if we could hear from our friends further south, I have no doubt they would enunciate the same idea. And, Sir, when we have come to the Southwest, we have had indicated to us by the gentleman from St. Louis, what they intend to do there; and Cincinnati, the metropolis of Ohio, I understand, means to do the same; but, Sir, when we came to the State of Illinois, one of the richest States of this confederation, what did we hear from the representatives of the great and proud city of Chicago? I must say, with regret, that they have not hesitated to proclaim upon this floor, that this nation is a bankrupt! Why, Sir, I can hardly credit it possible for a gentleman from that city,— one of the most prosperous cities in the world, a city that has almost doubled its population within five years,— to come into this Convention and say that the United States are bankrupt! I do not believe that delegate represents the views of the great and glorious State of Illinois.

What did we hear upon this floor only a few days ago from these gentlemen? What measure did they then advocate? Payment in cash; cash payment on delivery! Now, Mr. President, when we come to talk about paying the national debt, when it comes to paying contracts which were entered into with the most solemn obligations; what do we hear from these delegates? They indicate that we might possibly pay sixty cents on the dollar! Is that cash payment? Do they mean to say that while a man who has made a contract with them, or has borrowed money must pay them one hundred cents on the dollar, to go into their pockets; this great and rich nation is bankrupt, and that it ought to pay only sixty cents on the dollar? That is not the sentiment of the people of the United States, I am glad to say.

What have we heard from the southern section of this great nation? A section that has had so much trouble, but which with frugality, prudence and energy, expects to have a surplus of two hundred million dollars; — and this from States that we have been led to believe were utterly bankrupt! There, Sir, is a specimen of the energy, and I may say, of the honesty of those people. They have come here and declared their willingness to do their part and to assume their proportion of this enormous debt.

As I said, I am not prepared to enunciate any particular views of my own, but this I say, Maine means to pay her obligations to the utmost letter and spirit of the contract. We are in favor of the payment of these obligations in coin; we desire a resumption of specie payments at the earliest practicable moment; and we are ready to take the first step in that direction,— and when I say we are willing to take that step, we do not mean a step backward; that is, to refuse legalizing gold contracts; and I am surprised to hear from the same source from which the expressions already referred to have come, that this legalization ought not to be made. I am surprised that any intelligent business man should oppose a measure so reasonable. I consider it one of the surest steps towards resumption, and beyond that, I am perfectly willing to accept the measures which Congress may adopt, and which I trust will be selected from the very able propositions which have been brought before this body.

I believe that the great trouble of to-day is a want of confidence; but, if we would discard the opinions of politicians and of men of low impulses, if we would throw them aside, and let every honest man act on his own impulses, this matter would be settled at once. I recollect a circumstance that occurred in the early part of 1861, in connection with an institution over which I have the honor to preside, a Savings Bank. We have many prudent people in Portland; and one man by his prudence, had accumulated five hundred dollars, which he had deposited in the Savings Bank referred to. But something had disturbed his confidence in the institution, and one morning, when I was in the bank, he came in with his book and said tremblingly to the treasurer, "I've come to notify you that I want my money." "Very well," said the treasurer, who went to the desk and immediately began to count it out. The man looked on in amazement; said he, "Are you going to pay me the money now? If you are going to pay me, I don't want it;" and the result was that he re-deposited his money, and very large additions have since been made to it. That is the condition of the United States to-day. We want confidence; and with confidence I believe the whole matter will be settled. To achieve any great victory it is necessary that we have some great and noble chieftain to lead us; and I propose that our chief shall be *general confidence,* and God grant that all his efforts may be crowned with victory.

Mr. MUNN: I should like the privilege of one moment's explanation.

In my remarks yesterday, I unfortunately used the words, "bankrupt nation," but immediately qualified them by saying "a suspended nation;" and that is what I meant and intended to say. In the whole of my remarks I never conveyed the slightest intimation that this Government should not pay in full every cent it owes according to its contract and its obligation; and I would here say that if we, as members of this organization, misrepresent each other, and stoop to personalities, it is beneath the dignity of our Board.

Mr. MANSON: The present currency of the Government is not used as an equivalent for gold. In making our contracts we value it now at about twenty-five per cent. less than gold. The Government of the United States, might use the surplus gold in buying supplies for the army and navy; or, if it were to issue gold bills, bills that would be received for duties, which would be redeemed in coin in any subtreasury of the United States, then we could make our prices for such articles on a gold basis; and in the redemption of such bills the Government would suffer no loss. The amount of these bills should never exceed the amount of the surplus gold in the United States Treasury. They should be issued by the Government in exchange for gold; and the interest of our gold bonds should be paid in these bills or in gold, at the option of the holder of the bonds. To make these bills more desirable than gold, I would have Congress make it obligatory on all the National Banks to receive them on deposit, being responsible for the same or their equivalent in gold on demand. I would also have it enacted that the National Banks shall hold all these bills, or an equivalent in gold, in place of the present currency; that they shall reserve seven per cent. of their circulation on the first day of July, 1869, fourteen per cent. on the first day of July, 1870, and twenty-one per cent. on the first of July, 1871; and if there is not then sufficient gold reserved to make resumption practicable, twenty-eight per cent. on the first day of July following. The present currency of the Government I would retire as fast as practicable, allowing it to be received, as heretofore, for all dues except payments on imported goods; and in place of this currency, I would allow an increase of the national banking currency.

It seems to me that communities are the best judges of their necessities in regard to banking accommodation; and I can see no evil to be feared by the public in a multiplicity of National Banks. As much banking capital as can be profitably employed, is the exact amount needed by the community; and with the present bank laws, with additional restrictions according to the above suggestion, I think all fear of contraction and expansion would be groundless.

I would also call attention to the subject of the sale of gold. The Government for the past five years has sold gold through one channel. The gold operations of this country have been manipulated by a few parties in Wall Street; they have made the gold business their business; and I do not blame them; it naturally follows from the existence of the present system carried on by the Secretary of the Treasury. When a large amount of gold is to be sold, the market is depressed, and it is bought up by a few speculators. Now I would have the Secretary of the Treasury, whenever he has a surplus of gold, notify the Secretary of the Navy or of the Army that he can purchase one hundred thousand dollars or one hundred and fifty thousand dollars worth of supplies, to be paid for in gold bills or in gold. He would so advertise, and the prices would be regulated accordingly. Let the Government also issue bills which it will pay out for these goods, which bills may be taken direct to the Sub-Treasury, where gold will be paid for them, or be used in the payment of the duties on imported goods. The result would be that people would not want the gold; they would prefer the gold bills of the United States; and the Sub-Treasurer would have to put every dollar of gold of the United States into his vaults; and the effect upon foreign nations of the accumulation of that large amount of gold in the Sub-Treasury of the United States, would be to put out bonds on a par with any bonds in the world. Gentlemen talk about confidence in the United States! I would like to see the man of any other nation who has as much confidence in his nation, as the weakest-kneed Yankee has in the

United States! Not only have we confidence that we can pay our own debts, but we believe we could pay the debts of the world, if we had a mind to.

Sir, the Government will take care of itself. You need not worry yourself about the Government's bills. Let us multiply the National Banks; let us make them reserve so much of their circulation, as before suggested, to prepare for specie payments, and before 1872, their bills will take the place of all Government issues.* So gentlemen need not trouble themselves about the Government's resumption. The banks are the great monied institutions, and money is the great power, the greatest power in the universe — that we have to contend with.

To the banking institutions of the United States I would say, You have got to resume specie payments; and you must be satisfied with less profits for the next five years than you have had for the last five or ten years; no institutions have made so much money during the past five or six years as you have. I say that the banks are in duty bound to aid to the utmost of their power, in the resumption of specie payments.

Richmond Chamber of Commerce. Mr. BRANCH: At this late hour of the discussion of this subject, I should probably be the most presumptuous gentleman on the floor, if I imagined that I could say anything new, instructive, or interesting. Still, I think it proper under the circumstances, following the example of the widow with her mite, to bring my offering and lay it on the altar of our country. I would therefore speak for the section from which I come, and say that while we have no pet scheme, no particular method by which to arrive at the desirable result, the substantial people of the South, whether agricultural, mining, commercial, or manufacturing, are all deeply interested in the early resumption of specie payments by the United States Government. It is a matter of self-interest, if for no other and higher consideration than because we are a laboring people; and whenever the laborer shall receive gold as his hire, whether much or little, it will have more purchasing power than any rag that you may give him, can possibly have as a representative of value. Hence I was both a little surprised and sorry that my most excellent and intelligent friend from Philadelphia should seem so well satisfied with the present currency, and should think it a most excellent institution. While I will admit that as a purchasing power it is better than no money at all, I must say that it does not begin to compare with the old fashioned "yaller jackets," or what Benton called "mint drops." And while we down South don't know much, as a friend said to me, upon the question of depreciated currency, we think that what we do know, we know as well as anybody. We know a great deal more about a depreciated currency than you do! I tell you that I have seen, not a greenback, but a grayback, bearing upon its face a promise to pay five dollars in gold, at two per cent. premium. I have seen that piece of paper, representing five dollars, buy a barrel of flour, and four years afterwards, I had to take out of my pocket two hundred and fifty dollars worth of those promises, to buy a poor turkey to carry home to my family, and I have paid fifteen hundred dollars for a barrel of flour. Therefore, I tell you, Sir, with all modesty, that upon the question of a depreciated currency, what we do know, we know as well as any one. It was no uncommon occurrence with us, for a gentleman to send his money to market in a wheelbarrow, and bring back his purchases in a basket!

So this piece of paper, our legal-tender note, has no more substantial, intrinsic value than the pieces of worthless paper I have referred to. It has no intrinsic value. What then is its value? It is a promise to pay; and its representative value is based upon the ability to pay, of the party promising, and upon the disposition to pay; these elements make up the credit of any debtor. This piece of paper will become either better or worse; and unless we improve it, the probability is that it will get worse. It needs attention and improvement; and we must bring it to the gold standard, or it will depreciate, and continue to depreciate until it will be valueless.

One of the worst results of our present depreciated currency, is found in the enormous amount of non-productive labor, abstracted from the wealth and power of the country, in speculation. I believe, if a fair calculation could be made of the number of able-bodied men engaged in speculations based upon the unhealthy condition of our currency, from our villages, our towns, and our cities, one by one, up to New York, it would prove to be far greater than is generally supposed; and I think if a guillotine were set up in some convenient spot for their special benefit, it would prove an excellent thing for every one. There is hardly a village connected by telegraph with New York, in which you will not find men gambling in gold, and speculating in the fluctuations in the gold and stock market.

Take all that labor that is now consuming, but producing nothing, — the drones in the great hive of the country — and put it to the anvil, to the plough and in the mine, and in three years' the results of this labor, thus properly applied, will be sufficient to pay the national debt. What do you see in New York to-day? Such is the mania for gambling, that in order to gain admission to that gambling hell, the gold room, it costs ten thousand dollars. I do not of course, when I speak of this, intend any reflection upon New York; but because it is the great commercial centre, trade of every kind flows there. It is the disordered and distempered condition of our currency, which enables these gambling, grovelling vermin to thrive and fatten on a rotten currency.

Let us stop this. Let us have a gold basis, and quit this gambling. Let the people go to work; let them make wealth by honest toil. The mechanic, the artizan and the merchant must be willing to make less money on the solid basis, and make it by honest work.

I disagree in one particular with the proposition before us; that it is an easy matter to resume specie payments. I do not think it is. I never found it easy to pay an old debt; and I never knew a man who had suspended payment, and who in good faith determined to start again, who did not find it an uphill business, and did not find it necessary to economize rigidly as well as work diligently. And that is what we have to do as a nation, and as individuals, or we cannot pay our debt and resume specie payments. Therefore, let us retrench, nationally, as States, and as individuals; let us learn to make more and spend less. Let us understand that there is no new road to make money honestly. By the sweat of our brow have we to eat bread. If we can reduce our expenditures as a nation, as communities, and as individuals, we can slowly and steadily pay our debts, and get down to a metallic basis.

We need currency in the South. We have not half the amount of banking capital that we had before the war. In Virginia we have but three million five hundred thousand banking capital,— that is not half what some of your cities have. We cannot increase it; yet we need an increase much.

I beg to submit the following:

*Resolved*, That in the opinion of this Board it is desirable that additional banking capital, to the extent of at least one hundred million dollars, should be supplied to the Southern and Southwestern States, and to this end, that Congress should authorize an issue of National Bank notes to said amount, on the surrender of legal-tender notes, which shall be cancelled, and for which five-twenty bonds shall be held in pledge.

## St. Louis Union Merchants' Exchange. Mr. ALLEN:

I am satisfied, after listening to all that has been said, and to the various propositions that have been offered, that we are all in favor of an early resumption of specie payments.

I think, Sir, that it is advisable at this late stage of the proceeding, the matter having been so thoroughly discussed, that we should come to a vote on the subject; it appears to me that we are about ready to take a vote on the proposition of the St. Louis Board of Trade. I do not know how the delegates of the Union Exchange view it, I speak mainly for myself. I am in favor of the proposition as submitted by the St. Louis Board of Trade, the first part of which relates to the general subject of resumption of specie payments at an early day, and redeeming the paper currency; the second, that we should legalize gold contracts; I am in favor of that; and the third proposition, which relates to the time fixed for the resumption of specie payments and the redemption of legal-tender notes; I am in favor of that. But I would propose to amend the proposition very slightly, to make the "fourth day of July" the "first day of July, 1870," because this is the beginning of the fiscal year of the Government. I should propose, also, to amend the latter clause of the resolution, by omitting all details in regard to the manner in which this end should be reached. I believe, Sir, that if specie payments are resumed at the Treasury of the United States, all the other desirable results would follow; that is, that the banks would resume. But the Government and the banks must make the arrangements necessary to a resumption; let them provide the details. I think we can agree upon these three general principles to-day, and let the details take care of themselves. Without offering any further remarks, I will propose:

To amend the last clause of the resolution of the St. Louis Board of Trade, by striking out "fourth" and inserting "first." And to strike out all the last clause after 1870, where those figures first occur.

Mr. TAUSSIG : The resolutions submitted to you, are composed of three parts. The first is declaratory of the desirability of the resumption of specie payments, and the second and third show the mode in which it is to be done. As far as I understand the opinion of our delegation, it is that a simple declaration in favor of a resumption of specie payments, unless you show your earnestness for that desire, by designating a day on which it shall be done, and the mode in which it is to be done, will not amount to a row of pins. The simple declaration that it is our desire to resume specie payments, implies a reservation of mind that we shall do it only when it is convenient; hence the delegation in presenting the resolution, intend it to mean that it is not only desirable to resume, but to do this on a certain fixed day. Nor do I consider that the fourth of July, or the first of July or the first of January, 1871, is of so great importance, as that we should establish the principle that the Government should declare its desire and the sincerity of its desire to resume on a certain fixed day. Unless you do that, it amounts to a promise to pay without a date. In settling with your creditor by giving him a promissory note, he will want you to fix a date for the payment; as soon as you fix the date, that note has a certain rate of discount. It is upon this principle that a day ought to be designated; and it is upon this principle that we are satisfied that on that day on which it is settled specie payments shall be resumed, legal-tenders will be at par with gold.

In submitting the plan by which it is to be done, the St. Louis delegation have thought that a sliding scale of reducing the indebtedness slowly, would be concurrent with the decline of premium; that is to say, we have at the present day, if I understand the figures aright, in round numbers four hundred million dollars in greenbacks, and the average premium on gold is thirty-five per cent.; therefore, it takes one hundred and thirty-five dollars to purchase one hundred dollars worth of coin. Thirty-five per cent. on four hundred million dollars amounts to one hundred and fourteen million dollars; if, therefore, legal-tenders were at par to-day, two hundred and eighty million dollars would answer all the purposes for which four hundred million dollars are now used. Hence, if you decrease your currency at the rate proposed, eight per cent. a month, amounting to eight million three hundred and thirty-five thousand dollars a month, during these eighteen months, you reduce the premium on gold in a corresponding ratio. It is a scale that regulates itself. After this amount of currency is withdrawn, that which is left, in consequence of the reduction of the premium on gold, will purchase as much as the former amount of currency would have purchased.

Now, Mr. President, what we want is confidence. But we cannot have confidence unless we have a settled financial policy. Until now, our financial policy has been like that of a man sailing without a compass; there has been no point from which to start, and no objective destination at which to land; and unless we know where we start and where we are to land, and are assured that our financial operations are not to be disturbed by legislative enactments, and that a settled policy will be adopted, there will be no confidence.

What is the cause of all this financial trouble? At every session of Congress we have new measures started, and what between the upper and lower branches of the Legislature, and the Secretary of the Treasury, who is alternately bearing gold, and bulling it when ever he thinks bonds are high, between the big bug in Washington and those pestiferous mosquitoes in · Wall Street, stinging and biting you all the time, and keeping you in a state of perpetual discomfort, your commercial affairs continue to be in a most uncertain and unsatisfactory condition. For this reason the St. Louis resolutions start with a declaration of the desirability and the sincere intention of resuming specie payments, and then declare how it is to be done. The first of them is in favor of legalizing gold contracts. I wish to show the importance of that measure. I presume it has been the experience of every gentleman connected with banking institutions, that ever since the suspension of specie payments, there has been no gold whatever in the banks of the country; all the gold held by them consists of special deposits, which are liable to be withdrawn at any moment; therefore, when deposited it is sealed up, and there may be twenty million dollars to thirty million dollars of gold hidden away in the vaults, and kept out of circulation and out of use, because the depositor is satisfied that if he puts his gold on deposit, when the time comes round, and the bank does not ·feel like paying it back, it can protect itself behind the legal-tender act. But let gold contracts be legalized, and the banks will put gold into circulation, and the money market will be relieved. Another reason is, that our importers instead of having to buy foreign drafts for exchange and paying the current premium on gold, will give their own time bills, and the foreign importers will receive time bills.

I come now to the manner in which the resumption of specie payments is to be introduced. As far as this is concerned, although I think it would be well to reduce the currency in the manner proposed by the St. Louis delegation, still I must express my admiration of the wise and excellent plan submitted by our presiding officer; I would with the greatest pleasure vote for the measure he has proposed.

The only rule by which to calculate values, or to regulate them, is the rule of supply and demand. It is well known that this is not now the rule of commercial transactions in this country. It is a changing rule; every article, except gold, has only a fictitious value. This is not caused by the merchants themselves; they are but the victims of a perverse state of things. I say it is regulated by speculation, by speculative movements beyond the control of the merchants; and because they are under the power of such speculative movement, they are the losers to that extent. If you reduce the circulation of the country, will that increase the productive power of the country? The higher the prices of your home manufactures, the more you induce importations from foreign countries, where labor is only one-fifth of the price we pay; we pay five times additional price for labor because all values have risen.

I desire no stronger argument than the one presented by the gentleman from Chicago, who so ably defended his position in debate the other day, on the subject of cash payment on delivery. That gentleman stated, in illustration, that in 1857, I believe, when currency became redundant, the merchants of Chicago were determined that they would not ship any more grain and receive the rags of Pennsylvania and the rags of New York in payment for it; they determined that they would have gold. And the gold came. If a portion of the country is so powerful that it can command gold thus to come at any instant, upon the delivery of its wheat, surely the nation is sufficiently powerful to bring out a sufficiency of gold when it is determined that the volume of legal-tenders shall be reduced.

Mr. STANARD: I regret to find myself under the necessity of disagreeing with the majority of the delegates from St. Louis, and also with many, who are much older than myself, from the seaboard cities, relative to the Government's resumption of specie payments.

I believe the time has not yet arrived for the Government of the United States to fix a day definitely for the resumption of specie payments. I am of opinion that we have not lived long enough since the war to begin to talk of this matter. I believe that there exists no occasion for any great uneasiness to-day. A country that can stand up under the pressure this country has borne during the last eight years, and have its money at thirty-three per cent., need have no fear of the debt that is upon it; especially if the country is increasing in power and population as our country is at the present time.

I look upon this nation not as I would upon a bankrupt merchant, but as somewhat in the condition of a firm which has expended a good deal of its money in real estate, mines, lands and agricultural pursuits, and one of the partners of which having turned traitorous to the interests of the concern, and squandered money that should have been used in conducting the business, the other partner is unable to pay the indebtedness; but the creditors, having confidence in the integrity and ability of the remaining partner, come to him and say, "We will not close you out at this time; we will not sell you out under the hammer and force you to pay your debts to-day; but we will give you trust until you can develop the wealth of your mines, plow your uncultivated acres, and realize what you can from the property you have on hand; we will give you such time as will enable you to do this and pay all your debts."

Our Government is in exactly this situation to-day. She is amply good for every dollar she owes; and no man fears she is not. We have enough with which to pay our debts, and plenty to spare. But the policy of the Government to-day is not to fix any time for resumption; this, I believe, would cripple the industrial pursuits of the country; and would spread ruin among the merchants and the agriculturists. If we believe that we have to come to specie payments in a certain time, we shall feel that we cannot extend our railways, improve our rivers and levees, and put under cultivation the thousands of acres which are lying waste in the Southern States. It would cripple all our great enterprises. It would stop the immigration to this country, immigration which is increasing at so rapid a rate. If it continues to increase for the next twenty years as, according to the statistics I have examined, it has for the last ten years, in the year 1890 we shall have a population of one hundred and seventy millions of people to help pay this debt of ours. We shall have the benefit of their industry; and it will be far easier, (if we will not interpose any obstacles,) for one hundred and seventy millions to pay two billion five hundred million dollars than for the forty millions who now inhabit our country, to pay it.

I would have the broad acres lying uncultivated in the valley of the Mississippi, not one-tenth of which are now improved, brought into cultivation; I would have the lands of the Pacific slope developed, and the vast extent of country lying to the Southwest and Northwest improved: and this I would do by making a further expenditure of money, in sending railroads into that region of country to develop it. But some say, this is creating a greater debt. I say it is an economical expenditure, that will bring into the market for the Government thousands of acres of land; thousands upon thousands rich in mineral wealth will be developed, which also belong to the Government; but which are of no possible use to it to-day. I would make such improvements in this vast country,— and more than half of the enormous wealth of the continent lies west of the Mississippi — I would improve, develop, and bring out the resources of our country, in such a way as would make money for the Government. The investment would be profitable, and not be merely an expenditure. Suppose you were to sell the acres of ground belonging to the Government, each alternate section being given for the purposes of railroads, and the other to be cultivated; would not the industry and thrift upon those acres more than pay for the investment?

They tell us in the South, "We are short of money;" the cry comes up from that desolate region, "We need more currency to develop and aid the industries of our section of the country." How will they get the currency? Will not the industry of the whole country be crippled immediately, if the currency is withdrawn from it, and the trade of the country demoralized? We have no more currency than we need. Take into consideration, that forty million people require more currency than twenty-five million. Take into consideration that the whole Southern country is now using a national, instead of their old banking capital, and we need have no fears upon this subject.

I take it that the result of all this improvement of the Northwest, the Southwest and the West, keeping values near where they should be, and doing nothing to cripple the industries of the people, with the continual immigration, would be that we should produce breadstuffs at so cheap a price, that with the internal and national improvements making transportation cheap, we should be able to feed the rest of the world at a cheaper rate than it could feed itself. This being the case, instead of exporting gold to pay for our imports, our wheat, corn, hogs and hominy would be so cheap, that they would be exported instead. No man knows what this region of country is, till he sees it; and I would hold out such inducements, and so improve it, that the world might be fed from the produce of the Mississippi valley; and importers, instead of buying gold, and draining us of our gold, would take the cheap products of the country.

I have a resolution which I desire to offer. I do not believe we could, with any sort of propriety, at this early day, indicate a time when we could commence paying in gold. The resolution is as follows:

*Resolved*, That the National Board of Trade would recommend that the Government resume specie payments at as early a day as can be done without damaging or interrupting the great industrial pursuits of the country, and without impeding the great national improvements now in progress and under contemplation.

Mr. KREIKHAUS: There appears to be in this Board, a desire to return to specie payments at the earliest moment possible; the only difference of opinion is as to the mode in which it can be accomplished. Some gentlemen on this floor, recommend the contraction of the currency; but I question very much whether that will lead to the desired end. When we consider that only a few years ago, gold was at one hundred and seventy-eight per cent. premium, which is now only thirty-five, we see that the value of gold has very little to do with the circulating medium, or with the quality of the medium that circulates. Nor do I think that retrenching by private individuals will accomplish anything. These are things which cannot be regulated by legislation. Each individual must know how long his purse is, and be governed accordingly. Nor do I believe that imports and exports affect this matter as much as has been said. But I believe that public confidence is the only thing that will bring us back to specie payments. If the people a year ago, thought that gold was worth fifty per cent. premium, and to-day it is thirty-five, that shows that the value of gold fluctuates, not by the intrinsic value of greenbacks, but by the confidence placed in them by the people. I do not know that gold has any more intrinsic value than have greenbacks; I do not know but that a pound of iron is worth more than a pound of gold. I think the intrinsic value of gold is only imaginary. It is looked upon, all over the world, as the medium that circulates in exchange for commodities; but, Mr. President, its intrinsic value is no more than that of paper. I think then, the establishment of confidence in the circulating medium, or rather confidence in the stability of our government, is the only thing required in order to resume specie payments. If we could make every man in the United States believe that a dollar greenback is as good as a dollar in gold, we could resume specie payments to-morrow.

It has been asserted here that the large circulation of currency has caused the high prices. I differ very much with that opinion. I think that the high prices were caused in this way; during the war, the Government expended two billion of dollars for supplies necessary for the army and navy, and the people during that time, handled money as they were not accustomed to, and the consequence was an inflation of value in everything; and we have not come back to the standard to which we shall come, when this shall cease.

If we are to have the confidence of the people, it is necessary that the Government should have confidence in itself. No merchant can expect credit, who has no confidence in his own ability to pay; and therefore the first thing necessary, is for the Government to show its confidence in its ability to pay. The question is, how that can best be accomplished; and one way, by which I think it can be effected, is embodied in the resolution which I herewith offer:

*Resolved*, That this Board memorialize Congress, through its Executive Council, to enact such laws as will insure the early resumption of specie payments; and as a basis for these laws, it would recommend the gradual decrease of premium on gold, by resuming specie payments of legal-tender notes at a fixed discount, at once, and that this discount be decreased monthly, so as to insure the redemption of legal-tender notes at par on a fixed day.

St. Paul Chamber of Commerce. Mr. DRAKE: Said that he was amazed that representatives of old and important commercial bodies could talk so lightly of national disgrace, and could view the disordered condition of our currency with such composure.

He regarded a suspension of specie payments as a national disgrace, justified by the exigency then existing, but to continue it one month after the necessity ceased, was a national crime. It was the duty of this body, the representation of commercial honor and integrity of the country, to speak out in no uncertain words; they should declare it the duty of Congress to begin at once to make ready for resumption. The subject presented itself under three general propositions: First — Is it our duty to return to gold payments? To this proposition all agree, but with qualifications destroying the value of the proposition. Upon this question, some of our friends act as sinners usually do in the matter of forsaking their sins. They will all agree that they are sinners — that they should repent — but not now; their language is: "A little more sleep, a little more slumber;" "Let me for a little longer roll sin as a sweet morsel under my tongue." He claimed that it was not our duty to resume now, but it was our duty now to prepare.

The next question he would discuss, was the ability of the country to resume. He had no doubt that the country was able to resume at once, or as soon as the Government had provided for the redemption of its greenbacks; but he by no means deemed it expedient. His experience as a banker in Ohio, led him to believe a resumption a much easier matter than was generally supposed. The currency must necessarily be contracted, and the commercial demands for gold would be decreased, while the supply would be increased. When gold ceased to be hoarded as a commodity, it would come forth from its hiding places. When the banks of Ohio resumed from a suspension, no run was made upon the banks — on the contrary, their gold increased by deposits. Indeed, no run for gold ever occurred anywhere, except for want of confidence in the banks. A certain amount of gold was always required for the commercial and other wants of the country. It was then to be had whenever wanted. It was a mistake to suppose that hungry men stood ready to draw gold as soon as banks should resume. Such a demand had not been justified by past experience, and was not in accordance with the interests of the people. He was glad that the general expression had been in favor of marching steadily toward specie payments.

Some gentlemen seemed to regard the establishment of new banks as the panacea for all trouble. They wanted currency. He held that no country could have gold or currency, unless they had the products of labor to exchange for it. Every dollar above the actual business wants of the country, was injurious. It was the duty of the Government to fix the day for resumption and arrange to that end. We do not generally prepare for death, but if the fiat should go forth, "To-morrow you die," there is no one but would cry out at once, " God be merciful to me a sinner."

To resume to-morrow, would shrink mercantile values, to the great injury of the business of the country. If a day should be fixed, manufacturers and all classes would begin to put themselves upon proper bases. He reminded them that every moment they extended a legalized suspension, they were defrauding the widows and orphans of the country.

We should assume a high tone on this subject, and make ourselves heard in the councils of the nation. He was opposed to any Government circulation. The business of the Government is to coin money and to regulate the value thereof. A Government circulation would induce all sorts of speculation, and eternally embarrass the business of the country.

He had prepared a resolution which was more of the enunciation of principle and less in detail, than any presented, which he then offered:

*Resolved*, By the National Board of Trade, that the suspension of specie payments, and the substitution of paper money as a legal-tender, is a national misfortune, and was only justified by absolute necessity, and that its continuance after the necessity has ceased, will be a national crime.

*Resolved*, That it is the duty of Congress to provide for the withdrawal from circulation of the currency known as "greenbacks," and for the accumulation of gold by the National Banks, sufficient to enable them to resume on their circulating notes; that these measures should be begun at once, and be steadily continued as rapidly as in the judgment of Congress it may be done without violently or seriously disturbing the business interests of the country; and that a day should be now fixed beyond which suspension should not continue.

Toledo Board of Trade. Mr. DAVIS : We are all striving for one point, the resumption of specie payments, and the question is, how shall we reach it ? Some propose one plan, some another, but I think that the only way to resume, and the only way to continue, is to have sufficient coin in your vaults, and sufficient gold in the hands of the Government, that there shall not be at any time, a period when our Government bonds may be returned from Europe, and we not able to redeem them. They could cause us to suspend in twenty days; they have unquestionably the power to do so. Shall we resolve by act of Congress, or shall this Board recommend a specific time to resume, without being prepared for an emergency of that kind. I apprehend it will take a great deal of time to do this, we cannot resume by the simple passage of an Act. Now if we have but one hundred and fifty million dollars of gold, and if our crops should be short, and Europe full of prosperity, not requiring what we have to sell, what would be the result? The moment we resolve to resume, those in Europe who have bought our bonds at sixty to seventy cents on the dollar, would say, we can now afford to send our bonds and demand the gold. I claim, therefore, that unless we have three or four times this amount to protect ourselves on the first emergency, we shall be compelled to suspend again in twenty days. We must have the gold to meet our obligations.

In looking over all the resolutions, I am obliged to come to this conclusion, that Mr. FRALEY'S plan, as a whole, and the manner in which he proposes to reduce this currency, is the best. It is gradual, it is easy, and it would prepare the minds of the people for a return to specie payments. After looking over the whole ground, I shall recommend Mr. FRALEY'S resolution, as coming nearer my views than any other presented.

In addition, I have a resolution of my own which I had the honor of introducing at Boston, and which the President, Mr. FRALEY, at that time Chairman of the Finance Committee, very kindly permitted to go before the Board, and it was passed. Somebody has got to make the first step towards returning. Who are the proper parties to do it? The commission men, the merchants, or the bankers? I claim that it is the duty of the bankers to take the first step. We have to return to specie payments one of these days; and I claim that as their promises to pay are in circulation, and they have nothing to pay with, it is their duty, as prudent corporations, to begin to get something with which to redeem their own notes. I propose that the gold they get as interest on the bonds pledged for their notes that are out, shall be kept as a reserve; that it shall be put into their vaults, taking out the amount of greenbacks and distributing them to the public, until it reaches the amount equal to the reserve that is required to be kept by law. That is the first step. They then have gold, something to redeem with; this will begin to restore confidence among the people. Let the banks be fully protected, and have, say, twenty-five per cent. in coin, the legal reserve required by law in greenbacks, and what then would the Wall Street gentlemen and other speculators in gold say, as they look over the bank reports? They would say, it looks as if the banks intend to return to specie payments, and it is not prudent to buy one to two millions of gold for thirty days, to speculate upon. We want confidence that we can resume and sustain our position; but if you fix a date, and have an insufficiency of gold, you will certainly suspend within twenty days after resumption. As I said before, those bonds in Europe will be the great trouble. They will be returned, and in case of calamity they will be sold, perhaps for greenbacks, but they will again be sold for gold; a panic might occur, business men would get frightened, and make a run upon the banks and we could not sustain our position.

With these remarks, I propose to annex the following to Mr. FRALEY's resolution. As he said nothing about National Banks resuming, I propose to append this resolution to his:

*Resolved.* That this Board recommends to Congress to provide by law that from this date no National Bank shall be allowed to sell any part of the gold received from the Government as interest upon the bonds pledged for its circulation, until such time as the entire amount of the reserve required by law to be kept by the banks, shall be made up of coin.

New Orleans Board of Trade. Mr. BURWELL : Whatever may have been our opinions in the South upon the advantage to us of an impaired national credit, it is clearly now the interest of all that the currency and securities of the Government should be as near par as possible. Had the nation cancelled the war debt of the Northern States as it did those of the South, we should have had of course, less taxes to pay than at present. Having, however, accepted the situation with the incumbrances, it has been a matter of duty to throw no impediments in the way of reconstructing the national credit. It is, indeed, the interest of the Southern States that this credit should be entire. There should be another Pacific Railroad. The Southern portion of this continent and its islands may come under American domination. The Isthmus of Panama should be opened with an inter-oceanic canal. The levees of Louisiana should be repaired. In the vast future which spreads before the Republic, its financial credit may be useful to the South. The creation of the debt having done so much to destroy our prosperity, we cannot be as much injured by further public expenditures, in which we must in some manner participate. While it is far better to take a broad and dispassionate view of this important subject, we should not permit our passions to cloud the prospect of our prosperity. We have fought fiercely and faithfully for our rights as we understood them, let our friendships be equally sincere. While such are the reasons why the South should favor the restoration of federal credit, the State of Louisiana and the city of New Orleans are especially interested in bringing federal currency to the par of gold. We have already adverted to our dilapidated levees. Think of a crop of nearly half a million of hogsheads reduced by war and inundation to less than fifty thousand, and now after the lapse of three years scarcely amounting to one hundred thousand. And yet the American people pay for this reduced crop, perhaps double the money that they formerly paid for one-fifth of the product! While we are interested in a federal credit, which would by direct appropriation or by endowment enable us to repair this immense loss, are not you reciprocally interested in restoring our capacity for productiveness? Remember, that the sugar imported into the United States, cost last year more than fifty millions of specie. Recollect, that in restoring home productions you diminish these exported millions in the same proportion. Few measures, indeed, do more to appreciate federal bonds than the reparation of those levees. No policy could do more to restore the levees than the appreciation of those bonds.

The city of New Orleans has a further reason to desire the approximation of the currency to par. The sales of cotton in that market may be stated at an annual average of one hundred millions of dollars. Of this it would appear from the following statement, that at least eighty-eight per cent. was exported to foreign countries:

Total exports of cotton from the port of New Orleans for the four first months of 1868: . . . . . . 421,379 bales.
    Foreign, . . . . . 373,228
    Coastwise, . . . . . 48,151
                                                        421,379

Much of this cotton may have been exported from Northern ports to Europe. If we assume the average annual amount of cotton sales as above, it would appear that the factors who buy on foreign account must deal to the amount of more than eighty millions in federal currency, which is exclusively used in this market for the purchase of cotton, on foreign as well as domestic account. You, gentlemen, as practical merchants, will readily see the inconvenience as well as loss to which *bona fide* purchasers may be subjected in consequence of the fluctuations of this currency. Thus, a factor may buy on foreign account cotton to-day at twenty-five cents per pound, payable in currency at thirty-five per cent. premium on gold. Even before shipment gold may have varied so much as to disturb this cotton transaction greatly; for, it is to be observed, that the large proportion of this cotton is bought on account of parties who wish to hold or to manufacture it. So vexatious have these fluctuations proved to be, that a resolution was recently introduced in the Chamber of Commerce, by Mr. MUSGROVE, one of the principal factors on English account, and a Committee was raised for the purpose of enquiring into the practicability of making payments for cotton purchased in New Orleans — as it is in Texas — in gold exclusively. The Committee reported that this would be a very desirable system, but that it was impracticable for causes stated. There are many other reasons based on the direct communication between New Orleans and the continental and insular ports of America, why a currency so far below a gold value, and so subject to alternations, should offer embarrassment to a commerce with countries using only the precious metals as money of account.

I have shown why New Orleans and the South, dealing so largely in exportable values, are peculiarly interested in a sound and stable currency. It must not be inferred, however, that they are the advocates of a precipitate resumption of specie payments, still less so if that measure be accompanied with the withdrawal, or withholding of the just proportion of national currency which the business of the South requires. The reasoning is given to show the sincerity of my constituents in their wish for a solvent currency. The precise time and mode in which this is to be effected, is left with those who have the power and responsibility upon this subject. I cannot, however, sit down without reminding the National Board of Trade that the values exported from the South are estimated this year at more than two hundred and fifty millions of dollars, gold. This is a sum more than double the whole value exported from the rest of the Union. This must be in the highest degree useful in reducing the currency to par and in appreciating the value of the national securities. Is it not, then, the duty of the National Board of Trade to use its influence in restraining any further disturbance in the South of the relation between land and labor? If these extraordinary values have been produced amid political excitement, what must be the capacity of such a country and of such a people in a state of peace and protection? Certainly every holder of federal currency, every owner of federal bonds, should exercise, as far as possible, a conservative influence over the councils of the country, for the specie receipts on account of Southern staples have done much to save the Government from embarrassment, and can do much more to restore both its credit and currency.

**Buffalo Board of Trade. Mr. HAZARD**: Having reserved my right to speak, I desire now to say a few words, as I should think it a dereliction of duty if I did not offer the sentiments of the Board of Trade which I have the honor, partly, to represent.

I have been exceedingly interested and instructed, and I think any person might have learned a great deal during the last twenty-four hours in listening to the discussions of this body on this subject. A great many projects have been presented, and many of them have exhibited ability; others, perhaps, not so much, but all have been worthy of consideration. It seems to me we want no experimenting; certainly no tinkering with the currency of the country; and I think we want very little legislation. I regard the whole subject as a very simple matter; one that would cure itself; but it is quite right that the Government should take measures expressive of its determination to put the currency into such a shape that a dollar in paper will be worth a dollar in gold, and that as soon as possible.

I think, Sir, that many of the objections to a return to specie payments are based on the fear of its effect on the values of commodities, and the shrinkage that may take place. There must be a shrinkage, but the sooner we meet that like men, the better.

Some gentlemen have spoken in favor of legalizing gold contracts. But does any one say that a gold contract cannot now be made, and that among honorable men it is not binding? I do not see any necessity for any enactment. If gold contracts were legalized, it would deprive the country of the legal-tenders, the currency of the country, in the proportion in which they were used. If banks should have the power to issue bills payable in gold, or if individuals were allowed to issue bills payable in gold, it would deprive us of the currency of the country just in proportion as it was employed. The Government would, in fact, be passing an Act that would stultify itself by depressing the value of its own legal-tenders.

Whenever the banks resume specie payments they must have specie to resume upon. There should, therefore, be a gradual process of accumulation of gold in the Treasury of the United States, so that the Government would be in possession of a sufficient quantity to enable it to resume with confidence in its continuance.

In accordance with the manner of other gentlemen who have spoken, I have prepared a short resolution, which I propose to offer:

*Resolved*, That in the opinion of this Board, an early return to specie payments is not only desirable, but imperative on the Government; but this Board does not deem it expedient to recommend arbitrary enactments by the Congress of the United States, only so far as to gradually retire the legal-tenders and so to restrict the sales of gold that it may accumulate in the Treasury until the amount shall approximate to the proportion of forty per cent. of the amount of legal-tenders in circulation; and when the amount of gold in the Treasury shall reach that sum, then it shall be the duty of the Government to at once set an example to the country by taking measures for the immediate resumption of specie payments on its obligations.

Mr. GUTHRIE: I have listened with a great deal of pleasure to the discussions based on the various resolutions that have been offered. The question is an important one, affecting as it does the interests of every individual and every branch of business; and it is intimately connected with the interests of the nation at large. I am, I confess, surprised, that under the circumstances, there should be men of culture and experience here who advocate an immediate return to specie payments. Such a measure, it strikes me, would be fatal to all the interests of our country. As a nation we are largely in debt. We owe a debt of three thousand millions of dollars. And what have we got to pay it with? Two hundred millions, perhaps, in gold. We have a circulation of six or seven hundred millions of inflated currency, which in consequence of the war, we have been compelled to circulate. Now with this inflated currency and with the consequent inflation of the value of property, if we start out with the idea that we must resume specie payments immediately, we reduce the value of all property with which we have to pay this debt. The point I wish to make is, that in proportion as we reduce the liability we reduce the circulation. If you take any other step, you prostrate our manufactures, you check all our business operations and you hinder the development of the resources of the country. It is the fear of constant legislation on this matter that disturbs mercantile affairs more than anything else. There is a constant watchfulness and anxiety as to what Congress may do in regard to the financial operations of the country.

The return to specie payments is desirable and necessary; but we must move in the direction towards it with caution. The mighty energies of this country are pledged to pay every dollar we owe. We must look to the West and the Northwest, which roll up their millions of bushels of grain; we must look to the South, which has risen as it were from its ashes, and is already producing its hundreds of millions of surplus wealth; we must look to California and Colorado; and there can be no doubt that the persevering industry of this people, year by year increasing in their numbers and strength, will be equal to the emergency, and will accomplish the end we have in view. We cannot immediately resume without prostrating trade and commerce in all their channels. It may take us one or two, or three years, possibly five, to accomplish this desirable result; but I am in favor of resumption at the earliest practicable date.

I beg to offer the following:

*Resolved*, That in the opinion of this Board, the Government of the United States should, through its Congress, take such action as will enable it through its Treasury, at the earliest practicable moment, to resume specie payments.

### Albany Board of Trade. Mr. WILBOR:

I think we have had speeches enough on this financial question. What is wanted now, is an expression on the part of this Board, as to whether it is desirable or not that the Government should resume specie payments, leaving the time and manner of so doing, entirely to their wisdom. I think that Congress merely wants to know whether the great commercial interests of the country are in favor of specie payments or not.

I therefore offer this resolution:

*Resolved*, That the National Board of Trade is in favor of the early resumption of specie payments by the Government.

### Cincinnati Chamber of Commerce. Mr. GANO:

I feel a great deal of diffidence in rising at this stage of the discussion, to offer a few remarks in reference to finances. I feel, however, encouraged to do so, by the fact that men of large experience, and men who have given this subject a great deal more thought than I have, differ widely from each other in their views; and the more so, for another reason, that Cincinnati is claimed as the residence of both "Old Greenbacks" and "Young Greenbacks."

I admit all that has been said on the conservative side of this question, as expressing nearly my own views. I fully realize the necessity for a contraction of the currency, and I claim in reference to the payment of our national bonds, that where it is not specified in the law to the contrary, they should be paid in gold. I recognize also, the full force of what my friend, Mr. DAVIS, claims as to the necessity of increased production, which is well comprised in the phrase, *Ex nihilo nihil fit.* I offer the following as a suggestion for the consideration of men better able to judge of its merits than myself:

WHEREAS, All the commercial, financial and industrial interests of the country are kept in a state of continual embarrassment and uncertainty, and values of all kinds are exposed to unnatural fluctuations because of the absence of the application of the gold standard; be it

*Resolved,* That the National Board of Trade does hereby respectfully suggest to the Congress of the United States, a consideration of the propriety of enacting a law which shall provide that after the first day of July, 1869, no note shall be a legal-tender for a less amount than ten dollars; that after the first day of January, 1870, no note shall be a legal-tender for a less amount than twenty dollars; that after the first day of July, 1870, no note shall be a legal-tender for a less amount than fifty dollars; that after the first day of January, 1871, no note shall be a legal-lender for a less amount than one hundred dollars; and that after the first day of July, 1871, no note shall be a legal-tender for any amount. That in order to make such a plan effective, provision shall be made for the redemption of the legal-tender notes in coin, as they fall due at the dates named, and for their cancellation; but for the purpose of preserving a proper degree of elasticity in the movements of the currency, there shall be issued United States Treasury notes of like denominations to the legal-tenders displaced, which shall be redeemable in coin, yet subject to reissue, until the legal-tenders shall all have been redeemed, when their reissue shall cease, and they also shall be cancelled and destroyed on their return to the United States Treasury.

Those experienced in financial matters will, of course, apply to this, their knowledge as to the effect of a redemption of these notes. There will inevitably occur a pinch at first, but the movement towards it, when the Act shall have been passed, will be a conservative one. The National Banks will begin to protect themselves by saving their interest on national bonds. The Government will know how well it can protect these small legal-tenders; the people who hold them will possibly feel an inclination at first to get a little gold, to which they have so long been strangers; but finding that the gold does them no good, they will not hold it, or they will use it as currency.

Firmness will of course be necessary in inaugurating the change. The movement will begin to regulate values in the right quarters, in the exchanges between people of moderate means, who buy small quantities of things, and values will ultimately all be reduced to a gold standard. If a plan on this principle can be adopted, I think it will prove an eminently practical measure.

If propositions on general financial matters are in order, I would like to present the following:

*Resolved*, That Congress be requested to consider the propriety of establishing a commission, comprising the Secretary of the Treasury, the Chairman of the Ways and Means Committee of the House of Representatives, and the Chairman of the Finance Committee of the Senate, on whom shall be devolved the exercise of such discretionary and extraordinary power as may be necessary to be employed in managing the fiscal affairs of the Government.

And also this:

*Resolved*, That Congress be urged to so amend the National Banking Law, that quarterly reports, at specified times, be dispensed with, and that instead, each National Bank in the country shall be called upon by the Controller, at least once in each quarter, to show what its condition may have been on a designated day in the recent past, which reports shall be published as soon as made.

Mr. HOLTON: It occurred to me yesterday afternoon, just before our adjournment, that to facilitate our work in disposing of this important question, it would be well to refer to a Committee the various propositions which had been submitted to the Board; so that these might be crystallized, and that something practical and definite might be reported for the action of the Board. But as the discussion had not then closed, it seemed better on the whole, to postpone a motion to the effect stated. I now rise to make such a motion.

Mr. MEIER: The members of the St. Louis Board of Trade have not been heard.

Mr. HOLTON: I will willingly yield for the purpose of permitting the St. Louis Board to be heard.

Mr. FISK: It seems to me we may vote directly upon the St. Louis resolutions. Almost every speaker has given his views upon them, and has endorsed them in whole or in part. I think therefore we may come to a vote, taking up our first resolution, and if it needs to be amended, let it be amended now; and so with the rest.

Mr. HOLTON: I rose merely in the hope of facilitating business. I yielded the floor to the St. Louis Board for further discussion, but only on that point.

Mr. FISK: I am not going to discuss these resolutions. I was saying that almost every member on this floor agreed with them, but I confess I have felt very much as an Irish friend of mine at Cairo, must have felt at the time of the taking of Fort Sumter, when the national heart was aroused and every man was expected to declare where he stood. Our Irishman was met by a party, who enquired which side he was on. Pat was uncertain. "You must be for the Union or against it." "Then," said Pat, "I am for the Union." And they knocked him down. Shortly after he was met by another party, who put the same question; "I am for Jeff. Davis," said he, and down he went again. He was met by a third party, and again the query was put. Pat had learned discretion. "You seem to be in the majority gentlemen," said he, "just name which side ye are on, and I'll go with ye." There has been a good deal of that sort of discussion here. Still I think we all believe we have to climb Mr. ROPES's mountain, although we may go by different pathways. We all think we must have specie payments at an early day. Almost every resolution asks for it at the earliest practicable date. Now, Sir, we are here to tell Congress what that date shall be. Representing all the commercial interests of this great country, we are here to say to Congress, that the Government can resume specie payments on a certain day. We say the first of July or the fourth of July, 1870. If that is not far enough distant, say the first of January, 1871, but let us fix a date when we will do it. Let every man put his house in order, and if there is any one who cannot get his house in order by 1871, he had better sell out to some one who can.

As to the second resolution, it asks Congress to provide for the resumption of specie payments, by a contraction of at least one hundred million dollars. It seems to me that our system of contraction is akin to that proposed by our worthy President. We *must* contract a little; we are all resolved to go back to specie payments as early as possible, and we are convinced it may be done at no distant day, and of course we all want it done with the least possible squeeze to everybody.

Mr. MEIER: I have been much interested in the discussion which has taken place. I think our resolutions are not far from being right. Nothing has been said against them to convince me that we are in the wrong. As to any connection of the banks with the scheme of resumption, the Committee that drew up these resolutions, purposely omitted any reference to them. They are likely to have twenty-five per cent. of their circulation on hand in greenbacks, legal-tenders; therefore, as soon as resumption comes, they will have a reserve of twenty-five per cent., equal to coin. Ample time is given them to put their house in order. The strong banks will be gainers by the resumption; the weak banks may be in a different position; some of them may go by the board and fail, but I shall have no sympathy for them, and it will be better for the public that they wind up.

I hope that the resolutions will pass, and that they will not be referred to a Committee.

Mr. HOLTON: It is no part of my purpose to hinder this debate. I have listened with the utmost interest to all that has been said. I will, however, cheerfully yield the floor, if, as I think, Mr. WALBRIDGE, of New York, desires to speak. He is a gentleman I should like to hear.

Mr. WALBRIDGE: I desire simply to say that the views announced by my colleagues, right and left, are the views I was requested to represent.

Mr. HOLTON: I move that the resolutions from the St. Louis Board of Trade, together with the several amendments proposed, and the additional resolutions submitted, be now referred to a special Committee of seven.

Mr. HAND: I rise to second that motion. We have been in attendance here yesterday and to-day, listening to an innumerable number of speeches, and I might say, almost an innumerable number of resolutions. Now if the St. Louis resolutions only are acted upon, it cuts off all the other propositions. I think a Committee might, out of such a mass of resolutions, frame something that would be generally acceptable to the Board. It strikes me that a reference to a Committee is very much the best way of proceeding.

Mr. ROPES: I think this is the only way in which we can get at this subject. I should vote heartily for the St. Louis resolutions, rather than not vote for any, and I should vote for them in preference to most of the resolutions which have been presented. I admire the resolutions of our President, and those of Mr. GANO, but I am constrained to believe that they would fail in practical execution.

I said yesterday, that I should be content with merely stating my own views, and would not attempt to refute the various theories and arguments made contrary to them. I have felt, during the progress of this debate, that I would give a great deal to reply to them. I am not going to ask the indulgence of the house to do anything of the kind, but I am prepared, at any time, to *prove* the correctness of the views I had the honor to bring before the house yesterday, and to refute the multiplied assertions to which I have listened in opposition; and though I may not have an opportunity on this occasion, I may, possibly hereafter have an opportunity of doing so.

A member of Congress has told us here, that our action in this matter will have its effect on Congress. Does not this fact make it very important that we should put our action in just such a form as will carry the unanimous approval of this Board, and at the same time, that it will carry a large assent in Congress. If we can frame some practical measure, — the simpler the better — expressive of a determination to resume specie payments, and proposing some practical method of bringing it about, on which we all can agree, it will go to Congress with great force, as from the business men of the country, and from the multitude of resolutions brought forward, I think this might be done. I therefore hope the motion will prevail.

Mr. FISK: We ask that the subject be referred to a Committee.

The PRESIDENT: The question is on its being referred to a Committee of seven.

Carried.

Mr. STRANAHAN: I ask to offer the following resolution, and that it may be referred to the Committee when read:

*Resolved*, As the sense of this Board, that the National Congress should, at its present session, determine the time for the resumption of specie payments.

Mr. ROPES: Is it in order to offer resolutions in the same way.

The PRESIDENT: I did not understand for what purpose Mr. STRANAHAN rose, and was about to ask. The house has ordered the Committee. If it is the pleasure of the Board to elect this Committee, it would gratify the Chair.

Mr. DRAKE : I would make a suggestion, namely, that we should in some informal manner, test the sense of this body upon these propositions. It is very certain that if this matter goes to a Committee, the result will be the views of a majority of that Committee. I think therefore, we should, in an informal way, pass upon these general propositions.

The PRESIDENT : That would not be in order at this time.

The Board intimated its desire that the President should appoint the Committee of seven on finance.

The PRESIDENT : I am very much embarrassed in the selection; but according to the best of my judgment, I have selected, and will now name,

EDWARD D. HOLTON, Milwaukie,
A. MEIER, St. Louis,            J. S. ROPES, Boston,
J. S. T. STRANAHAN, New York,   G. W. DAVIS, Toledo,
CHARLES RANDOLPH, Chicago,      J. R. BRANCH, Richmond.

Mr. DAVIS : I move that the President's name be added to that Committee.

The PRESIDENT : That would be out of order.

After some informal debate, the Chair decided that additional resolutions on finance should be admitted without debate.

Mr. ROPES : I have drawn up my resolutions in the hope that I can get a majority of this Board to indorse them, and I hope a majority in Congress to pass them.

*Resolved,* That this Board respectfully and earnestly urges upon the Congress of the United States, the immediate passage of an act to enforce the resumption of specie payments by the Government and the National Banks, at the earliest practical moment, but not later than in July, 1871.

*Resolved,* That in order to reduce the volume of our paper currency to its just proportions, and to render practicable the resumption of specie payments without monetary disturbance, we recommend the immediate issue of five per cent. five-twenty gold bonds, at par, in exchange for all legal-tender notes which may be presented for that purpose at the Treasury, in multiplies of fifty dollars; and that, in order to avoid all risk of too rapid conversion and consequent pressure and panic, these bonds be again exchangeable for legal-tender notes, so that the process of withdrawal may be rendered safe, uniform and steady.

Mr. TURPIN: I beg to offer the following:

*Resolved*, That it is inexpedient for the Congress of the United States to fix a time in the near future, for the resumption of specie payments.

Mr. TAYLOR: I desire to present the following resolution:

*Resolved*, That simultaneously with the resumption of specie payments, Congress should take measures to withdraw from circulation, all notes of National Banks of denominations less than ten dollars.

Mr. WALBRIDGE: I was unable to reach this city until to-day, and therefore have not been present at the previous sessions of this body. I am now hourly expecting intelligence which may require me to leave. I would therefore respectfully ask, in behalf of those I represent, to be allowed to present my views on railroad interests at this stage of the proceedings.

Leave was granted.

Mr. WALBRIDGE: In the remarks I have the honor of submitting, I propose to discuss the influence that railways exert in the creation of wealth, and apply them in a more particular manner to those great national works which, in the United States, are to connect ocean with ocean, and open to settlement and commerce, vast tracts of the national domain, now deserts, and which must remain such till touched by the quickening hand of those mighty agents, the use of which is the peculiar feature and the glory of the present age.

The use of these agents — *the forces of nature* — marks the dividing line between the old and the new. The first use of steam as a motive power, is within the memory of the middle-aged. Previous to 1830, *muscular* action was the sole agent employed in the movement, on land, both of persons and property. In this respect, society had remained stationary from earliest history. The great ALEXANDER and the great NAPOLEON, employed precisely the same means, in their wonderful marches, for the transportation of men, supplies, and the material of war.

Under this old regime the cost and impotence of muscular action was so excessive as to restrict commerce in the more bulky articles — articles, too, of the chiefest account in social economy, food for example — within very narrow limits. Hence the extravagant importance attached to portable articles of high value, such as gold and silver. At an early period, a half dozen of articles made up the staple almost, of the commerce of the world. In this matter the experience of our own people covers the whole ground. Our markets are all within a narrow belt lying immediately upon the seaboard. Previous to the construction of improved highways they could be reached only from a very limited area. The report submitted to the Legislature of the State of New York, in 1817, and which led to the construction of the Erie Canal, stated the cost of transporting a ton of freight at that time, from Buffalo to the city of New York, to be one hundred dollars — a sum exceeding twice the value of wheat at Buffalo, and four times that of corn! The time required was twenty days.

Such is an illustration of the condition of the internal commerce of our country forty years ago. The nature of the soil in most of the States rendered the construction of ordinary highways very difficult. Neither railroads nor canals existed. Commerce was restricted, consequently, to water-courses, navigable by steamboats, barges, and even to batteaux. Over nine-tenths of our inhabited territory, the produce of the soil was without commercial value — that is — the cost of sending it to market far exceeded the sum it would sell for. The labor of the farmer, consequently, instead of being directed to objects that would produce the greatest value, was necessarily employed in the production of nearly every article going into domestic consumption. The family was obliged to be, in a great measure, self-supporting. The loss attendant upon a constant change of the objects of labor was so great that little more was produced than was necessary to meet the daily accruing wants. The accumulation of wealth was a process exceedingly slow, and its possessors were a mere fraction of society. All this is within the experience of nearly every one that hears me. Each one of you, of middle age, went forth to school, and from school to the world, clad in *homespun*. You could not buy the product of others because you could not sell your own. The labor upon the farm in which almost the whole nation was employed was, owing to the want of those mechanical aids now so universal, comparatively unproductive. There was no stimulus to improvements for the abridgement of toil, because, with the existing state of highways, there was hardly any demand, out of the family, for what could be produced.

Such is a brief picture of the past — of the *old regime*. In locomotion society remained stationary for six thousand years, and till, within the memory of all, the forces of nature came to its aid. The power gained by a substitution of *steam* for muscles, and by highways of comparatively straight lines and smooth surfaces, is almost incalculable. The locomotive upon the railway exerts the power of two thousand horses upon an ordinary highway — that is, it will move in a day as many tons, one mile, as two thousand horses. But the cost of providing the two thousand horses and a thousand wagons, with that of their maintenance, exceeds ten-fold that of the locomotive and cars of the capacity of two thousand tons With these brief data the arithmetic is simple, although the comparative results are most astounding. As incredible as they seem, they only mark the magnitude of the revolution which the physical sciences have wrought in favor of man.

We have said enough to show that in this country our internal commerce is a creation of the new agencies which the last half century has set at work. Our commerce, wealth, and our population, even, are simply the results of the new methods. They have advanced precisely in ratio to the value and efficiency of the agencies we have employed. These agencies, wherever introduced, have given a market to labor at its door. The corn that now supplies the Eastern markets, as well as those of Europe, is grown more than one thousand miles inland. This corn would not bear transportation over the ordinary roads of the West more than one hundred and fifty miles. Over the railroad it is borne seven-fold that distance, at the same time yielding an ample profit to the producer. Wheat will bear a transportation three hundred and thirty miles over an ordinary road. The great supplies to the Eastern markets are now grown one thousand five hundred miles distant. But for railroads the area from which the Eastern markets could draw their supplies of cereals, without an enormously increased price, would have been upon a radius of one hundred and fifty and three hundred and thirty miles, respectively. With these works, owing to the economies that are being daily made in transportation, every acre of arable land on the continent, no matter how far distant from the great seats of consumption, may be cultivated with profit.

Previous to the opening of the Erie Canal, in 1827, the tonnage crossing the Alleghany range in both directions, and from the Lakes to New York, did not exceed fifteen thousand tons. This tonnage consisted almost wholly of merchandise going West — the cost of transportation being a complete bar to the movement, East, of Western produce. The only outlet of the interior was the Mississippi river, with its tributaries, the navigation of which was most tedious and hazardous, and so expensive as to leave little profit, to either the forwarder or the producer. The opening of the Erie Canal was an epoch in the commerce of the country, but it exerted, for the first ten years, but little influence beyond the route immediately traversed. So late as 1836, the total amount of tonnage from the Western States coming through this channel to tide-water, equalled only fifty-six thousand tons. Before the Western States could avail themselves of it, they had to connect their territories with it, and with the Lakes by canals, or by the best earth roads they could construct. In 1846, the amount of Western produce reaching tide water by canal was four hundred and nineteen thousand tons. In 1851, the date of the opening of the Erie Railroad, and the removal of the restrictions on the transportation of freight on the New York Central Railroad, (which was first opened in the fall of 1842,) the tonnage of Western produce on the canal had reached nine hundred and sixty-five thousand nine hundred and ninety-three tons. This tonnage measured to a very great extent the commerce then existing between the Eastern and Western States. In 1867, the united through tonnage of the five great lines between the two sections — the Erie Canal, the New York Central, Erie, Pennsylvania, and Baltimore and Ohio Railroads — equalled six million tons, having a value of one billion two hundred million dollars.

At the date of the opening of the Erie Railway, and the enfranchisement of the Central Railroad, there were ten thousand miles of railway in operation in the United States. The total tonnage of the merchandise transported over them could not have exceeded five million tons, of the value of one hundred and fifty dollars per ton, or of the aggregate value of seven hundred and fifty million dollars. On the first of January, 1868, the mileage of our railroads had gone up to thirty-nine thousand miles. The tonnage of merchandise transported over them equalled fifty million tons, having, at the above estimate, a value equal to seven billion five hundred million dollars. In a period of seventeen years the mileage of our railways had increased nearly four hundred per cent., their tonnage one thousand per cent., with a corresponding increase in value. The population of the country, in the meantime, had increased from twenty-four millions to thirty-six millions, or at the rate of fifty per cent. In other words, the increase of the commerce of the country borne upon railroads, has been two thousand fold greater than that of our population. In 1851, the freight moved upon all the railroads equalled four hundred and seventeen pounds per head of population. Its value equalled say thirty-one dollars per head. In 1868, the tonnage equalled two thousand seven hundred and seventy-seven pounds per head, having a value of two hundred and ten dollars per head. The increase of the tonnage of railroads for the period named has been wholly a creation of these works, as there has, at the same time, been a very large increase of merchandise moved upon the water courses of the country.

In 1851, the cost of the ten thousand miles of railway then in operation in the United States, equalled two hundred million dollars. In 1868, the cost of the thirty-nine thousand miles equalled one billion six hundred million dollars. The investment since 1851, of one billion four hundred million dollars consequently, has been the means of an annual creation of a commerce having a value five-fold greater, or six billion seven hundred and fifty million dollars. Every dollar invested in our railroads is the direct means of creating, annually, five times the amount, so marvellously potent are the new agencies, that science, within the memory of us all, has brought to the aid of man. In their use we have at last hit upon the method of Nature — of Providence — and enjoy in some degree His infinite attributes, in wielding for our own use, the laws that uphold and control the material world.

The results achieved in a single State, will be found, on examination, to be quite as striking as in the aggregate for the whole nation, There were in the State of Illinois in 1851, two hundred and fifty miles of railway, the cost of which was about seven million five hundred thousand dollars. The tonnage of these roads, only just opened, could not have exceeded one hundred thousand tons, having a value say of fifteen million dollars. At the close of 1867, there were three thousand two hundred and fifty miles of railroad in operation in the State, having a tonnage traffic of at least five million tons, possessing a value of at least seven hundred and fifty million dollars. The cost of the roads equalled one hundred and thirty million dollars. The value of the commerce transported over them in one year, equalled, very nearly, six times their cost. In 1851, the number of pounds of merchandise transported by these roads, equalled about two hundred pounds per head of population. In 1867, the tonnage transported exceeded four thousand pounds, or two tons per head. The value of the tonnage per head in 1851, was about fifteen dollars; in 1867, it was equal to three hundred and thirty dollars per head. This unexampled increase was wholly due to the construction of railroads, as there has in the meantime been a very large increase in the tonnage on the water-courses of the State. It will be borne in mind that the tonnage of railroads of this State consists almost entirely of the products of agriculture which will bear transportation for only a comparatively small distance, over ordinary roads. These products are now forwarded, on an average, one thousand two hundred miles, before reaching a market.

The population of Illinois now makes one-fifteenth of that of the whole country. It now defrays one-fifteenth of the whole burden of the General Government. Its proportion of the Federal taxes equals twenty-four million dollars annually. Its ability to pay this vast sum is almost entirely due to the railroads that have been constructed within it during the past fifteen years. Toward their construction the Federal Government never contributed a penny. It did, however, in 1850, make a valuable land grant to the State in favor of the Illinois Central Railroad, which secured the speedy construction of this great work, and gave a wonderful impulse to the construction of other important lines. The additional price charged for reserved lands yielded to the National Treasury the same sum that would have been realized if the grant had not been made. If by the use of similar means we can create another Illinois as far as concerns its population, wealth, and value in the Union, we shall in an equal degree lighten the burdens resting upon us. A vigorous movement in this direction, consequently, is the dictate of sound statesmanship, as well as of enlightened self-interest.

By what means shall we repeat the example of Illinois? The first condition exists in a vast, fertile, and unoccupied public domain. But, unlike Illinois, Iowa, and Minnesota, it cannot be reached by navigable water-courses, that were the routes of pioneers, and enabled them to gain foothold in these States, and in time to acquire sufficient strength to undertake enterprises not necessary to the maintenance of their own existence. But for these water-courses, the Mississippi River and the great lakes, these States, to-day, would have been in the condition of the boundless unoccupied plains of the Upper Missouri, of the Red River of the North, and of the Rio Grande. These States had almost every possible natural means of access. The artificial means came in good time. The former, however, were the necessary antecedents of the latter. But for the natural, the artificial works could never have been constructed.

Now, the proper duty and function of the Federal Government is to correct this oversight of nature in not giving the means of access to vast portions of our public domain. In place of great water lines it must supply what is far better — a great trunk line of railway, to enable the pioneers to gain a foothold upon the soil. It is only by means of such works that such foothold can be gained, and strength acquired, sufficient, as in the Western States, to carry forward whatever enterprises may be necessary and proper for the promotion of their well-being. From the western end of Lake Superior to the base of the Rocky Mountains, some one thousand two hundred miles, is a vast fertile plain, but now wholly destitute of the means of transportation. The Missouri, though a valuable auxiliary to a railway, is of itself, wholly inadequate to meet the commercial wants of the country it traverses. A railway from the lake to the mountains, which could be built at an expenditure of twenty million dollars by the Federal Government, would open to settlement an area five times greater than that of Illinois. Now, with such an expenditure, we should repeat Illinois many times, and just as quick as the movement of an adequate number of people and the creation of new industries could be effected. As already remarked, the arithmetic of all this is perfectly simple. Supply the means of transportation, and the tide of population flowing over the new territory, will keep pace with the progress of the railway, so that when the mountains are reached, the territories now deserts, will present themselves to Congress with all the conditions necessary to entitle them to become members of the Union.

These remarks apply with equal force in favor of a great line of railroad crossing the continent upon the general routes of the thirty-fifth or thirty-second parallels. In this division of the Union, is a territory embracing many hundred thousand square miles, large portions of it of great fertility, and with a vast mineral wealth to compensate for any barrenness of soil, for the want of suitable highways, utterly cut off from settlement, and from commerce. Such a work would give an access to the northern provinces of Mexico, whose great wealth in mineral and soil is well known, as well as to our own Territories. In this direction we can repeat many times, Illinois and Missouri, as well as in the North. The Southwest is the region which is to supply animal food and wool, while the Northwest is peculiarly adapted to the growth of wheat, which has a very limited belt in this, as in the Old World. The two sections are complements that will supply all the prime articles entering into domestic consumption.

Such is a plain statement of the proposition before us. Can we afford to allow vast tracts of fertile country to remain wastes, simply for the want of a few millions of dollars to be expended in opening them to settlement? Certainly not. The process of aiding such works will be a paying one from the start. The immediate increase of consumption by the inhabitants of the newly-opened Territories, of the manufactures of the older States, will more than make up the proportion to the latter, of any expenditures they may be called to make; while the taxes paid to the Federal Government by the inhabitants of the new Territories and States will speedily repay all the advances to be made. When it is considered what the Government would gain in the transportation of troops, supplies, and munitions of war, it is not probable that it would at any moment be a dollar out of pocket, while it is certain that in a very short time it would be repaid more than ten-fold for all the advances made.

The experience already afforded by the progress of the Union Pacific Railroad, perfectly sustains all the positions I have taken. The States of Kansas and Nebraska, from the advantages and stimulus supplied by this great work, with its branches, are fast repeating the example of Illinois. Their increase in population and wealth is much greater than was that of Illinois, at a corresponding period in the history of the latter. No one who examines the subject, can avoid the conclusion that already, in a pecuniary sense, has the Government gained immensely by the aid it has extended to these works. They have built up two great States, whose populations are the most profitable consumers of the products of the Eastern States, and whose contributions to the national treasury far exceed the interest on the bonds issued in their aid. In a few years such contributions will annually exceed the *principal* of such bonds, when the Government will be receiving, annually, cent per cent. upon the investment it has made.

With such demonstrations before me, I cannot doubt the expediency of further aid by the Federal Government in opening up other sections far more fertile and valuable than that traversed by the Union Pacific Railroad. It cannot afford to allow an acre of valuable soil or mineral to be beyond the reach of commerce or of human life. All it has to do, is to supply a few great trunk lines. From these, offshoots will be made by private enterprise to every section, so as to supply the means of cheap transportation for any ton of produce or of mineral, that may be raised.

The Board adjourned to meet on Monday morning at ten o'clock.

# FIFTH DAY.

MONDAY, DECEMBER 7, 1868.

The Board met pursuant to adjournment.
The President in the chair.
Prayer was offered by the Rev. W. S. STUDLEY.
On motion of Mr. DAVIS, the reading of the Journal was dispensed with.

The SECRETARY: I am instructed to report that the Executive Council decided this morning to recommend to the Board a change in the order of business, so that when the propositions from the St. Louis and Lousville Boards of Trade are in order, the respective railroad propositions from the two Boards shall be considered as a single measure, and shall take precedence of the other measures presented by the same Boards.

Another recommendation from the Executive Council is the adoption of the two following by-laws, in addition to No. 1, adopted on the 3d instant;

No. 2. The annual assessment laid by the Executive Council shall be considered as due at the beginning of the year; and no constituent body shall be represented at any meeting of the Board, unless its assessment then due shall have been paid.

No. 3. The Executive Council shall recommend at each annual meeting the place at which it judges it to be expedient that the next annual meeting shall be held.

Mr. HOFFMAN: I move the adoption of the report presented from the Executive Council, both as to business and as to the by-laws.
Carried.

The Secretary then read the following action of the Dubuque Board of Trade:

WHEREAS, The Pacific Railroad, with its several branches, being of great national importance, in the successful prosecution of which, and in the faithful execution of the laws creating the same, the people of the whole country are deeply interested; and,

WHEREAS, It is asserted by very many of the friends of that enterprise in all parts of the country, that it has been diverted from its original destination westwardly, from its initial point, south-eastwardly down the valley of the Missouri River, to the irreparable injury and destruction of the entire system of railroads running south-westwardly through the State of Minnesota, and westwardly through the northern portion of Iowa, and through Wisconsin; therefore,

*Resolved,* That the National Board of Trade, which meets in Cincinnati on the third of December, be respectfully requested to recommend to Congress such action as may be necessary and proper to secure its restoration to the original route westwardly, as provided by law.

Mr. MONROE: I beg to offer the following in connection with the resolution just read:

WHEREAS, The foregoing preamble and resolution from the Board of Trade of the city of Dubuque, in the State of Iowa, have been addressed to this Convention for its consideration and action; therefore,

*Resolved,* That Congress be respectfully requested to adopt such legislation as may be necessary to carry out, and enforce the true interest, meaning and purpose of the Pacific Railroad law of Congress, and amendments thereto, in relation to the said north or Sioux city branch of said road.

The PRESIDENT: The question is on receiving these propositions and placing them on the official programme for action.

Mr. THOMAS: With respect to this action of our Board, it is fully understood that a two-thirds vote is required to secure action upon it.

Under a misapprehension on the part of a portion of the Government officers, the enactment in relation to that branch of the Pacific Railroad has been placed in such a position that further legislation is required to make it effective. We do not ask this Board to recommend to Congress any further appropriation or legislation in regard to that line. The legislation is all sufficient; the only action we ask is in favor of a brief supplemental law making the law in relation to that branch effective. The Board of Trade of Dubuque resolved to present the matter here before this National Board, and desired that it might be considered; and on behalf of the citizens of the Northwest, as well as of the whole country, I hope that the proposition will receive the favorable attention of this body.

Mr. BRUNOT: I ask the unanimous consent of the house to offer a short resolution, which I think will not produce debate.

Allowed to be read for the information of the house.

*Resolved* That the officers of the National Board of Trade are hereby instructed to memorialize Congress in favor of the passage of an act to prevent the carriage of petroleum, or other inflammable oils, as freight upon passenger vessels navigating the waters or clearing from the ports of the United States.

Mr. BRUNOT: Coming as I do from a city whence is shipped the daily product of more than sixty refineries of petroleum, I am well aware that some may think me over ready, in offering this resolution, to interfere with the profits of the carrying trade; but with me it is no question of money. Among the men in the ranks of the Christian Commission, during the late rebellion, there was one who, in ability, zeal and patriotic devotion to the cause of his country and humanity, had no superior, and who, since the war, has never flagged in the service of his Divine Master, and in labors for the benefit of his country and his race. ROBERT J. PARVIN was a passenger upon the ill-fated steamer *United States*.* I would not have given that one life for all the money paid for the carriage of that product since its discovery. How many such men were on board the *United States*, I do not know; but I do know that for every life lost, there are some lately expectant, loved ones at home now mourning the consequences of the terrible disaster. I need not attempt to paint its horrors — how the victims, terrified by flames, suffocating in smoke, leaped for safety into the merciless water, to find it only tempered with still more merciless fire! It is not necessary for me to do so to secure the passage

---

* Just before midnight, on Friday, the fourth of December, the steamers *United States*, bound from Cincinnati to Louisville, and *America*, bound from Louisville to Cincinnati, both of the United States Mail Line, came in collision on the Ohio River, and in consequence of the inflammable nature of their cargoes, took fire instantly, and in a few minutes were burnt to the water's edge. A large number of passengers on board the *United States* were lost, and among them were several gentlemen who had been present at the sessions of the Board during the first three days of the meeting.

of the resolution. Every member of this Board fully appreciates the necessity of a law which shall deter either the recklessness or the cupidity of men from leading to future repetitions of the disaster.

Mr. PORTER: In support of the proposition of the gentleman from Pittsburgh, allow me in the name of the Louisville delegation, to give some expression to the sense of our loss in the death of Mr. WILLIAM GARVIN.

He was not here as a delegate to this body, but came solely to watch its proceedings, which he did with the interest natural to an intelligent merchant.

He was a Christian gentleman, of unimpeachable integrity; a merchant for nearly half a century; he has passed from the scene of his arduous labors, leaving a reputation for commercial probity and generous liberality, as a rich legacy to his bereaved family.

The death of this excellent man, and the gloom which enshrouds this delegation, and our entire community, can be attributed only to the absence of such a law as the resolution before you recommends.

Mr DAVIS, of Cincinnati: I understand there is already a law prohibiting the carrying of inflammable materials, especially gunpowder, on passenger steamers; we might be memorializing Congress, when we already have a law upon the subject.

Mr. BRUNOT: That law does not extend to this particular article.

Carried unanimously.

Mr. CARPENTER: I rise to a question of privilege. I desire to offer the following resolution:

*Resolved*, That the National Board of Trade desire to express their grateful thanks in this formal manner, to the managers of the Western Union, Pacific and Atlantic, and Franklin Telegraph lines, for their politeness in tendering the free use of their wires to its members for social and family messages, and especially to the officers of the Atlantic and Pacific line, for favors conferred upon the Board.

Mr. STANARD: I move to strike out the last clause.

Mr. HAZARD: I do not think that any discrimination should be made. I second the motion.

Mr. THURSTON: I appreciate the kindness and courtesy of the gentleman from Boston, who offered the resolution. It may not be unknown that I stand in an official position towards the company named. In tendering the use of the lines, I did it for the purpose of facilitating the business of the Board; nothing more. All I asked, was that the lines should be used as fully and freely as the Board might choose. I think that also was the intention of the Western Union Telegraph Company. I do not see that any distinction should be made in the two companies.

Mr. CARPENTER: I withdraw that part of the resolution which is objected to, and would say that the reason for placing it in the resolution, was that several important documents had been transmitted by that company expressly for the use of the Board.

The resolution, as amended, was carried unanimously.

The PRESIDENT: The report on American Shipping is now in order.

I understand the state of that question to be this: The Committee made its report with resolutions. The Board directed that the report and resolutions should be printed, and re-committed it to the Committee, with power to call it up at any time. They desire to call it up now, seeing that the discussion on specie payments is closed.

Mr. HINCKEN: I regret to begin with an apology to the Board for the imperfect manner in which our report comes in the printed sheet now before them. There are some typographical errors in it, which, however, are not important, but it must go to the Board as it is.

The Committee to whom was referred this important question, have produced a report, upon which all the members of the Committee are agreed; and although the resolutions are not what the seaboard cities asked for, they are the best that we could get, upon which all could agree. We have accepted them, and offer them to the Board. I move the adoption of the report and resolutions.

## REPORT;

The Committee to whom was referred the resolutions of the Boston Board of Trade and the New York Produce Exchange on the foreign and domestic commerce of the United States, as introductory to the action which they would respectfully recommend to the National Board of Trade, beg to call the attention of the delegates to the following paper, prepared by the Secretary of the Board, Mr. HAMILTON A. HILL, of Boston, entitled,

AMERICAN SHIPPING; ITS DECLINE AND THE REMEDIES.

On one of the great occasions when the Jewish people were convened to give expression to their gratitude for the past, and to take counsel for the future, their thanksgiving was mingled with lamentation, and their anticipations were clouded with gloom, in view of the dire calamities by which one of the divisions of the nation had been visited and well-nigh destroyed. From the vast congregation, like the voice of a single man, arose a complaint loud and bitter, piercing the very skies: There is one tribe cut off from Israel this day!

Assembled as we are, at this the first annual meeting of the National Board of Trade, the representatives of the industry and the enterprise of the United States, our felicitations upon the pleasant and promising circumstances under which we have come together, and the congratulations mutually exchanged among us, on the fair degree of good fortune enjoyed at the present time by the agriculturists, the artisans, the manufacturers and the merchants of the country, are seriously modified and checked by the remembrance that one important national interest, honorable and honored in the past, has, to-day, no share in the otherwise almost universal prosperity; that while during recent years, others have been growing with unprecedented vigor, it has languished and decayed; and that while now, others are laying plans, broad and far-reaching, for still further development, it is positively struggling for existence, uncertain whether or not it is to have a future at all. We need hardly say that in these allusions we refer to American ocean commerce, to the past history and present condition of which attention is now invited.

In 1789 our shipping comprised about two hundred thousand tons. On the 30th of June, 1861, it had reached five and a half millions of tons, and was nearly as large as that of all the maritime nations combined, excepting Great Britain. At the latter date, the United States had attained a position in the first rank among the maritime powers;* our flag was seen in every port upon the globe; our

---

*In 1861 the tonnage of the globe was distributed as follows:

|   | Tons. |
|---|---|
| Owned by the United States, | 5,539,813 |
| " Great Britain and dependencies, | 5,895,369 |
| " all other nations, | 5,800,767 |
|  | 17,235,949 |

Of this total the United States owned nearly one-third, Great Britain over one-third, and all other maritime nations the remaining third. Mr. MORSE, United

merchants were competing successfully for the traffic, under canvas, of every ocean; and they participated with profit even in the carrying trade between different parts of the British empire. This great interest had been to that time a source of strength to our government, a source of wealth to our people. But since 1861, the almost uninterrupted growth of three-quarters of a century has been reversed, and a steady decline has been going on, which it would seem is still in progress, and which must be expected to continue, unless arrested by prompt, earnest and adequate measures of relief.

### THE TONNAGE OF 1861 AND 1867 COMPARED.

The total tonnage of the United States on the 30th of June, 1867, is given by the Register of the Treasury Department at three million eight hundred and sixty-eight thousand six hundred and fifteen tons. The total reported on the 30th of June, 1861, was five million five hundred and thirty-nine thousand eight hundred and thirteen tons, which was the highest point ever gained by us. The decline for the six years thus indicated, is one million six hundred and seventy-one thousand one hundred and ninety-eight tons, or about thirty per cent. But in order to be precise in our statements of fact, and intelligent, therefore, in our judgment, it is necessary to separate the national tonnage into two divisions — that which is employed in the internal commerce of the country, upon the rivers and lakes and along

---

States Consul at London, in a despatch to Mr. SEWARD, dated January 1, 1868, estimates that eight millions of this tonnage were employed in the international carrying trade; and he divides the amount thus:

|   |   | Tons. |
|---|---|---|
| Belonging to the United States, | . . . . . | 2,642,683 |
| " Great Britain, | . . . . . . | 3,179,628 |
| " all other nations, | . . . . . | 2,177,689 |
|   |   | 8,000,000 |

Mr. MORSE says: "Such was the sagacity and intelligence of our merchants, the capability and adventurous spirit of our mariners, and the taste and skill of our ship-wrights, that, in open competition with the old maritime nations of Europe who had been for centuries contending for ocean supremacy, they won for our young republic, not yet a century old, nearly one-third of the international ocean carrying trade of the civilized world." *Ex. Doc.* No. 283, pp. 5–6.

The British Almanac gives the tonnage of Great Britain, January 1, 1867, including twenty thousand nine hundred and thirty-seven tons foreign built, admitted to register during the previous year, as seven million three hundred and seven thousand eight hundred and fifty-one.

our coast, and that which is engaged in foreign trade. The figures for the former, or, as it is called, the enrolled and licensed tonnage, are as follows:

| | |
|---|---:|
| In 1861, | 2,897,185 |
| In 1867, | 2,514,380 |
| Difference, | 382,805 |

We have here a falling off of thirteen per cent. But, although the tonnage of 1861, as a whole, exceeded that of any year before or since, the enrolled and licensed tonnage reached its highest point in 1864:

| | |
|---|---:|
| In 1864 it was | 3,404,506 |
| In 1867 " | 2,514,380 |
| Difference, | 890,126 |

This shows a decline during the three years, in the internal waterborne transportation facilities of the country, of twenty-six per cent. But we do not here see the full decline. Since the 30th of June, 1864, a new method of measuring vessels has been in use in the United States, and many spaces are now included in the measurement, which before were not taken into the account. The proportion between the new system and the old, changes with every difference of model, and it is difficult to reach an exact estimate in reference to it; the authorities of the department think that from ten to fifteen per cent. would cover it. If we subtract only ten per cent. from the tonnage of 1867, to bring it to the same terms with that of 1864, we have the following result:

| | | |
|---|---:|---:|
| Domestic tonnage in 1864, | | 3,404,506 |
| " " " 1867, | 2,514,380 | |
| Less ten per cent., | 251,438 | |
| | | 2,262,942 |
| Difference, | | 1,141,564 |

We have declined, it would seem, in our domestic tonnage, thirty-three per cent. in the last three years; and these years, be it remembered, were years of peace, and of at least average commercial activity. If this is the condition of the coasting trade, which is jealously protected against all competition from without, what is likely to be the case in regard to the registered tonnage, that is, the tonnage engaged in foreign commerce, in rivalry with all the world? The official report gives us the following information:

| | | | | | |
|---|---|---|---|---|---|
| 1861, registered tonnage, | sail, | | 2,540,020 | | |
| " " " | steam, | | 102,608 | | |
| | | | | 2,642,628 | |
| 1867, " " | sail, | | 1,178,715 | | |
| " " " | steam, | | 175,520 | | |
| | | | | 1,354,235 | |
| Difference, | | | | 1,288,393 | |

This shows a loss of nearly fifty per cent. But, as before, if we would reach the exact truth, we must allow for the new system of admeasurement:

| | | | |
|---|---|---|---|
| Registered tonnage, 1861, | | | 2,642,628 |
| " " 1867, | | 1,354,235 | |
| Less ten per cent., | | 135,423 | |
| | | | 1,218,812 |
| | | | 1,423,816 |

The absolute decline therefore, in the foreign tonnage of the country, from 1861 to 1867, has been fifty-four per cent., or nearly a million and a half of tons.

### Growth of our Tonnage in the Past.

Let us examine this state of things in another aspect. From almost the beginning of our history as a nation, our traffic upon the sea has been steadily increasing, with occasional reverses, as between 1811 and 1814, and 1818 and 1825. Even during the period of the last war with Great Britain, our foreign tonnage fell off only twelve and a half per cent., although it should be said that during the two years previous to that war, it fell off twenty-two per cent. We have prepared the following table for the purpose of indicating the changes which have taken place in the registered tonnage of the country for the eight years from 1789 to 1797, and from 1797, by decades, to 1867:

| Year. | Regt'd tonnage | Change. | | | Rate of change. | |
|---|---|---|---|---|---|---|
| 1789 | 123,893 | . . . | | | . . . | |
| 1797 | 597,777 | Increase in | 8 years | 473,884 or | 384½ | per cent. |
| 1807 | 848,307 | " " | 10 " | 250,530 " | 42 | " |
| 1817 | 800,725 | Decrease " | 10 " | 47,582 " | 5¼ | " |
| 1827 | 747,170 | " " | 10 " | 53,555 " | 6¼ | " |
| 1837 | 810,447 | Increase " | 10 " | 68,277 " | 8¼ | " |
| 1847 | 1,241,313 | " " | 10 " | 430,866 " | 53¼ | " |
| 1857 | 2,463,967 | " " | 10 " | 1,222,654 " | 98½ | " |
| 1867 | 1,354,235 | Decrease " | 10 " | 1,109,732 " | 45 | " |

This table shows an average gain of eighty and a half per cent. for the periods given, including the remarkable growth which took place between 1789 and 1797, when, in consequence of the wars then prevailing among the maritime powers of Europe, our foreign tonnage increased three hundred eighty-four and a half per cent., and including also the decades between 1807 and 1827, when there was a decrease of five and a half and six and a half per cent. respectively. As the period from 1789 to 1797 may be considered exceptional, let us look at the growth of our foreign tonnage during the three decades between 1827 and 1857; the first of these shows an increase of only eight and a half per cent., and yet the average of the three is fifty-three and three-eighths per cent. In looking forward in 1857 through the coming ten years, it would not have been thought extravagant to anticipate an increase equal to the average of the previous thirty years. Let us see how much this difference really is, between what in 1857 would not have been an unreasonable anticipation, and the existing fact:

| | | |
|---|---:|---:|
| In 1857 our foreign or registered tonnage was, | | 2,463,967 |
| Add 53⅜ per cent. for the average growth per decade from 1827 to 1857, | | 1,315,142 |
| Our tonnage might have been expected to reach in 1867, | | 3,779,109 |
| Our actual tonnage in 1867 was, | 1,354,235 | |
| Allow 10 per cent. for new system of admeasurement, | 135,423 | |
| | | 1,218,812 |
| Showing a net difference of . | | 2,560,297 |

or, instead of a gain of fifty-three and three-eighths per cent., a loss of sixty-eight per cent.; and *leaving our foreign tonnage less than one-third of what in 1857 we should have been justified by past experience in estimating that it would be.*

### AMERICAN STEAM COMMERCE.

Our calculations thus far have not discriminated between sailing vessels and steamers. We will now turn to the foreign steam commerce of the United States, in which we shall discover a state of things still more unsatisfactory.

Our foreign steam shipping may be said to date from 1848, when it amounted to about sixteen thousand tons. In 1849 it was nearly twenty-one thousand tons. During the next year it more than doubled; and it steadily increased down to 1855, when it reached one hundred and fifteen thousand tons. From that time onward for several years it did not hold its own, its aggregate in 1862 being less by a thousand tons than it was in 1855. In 1867 it amounted to one hundred seventy-five and a half thousand tons; this included the mail service between the Atlantic and the Pacific States, but not the steamers on the northern lakes which call at British American ports. The following table will furnish an analysis of the growth of American ocean steam tonnage in the period referred to:

| Year. | Foreign Steam Tonnage. | Increase. | Rate of Increase. |
|---|---|---|---|
| 1848 | 16,068 | ... | ... |
| 1849 | 20,870 | 4,802 | 30 per cent. |
| 1850 | 44,429 | 23,559 | 113 " |
| 1851 | 62,390 | 17,961 | 40 " |
| 1852 | 79,704 | 17,314 | 28 " |
| 1853 | 90,520 | 10,816 | 13½ " |
| 1854 | 95,036 | 4,516 | 5 " |
| 1855 | 115,045 | 20,009 | 21½ " |

We here see that the average gain per annum from 1848 to 1855 was thirty-six per cent. If we take out of the account the year 1850, when the increase was one hundred and thirteen per cent., as being exceptional, we still have an annual average gain of twenty-three per cent. At this latter rate of increase, had it continued, the steam tonnage of the United States would have reached in 1862, three hundred thousand tons; instead of this, it was only, as already given, one hundred and fourteen thousand tons, less by one thousand tons than it was seven years previously, and sixty-two per cent. less than it would have been under the former ratio of development.

THE STEAM COMMERCE OF GREAT BRITAIN.

For the sake of comparison, we will now turn to the statistics of the foreign steam shipping of Great Britain, for the interval covered by the foregoing calculations. We invite attention to these, in the tabulated form in which we have placed them:

*British Steam Tonnage employed, in whole or in part, in Foreign Service.*

| Year. | Tonnage. | Change. | | Rate. |
|---|---|---|---|---|
| 1851 | 65,921 | ... | | ... |
| 1852 | 98,613 | Increase | 32,692 | 49⅔ per cent. |
| 1853 | 132,789 | " | 34,176 | 34⅔ " |
| 1854 | 158,635 | " | 25,846 | 19¼ " |
| 1855 | 231,541 | " | 72,906 | 46 " |
| 1856 | 263,439 | " | 31,898 | 13¾ " |
| 1857 | 288,882 | " | 25,443 | 9⅔ " |
| 1858 | 278,465 | Decrease | 10,417 | 3¾ " |
| 1859 | 298,650 | Increase | 20,185 | 7¼ " |
| 1860 | 307,240 | " | 8,590 | 3 " |
| 1861 | 338,389 | " | 31,149 | 10 " |
| 1862 | 357,773 | " | 19,384 | 5¾ " |

From these tables, it would appear that in 1851, the foreign steam tonnages of the United States and of Great Britain were almost equal, that of the former being sixty-two thousand three hundred and ninety tons, and that of the latter sixty-five thousand nine hundred and twenty-one tons. The difference between the two has been gradually increasing from that time to the present; although at first the variation was less marked than it has been in recent years. In 1855 the United States had only doubled its foreign steam tonnage since 1851; while that of Great Britain had gained nearly four-fold. But in 1856, as already stated, we began to fail even to hold our own, and in 1862 we had not recovered ourselves. On the other hand, Great Britain, except in 1858, had been steadily advancing year by year; and in 1862, had added more than forty per cent. to her steam tonnage of 1856, and had multiplied that of 1851 nearly six-fold. If, in the United States, the average rate of increase from 1848 to 1855 had been continued down to 1862, we should then have had within about sixty thousand tons of the foreign steam shipping of Great Britain. As it was, however, the British tonnage had grown to more than three times our own; and this most calamitous condition of affairs at the beginning of the civil war was, as was to be expected, aggravated by the events which followed. With the figures of 1862 before us, we need not be surprised by those of 1867.

### 1867 — Foreign Steam Tonnage.

| | |
|---|---:|
| Great Britain, estimate, | 775,000 |
| United States, | 175,520 |
| Difference, | 599,480 |

*This difference of nearly six hundred thousand tons is more than the combined commercial steam tonnage of the United States and Great Britain five years ago.*

### The Causes of the Decline in American Tonnage.

It needs no argument to show that the decline of our commerce upon the ocean, which the statistics we have attempted to collate so emphatically illustrate, is owing to causes as marked and as exceptional as the effect which they have produced. No ordinary fluctuations of supply and demand — no commercial vicissitudes, such as those of which we have had any experience — could have proved sufficient, not only to arrest an annual gain in our tonnage, which had been almost uninterrupted during seventy years, but also to reduce this tonnage by more than one-half. The American nation has been engaged in foreign wars, and it has been overtaken by financial revulsions; but neither the wars nor the revulsions of the past have ever affected its ocean commerce to anything like this extent. Where, then, shall we make search for causes adequate to accomplish such a result? In replying to this inquiry, we must again distinguish between the sailing and the steam tonnage employed in our foreign trade.

THE EFFECT OF THE WAR UPON OUR SAILING TONNAGE.

So far as relates to our sailing tonnage, we may safely affirm that nearly the whole of the decline which we now have occasion to deplore, is the result of the late war of rebellion, and of circumstances attending or growing out of it. In that conflict, the weakness of the national Government and of the loyal people — as is always the case with commercial nations, and in precise proportion to their commercial strength — was on the ocean. Our vessels were everywhere exposed to capture, and the Government was unable to protect them. Many were taken and destroyed; but these were few as compared with others which were sold and transferred to foreign owners. The flag of the weakest power in Europe furnished an immunity to property afloat which our own could not give. American merchants, therefore, were obliged to sell their shipping to those who could use it with safety and profit.* The almost complete cessation of ship-build-

---

* "The disastrous effects of the war of the rebellion upon our foreign trade claim our special attention, and they can hardly be overstated. During the continuance of the war every branch of Northern industry upon the land was promoted and strengthened. Production and manufactures prospered to an unwonted degree, and the tendency of every step in our national legislation was to stimulate that prosperity. It will be sufficient to refer to a single State to illustrate this. An abstract of the census of Massachusetts for the State fiscal years 1854-5 and 1864-5 respectively, prepared by Mr. E. B. ELLIOTT, shows that during the latter year, as compared with the former, the production of leather, boots and shoes, had increased nearly fifty per cent.; of cotton goods and calicoes had more than doubled; of paper had more than doubled; of clothing had nearly doubled; and of woollen goods had increased four-fold. Contrast, now, this statement with the statistics of the tonnage of Massachusetts for the same years. On the thirtieth of June, 1855, the total tonnage of this Commonwealth, foreign and domestic, was nine hundred and seventy-nine thousand two hundred and five tons; on the thirtieth of June, 1865, it was two hundred and forty-eight thousand eight hundred and thirty-six tons, or about one quarter of what it was ten years previously. Startling as the difference is which is thus developed, it is not difficult to account for it when we recall the experiences of the war. Not only did the shipping interest not participate in the stimulus received by other branches of enterprise, but it was exposed to the attack of the enemy, as all the others were not; indeed, it was the vulnerable point of the

ing for mercantile purposes followed as a necessary consequence. Thus, while the tonnage of the nation was rapidly disappearing by the ravages of the rebel cruisers and by sales abroad, in addition to the usual loss by the perils of the sea, there was no construction of new vessels going forward, to counteract the decline even in part.

Nor did the cessation of actual hostilities bring any relief to this crippled branch of our national industry. The annual decline was nearly if not quite as great during the two or three years which succeeded the restoration of peace as at any time during the continuance of the war; and we are not sure that it has yet been stopped. The returns of 1868 have not been made public; but *the registered sail tonnage of* 1867 *was less than that of* 1847, *making no allowance for the new mode of measurement, and less than that of* 1844, *making this allowance.* It is nearly four years since the last instance of capture and destruction on the high seas was reported; but the process of sale has not altogether ceased, and the loss by disasters and by ordinary wear and tear estimated at ten or twelve per cent. per annum, has been going on. And in the meantime, our shipyards have remained quiet and unused. Except for the coasting trade, very few vessels are on the stocks to-day; and these in most instances, are built for special purposes, and supply no evidence of improvement in the general business of shipbuilding and shipowning. Evidently, therefore, disastrous influences are still at work; and we must ascertain what they are, before we seek to apply measures designed to check and overcome them.

THE RELATIONS OF THE CURRENCY TO THE SHIPPING INTEREST.

One of these influences comes from the present depreciated condition of our currency. This affects the national industry in every department, but especially the shipping interest, because this is obliged to compete in the maritime centres of the globe, with tonnage built on a gold basis, and consequently at a comparatively low cost of labor and materials. This was forcibly stated by a delegate from

---

nation, and how much it suffered the figures we have quoted show only too clearly. What the raid into Pennsylvania and the burning of Chambersburg was, in one memorable instance, was, in effect, repeated upon every sea traversed by our merchant vessels. They were soon driven from the ocean; the only alternative for those that escaped the treacherous pirate was sale, either absolute or *pro forma*, to a foreign owner, whose flag could afford protection while ours could not. The disappearance of our shipping, therefore, need be no mystery to any of us." — *Hunt's Merchants' Magazine for April,* 1868; *vol.* 58, *p.* 285.

Milwaukie, at the Commercial Convention held in Boston last winter. " Why," said he, " are your ships rotting at your wharves? It is because we are away from the rock bottom on which the nations of the earth transact business. When we can get back to the right basis, we shall again have free commercial intercourse with the world." Of course with a redundant and irredeemable currency, we cannot compete in the construction of vessels, with the people of those countries in which a specie standard prevails to regulate prices and to give stability to values.

### THE TARIFF AND INTERNAL TAXATION.

Our present tariff and system of internal taxation, also, have operated prejudicially to the shipping interest of the country. The effect of the tariff has been, first, in protecting and promoting production at home, to diminish our foreign trade, and so, to lessen the demand for tonnage ; and, secondly, in connection with internal taxes, to enhance the price of many of the most important materials used in building and outfitting vessels. The legislation of the last few years, while developing almost every other kind of manufactures, has made it well nigh impossible for our mechanics to build ships for use in general commerce, or for our merchants to own them. A careful estimate shows that the duties paid on the foreign iron, copper, hemp and other articles entering into the construction and completion of an American vessel, amount to seven dollars a ton in gold. As against this, the policy of Great Britain and other maritime nations is to remit the imposts upon all shipbuilding materials and ship supplies, so as to encourage their foreign trade to the utmost. What hope of successful competition in the carrying trade of the ocean can there be for the American ship under these circumstances?

As the result of the depreciation of our currency and the severity of our taxation, we have it on the authority of the Hon. Mr. PIKE, of Maine, that a thousand ton ship would cost a builder of his State eighty-five thousand dollars in currency, while a similar vessel could be built in the adjoining British provinces for forty-five thousand dollars in gold. And as was truly said by this gentleman in the House of Representatives at Washington last winter : " It is apparent that our ships cannot compete with foreign ships, when the difference of cost is so great, unless a corresponding advantage is in some way given to them in the way of employment. But the House is aware that an American ship has no such advantages. She competes with her great rival on a free trade basis. The St. John ship comes into the port of New York and gets the same freight and is subject to the same insurance as the American ship. The only privilege the American ship has is that of the coast-wise trade, and that is hardly appreciable."

We have testimony to the same effect in a despatch on the commercial policy of Great Britain, addressed by Mr. MORSE, United States Consul at London, under date of January 1, 1868, to Mr. SEWARD, in which it is said: — "Taxation on importations is necessary for revenue, and to encourage and strengthen the growth of some of our industries by limiting foreign competition in our home markets; but it seriously cripples, and may fatally wound an interest, the position and value of which cannot be determined by ourselves. As long as our ports are wisely kept open to the reception of cargoes from foreign ships, as long as the freedom of the sea is maintained and we send our ships out thereon to seek business in its harbors and commercial ports, we must go into the freight markets of the world as nearly on an equality with all maritime powers as possible. In those markets the true practical value of American ships must be determined, whatever nominal or fictitious value our legislation may attempt to force upon them within our limits. This legislation can give a high comparative value to our coasting tonnage, because of that we have and can hold the monopoly, and admit no foreign competition. But when we go beyond the reach of the local laws which secure this monopoly — and all maritime nations practically secure to themselves this home trade in some way — the true value of such out-going ships is in reality controlled by the contestants for the prizes of commerce, and not by ourselves. If by any means of excessive taxation we place a cost value on American tonnage so far above that of our competitors, and if we continue the use of perishable materials instead of iron in its construction, we shall in time, by our own voluntary action, exclude ourselves from this most desirable and honorable international competition, acknowledge ourselves unequal to the contest, disperse our keels, call home our flag, and circumscribe that commerce which but so recently led all rivals in the race of the seas, to the comparatively narrow limits of our own coasts, rivers and lakes."*

### REASONS WHY OUR OCEAN STEAM COMMERCE HAS NOT FLOURISHED.

Let us recur now to the steam tonnage of the United States, registered for the foreign trade. The utter want of vitality which characterizes this branch of our mercantile marine, cannot be accounted for

---

* *Exec. Doc.* No. 283, pp. 10, 11.

by the reasons assigned for the decline of our shipping under canvas. These reasons are intimately related to the civil war of 1861 to 1865; but the foreign steam commerce of the United States, at the opening of that war, has been shown to have been less than it was seven years previously. In the spring of 1861, there were no ocean mail steamers, away from our own coasts, anywhere on the globe, under the American flag — except, perhaps, on the route between New York and Havre, where two steamships may then have been in commission, which, however, were soon afterwards withdrawn. The two or three steamship companies, which had been in existence in New York, had either failed or abandoned the business; and the entire mail, passenger and freight traffic between Great Britain and the United States, so far as this was carried on by steam, was controlled then, as it is now, by British companies. Clearly, therefore, our lamentable deficiency in ocean steam navigation antedates the war, and is not chargeable upon it. Undoubtedly, any endeavors to promote it now are made vastly more difficult than they would otherwise be by the expanded condition of the currency and the pressure of taxation, to which allusion has just been made; but, judging from the past, the removal of these disabilities, which would make it possible to renew our sailing tonnage, would not materially assist our people in the construction of foreign steamers. Why then was our attempt to participate in the advantages and emoluments of ocean steam commerce between 1848 and 1861 an absolute failure; and why have we been no less unsuccessful since?

At the outset the United States was behind Great Britain in the creation of a commercial steam marine. The Cunard company, so called, was incorporated and subsidized in 1838, and the West India and Peninsular companies were in 1840. These three packet lines were navigating the Atlantic, the Carribbean, the Mediterranean and the waters of the East, and another British company had occupied the Pacific coast of South America, several years before the *Washington* and the *Hermann*, our first ocean mail steamers, took their departure from New York for Southampton and Bremen. The Cunard vessels had been running ten years, and were making weekly trips, before, in 1850, the *Atlantic* went to sea as the pioneer of the Collins line. It looked then, however, as if, although late in the start, we might soon overtake our rival. In a single year, 1849–50, we had increased our foreign steam shipping one hundred and thirteen per cent. The sea-going qualities and performances of our mail steamers had been so admirable, that the Cunard Company was obliged to bring out new ships to compete with them. The development subsequently was steady, and perhaps healthful, until 1855; then the retrogression commenced. In September, 1854, the *Arctic* was lost; the *Pacific* left the Mersey for New York in January, 1856, and was never heard from again. Mr. COLLINS and his associates, already deeply involved, could not sustain these terrible disasters, and early in 1857, they went into liquidation. From the effect of their misfortunes, American ocean commerce has never recovered. We gradually withdrew from the competition for the carrying trade of the Atlantic ocean, which, before the days of steam, was almost entirely in our hands; and now, although the steamship departures and arrivals at New York to and from European ports are almost daily, they are without exception under foreign flags. Of the fifty or more steamers, with an aggregate tonnage of one hundred and twenty-five thousand tons, engaged in this trade at the present time, not one of them all belongs to the United States. The steamships which connect Boston and Portland with Europe, are owned abroad. So also, largely, are the vessels recently placed on the route between Baltimore and Bremen, under the enlightened patronage of the Baltimore and Ohio Railroad. Lines have recently been started between Charleston and New Orleans respectively, and Liverpool; but they are English lines. Thus are our ports, one by one, taken possession of for the benefit of foreign capital and commerce. Our strictly foreign steam commerce consists of one or two lines from New York to Havana; a monthly line, partly supported by the Brazilian Government, from New York to Rio de Janeiro; and a monthly service, performed by the Pacific Mail Company, from San Francisco to Japan and China.

THE POLICIES OF THE BRITISH AND AMERICAN GOVERNMENTS COMPARED.

We need not look far for an explanation of the foregoing facts. The British Government has had a policy in reference to ocean steam commerce, definite, comprehensive and persistent; the policy of our own Government on this subject has been uncertain, partial and spasmodic. The former regards an annual expenditure of a million sterling in the maintenance of its packet service as one of its most judicious outlays — one of its best investments; believing, as an English statesman once expressed it, that "swift ships bring swift orders for goods." The latter has, of late certainly, regarded it as a wiser economy to pay several hundred thousand dollars a year to foreign companies for the conveyance of its mails, than to make grants to its own citizens to encourage them to undertake this service. Only once has there been legislation at Washington in relation to this great interest, in any degree worthy of the issues involved; and even then, the principles which govern all judicious and sound encouragement of ocean steamship enterprise, would seem not to have been distinctly apprehended. It is not necessary at this time to discuss the treatment of the Collins Company by our Government, although it ought to be said that the failure of the line, sooner or later, was, in our judgment, inevitable, managed as it was, whether its subventions had been continued to it or not. For ourselves, we have never blamed the Government, which had been only too lenient from the first, for withholding further payments of money after the loss of the *Pacific*. We do not see how these could properly have been continued, except with new guarantees and under more safe restrictions. But, in our view, Congress made a most serious mistake at that juncture, in not immediately appointing a special committee to inquire into all the causes of the company's embarrassment, and particularly into all the circumstances, so far as known, of the destruction of its steamers. Such a committee might have reported with a scheme for the resuscitation of the line upon a more careful and conservative plan; or with a project for the organization of an entirely new company, which should profit by the misfortunes of its predecessor, and perform the service in the interest of the nation, which it had undertaken, but had proved itself unable to carry out. Instead of all this, Congress gave up the whole question in despair, and apparently acted on the presumption that where Mr. COLLINS had failed, no one else could succeed. Judicious investigation and wise discrimination might have led to new efforts on the part of our merchants, notwithstanding the discouragements of the past; and in 1861 we might have had a commercial steam marine which no privateers could injure, and which would have been of incalculable advantage to the Government and to the nation during the war.*

### MISTAKES OF THE MERCANTILE COMMUNITY.

We shall not, we hope, be understood as intimating that our mercantile community was altogether free from blame for the failure as late as 1861 to successfully establish steam commerce under the American flag. The mistakes of the Collins Company have been

---

* For a history of the course pursued by Congress with the Collins Company, see an article on Ocean Steam Navigation in the *North American Review* for October, 1864, pp. 490–502.

incidentally referred to ; unfortunately they were the mistakes of the American public at the time, quite as much as of the company itself. It is not likely that all of these will be repeated in our future efforts in this behalf; and yet it is to be feared that thoroughly intelligent and practical views on this subject do not as generally prevail among us as could be wished. Strangely enough, our merchants are still to a considerable extent unfamiliar with or indifferent to the paramount advantages of propulsion by the screw; although this has been adopted almost universally by the foreign lines. The experiment has been so thoroughly made before our eyes by British, French and German companies, that one would suppose it was hardly necessary for us to work out the costly problem for ourselves. This, however, we are doing; and we are beginning to find out what others could have told us, that paddle-wheel steamers cannot profitably be employed upon long ocean routes. Our slowness to learn this lesson, has had much to do with bringing us, as a nation, to our present mortifying position, in reference to the navigation of the ocean by steam ; and if persisted in, it will render all our attempts futile in time to come.

## The Remedies.

No intelligent and patriotic citizen can contemplate, not to say with indifference, but without feelings of the deepest anxiety, this condition of our ocean commerce ; and the National Board of Trade, established for the purpose of securing " the proper consideration of questions pertaining to the financial, commercial and industrial interests of the country at large," cannot but avail itself of the earliest opportunity to direct attention thereto. This Board is solicitous for the prosperity, no less of the national commerce, both foreign and domestic, than of agriculture and manufactures. It recognizes the intimate relations which subsist between the manifold and diversified pursuits of American industry and uses of American capital; and it appreciates the necessity which exists for the success of each of these, in order to the best security of all. Without seeking to discriminate as to the comparative importance of any of them over the rest, it must naturally feel an especial concern in behalf of that one which has for many years been suffering as none others have, and which, without the application of remedial measures, may be found at no distant period to be absolutely past help.

What remedies, then, shall this Board propose ? These have been suggested, in part perhaps, as we have been considering the depression of the shipping interest and its causes ; but they deserve to be noticed more specifically. In this connection it will be enough simply to declare that for the early restoration of our foreign commerce, as well as for the permanent well-being of every description of business at home, a sound and solvent currency is indispensable. No change in our navigation laws, making them conformable to the legislation of the most advanced and most highly favored mercantile communities on the globe, would afford more than temporary relief, if the American mechanic and the American merchant were still deprived of all the advantages which accompany a circulating medium equal to money. We must return to the gold standard before we can hope to compete with any degree of success with the enterprise of specie-paying countries. These considerations, however, in their general application will be more fully discussed at another stage of the meeting; they appear under a distinct head, at the instance of the Board of Trade of St. Louis, in the official programme of our proceedings, and we need not enlarge on them now. May we not safely assume that our industrial, our producing and our commercial classes will not much longer remain contented with the fluctuations and the contingencies of our present monetary system; and that they will determine to base all their operations henceforward on that "rock bottom," to which allusion has been made, as that "on which the nations of the earth transact business."

Apart then from the question of currency, two measures are, in our judgment, indispensable to the revival of our carrying trade: first, the remission of import duties and internal taxes on the chief articles required for the construction and outfit of vessels to be employed in foreign commerce; second, governmental encouragement, by a well defined system of subsidies to ocean steam lines.

### THE REMISSION OF TARIFF AND INTERNAL DUTIES.

First, *The remission of duties and taxes on articles used in building and outfitting vessels for our foreign trade.* This is the policy of Great Britain, of France and of British North America, our chief competitors in the carrying trade of the world. It has been deliberately adopted by them; and, as it has come to be regarded with unqualified favor by their public men of all parties, there is no probability that it will ever be given up. Under it their shipping interests have flourished as never before; and from it even greater benefits are anticipated than any which it has yet yielded. In the United States, previously to the civil war, we had a moderate tariff, and no internal taxes. We were able, therefore, to maintain our position, so far as related to sailing tonnage, with credit and with profit. But our ship-builders and our merchants were forcibly driven from the competition during the continuance of hostilities; and they have since found themselves utterly unable to regain their standing, in consequence of the taxation entailed upon them by the war. They must be relieved from this taxation, or all hope of the restoration of our tonnage must be indefinitely postponed. This is the alternative. Even if the principle of remitting the duties were not wise in itself, seeing that it has been definitively accepted by the leading commercial nations, we shall be obliged, unless prepared to withdraw altogether from the ocean, to govern ourselves in conformity with it. But the experience of those who have tested it, has demonstrated that it is eminently wise, and that while working no injustice to any other branch of industry, it gives a healthful stimulus to the enterprise of the ship-builder and the ship-owner. Its adoption also in this country, would be quite in harmony with the theory of protection, which is the basis of our present revenue laws. A prominent and an able protectionist recently made the remark to us, that the views supported by him include just as much the taking off of duties in certain instances, as of imposing them in others, and aim at providing for our deficiencies equally with caring for our productions; the purpose being always to place the American mechanic and manufacturer as nearly as possible on the same footing as the European. For a few years past, however, we have in effect had one law for the builder of ships, and another for the manufacturer in iron, cotton or wool. Against the former there has been discrimination, by duties imposed on the home-made article; in favor of the latter there has been protection, by duties imposed on the foreign fabric. Ought such inequality to continue?

### OBJECTIONS CONSIDERED.

It has been objected to the remission of duties which we recommend, that there are difficulties of a practical and administrative character which cannot be overcome. We have heard it said that there would be an embarrassment sometimes in deciding upon the amount of drawback to which builders would be entitled; and that there would be constant opportunity for perpetrating frauds upon the Government. Similar arguments might be urged against every description of tax and every method of collection; but surely it is not proposed to abandon a great national interest to permanent decline, because the measures indispensable to its relief and revival will involve an expenditure of labor in maturing them, and of skill in executing them. Are we prepared to admit that wherein Great Britain and

Canada have shown themselves able to administer a judicious law, the United States would prove incapable?

It is objected further, that to concede a drawback to our ship-builders, while refusing to allow our merchants to purchase vessels abroad, is to discriminate improperly against the latter. If this shall be the view of Congress and of the country, let our navigation laws be so modified as to permit the register of foreign tonnage, as well as to give the benefit of drawback to ships built here. There are many among us who are prepared for all this, at least temporarily, by way of experiment;* and some of the most intelligent ship-builders on our coast would like to see it tried. In Great Britain the drawback system and the admission to registry of foreign built ships have gone together, and both have contributed to the unparalleled increase of British tonnage. Since 1866, the same policy has been adopted by France, and with like success. As relates to the United States, the burden of proof is upon those who deny that the same agencies which have secured the results witnessed elsewhere, will lead to the same results here.†

---

*Mr. MORSE admits the principle, in his despatch to Mr. SEWARD; he says, "It may also be thought expedient to permit the purchase by American citizens, of such foreign built steamers of not less than two thousand tons burden, as may at any time within a given day, be immediately wanted to put on any established and regular line between the United States and any foreign country."

†Since the above was written, the annual report of the Secretary of the Treasury for 1868 has appeared; and as its recommendations in behalf of the shipping interest, strongly confirm the suggestions made in this paper, the writer takes pleasure in transcribing them:

"In his report for the year 1866, the Secretary called the attention of Congress especially to the condition of the shipping interest of the United States. In his report of last year, he again referred to it in the following language:

"'The shipping interest of the United States, to a great degree prostrated by the war, has not revived during the past year. Our shipyards are, with rare exceptions, inactive. Our surplus products are being chiefly transported to foreign countries in foreign vessels. The Secretary is still forced to admit, in the language of his report, that with unequalled facilities for obtaining the materials, with acknowledged skill in ship-building, with thousands of miles of seacoast, indented with the finest harbors in the world, with surplus products that require in their transportation a large and increasing tonnage, we can neither profitably build ships, nor successfully compete with English ships in the transportation of our own productions.

"'No change for the better has taken place since that report was made. On the contrary, the indications are that the great ship-building interest of the Eastern and Middle States has been steadily declining, and that, consequently, the United States is gradually ceasing to be a great maritime power. A return to specie payments will do much, but will not be sufficient, to avert this declension and give

The following emphatic language, from an influential commercial newspaper, confirms the opinions which we have endeavored to express:

"In Great Britain, in France and in the Dominion of Canada, everything seems to be done to favor and to promote ocean commerce. In the United States, a policy the very reverse of this has too long prevailed. We will not for a moment believe that our congressional legislation has been expressly designed to weaken and to destroy the foreign commerce of the nation; but we confess that, had there been any such purpose on the part of those who have framed the laws, these need not have been made essentially different from what they have been and still are. The very bunting which is used to display aloft our emblazoned nationality, is charged with a tariff duty of one hundred and twenty-five per cent.; and the chain cables and anchors, which are employed to hold our vessels in safety in the roadstead, are burdened with an impost exceeding the total cost, at which all merchants, except those of the United States, can supply themselves with them. And almost everything else entering into the construction and outfit of American ships is taxed with a like severity, amounting almost to prohibition. No wonder that our merchants are changing their investments from the water to the land, and that the foreign carrying trade is being abandoned to the more favored citizens of other countries."

OCEAN STEAMSHIP SUBSIDIES.

Secondly: *Governmental subsidies to ocean steam lines.* Here again we find ourselves called upon to decide between following the example of others, and giving up the expectation of competing even feebly for a share in the carrying trade of the ocean. Here again also, we have convincing testimony in favor of the course which expediency would seem to point out to us. And we have the added testimony supplied by the results of a course entirely the reverse of this, which we have hitherto maintained. The tables of British and American steam shipping, to which we have asked attention, illustrate with the

---

activity to our shipyards. The materials which enter into the construction of vessels should be relieved from taxation by means of drawbacks; or if this may be regarded as impracticable, subsidies might be allowed as an offset to taxation. If subsidies are objectionable, then it is recommended that all restrictions upon the registration of foreign-built vessels be removed, so that the people of the United States, who cannot profitably build vessels, may be permitted to purchase them in the cheapest market. It is certainly unwise to retain upon the statute books a law restrictive upon commerce, when it no longer accomplishes the object for which it was enacted.'

"What was said by the Secretary in 1866 and 1867 upon the subject is true at the present time, and he therefore feels it his duty to repeat his recommendations. The shipping interest was not only prostrated by the war, but its continued depression is attributable to the financial legislation, and the high taxes consequent upon the war. The honor and the welfare of the country demand its restoration."

utmost distinctness the two policies and their effects. Shall we heed the lessons which they teach?

Our national legislation on this subject, to be permanently efficient, must be based upon sound commercial principles, and it must be as broad as the country itself. A grant of money should never be made for the benefit of speculators or monopolists; nor should it be sufficiently liberal to permit, not to say encourage, gross and persistent mismanagement. No undue advantage should be given to one city over another. It should not be the object to start a single line, upon which all the liberality of the Government shall be lavished, and on the achievements of which all the world shall be invited to gaze. We do not want a second Collins company, brilliant and unsuccessful. We have made one costly attempt for the sake of glory; let us be actuated next time by a sober desire for gain. It is not so much an ocean steamship line, as an ocean steamship system, of which we now stand urgently in need. The West, the South, the North, need this. The interior needs it equally with the seaboard; Cincinnati, St. Louis and Chicago, no less than Baltimore, Philadelphia, New York and Boston. The system therefore, in all its features, must be the opposite of everything limited, local and special. The Atlantic Ocean should be treated for commercial purposes, as part of our territorial domain; and the importance of organizing and controlling transportation upon its waters in the interest of American commerce, should be regarded as only less than of doing this on the land. We must establish steamship lines for the purpose of supplementing the service of our railroads; and in all that is attempted in this behalf, the interdependence of the inland and the ocean traffic of the country must be kept in view. Only thus can we place the granaries and storehouses of the West in proper communication with the markets of the world.

At the last session of Congress, a bill was introduced by the Hon. Mr. ELIOT, of New Bedford, in the House of Representatives and is now pending, which, in our judgment, is the first proposal of a truly national character which has been brought forward for the encouragement of American steamship enterprise. This bill has reference to no particular company, and to no particular route. It comprehends the general necessities of the traffic at large, between the United States and Great Britain, France and the North Sea ports. It vests authority in the Postmaster-General, to make contracts for a specified period with responsible individuals or corporations for the conveyance of the mails in American steam vessels at a stipulated sum for each round voyage. It prescribes the size and general character of the ships to be employed, and fixes the rate of speed. It is to be hoped that, during the coming winter, this bill will be passed by both houses, substantially in the form in which it was presented; as, under the limitations and checks which it contemplates, one or more transatlantic steam lines would probably soon be established, and in a way which would enable them to maintain themselves in competition with the European companies, without any excessive outlay of the public money.

### Two Objections Replied To.

Two arguments only, worthy of notice at this time, are adduced in opposition to the policy now recommended. The first of these is the consideration of economy, and of the necessity for retrenchment in the national expenditures. The words economy and retrenchment have a plausible sound; but in themselves they are utterly meaningless,—just as adjectives are, when disconnected from their nouns substantive. Their value depends altogether upon what they are intended to qualify. In our view, a wise economy consists not always in the non-expenditure of money, but in the disbursement of money for purely national objects, and in measure adjusted carefully to the necessities of the case in each instance. The refusal of an appropriation of a million of dollars may or may not be an instance of economy. If the object to be promoted have no proper claim on the consideration of the Government, or if it ought to and could be secured by supplying say one-half of this sum, it would indicate sound financial sense to vote accordingly. On the other hand, if the proposed expenditure give assurance of adequate and ample returns not otherwise to be had, to refuse the grant would be short-sighted parsimony. We all know that in mercantile life, a man may appear to be very profuse, and yet be a wise manager; he may be very saving, and yet very improvident. And no less in public than in private concerns, economy and retrenchment are relative and not absolute terms; and therefore applications for the pecuniary encouragement of the Government should be judged strictly upon the merits of each enterprise by itself, and not simply or primarily as matters involving the outlay of money. We should sometimes ask, Can the country afford *not* to foster this or that project? instead of always raising the inquiry whether it can afford to do what is requested. All this is so generally accepted as true, that it would seem to be hardly necessary to repeat it here. But in fact this plea of economy is one which is urged immediately, at Washington, whenever the condition of our ocean steam shipping is brought to notice, and it is considered a valid and sufficient answer to every application for relief. Hence it is that this great interest has been allowed to languish for so many years, and that to-day it has almost ceased to exist.

The other argument brought against legislation favorable to the creation of an American ocean steam commerce, comes from those who object on principle to anything like protection to particular interests, or to the building up of particular interests at the public expense. This has its influence to a very considerable extent at the West; and largely also at the East, with thoughtful men of one school of political economy. It is said: Foreign companies are performing for us in a very satisfactory manner, the transportation and mail service between this continent and the rest of the world, and they are willing to supply the capital for extending this service as rapidly as it may be required. Why, then, should we not leave ocean steam navigation to those who, by experience and by many favoring circumstances, are abundantly qualified to sustain it, and whose governments are disposed to contribute large subsidies to help them, while we confine ourselves to pursuits in which we can engage to better advantage, and without competition from abroad? This statement of the question implies a readiness to give up to others all the emoluments of the carrying trade of the ocean, even that which grows out of our own relations with other countries; and this again involves the abandonment of our position as a first-class naval power, for, if any lesson is taught by history, it is that when the ocean commerce of a people has declined, its naval influence has suffered in the same proportion. But not to dwell upon this, we would say that when the principle of what is called protection to American industry is deliberately given up, and we are all left unassisted and untrammelled either to produce or to purchase whatever we please and wherever we choose, the ship-building and the ship-owning classes will conform to the established policy, such as it may be, and will take their chances with the rest. They only ask now that our revenue system may be in harmony with itself, an unit in all its applications. As already remarked, during recent years there has been one law for the ship-builder and another for the manufacturer. So also, by many, a principle has been laid down for ocean steam navigation, the very reverse of that which governs them in reference to all enterprise upon the land. They would leave the mail and passenger and merchandise traffic of the ocean to be carried on by whoever can do it the best, without regard to nationality; yet they would protect those among us who raise wool, or spin cotton, or manufacture iron, against all competition from foreigners. Such inconsistency could only result in confusion; and in the instance before us, it has proved almost fatal to the one unassisted pursuit. The exceptional case, also, will be seen to be that one of all others, which under an anti-protectionist policy, might plead that it ought to receive national aid; because, while in common with the rest, it has to compete with the capital and the industry of foreign citizens, it is obliged as they are not, to further compete, with the liberal endowments of foreign governments. On every ground, therefore, of consistency and justice, as well as of high expediency, it would seem that there should be nothing less than an uniform and universal law for the fostering encouragement of American industry in all its varied pursuits, whether upon the land or upon the sea.

### Ground of Encouragement for the Future.

We have thus cursorily reviewed the shipping interests of the United States, both in its past prosperity and in its present depression. The decline in our foreign sailing tonnage which we have traced, cannot be charged to any want of skill on the part of our artizans, or of ability on the part of our seamen, or of enterprise on the part of our merchants. It is not a retrogression following upon a time of undue expansion; it is not a reaction from a course of stimulating legislation. It began with the late civil war; it went on during its progress; and it has continued, notwithstanding the return of peace. It has suffered doubly during the last seven years, as no other interest among us has suffered, first, from the actual ravages of war; secondly, from war legislation. The effects of the former, time only can cure; from the severity of the latter, Congress can at once relieve it. Our lack of ocean steam tonnage is the result of other causes. We failed at the outset to foresee the controlling influence which steam was to exert in the commerce of the globe; and when, after a time, we sought to avail ourselves of the new agency, our plans were without breadth, and our purposes without steadfastness. As a consequence, we are, in this respect, twenty years behind our maritime compeers; and here again, Congress must intervene, if it is intended that the nation shall retrieve what it has lost. It is late, but not too late, to make the attempt. France did not seek to participate in the advantages of ocean steam commerce until within a comparatively recent period; but under the progressive and determined commercial policy of the imperial government, the French flag now boasts lines of steamers on the Atlantic, the Mediterranean and the Indian Oceans, which are maintaining themselves most creditably in competition with the long established British companies. There is still room for the United States in the steam traffic of the globe. The trade of the Atlantic has not, by any means, seen its full development; year by year and decade by decade, the intercourse between America and Europe, socially and commercially, is destined to increase. The trade of the Pacific is yet in its infancy. On both the oceans which bound our continental republic, steam lines are to be multiplied almost indefinitely. The responsibility rests with Congress to decide how many of these lines shall traverse the seas in the interest of American industry, and in the service of the national flag. Individual capital is inadequate to the exigency. Associated capital in consequence of the discouragements of the past and the disabilities of the present, it has been found impossible hitherto to divert in this direction. But when the merchants of the United States shall see that the Government feels anxiously concerned for the revival of our maritime commerce, and that it is prepared to second and support their efforts in its behalf, the means will be forthcoming, and the ability will not be lacking to establish and to sustain steam lines which shall prove themselves not unworthy either of the competition into which they will have to enter, or of the nationality whose traditional renown upon the ocean it will be made their duty to maintain.

The foregoing very able paper of Mr. HILL, is filled with facts and figures that show the decay of the shipping interest of the United States, and consequently the falling off of the demand for American built ships, the closing of the shipyards and the scattering of the workmen, to whose skill and ability in this branch of labor we are indebted for our success in promptly filling up our navy to the necessities of the late war. While it is unnecessary to repeat any of the facts therein stated, yet one very important fact has only been alluded to — it is that foreign capitalists are supplying us with carrying facilities for an extensive commerce.

During the month of November, just passed, thirty-eight foreign-built steamers left the city of New York for Europe. The smallest steamer, the *City of Cork*, one thousand five hundred and thirty-nine tons; the largest, the *Scotia*, three thousand eight hundred and sixty-five tons, an average of two thousand four hundred and sixty tons. Thus, ninety-three thousand four hundred and eighty tons left the city of New York bound for Europe, in foreign-built steamers. Suppose these steamers have brought as well ninety-three thousand four hundred and eighty tons of merchandise to our shores, it amounts to one hundred and eighty-six thousand nine hundred and sixty tons of freight, which, at an average freight of three dollars in gold per ton, (the steam rate of freight,) amounts to one million four hundred and ninety-five thousand six hundred and eighty dollars in gold, showing what we had to pay in the month of November as freight on our merchandise to the foreign capitalists who supply us with our carrying facilities. Besides those from New York, foreign built steamers have left other cities, bound for Europe, swelling this large sum still more. Besides steamers, sailing vessels under foreign flags, are bringing our sugar and molasses from the West Indies; the largest importers of the United States say that a very large proportion of these imports is brought in foreign built vessels.

Do foreign capitalists derive any advantage by carrying our merchandise? A German merchant, owner of stock in the Hamburg Line of Steamers, stated that the line had made twenty per cent. dividends, and been able to build out of their surplus a new steamer every year.

This line consists now of ten steamers, and one on the stocks.

There are now eight lines of foreign built steamers running from New York, owned by foreign capitalists, and protected by the flags of England, France, the North German Confederation, and the free city of Hamburg.

By acts of Parliament during the reign of the present Queen of England, all restriction has been removed, both as regards ownership of foreign built vessels and the nationality of the seamen required to sail them.

No other interests are prevented from hiring operatives wherever they can be hired to the best advantage. The emigrant just landed upon our shores, and before he has come into contact with the naturalization machines, may be employed by the cotton and iron manufacturers, but not by the ship-owner, who must wait until the foreigner is regenerated and has become an American citizen.

The English Government was not slow to recognize the superiority of American clipper ships, and allowed its subjects to become owners of American built ships, transferring them to its own fostering care, and protecting them by its own flag. The result has proved its wisdom. English clipper ships built on our models, now sail side by side with the ships thus purchased, and as fast as the American built ship is worn out, the newly built clipper, launched from the British yard, takes its place.

The following statement was made to the Legislature of the State of Maine, which shows that the duty upon materials entering into ship-building amounts to about seven dollars in gold per ton, or say ten dollars in currency:

"By a careful investigation of the duties upon materials entering into the construction of a ship, we find that they would amount in round numbers to seven dollars per ton in gold; reducing the cost of building a ship at present, sixty-eight dollars in currency, to a gold basis, in round numbers it would be forty-one dollars; deducting duties, seven dollars per ton, it would be thirty-four dollars per ton, which is as cheap as a spruce and hack ship could be bought for in the Provinces."

The Committee, therefore, recommend the adoption of the three following resolutions:

*Resolved*, That the National Board of Trade respectfully and earnestly urges on the Congress of the United States the enactment of such measures of relief to the foreign and domestic commerce of the United States as shall enable us to compete with the commerce of other nations on the ocean, and thereby permit the promoters of our merchant marine to regain for our country her proud position on the high seas, from which she has been driven by the late war of rebellion.

*Resolved*, That this Board, representing all sections and all interests of the United States, recommends to Congress the enactment of such laws as will allow American citizens the right to purchase, build or equip, in any part of the world, any boats or vessels, propelled either by sails or by steam, that may be required for commercial purposes, and as will admit such boats or vessels to register or enrolment under the American flag, on payment of a fixed duty on their cost; and it further recommends a remission of duty on vessels built in the United States equal to the amount of duty paid upon all materials entering into their construction.

*Resolved*, That in view of the great disadvantages under which American commerce has long labored, and of the severe competition to which it is exposed, this Board deems it expedient that American lines of ocean steamers should be aided by our Government temporarily at least by a preference in carrying the mails, and by a liberal compensation for the same.

EDWARD HINCKEN, New York,
CHARLES G. NAZRO, Massachusetts,
J. B. BROWN, Maine,
JAMES R. BRANCH, Virginia,
HENRY WINSOR, Pennsylvania,
E. O. STANARD, Missouri,
W. M. EGAN, Illinois,
*Committee.*

JOHN H. BOYNTON, *Secretary.*

The first resolution reported by the Committee was carried without debate.

The PRESIDENT: The question is on the adoption of the second resolution.

Mr. ROPES: I move the adoption of the first part of the second resolution in regard to the purchase and building of foreign vessels abroad, ending with the word "cost."

Mr. KIRKLAND: I second the motion.

Mr. BRUNOT: I rise to a point of order. If it is desired that the latter part of the resolution should be acted upon in a certain way, it would greatly modify the opinion of gentlemen in regard to the first. I desire that the resolution come before the Board as a whole.

Mr. GUTHRIE: I agree with Mr BRUNOT, that the action of the Board with regard to the first part, will modify their opinions with regard to the latter part.

Mr. NAZRO: It appears to me that this resolution is one of great importance for this body to pass. We are in a suffering condition with regard to our navigation, and it is important that we should take the earliest measures to facilitate the reconstruction of our commercial marine.

While there were many resolutions before the Committee to which I could not agree, when this proposition was brought forward it commended itself most clearly to my mind. While we propose to take advantage of the facilities given by other countries for building vessels, we desire to protect our labor by charging a proper duty on the vessels.

With regard to the latter clause, it seems to me it should go in: it is in accordance with the great American principle of not taxing raw material. It would be the course of wisdom towards our own mechanics, to have a remission of these duties, so that while foreign vessels come, and under a proper duty are admitted, we may also build, without paying a heavy duty on the raw material.

I hope the resolution will be passed as a whole, so that the Board may vote intelligently; I hope there will be no division.

The PRESIDENT: I decide that it is substantially two resolutions. Under that decision the first part of it is before the Board. The whole subject may be discussed; either the proposition immediately pending, or others bearing upon the general subject.

Mr. WETHERILL: I hope this resolution will not be divided. The matter should be settled in a spirit of compromise; those who are in favor of the resolution as it stands may not be inclined to vote for the latter part of it separated. The Philadelphia delegation desire to vote for it as it stands. They desire to amend it so that the products of American soil may be protected.

The PRESIDENT: If the gentlemen desire to make them one, it may be accomplished by agreeing to consider them one.

A motion was submitted to that effect and was carried.

Mr. BRUNOT: I move, Sir, to strike out from the resolution all after the word "cost," and I ask the indulgence of the house while I give my reasons.

After the adoption of the present Constitution of the United States, the very first act of Congress, passed, had prefixed to it a preamble, which was exceptional, I believe, as giving a reason for the enactment of a law. It declared why it was necessary that duties should be levied upon foreign products entering American ports. "Whereas," it said, "it is necessary for the support of the Government, for the discharge of the debt of the United States and for the encouragement and protection of manufactures, that duties be levied on goods imported by merchants," &c. From that day to the present, the idea of protecting the agricultural, manufacturing and commercial interests of this country by duties upon imports, has been a fundamental principle of the Government. The Commercial Convention which met at Boston a year ago and led to the formation of this Board, adopted resolutions asserting adherence to the principle of protection to American industry to be the duty of the Government, and an effective means by which to liquidate its debt. The principle was accepted by the two hundred and fifty or three hundred representatives of commercial bodies there assembled, almost without dissent. Now I do not propose to argue the question whether protection is right or wrong, but I claim it as a great principle which the Government has recognized from the beginning, and for the purpose of showing why this part of the resolution, which covertly strikes at it, should be stricken out. If any great principle or policy of the nation is proposed to be changed by the influence of this Board, how should it be accomplished? The first part of the resolution before us, recommends that foreign ships may be introduced by paying duties on their cost. This accords with our time-honored policy. The second part proposes to give a drawback to ship-builders equal to the duties paid on foreign materials used in their construction. Not content with the protective duty on competing ships, the builders of Maine want a special premium to induce them to use British timber, copper, hemp and iron, in preference to American. They would have us strike a blow at the principle of protection and at many industries for the sake of one. The purposes of this Board are national. We propose not to be used for the advancement of sectional, local, or individual interests. Nor should we permit utterances to go forth upon minor issues, which may be construed into attacks upon great principles which have not entered into the discussion. If it is proposed to attack the grand principle of protection to American industry, by which our country has attained to its present greatness, let the subject be introduced in the formal manner provided by the Constitution of this Board. Let it be discussed as thoroughly as a subject of paramount importance demands, and let your conclusions be set forth as comports with the dignity of the Board; but do not for the sake of a comparatively petty interest, be led to give your judgment to the injury of a great cause. Do not permit the sapper to strike his covered blows at the foundation of a great structure, on pretence of merely opening up his failing spring.

Our New England friends have ever been true to the interests of the whole country in all the great controversies of the century. It is well known that while right as to the interests of the whole country, they have never failed to take especial care of their own peculiar interests. Their industries have been well protected while others have sometimes suffered. The fisheries, for instance, not only received due protection, but bounties also. But I know of but one in all the list of American industries, in which the protective principle has been carried to the extent of legislative prohibition; I wish there were more. For the last forty-five years, if I am not mistaken in the time, no American citizen has been permitted, on any terms, to purchase a vessel and sail her under the American flag, unless she has been built within the bounds of the United States. It was wise legislation. Under it our commerce grew, and our ships sailed on every sea; our flag was borne into every port, and millions who looked upon it, came to share its protection upon our own shores. Generations of New England ship-builders grew rich by their monopoly of ship-building. It seems to me that of all the people in this broad land, the New England people, and of all industrial interests, the ship-building interests of Maine should be the last to attack the great principle of protection, to which they owe so much. I think it is a mistake for them, of all others, to come here with this proposition. The fact that in the clause which I have moved to strike out, we are asked to give the influence of this body to favor the business of one set or association of men, and to the probable damage of others, should be sufficient to carry my motion. At the Boston meeting, to which I have before alluded, there were present and asking for seats in the Convention, the able representatives of two important interests, the one commercial, the other industrial; the Ship-Owners' Association of New York, and the Ship-Builders' Association of the State of Maine. The Committee decided against the admission of the delegates on the ground that they came as representatives of special interests. The subjects they presented were nevertheless to be respectfully treated, and a Committee was appointed (consisting of a member from each State, I believe) to consider them and report. The Committee invited the intelligent representatives of the ship-builders and the ship-owners to address them, and were greatly instructed and interested. The gentleman from New York, on that occasion, adduced much of the matter which makes up the report which has accompanied his resolutions now under discussion. The Committee gave careful consideration to the subject, but refused unanimously, to adopt the views of the ship-owners and builders, who asked, substantially, what is expressed in this resolution. The Committee reported, in general terms, that it was desirable for Congress to devise, if possible, measures to restore the shipping interests of the United States upon the oceans of the world. But they refused to lend the influence of the body to the Ship-Building Association. They rejected this special recommendation to take off duties or give bounties to one interest of the country in preference to another, and their action was unanimously indorsed by the Convention. If the Ship-Building Association of Maine, or the Ship-Owners' Association of New York had private ends to accomplish when asking admission to the Boston Convention, I do not see how the mere fact that their delegates now present the same objects under cover of the New York Corn Exchange and the Portland Board of Trade, makes them national.

What I want here to direct attention to is, that it was impressed upon the minds of the Boston Convention that it was not expedient to admit commissioners or delegates from bodies organized for special purposes, advocating any special or peculiar interests. That idea was still more strongly impressed upon the body at Philadelphia, which met to frame the National Board, and after deliberate consideration it was embodied in the Constitution. It was provided that only bodies organized for general, and not for special or private purposes, should be admitted to representation here. The object of that was expressly, it seems to me, to keep out from the deliberations and discussions of this body, the consideration of questions of special or private interest —just such questions as this ship-building interest.

If we intend to secure respect for the deliberations of this body, if we intend that it shall accomplish the design of its organization, this use of it for private ends is one of the things against which we have got to most carefully guard. On this ground alone, I would be compelled to ask that that part of the resolution should be stricken out. We cannot consistently recommend this measure for the benefit of the ship-building interest, without allowing every other industrial interest in the country to come here with its special arguments and special advocates. For these reasons and others which I might advance, I trust my motion will prevail.

Mr. TREZEVANT: I am in favor of the resolution, and beg to propose the following amendment to the second portion of the resolution:

"And do further recommend a remission of duties on all materials entering into the construction of such vessels as shall be built in the United States."

There are other elements of commerce, and very powerful ones, in this country, besides those of the seaboard; and while I am exceedingly anxious to encourage the shipping interests of the Atlantic seaboard, from Maine to Florida, I am more than glad that an opportunity offers itself when the American shipping interests of the interior may shake hands with the seaboard. The internal commerce of the country, that which flows upon the Mississippi and its tributaries, is larger and more important than the entire maritime commerce of the country; and when we consider that the population of the country through which these waters flow, from the lakes to the gulf, is nearly half that of the Union; that in 1860 this population produced five-eighths of the corn, three-fourths of the wheat, one-half of the cotton and all the sugar of the country, we may well be desirous of furthering the interests of a population that furnishes this vast commerce of the Western waters.

Mr. KIRKLAND: I did hope when this report came up this morning for the consideration of this body, that there would be little or no debate upon it. It strikes me as being a proposition that is in no way sectional; it does not emanate from the ship-builders of Maine or from any particular section of the country; the cry comes up from the experienced merchants of the Atlantic seaboard, where our own ships are gradually rotting and disappearing, and their places supplied by ships sailing under foreign flags.

What we want now, after the devastation and almost annihilation of our steamers and other shipping from the ocean, as far as our foreign trade is concerned is, the adoption of some measures that will bring us back towards that proud preeminence that we occupied before the war. You are not asked to protect the ship-building interests of Maine, but the ship-building interests of the entire coast from Maine to California. To me it seems so eminently a national question that I am surprised at any opposition being raised to it in this body. Is not Congress, session after session, asked to change laws which experience proves to be detrimental to some particular section?

In Baltimore, from 1850 to 1858, there was an average of seventy vessels built per annum. Last year there were no vessels built there; our yards are all idle.

A gentleman on the Committee of Ways and Means in Washington, told me that what the Government wants is a tariff that will bring us duties wherewith to pay our debts. But can you pay your debts by driving your shipping out of existence? Is it not a fact that year after year our shipping is on the decline? Our merchants well know that the flag of our country is disappearing from the ocean, and our commerce year after year is being borne in foreign ships. In the Brazilian trade, in which I am interested,—at our coffee depot in Baltimore we have a railroad running up to it, so that the coffee goes direct from the ship to the car, and last year two hundred and thirty-five thousand bags were landed at that one wharf, and all from Swedish and British vessels; although the time was when it was a rarity to see a foreign vessel at that wharf. Moreover, American vessels used to make the trips in forty days, whereas now sixty days are required by foreign vessels. They were also more prompt in discharging their freight, and we have now from twenty-five to fifty per cent. more to pay for damages than when this commerce was carried in our own vessels.

How can this be remedied? Ought not American commerce to be restored? We have the enterprise, the ingenuity, the mechanical skill, and the capital; but so long as these laws remain in force there is no remedy.

I would move to amend the second resolution by adding after the word "duty," the words "and internal revenue tax."

Mr. WETHERILL: I fully approve of the resolutions now before this body, tending to advance the shipping interests of this country, and will cheerfully vote for all the resolutions presented to us by the

Committee to whom the subject was referred, with the exception of the second, which I desire to modify. I am fully aware of the condition of our commerce at the present time, and no one more deeply deplores its rapid decline than I do. I approve of the proposition of allowing, upon the payment of a proper duty, the purchase of ships in foreign ports. In the present depressed condition of shipbuilding, it is the only speedy way in which our commerce can be strengthened, and our flag once more assume the proud position it formerly held upon the sea. That the Government should moderately subsidize steamships by mail contracts, at liberal rates, or otherwise, I conceive to be proper. England with her two hundred and nine subsidized steamers, employing in that service about twelve thousand men, holds herself in readiness to support her supremacy, and to act in an emergency with a promptitude that would not be possible in any other way. In the construction of ships, however, I do not approve of the proposal that all duties upon materials entering into the construction of ships should be remitted by the Government. I favor a plan by which we should encourage the products of our own soil and of our own labor; and I am of opinion that all ships built in this country should use American, and not English iron; should be rigged with American, and not Russian hemp; should be sailed with American, and not India cotton; and that all materials used in the construction should be, if possible, of our own growth or the product of our own skill. To secure this result should be the effort of every member of this body; and that it may be accomplished without loss to the ship-builder, I am willing to place, to him, American iron on a footing with English iron, American hemp on a footing with Russian hemp, American cotton and other ship's materials, on a footing with the product of any other nation; and to do so, I will, at the proper time, offer the following amendment:

"And do further recommend that a bounty shall be allowed on all materials of American growth, or manufacture, entering into the construction of vessels built in the United States, equal in amount to the duties which would have been paid upon such articles had they been imported."

The PRESIDENT: The question is on the proposition of the gentleman from Memphis.

On being put to the vote it was declared lost.

The PRESIDENT: The question recurs upon the amendment suggested by the gentleman from Baltimore.

Mr. KREIKHAUS : I move the previous question.

The vote resulted: Yeas, 33 ; Nays, 11.

The PRESIDENT: The previous question is ordered. Mr. KIRKLAND moves to amend by inserting the words "and internal revenue tax" after the word "duty."

On being submitted to vote this was lost.

The PRESIDENT: The question now recurs upon the motion of the gentleman from Pittsburgh, to strike out all after the word "cost."

Mr. BRUNOT'S amendment was lost by the following vote: Yeas, 14 ; Nays, 38.

The PRESIDENT: The question now is upon the resolution reported by the Committee, the two resolutions being thrown into one. Under the old rules, when the previous question was called it cut off all amendments, and the previous question was merely upon the proposition as reported by the Committee, but by the recent changes in parliamentary rules, when the previous question is called the amendments are taken in order.

Mr. HAND : I call for the Yeas and Nays on the resolution as it stands printed.

The PRESIDENT : If any gentleman desires a division of the points involved in this resolution, he can call for such a division at this time.

A division of the resolution was called for by several delegates.

Mr. EGAN : I appeal from the decision of the Chair.

Mr. RANDOLPH : Is that question debatable?

The PRESIDENT: No, Sir. The decision of the Chair is, that this resolution as it stands involves two distinct propositions, and any member of this body has a right to call for a division ; such division being called for, the President directs the Secretary to call the Yeas and Nays. The decision of the Chair being appealed from, the question is, on sustaining the decision.

The Chair was sustained by the following vote: Yeas, 27 ; Nays, 24.

The Secretary proceeded to call the roll on the first part of the proposition ending with the word "cost."

Yeas: Messrs.—

| | | | |
|---|---|---|---|
| Allen, (Geo. N.,) | Davis, (Geo. W.,) | How, | Raum, |
| Bagley, | Dawson, | Ilsley, | Ropes, |
| Biggs, | Drake, | Kirkland, | Shryock, |
| Boynton, | Duvall, | Kreikhaus, | Stanard, |
| Bradford, | Egan, | Loney, | Stranahan, |
| Branch, | Fisk, | Malone, | Taussig, |
| Brannin, | Fraley, | Manson, | Taylor, |
| Brown, | Gano, | McGraw, | Thomas, |
| Brunot, | Grant, | Meier, | Thurston, |
| Buell, | Guthrie, | Michener, | Topp, |
| Burwell, | Hand, | Monroe, | Trezevant, |
| Buzby, | Harris, | Nazro, | Walton, |
| Carpenter, | Hazard, | Parr, | Walbridge, |
| Carrington, | Hincken, | Plumer, | Wetherill, |
| Converse, | Hoffman, | Porter, | Wilbor, |
| Crichton, | Holton, | Randolph, | Young—65. |
| Davis, (Geo. F.,) | | | |

Nays: Messrs.—
Cobia,      King — 2.

Mr. KING: I would vote Yea if Mr. WETHERILL's amendment was added.

The PRESIDENT: The first part of the resolution is carried by a vote of 65 to 2. The question is now upon the second part, upon which the Yeas and Nays will now be called.

The Secretary called the roll, with the following result:

Yeas: Messrs.—

| | | | |
|---|---|---|---|
| Boynton, | Dawson | How, | Ropes, |
| Bradford, | Duvall, | Ilsley, | Sage, |
| Branch, | Egan, | Kirkland, | Stanard, |
| Brown, | Fisk, | Kreikhaus, | Stranahan, |
| Buell, | Grant | Loney, | Taussig, |
| Burwell, | Guthrie, | Manson, | Topp, |
| Carpenter, | Harris, | Nazro, | Trezevant, |
| Carrington, | Hazard, | Parr, | Walbridge, |
| Cobia, | Hincken, | Plumer, | Wilbor, |
| Converse, | Holton, | Randolph, | Young—40. |

Nays: Messrs.—

| | | | |
|---|---|---|---|
| Allen, (Geo. N.,) | Davis, (Geo. F.,) | King, | Raum, |
| Bagley, | Davis, (Geo. W.) | Malone, | Shryock, |
| Biggs, | Drake, | McGraw, | Taylor, |
| Brannin, | Fraley, | Meier, | Thomas, |
| Brunot, | Gano, | Michener, | Thurston, |
| Buzby, | Hand, | Monroe, | Wetherill, |
| Crichton, | Hoffman, | Porter, | 27. |

Mr. SHRYOCK explained: If you will admit railroad iron, I will vote "Yea;" if not, "No."

The PRESIDENT: The proposition requires a two-thirds vote to carry it; it is, therefore, not agreed to.

The next proposition before the house is the third resolution offered by the Committee.

Mr. MEIER: I move to amend the third resolution by adding the words "if carried in the same number of days as by other lines, and giving preference to the fastest lines."

On being seconded, the amendment was submitted to vote and was lost. Yeas, 8; Nays, 25.

The PRESIDENT: The question recurs now on the resolution as reported by the Committee.

The Secretary called the roll, and the resolution was adopted by the following vote:

Yeas: Messrs.—

| | | | |
|---|---|---|---|
| Allen, (Geo. N.,) | Crichton, | Hoffman, | Randolph, |
| Biggs, | Davis, (Geo. F.,) | Holton, | Raum, |
| Boynton, | Dawson, | How, | Ropes, |
| Bradford, | Drake, | Ilsley, | Shryock, |
| Branch, | Duvall, | King, | Stanard, |
| Brown, | Egan, | Kirkland, | Stranahan, |
| Brunot, | Fisk, | Loney, | Taussig, |
| Buell, | Fraley, | Malone, | Taylor, |
| Burwell, | Gano, | Manson | Thurston, |
| Buzby, | Grant, | McGraw, | Topp, |
| Carpenter, | Guthrie, | Meier, | Trezevant, |
| Carrington, | Hand, | Michener, | Walbridge, |
| Cobb, | Harris, | Nazro, | Walton, |
| Cobia, | Hazard, | Parr, | Wetherill, |
| Converse, | Hincken, | Plumer, | Young—60. |

Nays: Messrs.—
Kreikhaus, Monroe, Porter, Thomas—4.

Mr. HOLTON here announced his readiness to report on behalf of the Committee to whom had been referred the resolutions during the debate on finance.

Leave having been given:

Mr. HOLTON: As I understand it, the Committee are simply authorized to make the report without note or comment.

Your Committee have but a very brief report to make. You all understand full well how numerous and varied were the propositions referred to us. Your Committee have given very protracted attention to the matter, and have endeavored to arrive at such conclusions as may meet your approbation, and at the same time will distinctly express the opinions of the majority of the Board.

I understand that no minority report will be made. Two gentlemen, however, ask to have their views expressed by me, or one rather, the other wishes me to give notice that he will make a subsequent report on his own account. Mr. RANDOLPH, of Chicago, desires it to be distinctly understood that he dissents from the resolution with regard to legalizing gold contracts. Mr. FRALEY desired the Chairman of the Committee to give notice that while he would not make a minority report, he would submit on his own behalf and upon his own responsibility, some portion, if not the whole of the resolutions which he submitted to the Board, and which were also in the hands of the Committee.

The following is the report of the Committee:

*Resolved*, That it is the sense of the National Board of Trade that Congress should, at its present session, determine the time for the resumption of specie payments.

*Resolved*, That this Board recommends to Congress to provide by law that no National Bank shall be allowed to sell any part of the gold hereafter received from Government, as interest upon the bonds pledged for its circulation, until such time as the entire amount of the reserve required by law to be kept by the banks shall be made up of coin.

*Resolved*, That we recommend that no further sales of gold shall be made by or under the authority of the Government of the United States.

*Resolved*, That, in the language of the resolutions passed by the Boston Convention, this Board recommends to Congress the enactment of a law authorizing contracts to be made in writing, which shall be payable in gold or silver coin, and securing the specific performance of such contracts.

*Resolved*, In the language of the same body, That the national honor and good faith alike require that the Government should not avail itself of the right to pay off the five-twenty bonds until by a general resumption of specie payments the public debt as it matures, can be paid in specie or its equivalent.

Mr. HOLTON : I move that the order of business be now suspended for the consideration of the question presented in our report.

Mr. NAZRO : Would any amendment to the report be in order at this time?

The PRESIDENT : Not until the Board have determined what they will do.

A vote being taken on the motion to suspend the order of business, it was carried.

The PRESIDENT : I desire to submit what I propose to add to the resolutions :

*Resolved*, That on and after the first day of March, 1869, the legal-tender notes of the United States, and the notes of the National Banks, shall be receivable for duties on imports, in the following sums and proportions: for the said month of March, five per cent., and for every month thereafter an increment of five per cent., until, by such increments, the whole amount of duties on imports may be thus payable.

*Resolved*, That the legal-tender notes of the United States so received for duties, shall be forthwith cancelled and destroyed.

*Resolved*, That the notes of the National Banks so received for duties, shall be forthwith redeemed by the several banks issuing the same, in the legal-tender notes of the United States, in six per cent. five-twenty bonds of the United States, or in coin, and on such redemption being made, the United States legal-tender notes so received shall be cancelled and destroyed, and the said bonds shall be cancelled, declared paid, and shall not be reissued.

Mr. NAZRO : I move to amend the report by adding at the close of the first resolution, "and at no later period than two years from the first of January, 1869."

Mr. TAYLOR: I understand that two amendments to the report of the Committee are now pending: is that so?

The PRESIDENT: No, Sir. I simply asked for the consideration of two propositions in addition to those of the Committee, the Committee having recommended that I should have such leave. The first resolution reported by the Committee is before the house, and Mr. NAZRO has proposed an amendment.

Mr. HOLTON: As Chairman of the Committee, I desire to state some points that governed the Committee having this matter under consideration. I shall not attempt any extended remarks, but before proceeding further, I desire to reserve my right to move the previous question, if I should deem it necessary.

Your Committee rejected all detailed plans; on the ground, first, that we could not arrive at any conclusion as to which was best, and secondly, on the general principle that it might be questionable as to the propriety of our presenting Congress and the Secretary of the Treasury with a detailed plan at all. After looking the subject carefully over, your Committee adopted the shortest and most concise of all the resolutions. The first is that of Mr. STRANAHAN, the second of Mr. G. W. DAVIS, the third of Mr. FRALEY, the fourth and fifth are the resolutions of the Boston Convention. Your Committee were very desirous to present a report which would cover the ground and which they hope may carry the unanimous consent of this body. I shall now ask that the courtesy of the Board be extended to my colleagues, for very brief remarks, not to exceed five minutes each. I may then move the previous question, with a view to bringing our business to a head and of saving a wide range of discussion, which I think, all will agree, we cannot entertain at the present time.

Mr. DAVIS: I move that the Committee have leave.

Mr. GUTHRIE: Should not the same privilege be granted to delegates?

The PRESIDENT: The question is as to whether the Committee shall have the privilege of addressing the body.

A DELEGATE: I trust the Chairman of the Committee will waive that request.

Mr. HOLTON: The proposition is withdrawn.

Mr. TAYLOR: I have listened with great interest to every part of this debate, and do not rise now to bring forward arguments upon this important question; but I think I shall be able to present a few facts, in the nature of statistics, which may be of interest to the Board. I congratulate the Board upon the result of our labors thus far, not only for what we have done, but for what we have left undone, and I anticipate that the results of our conference here will be as satisfactory as those reached in Boston in February last, and which, I am certain, exerted a material influence upon the deliberations of our legislators at Washington.

There has been no reference in this debate to the action of Canada upon a financial proposition entirely identical with the first resolution now before us. About three years since, the Government of Canada was involved in the Fenian difficulties, and its credit was so far impaired that the Minister of Finance did not care to rely upon the money market of London. In imitation of the example of the United States, the Canadian Government issued notes identical in many respects with the notes of the United States ; but not identical in one important particular. They were the notes of the Government of Canada, and legal-tender, but they were at all times convertible into gold and silver, and they so remain to the present moment. The question, therefore, becomes of practical importance ; how has the Canada Government sustained specie payment during these three years ?

Allow me to give the features of this legislation. The Bank of Montreal became the financial agent of the Government of Canada, retiring its own circulation, and to meet the notes issued in behalf of the Government, it was required to retain twenty per cent. of coin in its vaults. It was also provided by law that the whole difference between this twenty per cent. reserve of coin and the amount of Government notes, should be represented by the bonds of the Government of Canada ; and it became the imperative duty of the Minister of Finance whenever necessary in order to maintain specie payments, to sell these bonds in the market, and on any terms he might find necessary. What has been the result? I am informed by the Hon. A. T. GALT, Minister of Finance, one of the foremost men of Canada, that there never has been a run on the Bank, in any perceptible degree ; that while reserving that twenty per cent. of coin, they have never found it necessary to sell or hypothecate a single bond, and this in the face of embarrassments as great, relatively, as any that have befallen the United States. They have suffered from eruptions of Fenians, from commotions and from internal difficulties, exceeding anything known by our Government since the war. They are inaugurating an untried system of Government. Nova Scotia is almost in an attitude of secession ; and yet under these adverse and trying circumstances, the experiment of specie payments has been a triumphant success.

I ask myself whether the Government of the United States with twenty per cent. of coin in possession of the Secretary of the Treasury cannot, by the exercise of the same means preserve the credit of the Government in this emergency and support specie payments?

One word more. I cannot believe that there is any excess in the volume of the currency of the United States over that of the great commercial countries of the world. We have in circulation twenty dollars per capita of our population. Great Britain and Ireland have in use, two hundred and twenty-five million dollars of paper, and three hundred and seventy-five million dollars of gold, making an aggregate of twenty dollars per capita. France, which tolerates no bank notes less than ten dollars, has at this moment twenty-four dollars per capita in circulation in her great commercial and manufacturing nationality. California and Oregon have a million of people who use a hard money currency and treat your paper as merchandise; this million of people have in use twenty-five million dollars of money. We see then, that the paper money countries of Great Britain and the Atlantic States have twenty dollars per capita, and the hard money countries of France and California have twenty-four dollars per capita.

I cannot leave this floor without saying to the representatives of the National Banks assembled all around·me, that the American people will expect the volume of circulation necessary for their use to be divided in such a manner that the great bulk of the circulation under ten dollars, shall be in gold and silver. We give to the National Banks the field of circulation beyond ten dollars, the commercial media of the country necessary for exchanges; but the people will demand, and I think rightfully, — and I regard it our true interest to concur in it, — that the great medium of circulation necessary for the ordinary transactions of their daily life, shall be gold and silver, as in England, as in France, and even more as in California.

If a portion of that circulation below the denomination of ten dollars be represented by Government notes, if your National Bankers are desirous that it shall be so, this Government can protect such circulation of Government notes as Canada does, and redeem them easily. To the extent that the greenbacks below ten dollars thus circulate, you relieve the people of that proportion of interest upon the public debt.

I should regard it as a happy circumstance if this assembly of bankers and merchants come to this fair adjustment, this fair compromise, that the banks shall fill the great commercial circulation of the country, leaving all the lower denominations to be occupied by the coin of the realm or by the notes of the Government. By this plan you remove the popular prejudice against the National Banks, and these become enabled to extend the benefits of their circulation over the South and West, making them truly national institutions.

I offered a resolution to this effect, but shall cordially vote for the proposition of the Committee.

Mr. HOLTON: I feel constrained to bring this question to a direct issue upon our report; I feel that the time is come when we must act upon it. I therefore move the previous question.

Having been seconded, the motion was carried.

The PRESIDENT: The question now before the house is the amendment of Mr. NAZRO.

It received the following vote, and was lost.

Yeas: Messrs.—

| | | | |
|---|---|---|---|
| Allen, (Geo. N.) | Grant, | Nazro, | Taussig, |
| Crichton, | Hand, | Plumer, | Wetherill, |
| Fisk, | Kirkland, | Porter, | Young—15. |
| Fraley, | Meier, | Shryock, | |

Nays: Messrs.—

| | | | |
|---|---|---|---|
| Bagley, | Dawson, | How, | Raum, |
| Biggs, | Davis, (Geo. F.) | Ilsley, | Ropes, |
| Boynton, | Davis, (Geo. W.) | King, | Stanard, |
| Bradford, | Drake, | Kreikhaus, | Stranahan, |
| Brown, | Egan, | Loney, | Taylor, |
| Brunot, | Gano, | Malone, | Thomas, |
| Buell, | Guthrie | Manson, | Thurston, |
| Burwell, | Harris, | McGraw, | Topp, |
| Buzby, | Hazard, | Michener, | Trezevant, |
| Carrington, | Hincken, | Monroe, | Walton, |
| Cobb, | Hoffman, | Randolph, | Wilbor—46. |
| Converse, | Holton, | | |

The PRESIDENT: The question now is upon the original resolution.

Mr. GUTHRIE called for the Yeas and Nays, and the resolution prevailed by the following vote:

Yeas: Messrs.—

| | | | |
|---|---|---|---|
| Allen, (Geo. N.,) | Egan, | Kirkland, | Raum, |
| Bagley, | Fisk, | Kreikhaus, | Ropes, |
| Bradford, | Fraley, | Malone, | Shryock, |
| Boynton, | Gano, | Manson, | Stranahan, |
| Brown, | Grant, | McGraw, | Taussig, |
| Brunot, | Hand, | Meier, | Taylor, |
| Buell, | Harris, | Michener, | Thomas, |
| Burwell, | Hazard, | Nazro, | Thurston, |
| Cobb, | Hincken, | Plumer, | Walbridge, |
| Converse, | Hoffman, | Porter, | Wetherill, |
| Davis, (Geo. W.) | Holton, | Randolph, | Wilbor—46. |
| Drake, | Ilsley, | | |

Nays: Messrs.—

| | | | |
|---|---|---|---|
| Biggs, | Dawson, | Loney, | Topp, |
| Buzby, | Guthrie, | Monroe, | Trezevant, |
| Carrington, | How, | Parr, | Walton—15. |
| Davis, (Geo. F.,) | King, | Stanard, | |

Mr. TREZEVANT: I rise to a question of privilege. I desire to ask the courtesy of the house to allow Mr. BARKER, who was here before we arrived, but who gave way to Mr. CHALMERS, to be allowed to take a seat in the Board: my colleague, Mr. CHALMERS, having been obliged to leave the city.

Mr. RANDOLPH: I desire to state that Mr. BARKER'S credentials were similar to all the rest.

The request was not granted.

The Board took a recess for the purpose of accepting an invitation to lunch with the members of the Cincinnati Club.

## AFTERNOON SESSION.

The PRESIDENT: The question before the house is on the second resolution of the Finance Committee.

I would say that since the adjournment, I have consulted the Manual, and find that when the previous question is ordered, it is proper to vote upon each separate proposition.

The second resolution was then voted on, and was carried, the Yeas and Nays being demanded.

Yeas: Messrs.—

| | | | |
|---|---|---|---|
| Allen, (Geo. N.,) | Crichton, | How, | Raum, |
| Bagley, | Davis, (Geo. W.,) | Ilsley, | Ropes, |
| Bradford, | Duvall, | King, | Stranahan, |
| Branch | Egan, | Kirkland, | Taussig, |
| Brown, | Fisk, | Kreikhaus, | Taylor, |
| Brunot, | Fraley, | Manson, | Thomas, |
| Buell, | Gano, | McGraw, | Trezevant, |
| Burwell, | Grant, | Meier, | Walbridge, |
| Carpenter, | Hand, | Michener, | Wetherill, |
| Cobb, | Hazard, | Plumer, | Wilbor, |
| Cobia, | Holton, | Randolph, | Young—44. |

Nays: Messrs.—

| | | | |
|---|---|---|---|
| Biggs, | Drake, | Loney, | Shryock, |
| Boynton, | Guthrie, | Malone, | Stanard, |
| Buzby, | Harris, | Nazro, | Thurston, |
| Converse, | Hincken, | Porter, | Topp—18. |
| Dawson, | Hoffman, | | |

The PRESIDENT: The question is now on the third resolution.

The Yeas and Nays were called, with the following result:

Yeas: Messrs.—

| | | | |
|---|---|---|---|
| Bradford, | Duvall, | How, | Ropes, |
| Branch, | Egan, | Kreikhaus, | Stranahan, |
| Brunot, | Fisk, | Manson, | Taussig, |
| Buell. | Fraley, | Meier, | Thomas, |
| Burwell, | Grant, | Michener, | Trezevant, |
| Cobia, | Guthrie, | Plumer, | Wetherill, |
| Crichton, | Hazard, | Randolph, | Wilbor—31. |
| Davis (Geo. W.,) | Holton, | Raum, | |

Nays: Messrs.—

| | | | |
|---|---|---|---|
| Allen, (Geo. N.,) | Converse, | Ilsley, | Porter, |
| Bagley, | Davis, (Geo. F.,) | King, | Shryock, |
| Biggs, | Dawson, | Kirkland, | Stanard, |
| Boynton, | Drake, | Loney, | Taylor, |
| Brown, | Gano, | Malone, | Thurston, |
| Buzby, | Hand, | McGraw, | Topp, |
| Carpenter, | Harris, | Nazro, | Walbridge, |
| Carrington, | Hincken, | Parr, | Young—34. |
| Cobb, | Hoffman, | | |

The resolution was lost.

The PRESIDENT: The next proposition is that recommending to Congress the enactment of a law authorizing contracts in gold and securing the specific performance of the same. It now stands as the third in the series.

The roll was called as follows:

Yeas: Messrs.—

| | | | |
|---|---|---|---|
| Allen, (Geo. N.,) | Davis, (Geo. F.,) | Holton, | Ropes, |
| Bagley, | Davis, (Geo. W.,) | Ilsley, | Shryock, |
| Boynton, | Dawson, | King, | Stranahan, |
| Branch, | Drake, | Kirkland, | Taussig, |
| Brown, | Duvall, | Kreikhaus, | Taylor, |
| Brunot, | Fisk, | Loney, | Thomas, |
| Buell, | Fraley, | Manson, | Thurston, |
| Burwell, | Gano, | McGraw, | Trezevant, |
| Carpenter, | Grant, | Meier, | Walbridge, |
| Cobb, | Hand, | Nazro, | Wetherill, |
| Cobia, | Harris, | Parr, | Wilbor, |
| Converse, | Hincken, | Plumer, | Young—51. |
| Crichton, | Hoffman, | Porter, | |

Nays : Messrs.—

| | | | |
|---|---|---|---|
| Biggs, | Egan, | Malone, | Raum, |
| Bradford, | Guthrie, | Michener, | Stanard, |
| Buzby, | Hazard, | Randolph, | Topp—14. |
| Carrington, | How, | | |

The resolution was declared to have been carried.

The PRESIDENT: The fifth resolution, now the fourth, is the next in order.

The Yeas and Nays were called for.

Mr. KIRKLAND: I move that the Yeas and Nays be dispensed with.

Mr. PORTER: I ask that the Yeas and Nays be called.

The result was, Yeas 56, Nays 9, as follows:

Yeas: Messrs.—

| | | | |
|---|---|---|---|
| Allen, (Geo. N.,) | Dawson, | Holton, | Randolph, |
| Bagley, | Drake, | How, | Raum, |
| Boynton, | Duvall, | Ilsley, | Ropes, |
| Branch, | Egan, | King, | Stanard, |
| Brown, | Fisk, | Kirkland, | Stranahan, |
| Brunot, | Fraley, | Kreikhaus, | Taussig, |
| Buell, | Gano, | Loney, | Taylor, |
| Carpenter, | Grant, | Malone, | Thomas, |
| Carrington, | Guthrie, | Manson, | Thurston, |
| Cobb, | Hand, | Meier, | Trezevant, |
| Cobia, | Harris, | McGraw, | Walbridge, |
| Converse, | Hazard, | Michener, | Wetherill, |
| Davis, (Geo F.,) | Hincken, | Nazro, | Wilbor, |
| Davis, (Geo. W.,) | Hoffman, | Plumer, | Young—56. |

Nays : Messrs.—

| | | | |
|---|---|---|---|
| Biggs, | Buzby, | Parr, | Shryock, |
| Bradford, | Crichton, | Porter, | Topp—9.* |
| Burwell, | | | |

---

*It will be interesting to compare the third and fourth of the series of financial resolutions adopted by the Board, with the bill to promote the public credit, which

Mr. HOLTON: I hold in my hand a resolution which the Committee very favorably considered, but did not reach any action upon, proposed by Mr. GANO. I think the Committee intended, perhaps, to act upon it; at all events I offer it now:

*Resolved*, That the Congress of the United States be urged to so amend the National Banking Law, that quarterly reports, at specified times, be dispensed with, and that instead each National Bank in the country shall be called upon by the Comptroller of the national currency, at least once in each quarter, to show what its condition may have been on a designated day in the recent past, which reports shall be published as soon as made.

The resolution was carried by an unanimous vote.

The PRESIDENT: The next business in order, is the Postal and Telegraphic Service.

*Resolved*, That the National Board of Trade recommend the adoption by the General Government of measures to cheapen and extend

---

passed both branches of the Fortieth Congress the day before its adjournment, but which, failing to receive the Executive approval, did not become a law:

*Be it enacted, &c.,* That, in order to remove any doubt as to the purpose of the Government to discharge all just obligations to the public creditors and to settle conflicting questions and interpretations of the laws by virtue of which such obligations have been contracted, it is hereby provided and declared that the faith of the United States is solemnly pledged to the payment in coin or its equivalent of all the obligations of the United States not bearing interest, known as United States notes, and of the interest-bearing obligations of the United States, except in cases where the law authorizing the issue of any such obligation has expressly provided that the same may be paid in lawful money or other currency than gold and silver; but none of said interest-bearing obligations not already due, shall be paid or redeemed before maturity, unless at such time United States notes shall be convertible into coin at the option of the holder, or unless at such time bonds of the United States bearing a lower rate of interest than the bonds to be redeemed, can be sold at par in coin; and the United States also solemnly pledges its faith to make provision, at the earliest practicable period, for redemption of United States notes in coin.

SEC. 2. *And be it further enacted*, That any contract hereafter made, specifically payable in coin, and the consideration of which may be a loan of coin or a sale of property, or the rendering of labor or service of any kind, the price of which, as carried into the contract, may have been adjusted on the basis of the coin value thereof at the time of such sale, or the rendering of such service or labor, shall be legal and valid, and may be enforced according to its terms; and on the trial of a suit brought for the enforcement of any such contract, proof of the real consideration may be given.

telegraphic communication between the different parts of the country, by making it a part of its postal system.

Mr. DRAKE: In the absence of the Chairman of the Committee, I have been directed to take charge of this measure.

Mr. SHRYOCK: I desire to say something in relation to this matter. It is a subject in which I am deeply interested, although it may be a new one, not only to the Committee, but to other members of this house. It has been presented in its various forms, and as far as I have been able to discover, there are but few who are not perfectly willing that the Government should adopt it in some shape. It has worked well in England, France, Holland, Prussia and Russia. The people do not there pay more than one-tenth of what we pay for the transmission of telegraphic messages; and I am told by those who are familiar with its working, that it is three times more certain and reliable than it is with us. The great point is to arrive at a position where the greatest number shall derive the greatest good; and I am satisfied that it can be done by uniting the telegraphic system with the postal system of the country.

Objections have been raised to the effect that it would be giving too much into the hands of the Government, and creating too many office holders; also, that in times of national difficulty the telegraph would be in the hands of the Government. I entertained these opinions once, but they have all vanished from my mind. The people are the sovereigns in this country, and they will rule.

I will not detain the Board further, but will simply offer the following, as a substitute to that before the house:

WHEREAS, The telegraph system of the United States, as at present organized, does not seem to meet fully the wants of the country and is not governed by any fixed rule in principle in its tariff or charges, which may be safely said to be much too high for the service performed; and,

WHEREAS, Experience in the past few years in the telegraphic system, as worked by the Governments of England, France, Prussia, Belgium, and other countries of Europe, has demonstrated the fact that telegraphic communication can be so extended and cheapened as to place it within the reach of nearly all classes of the community;

*Therefore, be it resolved by the National Board:*

That the attention of the Congress of the United States is most respectfully called to the subject at the ensuing session, and should it be deemed advisable to build, buy or lease the telegraph lines now in operation, and attach the same to the postal system of the country, placing them under the control of the Postmaster-General; it is the sense of this Board that it will not only facilitate and cheapen their working, but prove of incalculable benefit to the whole country.

Mr. STRANAHAN : In justice to the minority of the Committee, I beg to state that the report was not unanimous.

Mr. BUELL : I desire to introduce a substitute as an amendment.

The PRESIDENT : You may move it as an amendment to the amendment already proposed.

Mr. BUELL : In that form then, I beg leave to offer the following :

WHEREAS, The spirit of a republican form of government requires that all private enterprises tending to the development of the country, shall be fostered, and not obstructed ; and,

WHEREAS, In the effort now making for the adoption by the Government of the telegraph, and its incorporation with the Post-Office Department, we recognize the introduction of a dangerous precedent, naturally leading to Governmental monopoly of many of the legitimate avenues for the employment of private capital ; therefore,

*Resolved,* That in the judgment of the National Board of Trade, the Government should not unite with the Post-Office Department the transmission of messages by telegraph, or in any way assume control of the telegraphic business of the country, but should leave to private enterprise and competition the efforts necessary to meet the wants of the country.

It seems to me that the endorsement of any proposition by the General Government will open an immense job, of which we have, already, had too many in this country. By the history of the past, I think we may be assured that the Government will not and cannot fairly compete with private enterprise. It seems to me that the Government of the United States might as well undertake the management of the express, or sleeping-car business of the country. This whole matter should be left to private enterprise, and let competition reduce the rates of telegraphing. I do not understand that the people of this country demand this change. The proposition as I understand it, is made in the interest of certain men, who desire the Government to organize a company, of which they are to be the incorporators.

Mr. LONEY : I move to lay this whole subject on the table.

The motion being put, was lost by the vote : Yeas 19, Nays 31.

Mr. DRAKE : I was willing that a vote should be taken without a word, but amendments have been introduced and remarks made, and I think it is proper that the Committee should be heard.

In reporting this resolution, the Committee believe that they express the wishes of a majority of this Convention, that Congress should take such steps as in its wisdom should be deemed best to cheapen telegraphing, and make it a part of the postal system. They purposely avoided entering into details as to whether Congress should purchase or construct telegraphs, or hire the service of existing lines. The gentleman on the other side, who offered an amendment, claims that Government should not enter into this branch of business, because it is in competition with private enterprise. I conceive that no argument can be made against the Government embarking in the business of transmitting telegraphic despatches, which does not apply with greater force to carrying letters by mail. What right has Government to say that I shall not establish a postal system between this city and Louisville? Yet the common judgment of the country justifies the Government in taking and keeping that in its own hands.

The time may arrive when the transmission of telegraphic despatches will so lessen the postal revenue, that Government will not be able to sustain the postal department; it has already made heavy inroads on its revenue. The object of this resolution is not only that the Government shall be protected, but that it shall protect the people in transmitting telegraphic despatches everywhere, and at cheap rates, a matter of as great importance, perhaps, as the transmission of letters themselves. It is because the telegraphic system has not reached this point, that this change is demanded. Telegraphing being a new business in the country, was undertaken by large monopolies; they gained the ascendency, and every effort that has been made to withstand them has resulted in failure. The capital of one monopoly, it is said, exceeds forty million dollars, and no sooner does any new enterprise attempt to establish itself, than it is crushed out. During a recent competition, a despatch could be sent from Milwaukie to Chicago for ten cents, but the new company was soon stopped.

I have nothing to say against telegraphing as a private enterprise, and I am not prepared to say that it has not rendered good service to the land. I admit that the prices are, under some circumstances, reasonable, and that there is reasonable despatch in transmission; but I want a system that shall be self-sustaining, that shall be extended all over the land, and that shall give the accommodation that is nationally desired.

This resolution is very general in its character. It is simply an expression of this body that telegraphing ought to be reduced, — how much I am not prepared to say — that will be for the wisdom of others to determine; and further, that in the judgment of this Convention it should become a part of the postal system.

I therefore take the liberty of moving the previous question.

Mr. THURSTON: I hope that motion will be withdrawn. I think the telegraph companies ought to be heard.

Mr. DRAKE withdrew the motion.

The PRESIDENT: The proposition is the amendment to the amendment offered by the gentleman from Albany, Mr. BUELL.

Mr. THURSTON: It is with much hesitation that I rise to oppose the report of the Committee in favor of the Government incorporating with its postal department, the telegraphic service of the country. This hesitation arises from the fact well known to the members of this Board, that I am the President of a Telegraph Company, whose wires extend over several thousand miles, and it may be thought that my opposition to the measure arises from interested motives.

Actuated by the fear lest this misapprehension might arise, as well as by the belief that there are many more important questions awaiting our action, which may not be reached from want of time, I voted to lay the recommendation of the St. Louis Board of Trade upon the table.

In this encroachment of the Government upon the domain of private capital and private enterprise, we are following the lead of monarchies. In Great Britain the Government has lately monopolized the telegraph by the purchase of all the telegraph lines. The price paid is, first, twenty years purchase of the net profits of each company, based upon the profits of the year previous to the purchase; secondly, payment for the estimated aggregate value of the capital; thirdly, compensation for the loss of the prospective profits of the company on its ordinary shares; fourthly, each and every officer and clerk who has been five years in the service of a telegraph company, will, if he has no offer of appointment from the Postmaster-General, of equal value to that held by him under the company, receive during his life an annuity, graduated according to the number of years he has been in the telegraph service, but equal to two-thirds of his previous emoluments. Should the United States absorb into its postal service the telegraph lines of this country, it is not unlikely that the plan of purchase would be more or less formed upon this

English method. Be that as it may, it cannot but be evident that there is in this scheme sufficient opportunity for profit to make it to the interest of telegraph officers to favor, rather than to oppose it. I feel free to say as a stockholder and as an officer representing a body of stockholders, that any absorption by the United States Government of the telegraphic lines of this country under a recompense one-quarter as liberal, ought, on purely selfish grounds, to receive my support; but, Sir, as a tax-payer, as a commercial man, as a good citizen, and as one who would see the patronage of the Government decreased instead of enlarged, I view the proposition with apprehension and oppose it from principle.

I believe the adoption of this plan would be a dangerous precedent, tending to the occupancy by the Government of many of those avenues in which personal enterprise and private capital now seek employment, and that it would be in opposition to the very spirit of a Republican Government. Such a Government is for the protection of the liberty, the life, and the property of its creators, and it was never contemplated that it should come in competition with the enterprise of those who formed it. With the guarantee of free speech, and of a free press, these should go hand in hand as a guarantee of the widest field for the exercise of private enterprise, the use of private capital, and the encouragement of competition in all branches of business.

Competition in this country has brought about nearly all the great improvements in which we rejoice. Why not leave to the means which have accomplished so much, such further improvements as the growth of the nation and its business may demand? There are already four telegraphic lines running from Washington to New York; three from the East to Chicago; three constructed and constructing to St. Louis from the East; two reaching to Memphis from Portland, Maine, and extending to New Orleans and Mobile; not to mention the various side lines to less important cities. Under this competition, the rates of telegraphing have been largely reduced during the past two years; the reduction ranging from forty to sixty per cent., and in some cases even more. It has been said by the gentleman from Minnesota, who supported the measure, that the country has been suffering under a monopoly in the telegraphing business. That, Sir, was true. He also said that against the power of this monopoly no competing line could stand a year. In that he errs. The Pacific and Atlantic Telegraph Company, of which I have the honor to be chief officer, has successfully and profitably maintained itself against the monopoly referred to for nearly four years, and I can see no reason why it should not continue so to do.

The gentleman from Minnesota said that already the telegraph is encroaching upon the revenues of the Post Office Department, inasmuch as it is transmitting messages which would otherwise go by mail. Does not this indicate that the very end is being reached by private enterprise, which it is claimed the Government must step in to accomplish by taking possession of the telegraph lines? And I would have you recollect that great as have been the reductions in the rates of postage, it is to attempts made through individual enterprise to lessen the cost and shorten the time for the transmission of letters, that cheap postage is in some measure due. Whether the postal service of the country would not be as well, if not better performed by private enterprise, is yet a mooted question. And in view of the postal deficiency of the last year, there would seem to be great propriety in leaving to competition the cheapening of the transmission of telegraphic messages until the postal department at least maintains itself.

It has been charged that the deficiences in the post office revenues are the result of iniquitous contracts. Be that as it may, are there any who claim that the introduction of the telegraph service into the departments of the Government is going to make all its agents honest? If so, I must confess I am so much more interested in the millenium than I am in telegraphs, that I should at once advocate the Government absorbing all the telegraph lines in the world. But on the contrary I look upon the incorporation of the telegraph with the postal service as creating so many more possible means to breed corruption, if the charges made are true.

The precedent, I conceive, is altogether a dangerous one. Already in England, since the purchase of the telegraph lines, a plan has been urged for the purchase of all the railroads of that country. Would not the absorption of the telegraph lines by this Government lead to the same cry here? And if the Government shall, on the cry of any great or small body of its citizens that certain facilities or luxuries cost the public more under private enterprise than if furnished by the Government, proceed to act as is proposed in telegraphs, what may it not monopolize?

The plea for the Government to do the telegraphing of the country, is that the people may have it cheaper. Now, Sir, who are the people who use the telegraph? Why, Sir, nine-tenths of all the messages are sent by merchants, manufacturers, bankers and speculators, who use the telegraph because they can make transactions more quickly and more profitably than by using the mail. It is a mere matter of dollars and cents. If then there is an over taxation for the use of the wires, does it not fall in the right place? The great mass of laboring men, agriculturists and mechanics, rarely have need to resort to the telegraph office. Why should the Government go into an experiment at a probable loss, and increase the taxation of the great mass of the people, who seldom use the wires, for the benefit of the commercial masses, who use the telegraph as a money-making facility?

While I would be the last to utter a word that might prevent the Government from increasing the business of the country and augmenting the facilities for its transaction, yet from my knowledge of the classes between whom telegraphic messages chiefly pass, it would seem to me that the absorption of the telegraph lines into the postal department, would be legislating for the benefit of a few, at the expense of the many. And the very class which would expect to be most benefited would, I fear, find the telegraph robbed of all that celerity, secrecy and reliability which now render it valuable to business men.

The Government cannot be sued for loss resulting from delay in the transmission of a letter, and it is not to be presumed that one could sue it in case of loss resulting from delay in delivery, or error in transmission of a telegraph message. Yet for such delay or error, telegraph corporations can be sued and recovery made if the case is proven. Again, who will doubt that there are many men who would give a large sum annually to be placed at the head of the telegraph offices in our large cities? When we recollect that fortunes are sometimes the result of a few minutes' earlier possession of news affecting monetary values, none will ask why such a position would be worth intriguing for and purchasing. All know the liability of wires to get out of order, to break, to become entangled, and in other ways to be rendered useless for a time. While the telegraph service of the country is in the hands of competing companies, there is every inducement to the officers to shorten the time of all such interruptions. Prestige, patronage, dividends, all depend upon uninterrupted lines. But committed to the hands of Government employees, who that knows anything of delays in the postal service will doubt that the repairing of interruptions would be, to say the least, a much slower operation than under the spur of competition.

It would appear, then, that from the inability to sue for damages, all reliability would be gone. Secrecy too would be endangered, not only for reasons stated, but because every operator at each station along the wires being able to read the messages, by sound, as they passed, the private and political secrets of all who used the wires would be at the mercy of the partizans of the administration in power. It would place a dangerous opportunity in the hands of ambitious, corrupt or designing men, who might belong to the governing party, to perpetuate their rule or politically to destroy their opponents. In the mail all correspondence is safe in its envelope, and cannot be tampered with without danger of detection; but correspondence passing over the wires is open. Celerity would be perhaps lost, from slowness to put a stop to interruptions, under the routine system of Government encouragement compared with the incessant whip and spur of general competition. The result would then most probably be that the telegraph would lose or suffer greatly in the three important particulars named, which now render it so efficient and useful.

The question really is, whether those who use the telegraph would be benefited by its transference to the Government. Supposing the Government telegraph retains all the celerity, secrecy and reliability of corporate telegraphs, wherein is the service to be bettered? There is no evidence in any existing branch of the Government, that it would employ any better men than corporations do. On the contrary, is it not notorious that political influence causes the appointment of very inferior men? On the reverse, the object of corporations being to make money, the best men are chosen. To all this, it may be replied that the Government may contract with the existing telegraph companies, to carry messages for the Government, as they now contract with the railroads to carry the mails. In this there is a wide difference. The telegraph companies can carry nothing but messages, while the mails form but a small proportion of the transportation of the railroads. The compensation for the mails is but one item in their revenues, and while they are debarred from carrying letters on corporate account for the public, yet this does not cut off their entire source of revenue.

With the telegraph corporations debarred from carrying messages for the public on corporate account, as would be the case, after the Government had assumed the carrying of messages, if the postal laws are to be carried out as they now stand, their business would be closed and their revenue would cease. The line that might receive the contract, would do all the carrying as a Government telegraph, and all other lines would die out or be absorbed by it, and when its contract expired, it could refuse another contract, except at an exorbitant price, and so hold a monopoly of the business.

There is now a bill before the Committee of Post Roads and Routes, known as the Ramsey bill, under which it is proposed that the

Postmaster-General shall contract with the various telegraph companies for the transmission of messages. Deftly, shrewdly and cunningly drawn, the bill to the general reader, or to those who run and read, seems innocent enough. Yet its whole purpose is the reëstablishment of telegraph monopoly and ultimate high rates.

This bill proposes to charter the United States Postal Telegraph Company, naming several persons as the corporators, for the purpose of constructing lines of telegraph and of operating and maintaining them upon the post roads and routes of the United States. It provides for the capital stock, and in every way creates a telegraph corporation. The same bill then goes on to authorize the Postmaster-General to establish a Postal Telegraph system, and specifies that he shall receive bids from companies for the transmission of messages; and that the rates for messages of twenty words or figures, or less, shall not exceed twenty cents, and five cents for each additional five words or figures, for every five hundred miles or less, of transmission. It also provides that messages may have priority over others by the payment of extra rates. The bill finally provides that if this Postal Telegraph Company, whose incorporation is so shrewdly interwoven with powers and instructions for the Postmaster-General, shall refuse or neglect to contract with him to carry messages at the rates proposed in the bill, its incorporation shall become void. Is it in any way necessary to inquire why this incorporation of a Telegraph Company is so cunningly connected with this authority to the Postmaster-General to join the sending of telegraphs with the carrying of letters in his department? Why should the rates be fixed, and the life of the corporation hinge upon its contracting at such rates? More especially let it be noted that in a pamphlet published by Mr. GARDINER G. HUBBARD, one of the corporators named in the bill, it is said: "It is not claimed that either the Western Union or any other company, or even the Government itself, could transmit messages through the country at the rates proposed in the bill without loss." Is it to be presumed that the present companies will contract at losing rates? Is there not room for suspicion that the projectors of the United States Postal Telegraph prefixed the rates at losing figures that they may be the only contractors bidding. Is it not equally clear, that under the contract they would have a monopoly? For must not the same general laws apply to telegrams, as part of the postal system, which are now in force for the carrying of letters? If the Government assumes the transmission of telegrams as a part of its postal system, under the laws of the department, independent companies could not send messages any more than individuals can now carry letters.

If it is contemplated, in good faith, that the Government shall take control of the telegraph for the benefit of the public, why is it necessary, to enable the Postmaster-General to assume his new duties, to legislate in such a way, that it is hard to say what. belongs to the Postmaster-General and what to the Postal Telegraph Company? Is a corporation to stand between the people and the Government — a sort of middle-man, who by first contracting at confessedly losing rates, obtains the monopoly of the transmission of messages and by so doing smothers all competition; and then is at liberty, according to the bill, to break the contract by forfeiting the trifling sum of thirty thousand dollars? A cheap price for a monopoly. Or, if not choosing so to do, the company is allowed by the bill to charge such extra rates as it may think proper for messages requiring immediate despatch. As if most messages by telegraph did not require immediate despatch; or else why use the wires? And as if, in a short time, the great majority of messages would not from necessity or priority, be costing extra rates? Is it necessary to dwell on the corruption possible under such a plan? To the avoidance of all this, it may be urged that the Government should buy all the lines. This would involve the expenditure of thirty or forty millions of money, and consequent taxation for the interest on this sum, to say nothing of bringing into existence a host of new political office holders; or of the probability, — taking the postal service as a criterion — of future taxation for deficiencies; while to the extension of the lines into all remote districts, to suit the demands of party politicians, there would be no end.

It seems to me that the whole aspect of the question of incorporating the telegraph with the postal service of the nation, is most unfortunate. The tendency of such a movement would be to lessen its value; to increase the Government patronage, to create expenditures of money, increase of debt and taxation, and additional taxation to supply deficiencies — if the lines are purchased by Government; or, if placed upon the contract system, it would eventuate in the suppression of competition, and the establishment of a dangerous monopoly. But left to competition, the result in the future will be in the same direction as at present, — a continuous reduction in rates to as low a point as is consistent with reasonable returns for capital invested — and such has been and is the policy of the Pacific and Atlantic Telegraph Company.

The sole good to be gained by the proposed change, is a cheapening of the cost of telegraphing throughout the United States; because in a few small and closely populated countries in Europe, telegraphing appears to be cheaper than it is with us. But is it really cheaper? It must not be overlooked that the distances here are far greater between populous towns, than in Europe, and that the country, save in a few sections, is more sparsely settled. The area of Belgium is only about one-quarter of that of the State of New York, and its greatest length is one hundred and seventy-five miles, while three-fourths of its population live within fifty miles of Brussels. In what section of our country is population so condensed? There the rate is ten cents for an average distance of seventy-five miles, for an average message. In the United States, competition has brought the rates quite as low. From Pittsburgh to Baltimore and to Philadelphia, a distance of about three hundred and sixty miles to each point, the rate is only thirty cents, or about seven and a half cents for each seventy-five miles of transmission; while after nightfall, twice the number of words can be sent for the same price. Between New York and Pittsburgh, a distance of about five hundred miles as the wires run, the rates are forty-five cents, or six and three-fourth cents for each seventy-five miles of transmission.

Between Louisville and New York the rates are one dollar, and the distance by wire is nine hundred and seventy-five miles, or about seven and three-fourth cents for each seventy-five miles. These rates have been established through the force of competition, not only where the distances are four, five, and ten times greater than the average distance of transmission in Europe. but where on many routes the population is very sparse in comparison with that of Belgium, in which nation the rates for telegraphing are the lowest. The rates in England, Switzerland and France when compared in the same manner with those established by the competition of the Pacific and Atlantic Telegraph Company with other companies in this country, show the same results.

And it must not be forgotten in the comparison, that the cost of skilled labor, and in fact all labor employed on the telegraph lines in the United States, far exceeds that of England. In England, managers of large offices think themselves well paid at from forty to fifty dollars a month; here they receive from one hundred to one hundred and fifty dollars. In England, in many important offices, the operators are boys, receiving only from two to three dollars a week, while from twenty to forty dollars a month is the usual salary of a man. Here the messenger boys get from three to five dollars a week, and operators in all but country offices, range from sixty to one hundred dollars a month. In France, Belgium and Switzerland, the compensations are even lower than in England. It is not, I presume, contemplated, in order that telegraphing with us may be brought lower than it now is, that the wages of our telegraphic employees should be reduced to the European standard. The rate for transmission has been reduced by competition to a lower rate per mile than in Europe, under all the disadvantages of high wages, long distances and sparse population; and the same competition is still reducing rates. The Pacific and Atlantic Telegraph Company have found that reduced rates bring increased revenues; and self-interest is fast developing, not only an increase of lines, but greater facilities and still lower rates. What profit then is there to either the business man, or the Government or the people, in giving ear to those, who having but cursorily examined the subject, cry out that the Government should absorb the telegraph business, on the plea that it will cheapen rates to the standard of Europe? That is already done, or being done, without the expenditure of money by the Government, and consequent increase of taxation or increase of the Government patronage and its attendant evils. Why should this rightful avenue for the employment of private capital and industrial enterprise be shut up by a Government monopoly, establishing a dangerous precedent, and incurring the liability to all the other evils named; when all the good results claimed from such a policy are being accomplished by private means?

I have stated my convictions on this subject; and have, I trust, shown that it is neither expedient, nor wise nor just for the Government to assume as its prerogative the sending of telegraphic despatches for the people. I hope I have also shown from present charges, where competing lines exist, that the rate for transmission is really less per mile in the United States than in Europe, even under the disadvantages of higher wages and sparser population. I think all who will dispassionately consider the subject, will agree with me that the further reduction of telegraphic charges had better be left to the same power which has tunneled our mountains, constructed our railroads, opened our mines, and built up our manufactures — the power of competition, driven by the impatience, the energy, and the brain of the American people.

Mr. TAUSSIG : I suggest that there are many delegates who have engagements requiring them to return home, and who must leave this city soon; they are desirous of voting on some measures of importance yet to come up, but if we discuss every question so elaborately, we shall never get through.

Mr. LONEY : I move to indefinitely postpone the whole subject.

Mr. DRAKE : I move the previous question.

Carried.

The PRESIDENT: The question is upon the amendment of the gentleman from Albany.

On being submitted to vote, it was lost.

The PRESIDENT: The question now is upon the amendment of the gentleman from St. Louis.

The Yeas and Nays being called, the vote stood, Yeas 14, Nays 48, as follows:

Yeas: Messrs.—

| | | | |
|---|---|---|---|
| Biggs, | Crichton, | Hazard, | Thomas, |
| Branch, | Davis, (Geo. F.,) | Parr, | Topp, |
| Burwell, | Gano, | Shryock, | Trezevant. |
| Carrington, | Grant, | | 14. |

Nays: Messrs.—

| | | | |
|---|---|---|---|
| Allen, (Geo. N.) | Dawson, | How, | Plumer, |
| Bagley, | Drake, | Ilsley, | Porter, |
| Boynton, | Duvall, | King, | Randolph, |
| Bradford, | Egan, | Kreikhaus, | Ropes, |
| Brown, | Fisk, | Loney, | Stanard, |
| Brunot, | Fraley, | Malone, | Stranahan, |
| Buell, | Guthrie, | Manson, | Taussig, |
| Buzby, | Hand, | McGraw, | Thurston, |
| Carpenter, | Harris, | Meier, | Walbridge, |
| Cobb, | Hincken, | Michener, | Wetherill, |
| Cobia, | Hoffman, | Monroe, | Wilbor, |
| Converse, | Holton, | Nazro, | Young—48. |

The PRESIDENT: The question now is on the original resolution.

The Yeas and Nays were called with the following result: Yeas 28, Nays 35;

Yeas: Messrs.—

| | | | |
|---|---|---|---|
| Biggs, | Crichton, | Holton, | Randolph, |
| Branch, | Davis, (Geo. F.,) | How, | Ropes, |
| Burwell, | Drake, | Kreikhaus, | Shryock, |
| Buzby, | Egan, | Malone, | Stanard, |
| Carpenter, | Gano, | Michener, | Topp, |
| Carrington, | Grant, | Nazro, | Trezevant, |
| Converse, | Hazard, | Parr, | Wetherill. 28. |

Nays: Messrs.—

| | | | |
|---|---|---|---|
| Allen, (Geo. N.,) | Davis, (Geo. W.,) | Hoffman, | Porter, |
| Bagley, | Dawson, | Ilsley, | Stranahan, |
| Boynton, | Duvall, | King, | Taussig, |
| Bradford, | Fisk, | Loney, | Thomas, |
| Brown, | Fraley, | Manson, | Thurston, |
| Brunot, | Guthrie, | McGraw, | Walbridge, |
| Buell | Hand, | Meier, | Wilbor, |
| Cobb, | Harris, | Monroe, | Young—35. |
| Cobia, | Hincken, | Plumer, | |

The PRESIDENT: The next order of business is the proposition from the St. Louis and Louisville Boards of Trade, with reference to Pacific Railroads.

Mr. WALBRIDGE: I desire permission to read a resolution, on which I think there will be no debate.

Permission was given to read for the information of the house.

*Resolved,* That it is the duty of the Federal Government to prescribe the conditions upon which telegraph lines from foreign countries are to be allowed to land in this country, without the intervention of any State legislation.

The PRESIDENT: That resolution would not now be in order.

Mr. MEIER: I beg to offer the following resolution on behalf of the St. Louis Board of Trade, which has also been agreed to by the Louisville Board of Trade:

### THE PACIFIC RAILROADS.

*Resolved,* That this Board respectfully and earnestly urges upon Congress the patriotic duty of granting immediate and adequate aid to perfect our system of Pacific Railroads;

First. By the extension southwestwardly of the Kansas Pacific Railway from its present terminus on the great plains, nearly seven hundred miles from St. Louis, to a point in New Mexico, on or near the thirty-fifth parallel.

By the construction of the Atlantic and Pacific Railway from Fort Smith westwardly through the Indian Territory and Northern Texas to the said point in New Mexico, at the base of the Rocky Mountains.

By the construction of a line by the Southern Pacific Railroad Company of Texas, from Marshall by the valley of Red river, to a proper point on the Canadian river, to connect there with the above road.

By the construction of a trunk line of railroad through New Mexico, Arizona, and Southern California, on the general route of the thirty-fifth parallel to the Pacific coast.

This system is demanded in view of the climate, the fertility and the mineral wealth of the country traversed, the duty of extending protection to the settlements in these territories, and the commercial necessities of all parts of the United States, the South being thereby put into the best communication with our mineral territories and the Pacific Ocean, by the proposed extension of their railway system westwardly from Memphis, Arkansas, Mississippi and Louisiana; and the Middle and Northern States being afforded a short connection through a mild climate with the Pacific and with the mines of Southern Colorado, New Mexico, Arizona, the Northern States of old Mexico and Southern California, by the extension of the line from Kansas.

Second. By the construction from Lake Superior to Puget Sound of the Northern Pacific Railroad, already chartered by the Government, which will give a short line of connection between the East and the Northern Pacific coast.

These lines, in connection with the Union Pacific and the Central Pacific Railroads form a complete system of Pacific Railroads entitled to national aid.

In presenting the resolution, I beg leave to accompany it with a few remarks. The system of Pacific Railroads, for which the Government aid is asked, embraces, it is believed, all the lines from the Mississippi river and Lake Superior to the Pacific Ocean, that will be wanted for many years to come. It affords through lines from the Atlantic to the Pacific Ocean by three routes, about equi-distant from each other, and gives, by means of railroads in different States, already existing, or being constructed by private capital, a connection with all the important towns in the country, and the States East, South and North, and thus completes a system entitled to the Government's aid, as private means alone are not adequate for such a vast undertaking.

Very thorough surveys, made by the Union Pacific Railway Company, within the last two years, under the direction of General PALMER, with five different corps of engineers, at an expense of about a quarter of a million of dollars, have demonstrated very clearly and fully, that a good and practical route for a railroad from the present terminus of said Pacific road in Kansas, about seven hundred miles west of the Mississippi river, *via* Colorado, New Mexico, and thence, on the thirty-fifth parallel, through Arizona to the Colorado river, and crossing that river, in a northwestern direction by the Tehuatchepay pass, and through the Tulare Valley to San Francisco, can be had running in a latitude that secures it from interruption by snow in winter, and passing through fertile regions, rich in agricultural lands and minerals, and capable of sustaining a large population.

The distances by the above road, by actual measurement, which may undoubtedly be reduced by more detailed surveys, are as follows:

From Kansas City to Meridan, four hundred and five miles; from Kansas City to the Rio Grande, eight hundred and seventy-one miles; from Kansas City to the Colorado river, one thousand and seventy-six miles; from St. Louis to San Francisco, two thousand two hundred and ninety-nine miles; from New York, *via* St. Louis, to San Francisco, three thousand three hundred and forty-nine miles; from Chicago, *via* Kansas City, to San Francisco, two thousand five hundred and fourteen miles; from Meridan to the Rio Grande, four hundred and sixty-six miles; from the Rio Grande to the Colorado river, five hundred and eighty miles; from the Colorado river to San Francisco, five hundred and seventy-five miles; and the distance from New York, *via* St. Louis, Kansas, and New Mexico, to the Pacific, would be about two hundred and forty miles shorter than by the Central Pacific, Union Pacific and other railroads from San Francisco, *via* Chicago to New York. The proposed resolution makes the foot of the Rocky Mountains, on the eastern slope, a point of meeting for the roads intended to be built from Fort Smith along the Canadian river, and from Marshall, Texas, along the valley of the Red river, and a grand trunk line is thence proposed westwardly, near or on the thirty-fifth parallel, through New Mexico, Arizona and California, to San Francisco. It is a system that connects all the Southern, Eastern and Northern States with the States and Territories West, and with the Pacific, and is, therefore, strictly a national work, deserving the assistance of the nation, and which cannot be carried out without its aid.

The aid asked is a land grant, and the loan of the Government credit. The returns of the Union Pacific Railway, Eastern Division, show that half the amount retained by the Government for the business done, has more than paid the interest on the Government bonds, and already a fair amount has been credited on the principal owed by said company — enough, if this continues proportionately, to liquidate the indebtedness to the United States many years before the bonds issued for the same mature. As the road, on its extension, reaches a fine country, having already a large population and a considerable business, to which a large increase for the Mexican trade may be expected, it is fair to suppose that this favorable result will continue. The issue of United States bonds for this road is only the loan of its credit, while the Government, by the enhancement of value of its Western Territories, its products and its mines, is largely the gainer, and also by the saving in transportation for its armies, munitions and mails. The saving of a few regiments of troops in the Western Territories will amount to more than the interest on all the bonds asked for this road, if the Government had to pay the whole. Railroads, the great civilizers of the world, are the best means to put a stop to our Indian difficulties. The savage cannot keep pace with the locomotive and the telegraph; he has to submit or he will be annihilated. A false philanthropy will not sustain him any longer, and his cruel outrages must cease.

It is true our national debt is large, and should not be increased, except for such objects as require it, imperatively; but for a measure such as is now before the Board, we can certainly loan the national credit, for we are not poor enough yet to refuse it. The opening of our mines, and the developing of the great agricultural resources that now lie dormant in the West, for the want of proper communication, will be the best means to liquidate our debt. As a military measure, it has the approval of General GRANT, as well as of Generals SHERMAN, SHERIDAN and HANCOCK, and other military commanders.

The line from Lake Superior to Puget's Sound has greater merit than has been generally supposed. It is less mountainous than the Union Pacific, and traverses a rich country adapted peculiarly to the cultivation of wheat and small grain generally, and it is the shortest route to travel to Japan and China. Of its merits, I leave it to gentlemen better able than myself to speak to this honorable assembly, and only express the hope that, after a careful consideration the resolution offered may be passed by you, thus showing to the world your appreciation of this great national undertaking. Our Pacific railroads are now the admiration of the Old World, and their completion is an imperative necessity for the people of this great nation.

I wish to reserve the privilege of moving the previous question.

Mr. WETHERILL: The early completion of the Kansas Pacific Railroad as proposed by the resolution now under consideration, is of vital importance to the development of the vast region west of the Mississippi; and it is hoped that we shall settle upon a well defined Pacific railroad system, by which the entire wants of the country may be fully secured. Congress, notwithstanding the country was involved in civil war, with its disastrous consequences, a damaged credit and distracted finances, saw fit to loan to the Union Pacific Railroad a sum sufficient to secure its ultimate completion, and thus initiated a plan of connecting California by a system of railroads commensurate with the wants of the country, and by which the national commerce would be largely increased, and our frontier boundaries thoroughly protected in time of war. A part of that plan was the completion of the Kansas Pacific road, now finished some four hundred miles west of Kansas city. The rapid progress made in its construction, the substantial manner in which it is being built, and the profitable results of the enterprise, have conclusively shown that the loan thus far made by the Government will not prove a gift as the creditors were at first inclined to believe, but that the Government will eventually realize the full amount of the interest annually from the company and that the earnings will also provide for a sinking fund, which will in a given time actually pay the full amount of the principal at maturity.

With this view of the case, with the road now in running order, confirming this statement, every objection to the endorsement of this resolution should be removed, and I deem it but an act of simple justice, that we should ask Congress to at once grant a sufficient subsidy to carry on vigorously this great enterprise.

No one without visiting the vast region developed by this road, can conceive of its extent, its fertility, its exhaustless mineral wealth. Commencing at Kansas city, the course of the road is due west some four hundred miles. This portion of the road is finished, and in running order. Then south some three hundred and odd miles to Santa Fe; then westward to the ocean. Thus the rich prairies of Kansas, the valuable trade of Santa Fe, and its vicinity, and the mineral deposits of Arizona, are secured and made productive. Twenty years ago the State of Kansas belonged to the Indians; now its increase in wealth and population, proves conclusively that in a few years it may rival the State of Illinois. The rich valleys of that State will soon teem with an active, hardy, thrifty population, and thus insure to the completed part of the road an ample support. As the work progresses, towns spring up on every hand with astonishing rapidity; the land offices of the company are filled with sturdy emigrants, selecting in the far off West their future homes, the old frontier forts, formerly an endless expense to the Government, become useless and are dismantled, for rapid emigration soon comes to need no protection from hostile Indians.

Let us look for a moment at the enormous expense which the progress of a work like this relieves the Government from paying. I am told it costs at Washington to keep a regiment of infantry one million of dollars, annually; add to this the additional expense when stationed on the plains, and we perceive that if the building of this road will save the expense of two regiments of infantry it will equal in amount the interest of a loan from the Government of nearly fifty millions of dollars. If this road in its progress disbands forts, it will soon show its immense value to the Government by relieving at least two regiments, and will thus return a full and ample consideration for any outlay or loan of credit that the Government is requested to make. Again, it is well understood that any war against hostile Indians is from the character of the country very annoying and difficult, as well as enormously expensive. The completion of this road will remove much of the trouble to which we are now subject. Arms, ammunition and troops can be readily carried from point to point, and hostilities and depredations can be more easily subdued. General SHERIDAN says, "no one, unless he has visited this country, can well appreciate the great assistance this railroad gives to economy, security and effectiveness, but in addition it almost substantially ends our Indian troubles by the moral effect it exercises, and the facility it gives the military to control them." Another great saving to the Government is the lessened cost on transportation of both supplies and the mails; the total saving upon these items this year for New Mexico alone will be, upon transportation of stores, eight hundred and fifty thousand dollars; of troops, one hundred and twenty-five thousand dollars; of mails, seventy thousand dollars; in all about eleven hundred thousand dollars. The amount asked for under this resolution to complete the road to Santa Fe, is about fifteen millions of Government bonds. The interest on this amount is nine hundred thousand dollars; the sinking fund necessary to meet these bonds when due, will be about one hundred and ninety thousand dollars, in all one million and ninety thousand dollars. Thus the saving to the Government as above stated will equal the interest on the bonds advanced and pay them when they mature. It seems clear to me that the request should be granted and that we should use our influence to secure so desirable a result.

Mr. DRAKE: I move to amend by inserting the following after the second section:

"By the extension of the Sioux City branch of the Union Pacific Railroad from Sioux City to the western end of Lake Superior."

Mr. RANDOLPH: I do not think I should have said anything on this subject but for the remarks of Mr. WETHERILL. If we examine the programme originally marked out for us, we find that the St. Louis and Louisville Boards of Trade offered certain railroad propositions; now if I take the resolutions that have been submitted and compare them with the propositions on the programme, I think I should say that somebody had been sold out. We find that these propositions seem to concentrate in St. Louis. I admit that the gentlemen have allowed a side track to run in the neighborhood of Shreveport, but, substantially, this is a St. Louis project. As such I shall not attempt, if you please, to fight or oppose it. I expect, and do not doubt, if these roads are built, as well as the Southern Pacific Railroad of which I shall speak presently, that we in Chicago shall reap quite as much advantage from them as the city of St. Louis; for I believe our connections extend quite as far in that direction as theirs do, consequently I do not wish to be understood as saying anything from local considerations in relation to this subject.

In regard to the Northern Pacific Railroad, one of the arguments of the gentleman in favor of his Southern road, and the argument of my friend from Philadelphia was, that the Union Pacific Road was so far north that it was practically of no use six months in the year. If that be true, how many months in the year can we use one three or four hundred miles further north? I remember well at Philadelphia when Mr. BLOW brought up this extension of the Kansas Pacific Road, that upon Mr. WALBRIDGE'S making a suggestion to hook these projects together, Mr. BLOW treated the matter with contempt; he would not consent that a live and vigorous project should be linked fast to one that had no existence save in the minds of speculators. There seems to have come a wonderful change over the mind of the gentlemen from St. Louis. It is now perfectly proper to hitch the Northern Pacific on to the Kansas road, although I am not aware that any new life has been infused into it.

In regard to the Union Pacific Railroad showing that it is successful, that the Government subsidy is likely to be returned, and that the Government assumed no risk,—

Mr. MEIER: That was as to the Kansas Pacific Road.

Mr. RANDOLPH: The returns that were read were from the Union Pacific Road, which show that it is successful, or is likely to be, and the Government aid is not risked or likely to be lost. I have no doubt that it will be returned, and that in the end the Government will be amply repaid, not only for the land it has granted to that line, but also for the subsidy. But does it follow because that line is prosperous, and the Government may have done a good thing once, that therefore it should increase the number of these lines?

Let us look at the circumstances under which the Union Pacific line was organized and commenced. We know that about that time the clouds in our political horizon were lowering. It was seriously threatened and about to be carried into execution that a portion of the States of this Union would secede. Every thinking man in Congress shuddered at the thought. We had an extended territory which lay west of the Rocky Mountains, extending over a vast area. We all recognized that there was very serious difficulty in local institutions in that territory. This difficulty it was which caused our Southern friends to attempt to set up for themselves and destroy our national Government. We cast our eyes across the Rocky Mountains and saw settlements springing up that had not even the same interest to bind them to us that the Southern States had; it became, therefore, a matter of anxiety with the Government to retain these States within the Union — for, Sir, it is safe now to say, that had the Pacific States in the early part of that struggle attempted to set up for themselves, it might have been exceedingly difficult for us to prevent them. It became necessary then that the Government should do something to harmonize the national feeling, to draw the people together and make them feel that they were one and the same with us. This, I apprehend, was the great, controlling fact which induced the Government to subsidize the Union Pacific Railroad, in order that it might be pushed through certainly and promptly. Another feature of the case, altogether outside of this was, that the movement was an experiment. Private capital, not knowing what return would be made, hesitated before embarking in a project of such magnitude. Government was willing to grant subsidies of land; but what were lands worth in the wild interior? The appropriation of Government lands was not considered worth anything; money would not come out. Something else must be done. Government, therefore, appropriated money; passed a law granting a loan of its credit to the extent of sixteen thousand dollars, thirty-two thousand dollars, and forty-eight thousand dollars per mile for the various sections of the road. The smallest amount for the level section, the middle sum for the higher section, and the largest grant for the mountainous section. Had the road been built with private capital entirely and economically, undoubtedly fifty per cent. added to this appropriation would have built the road. The road, however, has cost more. It was expected that it would be pushed through with great vigor regardless of expense, and the expenses have been large; but taking into consideration the cost of other railroads over similar territory in the West, it is safe to say that fifty per cent. added to the Government appropriation would have constructed the road.

This one line having been built,— and as I think, we are all convinced it was a matter of necessity that if put through at all it should be put through on some such basis,— we are asked that we shall build other lines. It is said that competition is necessary. Here is a corporation composed of a few gentlemen, who have secured the charter. They have this amount of Government bonds to build the road, with the right to give a first mortgage over the bonds to an equal amount, which has the preference of the Government subsidy; secondly, they have thirty-two thousand dollars, sixty-four thousand dollars, and ninety-eight thousand dollars per mile to construct their road, without one dollar of stock; and it is proposed that the same thing shall be repeated.

Have we not been placing in the hands of a few gentlemen an enormous franchise, such as this country has never seen, and which, under ordinary circumstances, should never be permitted? If we place a similar franchise in the hands of another dozen gentlemen, is it likely that for the through trade there will be any considerable competition between the two parties? I think not. I do not think the matter of competition is of much account in that view of the case. It would have seemed almost impossible that the New York Central and the New York and Erie Railroads could so combine as to make a monopoly; but we see to-day, from reports in New York, that an effort is being made to that end, and that it is not unlikely that those two corporations will be combined, not under the control of a few individuals, but of one man.

We do not know who are interested in these other Pacific roads. It may be the same gentlemen who have each such a large slice in the other; some of them, I believe, are admitted to be thus interested.

My objection to the entire project is, in the first place, that it builds up, at the expense of the Government, an enormous monopoly. It throws into the hands of a few individuals an immense fortune at comparatively little cost to themselves, and it builds up a monopoly that has no interest whatever in developing this country.

Another objection: this Board is asked to endorse a plan which seems to be in the interest of a portion of the territory south of the mouth of the Ohio. Our Southern friends have a great interest in getting, by some means, a line of direct communication, which shall terminate in the Southern States, for their especial benefit. This nominally does so. It has a terminus in Shreveport. But they look upon this as simply giving them a sort of side connection; the real terminus of the Union Pacific Railroad is intended to be at St. Louis.

Another objection I have to urge, and one which at the present moment seems most important, is, that it is not in consonance with our professions to recommend such an expenditure, now that we are attempting to come back to a specie basis, and have just passed resolutions clearly indicating the sense of this Board to be in favor of returning to a specie basis at a very early day. The reason why we are not upon a specie basis to-day, is because the credit of the Government is more or less impaired. Our bonds are selling in Europe at about eighty cents on the dollar. I have not the slightest idea that we shall ever recover ourselves until these bonds are nearly or quite at par with gold in Europe. The various processes that may be adopted to arrive at that result, I am not allowed to refer to, as it would not be germane to the present subject. Our first duty is to bring up the Government's credit. I do not believe that to be possible while foreigners see that our Government is swift to vote appropriations of this kind to build up corporations which are to become huge monopolies. It would show that the Government was doing what no wise or prudent merchant would do, who had his paper largely upon the market.

Another objection is that this is only one of a series of internal improvements which are pressing more or less upon the country. We at the North feel that if the Government is going to make appropriations for internal improvements at all, it should make them where the amount of money it is proposed to spend, will produce the greatest amount of good, and benefit the largest number of people, having in view the ultimate returns and profits, either to the Government or to the people. Here is a project to run a railroad through an uninhabited country — and one which for years will remain uninhabited — New Mexico and Arizona. It is not desirable for emigration to penetrate so far for years to come. I say this after very careful consideration. That portion of our territory may possibly at a future day, be rendered productive by some process of agriculture and management of the soil; but at present, I apprehend, it would be entirely too expensive to endeavor to produce anything from the soil of Arizona or New Mexico. I think the Government should do what it can to improve that portion of our territory which is already open, and to a considerable extent, inhabited, inviting emigration thither from the Eastern States and from

Europe. St. Louis has Kansas lying behind it, as rich as any territory through which this road would be likely to pass, and very much nearer to a market. Missouri itself can more than treble its population and not be crowded, and be made more profitably productive than the new lands beyond. I appeal to Missouri delegates, whether that is not true.

The Southern portion of our country is the most hopeful field for remunerating labor, and for certain success to the emigrant, I would recommend this portion to be settled, and thickly settled, before I would ask people to go to New Mexico and Arizona. I do not believe it is wise to oppress the Government credit to fill up that part of our territory at the present time. Let us fill up that which is already open, before we expand further in the direction proposed.

In regard to Mr. DRAKE's amendment, I would say that I think he is a little mistaken in regard to the way in which he would go from St. Paul to San Francisco by way of the Union Pacific road. I don't think he would go to Chicago unless he had some business there. There is a line in construction from St. Paul, which will be very little longer, and which will certainly be built without any Government subsidy. The line from St. Paul, almost in a due line south, crosses the extension of the Union Pacific road at about the middle of the State of Iowa. I think that would be the most direct road for my friend to take, if he wanted to go to San Francisco.

Mr. TOPP: Before I propose a motion to amend the resolution, in order that I may be correctly understood and my motion properly appreciated, I beg to say to this distinguished assembly, that I have for many years been an earnest advocate for internal improvements. I believe I was the first who ever publicly contended for them in the legislature of Tennessee. At all times and under all circumstances, I have looked upon these improvements, and on railroads particularly, as great blessings to the land; they are in fact the *avant couriers* of civilization. If you look for the most enlightened nations on the earth, you will find them to be those which have built the most railroads.

With regard to the territory west of the Mississippi river, I beg gentlemen to look at it, extending from the forty-ninth degree of latitude to the twenty-ninth west of the newly settled States; abundantly large for a mighty empire, and to obtain one-tenth part of which, any nation in Europe would drench its land with blood.

The question is, what shall we do with that territory? Shall we suffer it to lie idle, with its vast resources and wealth undeveloped? Shall we leave it for the owl, the wolf and the panther? Or shall we develop it? That is the question. I do not come here to oppose any particular railroad scheme. I listened with the greatest pleasure to the admirable address delivered before you on Saturday by the gentleman from New York, Mr. WALBRIDGE; and I concur with every word he said. If you want to lay a road from Lake Superior to Puget Sound, that would open up territory which would make five States, each as large as Illinois, and perhaps as productive. What argument can any gentleman advance against this? Again: we have seen a great railroad line constructed from Omaha; neither mountain, nor savanna, nor deep flowing river, nor arid waste has been sufficient to restrain the enterprise of our countrymen in that direction. That road has been carried forward with an energy worthy of all praise; and I would not, now that it is nearly completed, utter one word of discouragement concerning it. I say that it is a great work, and that it will prove a great blessing to the country.

Mr. MEIER, of St. Louis, asks me to go for the Eastern branch of the Pacific Railroad, and I say, in reply, I am for his road with all my heart. But I want to amend the resolution offered by him, by moving to strike out the words "Atlantic and Pacific Railway;" and to insert in their place, "Memphis, Little Rock and Fort Smith Railroad." And my reasons are, that I do not believe any of the gentlemen here would willingly do injustice to any part of our country. What is the proposition coming from St. Louis? As to the main Eastern branch, we are in favor of it; but Sir, I am not willing that St. Louis, at our expense, shall have two railways. And hence the object of my amendment. While holding out promises to the South to enable it to connect with them, the real object, intent and meaning of that Atlantic and Pacific Railroad will be to cut off the South.

Mr. TAUSSIG: There are not two railroads from St. Louis.

Mr. TOPP: Yes, Sir, there are two railroads from St. Louis. Gentlemen, remember the South is not represented here; you are mostly from the East. You have the power in your hands, and can do as you please with your endorsements. We of the South are powerless; we have but one or two representatives here from Tennessee; from Virginia one or two, from Georgia none, from Florida none, and from other Southern States there is nobody here to speak for them. Is it the object or the intention of this Board to cut off the whole South from its rightful opportunities?

A DELEGATE: No, Sir.

Mr. TOPP: So I say; it ought to be the intention of all honorable men to do equal justice to all parts of the Union. All we want is a reasonably fair chance. We have formidable difficulties under any circumstances to encounter in building our railways.

I am sorry, from the bottom of my heart, that I cannot present to you a glowing prospect from the South, or the high prosperity that some of you were asked to believe in the other day. I read her position through other and different glasses. We have at Memphis been attempting for the three or four years preceding the war, and since, to build a railroad from Memphis to Little Rock, and thence to Fort Smith. For twenty years, this project has been a cherished one with us in Memphis, and about it there has been no dispute. We have been working on as best we could, notwithstanding all our difficulties at home, and you know they have been grievous. We are desirous of extending our railroad system to Fort Smith, to the borders of the Cherokee nation. But first we have forty miles of Mississippi overflow to encounter; then we have three large navigable rivers to cross and bridge, and various other obstacles on the White river and its branches. From Little Rock we have a broken, rough and difficult road to Fort Smith. We intend to put that through with all the energy in our power. We have not asked any aid from the Government for that, difficult and bad as it is. But the very moment, to use the language of my friend, that we have reached the top of Mount Pisgah to look at the promised land, up comes St. Louis and says, "you cannot have that; somebody else has the charter." Somebody else, who never stuck a stake, and never drove a nail. After we have gone through the lagoons and overflows, and over the rivers and mountains we enter on a most beautiful country; I doubt, Mr. President and gentlemen, whether there is to be found on this continent a country superior to that. Taking it in all its aspects, it is a country through which it is easy to construct railroads; besides being a rich country; and there is the point for which the Government proposes to give us subsidies to aid us; and right there my friend over the way, not Mr. MEIER, but Mr. FISK, says, "stop there, you cannot have that territory."

Mr. FISK: I have not said a word about it, except in private conversations, and I should very much dislike to embarrass the gentleman by repeating what he said to me.

Mr. TOPP: I want every delegate to understand this matter.

Mr. TOPP, by the aid of a large map, indicated the line he desired the Board to endorse, and illustrated the benefits which would result from its construction.

Does any gentleman believe if St. Louis gets a subsidy and land grants, with these various lines connecting with St. Louis, that we would have the slightest chance for trade or travel, or anything else? Every man knows the effect and working of long lines of railroad. Construct a little line and how soon it is swallowed up by the big one. Where will all the trade go to? Up to St. Louis; this is the English, the very alphabet of the question, and for one I am not willing to concede what St. Louis is asking for. Let the South have some interest in these enterprises; if she does not, there will be one of the tribes of Israel left out of the compact.

Mr. FISK : I think, Sir, St. Louis has great reason to congratulate herself to-day. We have always been putting on a great many airs, and the gentleman from Memphis says that we are entitled to do so. Mr. TOPP has made a first-rate speech for the Atlantic and Pacific Railroad. He tells us of the difficulties of the country lying west from Memphis to Fort Smith, and that beyond is a rich, fine country, where railroads can easily be constructed, and that Government has granted subsidies, and that these are claimed by the St. Louis corporators. That is not so. The St. Louis corporators are scattered over all this broad land. When it was chartered by the Government in 1866, among the corporators was included the honorable gentleman who has just sat down.

Mr. TOPP: It was some speculating scheme to which my name was attached, but about which I never was consulted.

Mr. FISK : Many honorable names from Tennessee were originally in the charter A meeting was held in Memphis to engineer the matter, and the gentleman was invited to take part; but he failed to do so. The gentleman says that after twenty years of struggling endeavors to build a railroad from Memphis to Little Rock, they have failed. It is not for me to tell him just why Tennessee failed in getting to Little Rock. I may tell him that if he does not get out of the way, we shall run to Memphis. But this is no St. Louis railroad. St. Louis will not have any benefit from it until it has spent five times the amount of money it would cost to build the railroad from Memphis to Fort Smith. St. Louis is spending three millions in its scheme. Let Memphis do the same.

I am surprised that Mr. RANDOLPH should say one word against the Northern Pacific; when Chicago is striving with all its might to reach out towards it. The best advocates I have heard for the thirty-fifth parallel, have been from Chicago.

Mr. RANDOLPH: I did not oppose it from any local standpoint, but because the scheme would retard our return to specie payments.

Mr. FISK: Instead of being in the way of specie payments, I contend that by developing the resources of our country, it would be in the direct line towards them. We are in the condition of a suspended merchant, seeking for something with which to pay his debts; and I look upon the completion of these roads as a matter of national economy. Why, the Government saved nearly a million of dollars last year in the transportation of freight. The cost of one regiment of infantry is over one million dollars a year, and for a cavalry regiment almost two million dollars. General SHERMAN has testified that if the road were built, one-half of the Indian forces could be dispensed with, and from three to five hundred thousand dollars a year be saved in transportation. Experience has shown in Kansas, that by building a road we are enabled to dispense with troops altogether. This one question of peace, of quieting the savages, to say nothing of the opening of that great region, that "promised land," ought to be sufficient to secure the earnest support of every lover of his country here to-day; of every man who would do anything to develop the material resources of the country; of every man who desires that Christian civilization shall spread over that great Western country.

My friend has intimated that had the Pacific coast seceded from us, it would have been a difficult thing for us to save it. That sentiment, I hope, finds no response here, no matter on which side our sympathies or our swords may have been cast. It would have been an easy thing to hold the Pacific coast. It would be an easy thing to hold any section of this country that might undertake to break away from the beautiful banner under which we are all now gladly united. Nothing shall bind together East and West, North and South more than the bestowment of all needed aid and encouragement for these railways; but let them be placed in good hands. All that Mr. TOPP has said about that country that lies beyond Fort Smith, is perfectly true, and he and I agree exactly that the South should be taken care of. He asks that we should recommend to Congress that a subsidy be granted to the Memphis, Little Rock and Fort Smith company, and we ask that Congress should give it to the company already chartered.

Mr. WALBRIDGE: I am somewhat surprised at the remarks of my friend from Chicago, when it is remembered that the first grant of land from the Government for the construction of a railroad was to the State of Illinois. At the foot of Lake Michigan there are railroad structures not surpassed by any on this continent; and it is mainly those lines which have, in thirty years built up a city of nearly three hundred thousand souls, which have made it the first city of the West, one which might not have had existence but for the aid given by the Government.

The Government at the commencement of the war, as stated by my friend from Chicago, conceived the project of holding together the widely separated parts of this great country, not by one, but by three lines of continental railroad; not that the Government intended to subsidize these three roads, but to designate the particular routes, one northern, one central, and the other southern. The central has received its aid; its work has been prosecuted with an energy unsurpassed in ancient or modern times; and it has been the instrumentality which has to a great extent built up the cities of St. Louis and Chicago.

We only ask now, that the original proposition shall be carried into effect. We ask that this Northern line from Puget Sound to Lake Superior shall have the same aid that has been given to the Union Pacific road.

When we made peace under the apple tree at Appomattox Court House, we buried the hatchet; and we resolved that thenceforth Southern men should be heard. We are not here to wash the dirty linen of any corporation; we are here to represent our whole country. This National Board of Trade sits to further national projects, to advocate national interests, and to sustain national rights. It is only the execution of the original design, that these three lines should be laid across the mountains. It is the interest and the duty of the Government to bind the Union together, and to open up to commerce those vast avenues which otherwise will remain closed. It is not for a moment to be supposed that when the Union Pacific Railroad is completed, the commerce of Europe and Asia can be carried upon a single road. Gentlemen are here asking for and insisting upon a Southern road; and I urge as a matter of simple justice that they should have it.

Mr. TREZEVANT: I am here to get all the aid for the Southern railroad that I can; I am here to ask the Government to expend as much money as it will. We want some money at the South, and Heaven knows we don't care much where it comes from. Our friend Mr. FISK, may preach as long as he pleases; but we shall never see our railroad built without dollars and cents.

Mr. MEIER: I move the previous question.

The motion was seconded and carried.

The PRESIDENT: The question is upon the amendment to the amendment proposed by the gentleman from Memphis, striking out "Atlantic and Pacific," and inserting, "Memphis, Little Rock and Fort Smith."

A division was called for. Yeas, 11; Nays, 29.

The PRESIDENT: The next question is on the amendment by Mr. DRAKE, adding to the second paragraph, "from Sioux city to the western end of Lake Superior."

The amendment was lost.

The PRESIDENT: The question now is on the resolution as originally proposed by Mr. MEIER.

The roll being called, the resolution was adopted, the vote standing as follows:

Yeas: Messrs.—

| | | | |
|---|---|---|---|
| Allen, (Geo. N.,) | Converse, | King, | Stanard, |
| Bagley, | Davis, (Geo. W.,) | Kirkland, | Stranahan, |
| Biggs, | Drake, | Kreikhaus, | Taussig, |
| Boynton, | Fisk, | Loney, | Taylor, |
| Branch | Fraley, | McGraw, | Thomas, |
| Buell, | Grant, | Meier, | Topp, |
| Burwell, | Guthrie, | Monroe, | Trezevant, |
| Carpenter, | Hand, | Nazro, | Walbridge, |
| Carrington, | Harris, | Porter, | Wetherill, |
| Cobb, | Hazard, | Shryock, | Wilbor—41. |
| Cobia, | | | |

Nays: Messrs.—

| | | | |
|---|---|---|---|
| Bradford, | Davis,(Geo. F.,) | Holton, | Parr, |
| Brunot, | Egan, | How, | Plumer, |
| Buzby, | Gano, | Ilsley, | Randolph, |
| Crichton, | Hincken, | Malone, | Ropes—16. |

Mr. ROPES: (in explanation of vote,) I vote *No* because the proposition demands immediate aid, which I think the Government cannot properly give at this time.

Mr. GANO: I feel it my duty with my understanding of the matter, to vote *No*, for the reason that I am decidedly opposed to the Government's building up such enterprises for private advantage as these have proved to be in the past and are likely to prove in the future.

Mr. DAVIS: For the same reason as given by Mr. GANO, I vote *No*.

Mr. HOLTON: Since I don't know the country, and as the Government has difficulty in meeting its present demands, I vote *No*.

Mr. HOFFMAN: I beg to be excused from voting.

Mr. BRUNOT: I wish to vote for this measure, but not knowing enough about it, I can only vote for a general recommendation to Congress.

Mr. STANARD: I move to take a recess till half-past seven, P. M. Carried.

## EVENING SESSION.

Mr. WILBOR: I beg to offer the following resolution of thanks.

*Resolved,* That the Board tenders its thanks to the Fire Department, of the city of Cincinnati, for the fine exhibition given of its promptness and efficiency.

Unanimously agreed to.

The PRESIDENT: The next business in order is the proposition from the St. Louis Board of Trade, respecting ports of entry.

We recommend the passage of a law declaring the cities of Chicago, Cincinnati and St. Louis ports of entry, under such restrictions and regulations only as shall protect the Government against fraud.

Mr. TOPP: I beg to amend by adding Memphis.

Mr. FISK: The St. Louis Board of Trade simply presented a resolution making Chicago, St. Louis, Cincinnati and Louisville, ports of entry. Our delegation desire to amend this so as to cover all interior and Western cities having a population of two hundred thousand and over:

That the National Board of Trade recommend to Congress the immediate passage of a law declaring all interior and Western cities having a population of two hundred thousand and upward, ports of entry, under such restrictions and regulations only as shall protect the Government against fraud.

Mr. KIRKLAND: I would further amend:

That we recommend the passage of a law declaring that all cities and towns interior or otherwise, be made ports of entry, under such restrictions and regulations as will protect and guard the Government against fraud.

Mr. TOPP: I hope the house will not adopt the resolution proposed by the gentleman from St. Louis. Memphis has not a population of two hundred thousand. It seems to me it would be an arbitrary rule to fix, for Louisville, too, would be thus cut off. It matters not whether we have fifty thousand or one hundred thousand inhabitants.

Mr. ALLEN, of Philadelphia : I have no objection to these various amendments, but I have a resolution bearing upon this very subject. The Conventions, it will be recollected, in Boston and Philadelphia, adopted a memorial which was sent to Congress. The House of Representatives passed a bill in accordance with our request. It went to the Senate, and they reported a bill which covered all the ground, but guarded the interests of the Government better than the House bill.

Mr. KREIKHAUS : I move that we accept the suggestion of the gentleman from Philadelphia.

Mr. ALLEN : I am perfectly willing to include Memphis, Louisville, Toledo and Milwaukie.

Mr. KIRKLAND : I think my resolution is sufficiently comprehensive to bring in all those interior cities and towns in which the Government may think it can safely establish a Custom House. Most, if not all, of the cities that have been mentioned, have Custom Houses. I can sell a cargo of sugar, silk, coffee, or tea, to a merchant in Chicago, Cincinnati, St. Louis or Louisville, and transport it in bond to either of those cities, where there is now a Custom House, at which those duties can be paid by the parties to whom the goods are consigned. If the Government in its wisdom can devise such safeguards as shall protect and guard the revenue, merchants in those towns and cities that have Custom House machinery might be allowed to order direct from China, Japan, or Brazil. It is true the ships cannot go to St. Louis or Chicago ; but if I understand the provisions of this bill, a merchant in Chicago or St. Louis may have a cargo put into railroad cars and sent to him there, and have the duties adjusted. It is asked that instead of molasses, for instance, being guaged at New Orleans, it may be put in a railroad car and sent to Cincinnati or St. Louis, so that on any loss that may occur between the seaboard and the place to which it is consigned, there shall not be any charge, but the duties shall be paid on what is received.

We would not recommend Chicago, Cincinnati or St. Louis, to the exclusion of other cities. If the Government can protect its revenue so as to give to any of the interior cities this privilege, I say, on behalf of Baltimore, that we have no jealousy in the matter ; we do not wish to interpose obstacles to prevent any interior city from having any advantage to which its rights may entitle it.

Mr. BURWELL: I regard this as a serious measure, involving as it does a large amount of imports, which are here sought to be transferred to interior cities, and which are now received through the mouth of the Mississippi. I am of opinion that the cities should be named, that this Board would recommend to be made ports of entry.

The gentleman from St. Louis complains of the expenses attending the importation of goods by way of New Orleans. But our Custom House is now more liberal than formerly, and much more liberal than New York, I understand. Railroad iron has been specified as being subject to heavy charges. Under the old regulations, railroad iron has been imported, the customary charges amounting to seven dollars per ton. But within the last two years, St. Louis has revolutionized the whole trade. Instead of unloading and having the goods stored, barges now drop along-side the vessels, and the transference is made without delay, and at a great saving of expense. Our Chamber of Commerce has adopted resolutions lessening the tariff of charges, and it is prepared to offer facilities to expedite importations into interior cities.

I think if we adopt so general a proposition as has been suggested in regard to this matter, we may render ourselves ridiculous. The time may come when the smaller towns and cities may have the same advantages that are now confined to the larger ones; but if we make our recommendation so general and so indefinite, Congress may pay no attention to our request.

Mr. HINCKEN: I think this question is taking up much more time than it should do. It is a simple proposition, and of interest only to the people of the interior. We of the seaboard have no objection, if they can pay their duties without loss.

Mr. ALLEN: We have the bonded system now. The benefit we seek will be for those who import goods outside of New York. The goods imported there, are appraised there, and shipped in bond to Louisville, Chicago, or Cincinnati; but in case of loss or damage on the way, we can get no redress, unless they are sent back to the Custom House at which they were appraised. The Congress of the United States have already done what they are here asked to do; they have gone into this matter, and the Committee of the Senate have reported upon it favorably; and I think we need do no more than we did in June, namely, ask Congress to pass the bill, when all these cities will obtain the advantage of it.

Mr. NAZRO: I was a strong advocate of this measure at the Convention held in Boston. I should, however, go between this bill and the motion of the gentleman from Baltimore. I think that his amendment is a little too broad, and moreover we don't want to go to Congress with a scheme that is impracticable. If it can be amended with some restrictions, it would be better to name a few of the principal cities to be made ports of entry. I trust the motion will not prevail in the shape in which it now is, but that some amendment to the Baltimore amendment will be adopted. We should take a view of the whole country. I would not single out three or four cities, and say that in the opinion of this Board, no others should be made ports of entry. I trust there will be some modification by which the size of the place or the number of inhabitants will be taken into consideration.

Mr. STRANAHAN: I beg to offer the following:

*Resolved,* That this Board recommends the passage of a law declaring the most important towns and cities in the West, ports of entry, under such restrictions only as shall protect the Government against frauds.

Mr. HOLTON: Will the gentleman amend by saying important cities of the West "and South"?

Mr. STRANAHAN: Yes, Sir.

Mr. TOPP: I withdraw my amendment.

Mr. STRANAHAN: I offer my resolution as a substitute for the original resolution and the amendments of the gentlemen from Baltimore and Philadelphia.

Mr. ALLEN: I withdraw my amendment.

Mr. KIRKLAND: I withdraw mine.

Mr. FISK: We will accept Mr. STRANAHAN's.

The PRESIDENT: The question before the Board is the proposition of the gentleman from New York.

Mr. PORTER: I must oppose the resolution. It is in reality only the resolution that came from the St. Louis Board of Trade. It says this Board recommends to Congress that the principal interior cities of the West and South shall be made ports of entry. St. Louis and Cincinnati declare, as does Chicago, that that refers to St. Louis, Cincinnati and Chicago, and Congress will certainly so receive it, because they have shown to us by the bill to which Mr. ALLEN has referred, that this is what they were about to do before, and they will consider that this Board, after adopting Mr. STRANAHAN's proposition, would make St. Louis, Cincinnati and Chicago alone ports of entry.

Mr. TREZEVANT : As I learn from the gentleman from Philadelphia, the proposition before Congress now names three cities. The resolution introduced by the gentleman from New York, is an enlargement of that proposition, and can be looked upon in no other light. "Important cities of the South and West;" Memphis, I apprehend, is an important city. I think Memphis is safe without being named; I am certainly willing that it should be recommended as an "important city," and if the national legislature does not so regard us, it is for us to log-roll to get Memphis included.

Mr. DAVIS : I move the previous question.

Carried.

The PRESIDENT : The question now is on Mr. STRANAHAN's resolution.

The resolution was carried.

The PRESIDENT : The next business in order is the recommendation from St. Louis on the navigation of the Mississippi.

Mr. SHRYOCK : By consent of the delegation from St. Louis, this proposition has been assigned to me, and I would claim the indulgence of the house to be briefly heard on this great question. It is one so broad and extensive, and one in which every member of this house is interested so deeply that I am satisfied the resolution will not be controverted by any one. The gentlemen behind me (from New York,) are interested in the commerce of the Mississippi River, the gentlemen from St. Paul are interested: and gentlemen from the frozen rivers of New England, along the coast down to the Rio Grande, are interested also.

The wealth of this country in a large measure comes from the commerce of the Mississippi River, and the fourteen States washed by its waters, entitled to the name of the Middle States, are worth one-half of all the wealth of this country; its people pay one-half the taxes, and it contains seven hundred and eighty-five million acres of the finest lands that are found in this or any other country. The commerce of this river is three or four times greater than all the foreign commerce of the country, hence the importance of this great channel of commerce and of communication between the North and South. It is a project in which Chicago and Boston are equally interested.

I beg to present the following resolutions without further remark:

WHEREAS, The Mississippi River being our great natural highway and medium of water navigation from the Falls of St. Anthony to the Gulf of Mexico, free forever for the commerce of all the States, and as such should be jealously guarded by the General Government: and

WHEREAS, Any impediment to its free and safe navigation is injurious to the general welfare of the country: therefore,

*Resolved*, That we consider it not only wise and proper, but an imperious necessity, for the Government to finish the work already commenced for its general improvement on the Mississippi Rapids, and to make such additional appropriations as will in the end remove all barriers to the safe and free navigation, and effect a radical improvement of the Mississippi and Ohio Rivers, whether these barriers exist from natural or artificial causes.

*Resolved*, That this Board desires to reaffirm the resolutions set forth and adopted by the River Improvement Convention at its late session at St. Louis.

*Resolved*, That no consideration of economy or retrenchment, present or prospective, should prevent appropriations by Congress on a scale commensurate with the national importance of the work.

Mr. TREZEVANT: I desire to offer a resolution, which may be considered a substitute for the one offered by the gentleman from St. Louis:

*Resolved*, That the leveeing of the Mississippi River, from Cairo to its mouth, and the removing of obstructions to the navigation of the same, are works too costly to be undertaken by States, counties, or individuals, yet too essential to the general prosperity of the whole Union to be longer deferred.

*Resolved*, That this Board of Trade most respectfully urges upon Congress the necessity of making such liberal appropriation as will place the fertile lands of the Mississippi Valley beyond the danger of inundation, and give safety to its commerce.

I regard this matter as second to none which the Convention may consider or discuss. The more it is examined, the more gigantic does it seem in its proportions. The commerce of this mighty stream — the Mississippi — is more extensive and valuable than that of any other on the globe. It has a navigation, for itself and branches, of more than twenty-five thousand miles; and the commerce floating upon its bosom is more valuable than the internal commerce of all Europe. The interest felt in it, is not confined to the States lying on its banks, but it pervades all the people from the Lakes to the Gulf.

The area of country directly interested in it, is equal to those of France, Austria and Prussia combined — nations that contain more than one hundred millions of people.

I ask the attention of the Board to the following table which I have compiled with much care, from the census return of 1860:

| Returns for 1860. | | In the United States. | In the States upon the Mississippi and its branches. |
|---|---|---|---|
| Population, | | 31,500,000 | 14,500,000 |
| Real and personal estate, | | $16,000,000,000 | $7,500,000,000 |
| Horses, mules, cattle, sheep and swine, | | 81,000,000 | 50,000,000 |
| Corn, | bushels, | 830,000,000 | 580,000,000 |
| Wheat, | " | 171,000,000 | 98,000,000 |
| Potatoes, | " | 110,000,000 | 40,000,000 |
| Sugar, | hhds., | 302,000,000 | 298,000,000 |
| Tobacco, | lbs., | 430,000,000 | 225,000,000 |
| Cotton, | bales, | 5,196,000 | 2,510,000 |

At the beginning of the century, the States that now produce these valuable products in such quantities, were a wilderness. This table shows what they are now. I undertake to say, such a picture of progress has never been known before in any age or country. But this is not all. Let us look at the increase of population in the Mississippi Valley from 1850 to 1860. Take the ten States of Ohio, Indiana, Illinois, Iowa, Kentucky, Wisconsin, Tennessee, Arkansas, Mississippi and Louisiana, and you find the population increased sixty-seven per cent. from 1850 to 1860, while the most prosperous States of the Atlantic, (Connecticut, Massachusetts, New York and New Jersey,) average but thirty-two per cent.

Now, look at the increase of wealth. That of the States named in the valley, was two hundred and ninety-nine per cent. from 1850 to 1860; that of the other States named, only one hundred and seven per cent. in the same time. These figures indicate where the population and wealth of the Union are; and these always command political power. By the beginning of the next century, this Union will contain more than one hundred millions of people; and two-thirds of them will be in this valley, and in their hands will be the control of this Government. Now Sir, let me ask, what relation this great river and its improvement have to this vast population and wealth. It will always be the artery of their commerce; and the products raised on its banks, from Memphis to its mouth, will forever constitute the chief national exports. Valuable as are the mines of California, they dwindle into insignificance when contrasted with the cotton raised on the banks of this stream. And yet, it is beyond the power of States or individuals to prevent the inundations constantly attending its annual rises. Millions of acres are annually destroyed just when the crop is promising; and millions more are prevented from being reclaimed by the same flood which annually pours down both from the Alleghany and from the Rocky Mountains. The wealth of the nation — that export wealth which is so valuable in settling the balances of trade — is thus constantly jeopardized; and even the shipping interests of the Atlantic are damaged. Would not the Atlantic States feel that their shipping would be much more profitably employed if we could raise five million bales of cotton? The State of Mississippi alone can raise five millions, in twenty years after her fertile bottoms shall be protected from overflow; for now, not one acre in five, of these rich lands, is cultivated. I trust, Sir, that all will perceive, from the views I present, that all portions of the Union are deeply interested in protecting this vast and rich region from inundation. The planter, the merchant, and the manufacturer, all feel it alike; and I can present the subject in no stronger light than by asking this question: How should we settle the balance of trade against us, if cotton should no longer be among our exports?

Mr. HOLTON: I rise to call the attention of the Board to what seems to me an immense evil in our present action. We have to-day passed upon a measure by which we have recommended to Congress the appropriation of many millions of dollars, possibly one hundred million dollars, for lines of railroad that we know little or nothing of, respecting which no statistics have been furnished us, and about which some are ignorant of the geography or even of the latitude of the regions through which the projected lines are to pass. Yet we sit here and pass resolutions in reference to improvements which will need millions on millions of money to complete.

If I understand the resolutions of the gentleman from St. Louis, it is that we shall, without any regard to the condition of the public Treasury, recommend Congress to enter upon the improvement of the Mississippi and all its tributaries.

Mr. SHRYOCK: The gentleman is mistaken.

Mr. HOLTON: I am glad to be corrected. The gentleman from Memphis would have us by his amendment recommend to Congress the improvement of the levees of the Mississippi from Cairo to the mouth of the Mississippi. I confess, Sir, these propositions frighten me. I am not prepared to recommend these gigantic schemes for the adoption of Congress; first we are without the statistics upon which such a recommendation should be based, and secondly we cannot lose sight of the fact, that the country is burdened with an enormous debt. It involves us in a dilemma from which our utmost energies will be required to free us. There is no man to whom I will be second in my belief of the natural and industrial capacity of our country : its God-given elements of wealth and greatness demand alike our admiration and our gratitude, but, Sir, let us not recommend measures here which might permanently cripple our resources and strike a deathblow at our real prosperity.

I desire to do nothing to restrain individual enterprise ; and I see nothing in the proposed improvements more arduous or difficult than has been again and again accomplished by the enterprise of private citizens. Look at this State of Ohio with her complex net-work of railroads stretching all over the State, and all the result of private enterprise. Our recommendations, Sir, have been given hitherto with a view to encourage private enterprise. We have recommended that the disabilities under which the shipping interest now suffers should be removed ; we have recommended that private property on the high seas should be respected at all times. Our recommendations have had in view the removal of restrictions on *private enterprise.* These seem to me laudable subjects for the National Board of Trade to consider; but we are now asked to appeal to Congress to spend millions on millions of dollars without the preparation and effort that I think should be first demanded of private citizens. We are but an advisory body at best, and unless we are very careful, our recommendations will command neither attention nor respect. The Boston Convention, in which this Board had its origin, was attended by nearly three hundred business men of the country. It committed the whole question of internal improvements to a Committee of twenty-eight, representing as many different cities of the United States. This Committee reported three or four measures,- but they were general, such only as I trust this National Board will consent to recommend. First, there was the ship canal from the lakes to the seaboard ; second, the improvement of the navigation of the Mississippi River ; this latter recommendation the Government accepted and is at this very day prosecuting. Another was that Government should, at the fitting time, take up its line of march from Lake Superior to Puget Sound, to that empire to which we are to succeed. Another was to meet the necessities of our friends at Memphis and elsewhere, by building a road to the Pacific Ocean central to the Southern States, at the proper time. But those recommendations did not look to the advancement of any private interests, but of great national interests, and for the encouragement of private enterprise. The Boston Convention distinctly accompanied its recommendations with the assertion that in its judgment the Federal Government could not and should not enter upon the execution of these recommendations in the present condition of the national Treasury.

It seems to me it would be the best plan if we have any agency by which it can be done, to commit these subjects to a proper Committee, which would bring the matter before us at a future meeting, with such facts and reasons as would carry certain conviction if they are to be adopted by the Board. As for the resolutions as they now stand, I cannot vote for them.

Mr. RANDOLPH : I shall not oppose the proposition coming from the St. Louis Board except in one particular. This resolution proposes to commit this body to recommendations of the extent of which they have not as yet given us the slightest idea. Besides I see nothing in this resolution of St. Louis that was not raised by a gentleman from New Orleans at Philadelphia last June. I think this Board will lose its influence if it tells the same story over and over again. When we say a thing once, and say it in the right manner, any repetition will be mere surplusage.

As to the proposition from Memphis, I understand that has reference to entirely different matters. It proposes that Government shall go to work and build up the levees and reclaim a vast amount of private land, resulting, as it must, in the acquirement of vast fortunes by the owners. I do not think this Board will recommend a proposition of this character. I understand there is another proposition to be presented in regard to these levees, which I might vote for, but not for this, and I hope action will be laid over, that the expression of this Board may stand as expressed at Philadelphia.

Mr. MONROE : By an arrangement with the gentlemen from St. Louis who had the proposition for river improvement under their charge, and the gentlemen from Louisville who had the Central Water Lines of Virginia in charge, and with the approval of my colleague, who represents the Wisconsin and Fox River improvement, it was agreed that these subjects might be considered together, and I drew up and submitted to them some resolutions to that end. At the proper time I will offer them as an amendment to the resolutions from Louisville, and with the permission of the house will now read them.

[ See resolutions in Mr. MONROE's remarks, December 8th.]

I read these for the purpose of showing that it is intended to present the improvement of the Western rivers and their connections with the Atlantic Ocean and the Gulf of Mexico as a system of water communication between the East and West, and I propose at the proper time to offer these resolutions in regard to the improvement of Western rivers, believing that by so doing it will supersede the necessity of separate action.

Mr. WETHERILL : I desire to ask what would be the probable cost of the improvements suggested in the scheme of Mr. MONROE?

Mr. MONROE: When I have an opportunity I will not only state the exact cost as nearly as can be estimated, but also the probable income. I may here say, that the amount of money already expended, as reported by the engineer, is about twelve million dollars; and the amount that will be required will be about twenty-six million dollars more.

Mr. STANARD: I want to say a word about the Mississippi River. But first, I would say that I trust those gentlemen who are from the east of the Mississippi, from the lakes and the seaboard, will excuse us of St. Louis for presenting so many matters here, and occupying so much of the attention of the Board. It will be remembered that for many years the Government of the United States have been making very large appropriations for improvements upon the lakes and along the seaboard, building light-houses, opening channels, &c., and it is not strange now if the West should come before you, when we believe that, to a very great extent, the Eastern country is comparatively finished up. Taking into consideration the fact that but two delegations here represent the vast country which lies west of the Mississippi River, — over half of this continent — you will excuse us if we talk considerably about this great valley, and the people who inhabit it, and those who will hereafter occupy it. I do not doubt that you think it is a very great country from the speeches which have been made and from the statistics which have been presented; I have such an estimate of that country myself.

But I wish to speak particularly of the Mississippi. This is the greatest river in our country, or indeed in the world. It is navigable without its tributaries to the extent of over three thousand miles; and if anybody knows how long the Missouri River is, I should like him to tell me; perhaps three thousand miles from St. Louis; and then you have the Ohio and its tributaries. And all that is asked in the resolution from St. Louis is that sufficient appropriation shall be made to keep this river in navigable condition, so that the commerce along its borders may be transported to the market. We do not anticipate or make any special call for appropriations; it is well known that appropriations were made for the improvement of the rapids of the Des Moines; — but what we desire is that Congress should complete the work, and have a canal round the lower rapids, so that navigation will be certain; and as the appropriations which are now made are not sufficient to complete the work, we desire further appropriations. It is important, as every one knows that knows anything about it, that the mud and dirt which settle in the mouth of the Mississippi at New Orleans, should be cleaned out; it cannot be done as a permanency, or for any given length of time; it requires constant work to keep the mouth clear of mud and sediment; and what we desire is that Government shall make such appropriations as will give us uninterrupted navigation to the sea. Therefore we ask that from time to time such appropriations shall be made as may be necessary for the uninterrupted transportation of the commerce of that great river.

The gentleman from Milwaukie must not accuse us of springing questions upon this Board. These matters were duly reported sixty days before the meeting, and were sent to all the constituent bodies; therefore, if the gentleman desired to investigate the claims of the projects and the desirability of these appropriations, and did not do it, he has no one to blame but himself. And with relation to the vote of the gentleman this afternoon, upon appropriations for the extension and building of those lines of railroads; it seems to me that any gentleman knowing nothing of the great country west of the Mississippi, might have taken sufficient pains to inform himself somewhat upon the geography of the country to enable him to vote understandingly. We do not desire to spring anything upon you; but we do submit to the consideration of this Board the fact that these are matters of national interest, and therefore possessing sufficient importance to recommend them to your attention. If you are not interested in the country west of the Mississippi, your children and children's children will be. For as our population increases, where will the people go? Where will they settle if not in the Valley of the Mississippi? I expect to live to see the day when this valley will have a population of more than one hundred millions;—and I consider this no extravagant assertion.

It is certain, that we are not here to advocate anything of a sectional character; neither are these things matters of no moment. There is a vast country rapidly filling up. The Government has millions of acres of land which it is desirable to bring into the market; and giving away alternate sections, will be the means of putting the other land in the market, and getting the money for it, while at the same time great good for humanity will be accomplished, not only by promoting the commerce of the country, but by helping forward the progress of civilization.

Mr. DAVIS, of Cincinnati: I have two objections to the resolution from St. Louis now before the house, and which I would move to amend by striking out that part referring to the action of the Convention at St. Louis. The original resolution spoke of the Mississippi and its tributaries. In the Ohio River we are thought to have some interest; the Louisville Canal, I should think, is a matter of some interest and importance; I know it has been talked of ever since I was a boy; and I therefore move to add, " and the Ohio River."

Mr. SHRYOCK: The resolution referred distinctly to the Ohio River.

Mr. DAVIS: The appropriations for which these Pacific Railroads have been asking, are immense; and I tell you that if one-hundreth part of the amounts they have received had been given to the improvement of these rivers, the rivers would now be unobstructed. Any one of the river steamers will carry more freight than can be carried on six railroad cars. A hundred tons; what is it? A thousand tons; what is it? Try to put a thousand tons on a railroad, and see how it will tax its energies. St. Louis tried taking freight by land and found it could not succeed.

These rivers are of vast importance. We have no commerce compared with that of the Mississippi Valley. It is larger even than we have yet heard; it will influence and affect more of the inhabitants of our country than any other commerce we may have. Notwithstanding the railroads we now have, the river commerce is not only not lessening but increasing all the time.

I do not blame gentlemen for desiring to vote intelligently; I think that we should have the necessary statistics worked up, not only for our own information, but to present to Congress for its particular benefit and use. But of what benefit are the railroads as compared with these rivers, in the transportation of freight? Therefore I would say while we do one thing, let us not leave the other undone.

I move to strike out the resolution endorsing the action of the River Improvement Convention at St. Louis; as an amendment to the amendment of the gentleman from Memphis.

Mr. BRUNOT: After the glowing descriptions which we have just heard of the productive capacity of the South, the magnificence of the great Northwest, the wonderful progress of our whole country in all the elements of greatness, and the glory of our achievements, let me ask your attention for a few moments to our shame. Since 1787 the United States Government has claimed exclusive jurisdiction and custodianship over the great rivers of the country. Nearly sixty years ago — before the era of steam navigation — it began to improve the Ohio River. The plan adopted seemed suitable to the requirements of the traffic. It was based upon the idea that as the width of the water channel could be decreased, the depth would be increased, and to that extent facility would be given to the passage of the craft then in use. Several wing dams were constructed upon this plan in the Lower Ohio. In 1837, the same plan substantially was adhered to by Major SANDERS, the Government Engineer then in charge, and the present works are but a continuation, on a more extended scale of the system first adopted.

The utmost that was hoped for from the plan by Major SANDERS, was, that it would produce a depth of two and a half feet in the channel, at low water. The utmost that is now claimed to have been effected at the points where the works have been completed is, that in an ordinary low water navigation stage, an additional depth of eight to twelve inches has been obtained, but in the times of extreme low water, no material change has been effected. The period of actual cessation of navigation has not been appreciably decreased. In the season of drought the Ohio River in its natural state was absolutely worthless for all purposes of through navigation, and during the same season it is absolutely worthless yet; arts, manufactures, means of land transportation, ocean navigation — everything, has made a progress during the last thirty years, which words cannot picture to the mind. This has alone stood still; not one step in advance has been permitted. The same old plans of sixty years ago, and which for twenty or thirty years have been abandoned by every other civilized nation on the globe, are still persistently adhered to by a Government which, in everything else, is alive and wide awake.*

Yet just as certainly as the genius of civilization has been able to seize upon the ore in our mines, the timber in our forests and the stone in our quarries, and therewith to supplant the inefficient turnpike and its Conestoga wagons by that magnificent channel of

---

* General WILSON, the engineer now having charge of the Upper Mississippi, proposes plans which, if carried out, cannot fail to accomplish all that could be desired for the radical improvement of the Des Moines Rapids. The appropriation last year to this object is the first and only indication on the part of Congress of an approach to some proper appreciation of either the capacity or the requirements of the Mississippi.

commerce — the iron railway — just as certainly and effectively is it within the compass of the same power to seize upon the timber on the hills, the stone in the quarries, and the water in the channel of this grand stream, and construct from them an artery of commerce which shall be as superior to it in its present state as is the railway to the common road.

Such a radical improvement of our great rivers is what we want, and the desideratum will never be reached by adhering to the old time schemes. Distinguished engineers have proposed various plans by which they believed the object would be accomplished. The late CHARLES ELLET proposed to effect it by a system of reservoirs in which the surplus waters of the rainy season would be held in reserve to supply the demands of navigation in drought. Another, the eminent engineer now in charge of the Ohio River, (W. M. ROBERT, Esq.,) years ago advocated a system of locks and dams with chutes, the former for low water, the latter for free navigation in high water. Another proposed a system of open dams and sluices in combination with locks. Another a combination of the reservoirs and the sluices. Each of these plans has its hundreds of practical minds conversant with the subject, who believe their favorite the best, and, of course, each has its doubters or active opponents.

The great advances which have been made in the modes of land transportation have been the result of experiment. Every improvement upon the railway or steam engine has resulted from the trial of somebody's plan. But for this, fac similes of the first steamer would still be laboriously puffing into your ports. The practical experiments which have led to the present perfection in the steamer and the railway, were within the compass of individual means and enterprise. In this matter of the improvement of the navigable capacity of our great rivers, practical experiment is beyond the compass of individuals. Government alone, which rightly claims their control, has either the means or the power to operate on so large a scale. The feasibility or practicability of any of the proposed plans can only be demonstrated by trial, and if the Government will not rise to an appreciation of this fact and make the trial, the Ohio River must remain as it is forever.

Other nations have made great advances in the improvements of their river navigation. With the French no branch of engineering science has had the precedence over this, and they have developed several plans which have accomplished for their rivers just what we desire for the Ohio. Improvements have been constructed upon the Seine and the Marne within the last few years, which admirably effect their purpose, and oppose no obstacle to free navigation in ordinary stages of water. They each consist of a lock, a dam with a navigation pass, and a regulating sluice. During high and moderate stages of the water, the navigation pass is free and the regulating sluice open. When the water begins to fall in the navigation pass below the desired level, it is kept up by closing gradually the regulating sluice. When the quantity of water is too small to afford the required depth by this means, both passes are closed and the lock is used. When it rises again, the passes are opened and the lock is dispensed with.

It is common to assume that plans which are adapted to the rivers of Europe must necessarily be too diminutive for the grander streams of North America. We compare the Mississippi or the Ohio in their floods with the Seine or the Rhine in their normal condition, forgetting that it is not the Ohio or the Mississippi in their flood tide that we desire to improve. The Ohio above Cincinnati, or the Mississippi at points above Alton, do not in drought differ greatly from the rivers named at similar stages. The so-called improvement of the Ohio River, when completed on its present plan, will have in its navigation passes, a depth of say two and a half feet. The French rivers have by means of their improvement, (in low water) a depth of four to seven feet.

What has been done by the French engineers for their rivers can be done more perfectly by American engineers for ours. What has been done by the French Government can be better done by the Congress of the United States. The engineers in charge of the work upon the Western rivers appreciate the importance and magnitude of the improvements required, and the capacity of the streams. They have the genius to plan and the ability to execute. The Congress of the United States has never yet appreciated the importance of the work to the nation, the grand results attainable, or the fact that the means required to accomplish such results, must be commensurably large.

When the States of Ohio, Indiana and Illinois deemed it for their interest to connect the lakes by water with the Ohio River, they did it. When the State of Pennsylvania desired to use the water of its mountain streams to effect a comparatively insignificant water navigation between the head of the Ohio and the Schuylkill, it set about the work and accomplished it at a cost of thirty millions. When the State of New York desired to make a similar connection between the Hudson and the lakes, it spent forty millions and did it. But when the Government of the United States, crying hands-off to citizen, corporation and Commonwealth, undertakes to perfect its navigation — it deals out each decade of years, two or three hundred thousand dollars, or the smallest possible sum which will for the moment quiet the periodical importunities of the Western people!

The highest estimate of cost made by the friends of either of the plans yet proposed for the radical improvement of the Ohio River, is twelve millions of dollars. The highest estimate on any of the plans by those who oppose them, is twenty to twenty-five millions of dollars.

Is not the radical improvement of the Ohio and Mississippi Rivers a national object? You have in the East a great river — great in width, great in depth, great in the commerce which floats upon its bosom — but insignificant in length. Suppose that by some freak of nature the Hudson should be reduced for three months in the summer to an almost worthless navigation — what expenditure would be thought too great to restore it to its normal condition? Would ten, fifty, a hundred millions be thought too much? We have here — from St. Paul to the mouth of the Ohio — from Cairo to Pittsburgh, eighteen hundred miles of river, with banks more fertile than the Hudson, richer than it in mines and forests and wealth-producing elements, capable of being made as useful for navigation, yet now useless for one-fourth of the year.

This Board has expressed the desire that the Government shall enter upon the construction of three great lines of railroads to the Pacific coast. When their trains shall reach the Mississippi Valley laden with the products of the mountains, of the great Pacific States beyond the mountains — of the great sea beyond the States — and of the great empires beyond the sea — they will find the existing railway avenues thence to the Atlantic cities overburthened by the traffic which they have created along their own tracks. Let the national rivers stand ready to carry off the surplus from the national roads. If the National Board of Trade shall but succeed in impressing upon Congress the necessity of entering at once upon the work of a general improvement of the great rivers of the country, this alone will amply repay for all the labor and pains spent in its organization.

Mr. WETHERILL: I should like to say in reference to the remarks of the gentleman from Milwaukie, that most of the members of this Board entirely agree with him that we should be careful as to the resolutions we may pass. We should ask for expenditures of money just as cautiously as though the money were to be placed to our own debit; otherwise, I doubt if any resolution we may pass, will have any effect. But at the same time, I differ with the gentleman; for I contend that the expenditure which we have already declared ourselves in favor of, is of vast importance to the country, and will repay ten-fold for the outlay. When I recollect the immense extent of country west of the Mississippi, — perhaps a thousand millions of acres — with its abundant river and ocean communication, I know that the expenditure asked for its improvement, would be better secured than is any mortgage upon any house in Cincinnati. There is all the wealth of this country. That land belongs to the country; and we are bound to do all we can to develop and improve it; for upon it, and the amount of labor we can put upon it, depend our success and our wealth hereafter. In keeping open the Mississippi, we add to the national wealth; because, Sir, no country can succeed unless every avenue is opened which is necessary to bring the manufactures of its people and the products of its soil to the seaboard at the lowest and cheapest rate. With that view, I shall vote for these resolutions.

I recollect that four years ago the great Northwest thought the life of the United States depended upon keeping open the Mississippi. They were willing to spend any amount of money then, in the accomplishment of that object; and now that it needs improvement, and when Congress is committed to that improvement, why should we hesitate to endorse what it is willing to do? If we should go to Congress and ask if the majority are in favor of this improvement, they would say yes; and it is our duty to support the members of Congress in this conviction. If Congress is to expend sixty million dollars on the Union Pacific Railroad, eight millions on the Kansas road, and do what it can to keep unobstructed the great and mighty rivers of this country, it seems to me this Board of Trade would belittle itself if it should oppose this great and needed improvement.

As to the expenditure; when I look around me and see that we represent the merchants and the manufacturers of the country, I contend that we have as much interest as any one in the expenses of the Government. We work for what we make; it is the merchants and manufacturers who keep the revenues full, who keep the Government in motion; and when we agree to expend money, we also know that we must raise the interest. We, therefore, who are the parties most deeply interested in the matter, should be careful of the expenditure, but we should not be niggardly. I hope, therefore, we shall vote for the resolutions.

Mr. GANO: I wish to offer the following proposition, as a substitute for the whole.

Mr. SHRYOCK: I will accept anything that is for the improvement of the Mississippi River.

Mr. GANO: It embodies part of the original paper presented by the gentlemen from St. Louis, but proposes to erase a part of the first resolution:

WHEREAS, The Mississippi River being our great natural highway and medium of water navigation from the Falls of St. Anthony to the Gulf of Mexico, free forever for the commerce of all the States, and, as such, should be jealously guarded by the general Government; and,

WHEREAS, Any impediment to its free and safe navigation is injurious to the general welfare of the country; therefore, be it

*Resolved*, That we consider it not only wise and proper, but an imperious necessity, for the Government to remove all natural and artificial barriers to the safe and free navigation, and effect a radical improvement of the Mississippi and Ohio Rivers.

*Resolved*, That the thanks of the National Board of Trade be tendered to Congress for the attention given, during its last session, to the wants of our Western river commerce, and that that body be respectfully urged to enact the appropriation bill already passed by the House of Representatives, and approved by the Senate Committee on Western river improvements, and now before the Senate.

Concerning the second resolution offered by the gentleman from St. Louis, I would say that I know something of the history of the River Improvement Convention and its acts, because of the intimate relation to it of our Cincinnati Chamber of Commerce, which approved of the action of the Convention. Its course was in a great degree a compromise; it was found necessary to take that course in order to get anything done. We assented to all the measures approved by the Central Committee of that body, to secure from Congress such appropriations as they could, in accordance with the resolution adopted. It has been before Congress, and the General Government has had surveyors in the field.

The appropriation bill before Congress, under the auspices of the St. Louis Central Committee, is very nearly in accordance with the desires of that body, so far as I understand. It is a generous one, and has the approval of the Senate Committee, but was not passed for reasons which all will comprehend, who understand the political situation at that time. They did not wish to load the Government too heavily with appropriations; but a sum was appropriated sufficient to carry on the work for the present season.

The PRESIDENT: The proposition is now on the substitute read by Mr. GANO.

Mr. HOLTON: I rise to second the motion. I understand these resolutions as simply confirming the recommendations made in Boston and in Philadelphia. There is no doubt as to the opinion of practical mercantile men on this subject. As Chairman of the Committee at Boston, I may say that we recommended the improvement of the Mississippi River, and such rivers as run through several States, thereby rendering it incompatible for the individual States to make the improvements.

On the other hand, I must oppose calling for appropriations of money for everything; and I hope that some CALHOUN will put his foot upon this idea of running to the Treasury for money for every special improvement.

Mr. PORTER: I move to strike out from the substitute the words "whether natural or artificial." I do not see the necessity for the words, and if they are to be interpreted literally, it would take away from Cincinnati the beautiful structure which spans the Ohio at this point, — for in some respects that is an obstruction to the navigation of the Ohio River.

Mr. STRANAHAN: I second the motion, for the purpose of getting an explanation of what is meant by an "artificial" obstruction.

Mr. SHRYOCK: I am very much amazed at the debate which has sprung up on this question. I framed the resolution in such a manner as I thought would avoid discussion; but it is my determination, both before this body and everywhere else, to raise my voice in opposition to any bridge, or anything else that will obstruct the Ohio or the Mississippi, or cause the slightest danger to the commerce of these rivers. From the mouth of the Ohio almost to its source, bridges are being thrown across, which threaten almost the destruction of its commerce. Bridges are being built over this river as a part of a great railroad system, which is intended to destroy the navigation of the Mississippi. If it were necessary, I could prove that proposition.

My object in rising was to explain that bridges less than five hundred feet span, I would regard as artificial obstructions. I have an immense number of statistics which I might have presented in reference to this matter, but I took my seat after presenting the resolution, not wishing to unnecessarily consume the time of the Board. But I might as well have stated the facts so that every member living on the water-shed of the Alleghanies might know the facts bearing on this important question. I do not want to be driven to believe that unless their individual axe is on the grindstone, members of this body will refuse to act. The commerce of the Mississippi is five, perhaps ten times as great as that of all the rest of the country. The people of the Western country feel they have a right to demand this river improvement. At the present time it costs more to carry a bushel of wheat from St. Paul to St. Louis than it ought to do to take it to New York city, and if the improvements called for, are made, a bushel of wheat can be carried from Milwaukie to New York for twenty-five cents. Our friends of the seaboard seem to know but little of the wants of the great West, and I can understand their refusal to ask Congress for appropriations that will tend so materially to the prosperity of the Western States; but I am amazed that gentlemen who live in the Mississippi Valley should refuse their consent to whatever may be necessary to secure the unimpeded navigation of the Mississippi to the Gulf. California is sending her wheat and flour in English ships to New York at greater profit than the people of Iowa can send theirs. California last year sent two hundred thousand barrels of flour, and thirteen million bushels of wheat to New York, in competition with us, and California is now the greatest competitor we have. Now the hardy sons of toil here in the West demand the removal of obstructions to forwarding the products of the soil, and it is a demand in which, it seems to me, the inhabitants of this country, from the seaboard of New England to the Rio Grande, should unite.

The PRESIDENT: Does Mr. GANO accept the proposition of Mr. PORTER to amend his proposition by striking out the words "natural and artificial?"

Mr. GANO: I do not feel at liberty to do so.

Mr. RANDOLPH: I did not expect to say more: I expected to vote for the propositions, but after what has been said by the gentleman from St. Louis, I cannot vote for them. From the peculiar language in which they are framed, they are calculated to deceive. I do not suppose there were five gentlemen in this room, who, when they were read and re-read, for a moment anticipated that it was intended to destroy all the bridges which span the Ohio, and to destroy the railroad capital invested in them. It seems to me it is an outrage upon this Board for the gentleman to present such resolutions and ask for the expenditure of money, when such a recommendation is covered up, as is the case in these resolutions. I move that the resolutions be laid upon the table. I think the action we took at Boston, committing this Board to the improvement of the rivers of the West, is as far as we need go, and this proposition, I repeat, I think is an outrage upon the Board.

Mr. STANARD: Will the gentleman withdraw his motion for an instant?

Mr. RANDOLPH : I will, temporarily, to allow Mr. STANARD to speak.

Mr. STANARD: I will say that I am in favor of no such measure as the gentleman from Chicago attributes to us. I am in favor of bridging the Ohio wherever railways find it necessary to bridge it. I am fully alive to the importance and necessity of extending our railways west of the Mississippi River, and we have been recommending legislation on this subject, and it is something very foreign to St. Louis, and to the people who live in the Valley of the Mississippi, to undertake to do anything to cripple communication by railroad, or to impede the progress of railroads in the Western country, by objecting to bridges, or indeed in any other way. I exceedingly regret that the matter has come to this pass, and I ask that Mr. SHRYOCK be allowed to explain if St. Louis endorses the sentiment to which he has inadvertently given expression in this Convention.

MR. SHRYOCK : I am very much obliged to my colleague for giving me an opportunity to make an explanation. I certainly did not intend in these resolutions to cover up anything, and I will say that you may build a bridge every fifty miles, provided it will not impede the commerce of the river, and make its navigation dangerous.

Mr. STRANAHAN : I ask that the words "and artificial" may be withdrawn, because we do not understand them.

Mr. GANO : I will withdraw them.

The motion on Mr. GANO's substitute was now put and carried.

A motion was made to adjourn, but was lost.

Mr. SHRYOCK : I wish that it may be understood, Sir, that the proposition offered on the improvement of the Mississippi, does not cover all we wish to offer under that head. If the session of the Board is prolonged till to-morrow, and this matter can be kept open, there are several propositions we desire to present under the head of river improvements.

The PRESIDENT : The next question before the Board, is on water communication between the Atlantic Ocean and the Mississippi Valley.

Mr. MONROE : Is the river improvement question disposed of ?

The PRESIDENT : Yes, Sir, for the present.

Mr. PORTER : In presenting this question before the National Board of Trade, I desire to say, Sir, that when the Louisville Board of Trade determined to send up these resolutions to this body, we were not aware that so many propositions would be brought before the Board, asking for Government aid; had we been aware of it, I am satisfied that the Louisville Board of Trade would not have sent up these resolutions. But, Sir, as they have been sent up, and feeling myself instructed to support them, and because the measure has in itself some merit, I offer, as the resolutions which we desire to have adopted, the original series notified to the constituent bodies, the first being withdrawn, the second substituted for the first, and so on:

1st. *Resolved*, That cheap transportation for its heavy products to the markets of the world, is not only a necessity to the West, but is equally demanded by the best interests of the whole country.

2nd. *Resolved*, That the most feasible plan to secure this end is to provide a direct and continuous line of water communication between the Mississippi River and the Atlantic Ocean, in a latitude favorable to the safe carriage of grain in bulk, and yet comparatively free from obstructions by frosts; that such a communication can be readily secured by the Ohio, Kanawha and James Rivers, through Virginia and West Virginia to the Atlantic Ocean, near the mouth of the Chesapeake Bay.

3rd. *Resolved*, That said line of water communication is a work of great national importance, and as such is entitled to receive such aid from the General Government as will secure its completion at the earliest possible period.

4th. *Resolved*, That the Executive Council is hereby directed to memorialize the Senate and House of Representatives of the United States in behalf of this body, and ask them to take the subject of said water line communication into favorable consideration at an early day, and to grant such aid as may be necessary to secure its early completion.

I desire to explain that Mr. MONROE, of Dubuque, presented the main features of this proposition to our Board, which considered that it possesses great merit; and if this Board were not called upon to recommend too many advances for other purposes, we should like to have this acted on. I leave the matter with the Board without any argument in favor of it.

Mr. MONROE commenced his remarks on the water line communication, but gave way to a motion to adjourn, it being now ten o'clock, reserving his right to the floor at the next session.

The Board then adjourned to meet on Tuesday, December 8th, at ten o'clock, A. M.

# SIXTH DAY.

TUESDAY, DECEMBER 8, 1868.

The Board met pursuant to adjournment. Mr. President FRALEY in the chair.

Prayer was offered by the Rev. A. D. MAYO.

The reading of the Journal was dispensed with.

Mr. GANO: I ask the privilege of presenting the following resolution. It was prepared yesterday, but I had no opportunity of offering it:

*Resolved*, That the members of the National Board of Trade deeply deploring the frightful calamity which resulted from the collision of the steamers *United States* and *America*, on the Ohio River, on Friday night, December 4th, by which so many lives were lost, and such great suffering was imposed on the survivors; cannot omit to express their sense of horror as to the event, and to tender to the relatives and friends of those who were so suddenly brought to a terrible death, their heartfelt sympathies.

Passed unanimously.

Mr. GANO: I also ask the privilege of presenting some matters of reference which I deem it of importance for this Board to consider.

The Cincinnati Chamber of Commerce suggests the propriety of an effort to secure uniformity in trade statistics, trade reports and standards of measures of commodities, so that all constituent bodies shall be able to show weekly, monthly and yearly statistics computed for the same dates, by the same measures, and in like forms; and proposes the following:

*Resolved*, By the National Board of Trade, that its constituent bodies be requested to submit propositions or suggestions in regard to this matter to the Executive Council, which body shall, after due consideration, make recommendations and submit a plan by which trade statistics, trade customs and standards of measures may be made uniform for the entire country.

Also the following: —

The Cincinnati Chamber of Commerce submits a suggestion of the propriety of an effort to secure a reform of the irregularities in the laws of the States of the Union which pertain to the organization of corporations and of joint stock associations — especially of the parts of those laws which refer to the liabilities of the subscribers to the stock of joint stock associations.

The PRESIDENT: In reference to the first proposition, relating to the cental system it has already been referred to the Executive Council, and they have taken action upon it so far as calling the attention of Congress to it.

In regard to the others, under the ruling of the house three days ago, the propositions cannot be received. This house, by an order made with great unanimity, decided that no proposition except such as came from a Board could be received and referred; any such proposition, notice having been given sixty days previously, might be referred by a two-thirds vote, but that all other propositions should be rejected. They cannot, therefore, be received, unless the house will reconsider their decision.

Mr. DRAKE: May it not be done by unanimous consent?

The PRESIDENT: The Board admonished the Chair that such a course was contrary to the constitution of the body. We cannot get the proposition before the body except on a motion to reconsider.

Mr. TREZEVANT: I have no idea we shall have any diversity of opinion on this matter. I have a proposition which I think important, but I am not disposed to press it. As we are now finishing the business of the Board, I beg Mr. GANO will not press it.

Mr. ALLEN: I move that the order of business be suspended to enable Mr. GANO to offer his resolutions.

The PRESIDENT: That would not be in order: it cannot be got at except by a vote to reconsider.

Mr. DAVIS: I understood the Board to decide to admit new matter by a two-thirds vote.

The PRESIDENT: That would require forty days notice, and anything else was decided to be unconstitutional.

Mr. MONROE: When the house adjourned, I had the floor. I beg to be allowed to proceed; I will occupy but a short time.

Mr. BRUNOT: The gentleman's proposition might possibly be disposed of in a few moments, but if that is considered, the proposition of the gentleman from Memphis will be brought before the house, and that to remit the duty on railroad iron, and these would not be disposed of in a week; and even if they were, something else would be next taken up. I hope the gentleman instead of insisting upon presenting his paper to the Board, will just hand it to the Executive Council and it will then receive all the consideration he desires for it.

The PRESIDENT: The Secretary informs me that Mr. GANO's resolutions are from the Cincinnati Chamber of Commerce; they will, therefore, be considered. The question is on receiving these propositions.

Unanimously carried.

The PRESIDENT: They will be received and placed on the calendar at the foot of the list.

Mr. PORTER: I move the adoption of the preamble and resolution in reference to a Water Line Communication between the Atlantic Ocean and the Mississippi Valley, which I yesterday submitted.

The PRESIDENT: No motion can be submitted while Mr. MONROE has the floor.

Mr. MONROE: Under the circumstances I cannot yield the floor, but I am willing the resolutions should be read for the information of the house.

Mr. PORTER read:—

WHEREAS, The subject of the resolution submitted by the Board of Trade of Louisville, and now under consideration, is one of great importance, and has been but recently brought to the attention of the majority of this body, and should be fully examined and maturely considered before final action; therefore,

*Resolved*, That the whole subject be referred to a Committee of fifteen, with instructions to fully examine the same and report to the Board at its next meeting.

Mr. MONROE: Last night I offered as a substitute for the resolutions of Mr. PORTER, of Louisville, the following preamble and resolutions, which I again beg to read:—

WHEREAS, The removal, by order of the General Government, of all impediments to the navigation of the Mississippi River and its tributaries, is now, by all sections of the country, admitted to be a national duty; and

WHEREAS, Cheap transportation of its heavy products to the markets of the world, and of their return supplies, is not only a *necessity* of the West, but is also demanded by the best interests of the whole country; therefore

*Resolved,* That the most feasible plan to secure this end, and thereby fully realize the benefits of such river improvements is, to provide continuous lines of water communication between the Mississippi River and the Atlantic Ocean; and that this plan can be most readily and advantageously accomplished by means of the Wisconsin and Fox Rivers improvement, connecting the Mississippi with Green Bay, and thence, by the Lakes, Erie Canal and Hudson River to New York, on the one hand; and by the Ohio River, the Kanawha and James Rivers, and the James River and Kanawha Canal to the Atlantic seaboard, near the mouth of the Chesapeake Bay, on the other; both of which routes are in a climate favorable to the transportation of grain in bulk, and the latter comparatively free from obstructions by ice.

*Resolved,* That while each one of these proposed routes has advantages over the other in directness, cheapness, and facility of transportation, to and from the region of country near the same parallel of latitude, and most directly tributary to it, there is a large margin of highly productive country, extending through the States of Ohio, Indiana, Illinois and Iowa, about one hundred miles in width and nearly one thousand miles in length, whose transportation will be competed for by both routes on nearly equal terms, which competition will compel facilities to be furnished, and charges of transportation to be reduced to the lowest paying rates, to enable each route to meet the competition of the other.

*Resolved,* Therefore, that these two proposed routes are not antagonistic to each other, but they are both demanded by the wants of the West, and the interest of the whole country, and each one will be rendered more valuable, not only to the region of country whose transportation is to be competed for, but to the country more directly tributary to it by the completion of the other.

*Resolved,* That these proposed improvements, when completed, will not only return to the West alone, in the reduction of the charges of transportation, for each year, more than double the entire amount of the cost of construction; but, at a low rate of tolls, will pay both the principal and interest on the cost of construction in a reasonable time.

*Resolved,* That the aid required of the Federal Government to complete these improvements, will add nothing to the national burthen of indebtedness, but on the contrary will diminish it, by greatly enhancing the means of payment.

*Resolved*, That both these contemplated routes are works of great national importance, directly beneficial to more than half the country, and indirectly to the whole, and are therefore entitled to receive such aid from the General Government as will ensure their speedy completion.

Mr. MONROE proceeded to address the Board, but not having concluded under the ten minute rule, on motion, leave was given to print his remarks, as follows:—

Mr. President: The great question, paramount to all others before this body, is that of transportation between the Valley of the Mississippi, the Atlantic seaboard, and the markets of the world.

There are now about twenty-five millions of tons of freight annually, wanting transportation back and forth from the Mississippi Valley to and from the Atlantic and Eastern States, and the present charges of transportation average at least twenty dollars per ton; aggregating the enormous sum of *five hundred millions of dollars*.

The whole of this is a loss in the annual value of the products of the country, except the amount of clear profit to the carriers. From Dubuque, only one hundred and eighty-eight miles by railroad west of Chicago, the charges to-day for fourth class freight (which pays least,) to New York, is twenty-three dollars, or at the rate of sixty-nine cents on a bushel of wheat. The third, second and first classes range from thirty-one dollars to forty-nine dollars per ton. The river is the proper line of comparison, as freight must come to it by railroad, which to that extent must continue to be the mode of transportation. This point too is a much more favorable one for comparison with the present modes of transportation, than the average; as it is nearly in the direct line of the principal transportation East and West; any considerable ascent or descent of the river from it increases the distance, and consequently the cost. Wheat is worth here about one dollar per bushel; it consequently costs about seventy per cent. of its value to carry it to market. From one hundred miles in the interior the farmer who has one thousand bushels of wheat, has to give five hundred bushels to carry the other five hundred to market; on all the other cereals the per centage on the value for transportation is still greater. West of the Missouri even, from Sioux city, Omaha, Leavenworth and Kansas city, there is a country extending for hundreds of miles still further from the Atlantic, with immense capacity for the production of wheat and corn, beef and pork; which must either remain uncultivated or be furnished some better and cheaper outlet. The vast region to the west of the Upper Mississippi, must remain valueless as a grain producing region, though of almost boundless capacity, for the smaller cereals, unless a less costly route be furnished to market, than the one by railroad, or even by railroad and the lakes.

Nor are the railroad charges necessarily extortionate; they are much lower than the average of charges, and from the far West, oftentimes lower than the roads can carry at a profit.

The two great railroads of New York, the Erie, and New York Central, struggling, as they have been, in competition with each other, and trying even to compete with the Erie Canal, ought to be regaded as able to carry freight on as favorable terms as any other lines for the transportation of ordinary produce, freight and merchandise; and which are also used as lines of travel. Roads constructed as coal roads, and with grades and curves to suit an immense freight may, and in some instances do, carry at a lower rate. But these latter bear no resemblance to the nature of the structure and operating expenses of such lines as must be relied on for the freight and passenger business, to and from the Atlantic and the West.

Taking the two principal New York roads then, as an average of what such roads can do, let us see what are the rates of transportation.

It appears from the official report of the State Engineer of the State of New York for the year 1866, showing the operations of these two roads, that the rates per ton per mile charged for that year, were as follows:

New York Central, $2.92, or for the whole distance, four hundred and forty miles from Buffalo to New York, the sum of $12.85.

Erie Railroad, $2.45, or for the whole distance from Erie to New York, four hundred and sixty miles, the sum of $11.27.

On pages 433-4 of the State Engineer's report of the State of New York, the rates of transportation on these two roads from 1856 to 1861 inclusive, range from $1.73 to $3.13, and average about $2.30 per ton per mile, making an aggregate on the whole distance, of upwards of $10 per ton.

While on page 130 of the report for the year 1864, the charges for the years 1862 and 1863 are as follows:

1862. Erie Railway, $1.89 per ton per mile, of which 61.93 per cent. was the actual cost of transportation, and of course 38.07 per cent. the profit.

1862. New York Central, $2.22 per ton per mile, of which $1.39 or 59.93 per cent. was the actual cost, and only 40.07 per cent. was the profit.

For the year 1863 the charges and the expenses of transportation were somewhat higher, making the percentage of cost and profit about the same.

Taking the thirteen principal roads of New York, the average of charges are about $2.78 per ton per mile, of which about 55 per cent. were the actual cost of transportation and of course about 45 per cent. profit.

In a recent correspondence between the very able and distinguished President of the Virginia Central Railroad Company (now in conjunction with the Covington and Ohio Railroad, the Chesapeake and Ohio Railroad,) in answer to enquiries from myself, made with a view to ascertain how far that line of road could be used as a temporary portage from one water line to the other of the James River and Kanawha Canal improvement, while the intermediate portion of the canal was being constructed, he in reply, after showing the great advantages possessed by the line of railroad in the character of its location as to grades and curvatures, (the highest grade going East, with the freight, being twenty-nine and a half feet to the mile, and that only at one place,) the large radius of the curves, and the great percentage of straight road; and after first conceding that "no one will deny that the continuous water line is the cheapest and ultimately will be adopted," proceeds to answer the enquiries in regard to a single track, as follows:

"In answer to your questions, after full consideration of the subject, with the aid of H. D. WHITCOMB, the very intelligent and experienced Engineer and Superintendent of the Virginia Central Road, and reference to the report of CHARLES B. FISK, lately the Engineer of the State of Virginia on the Covington and Ohio Road, I give you the following answers:

"1st. The cost of grading and superstructure of a single track road from Covington to Loup Creek Shoals with buildings and fixtures complete for a single track, . . . . . . . . . . . . . . . . . . . . . $6,084,049
Equipment for moving one million of tons, . . . . . . . . . 2,700,000

$8,784,049."

After claiming that the capacity for a single track would be more than one million of tons, he proceeds to answer the second interrogatory thus: —

"2nd. *If an abundance of freight be offered so that the trains can always be loaded going eastward, and one-half going westward, the actual cost of moving freight exclusive of interest on capital, would be about one cent per ton per mile.*"

"3rd. An ordinary thirty ton locomotive will draw with ease over the Covington and Ohio Road going eastward four hundred and eighty tons, encountering only ten miles in the two hundred and twenty-four of thirty feet grade at the Alleghany, and a few miles of sixty feet going west; it will draw two hundred and twenty-eight tons. Note, these grades are concentrated at a single point, and therefore assistant power may be used with great facility, practically increasing the capacity of the road."

Thus it will be seen that the President of that Company, with every desire to make as fair a showing as the facts would warrant, only claimed that under the favorable circumstances stated, the "*actual cost of moving freight exclusive of interest on capital*, would be about one cent per ton per mile.

Now even under these circumstances, in order that there should be as much as forty per cent. profit, on the gross receipts, the charge for transportation would have to be one dollar and sixty-seven cents per ton per mile.

It is very obvious that even with currency at par, the conclusion arrived at by a convention held in New York, representing the principal railroad interests of the United States, that railroads for ordinary transportation of freight and passengers, cannot be constructed and operated at a lower charge than two cents per ton per mile, is fully warranted.

These charges will average from the Mississippi River about twenty-four dollars a ton, or about seventy-two cents for a bushel of wheat. There may be exceptional cases under peculiar circumstances, when the charges may be temporarily somewhat lower; but the charges oftener exceed that amount, than fall below it.

During the season of water navigation through the lakes and Erie Canal, and with railroad transportation only to the lakes, these charges could be considerably reduced, and are much lower, when there is not a pressure upon the tonnage capacity of the vessels on the lakes, and on the capacity of the Erie Canal. During the earlier part of the navigation season, especially during the summer months, the charges on freight from Chicago to Buffalo range from about five cents to ten cents per bushel on wheat, and from Buffalo to New York through the canal, from about eleven cents to fourteen cents, tolls included, and about in the same proportion by the way of Oswego; while during the months of September, October and November, when the bulk of the western crop is seeking a market, the charges go up from ten cents to even twenty-six cents on the lakes, from Chicago to Buffalo; and by the canal from Buffalo to New York from fourteen cents to as high as thirty cents per bushel, and in the same proportion by way of

Oswego, averaging more than double the rates at which freight can be carried, and is carried, when there is no pressure upon the carrying capacity, either of the tonnage on the lakes, or of the Erie Canal, and then rates of charges are of course increased or diminished in like proportion as to all other freight.

On pages 128–9 of the official report of the State Engineer of New York for the year 1864, will be found the authority for the years 1861 and 1862, in the form of tabular statements and otherwise, fully warranting the foregoing conclusions, as to those two years; and the practical operation, both before and since, of the same causes, has been substantially the same.

The effort to escape still higher charges by railroad, presses the products of the West upon the water line, and thus enables the carriers, whether by lake or canal, to increase their charges, and the canal company is also thus enabled to increase its rate of tolls, of which advantage both carrier and canal company are not slow to avail themselves.

With the increasing products of the West and Northwest, this evil will continue to increase. Even the advantage of a water line connecting the upper Mississippi with the lakes, and thereby cheapening the transportation to one-third the present charges, will be to a great extent neutralized, by the increased pressure, and consequently increased charges from the lakes onward — unless aided, and the pressure relieved, and held in check by the competition of other cheap and continuous lines of transportation.

The next question is, can this great and constantly growing burden be removed, and to what extent and how.

By the resolutions offered as a substitute, and under consideration, it is proposed, in connection with the proper improvement of the navigable waters of the West, to adopt and carry into effect a national and comprehensive system of continuous water communication between the Mississippi Valley and the Atlantic Ocean.

This system embraces, first, such improvement of the channel and removal of obstructions in the Mississippi River as will make an easy, safe and convenient outlet from the Mississippi to the Gulf.

Second, The connecting of the navigable waters of the Ohio, from the mouth of the Kanawha River, with the seaboard, by means of the James River and Kanawha Canal; thus forming a central route, extending, in connection with the Ohio, Mississippi and Missouri Rivers, in a very direct line, about two thousand miles, across from East to West, on very nearly the same parallel of latitude, and about equidistant from our Northern and Southern boundaries; and

Third, The connection of the upper Mississippi, by way of the Wisconsin and Fox Rivers to Green Bay; thus forming, in connection with the lakes and New York canals (Erie and Oswego) and the Hudson River, a cheap and continuous water route through the Northern portion of our country to New York.

This is the system proposed. What will it accomplish as a whole? at what cost? and what part will each one of these proposed routes contribute towards the general results?

These questions I now propose, as briefly as the importance of the subject will permit, to consider.

A comparison between the cost of railroad transportation, and canal and other water transportation, is a preliminary to this enquiry.

I have already said something in regard to the cost of railroad transportation. The experience of many years, in the State of New York, with its thirteen principal railroads, and twelve canals, furnishes sufficient data for a satisfactory comparison.

The official report of the State Engineer of the State of New York, already referred to, contains not only a report of the operations of the next preceding year, but also an invaluable review of the operations of the canal system, from its commencement in 1817, with comparative statements between it and the railroad system, as to the cost of keeping them in repair, operating them, and the relative charges of transportation.

At the beginning of the report there is a map, containing, among other things, a statement that previous to the enlargement, the cost of keeping the canal in repair was seven hundred and twenty-five dollars per mile per annum, while since the enlargement it has been only four hundred dollars, and showing further that the cost of transportation previously, exclusive of tolls, was one cent per ton per mile, and only four and a half mills since. It is further shown in the report, that the cost of keeping in repair, and the cost of transportation, are proportionately diminished as the capacity of the canal is increased.

On pages 450–1 there are comparative tables, showing the average cost of transportation, tolls included, on all the New York canals; and on the Erie and Central railroads for a period of ten years, ranging on the Central road from one dollar and ninety-six cents to three dollars and thirty-six cents per ton per mile, making an average of about two dollars and sixty cents; and on the New York and Erie, from one dollar and eighty-four cents to two dollars and forty-nine cents, and averaging about two dollars and twenty cents.

While on the canals of New York (embracing not only the Erie and other principal canals, but the others, twelve in all, with charges as to some of inferior capacity, ranging from one cent to two and a half cents per ton per mile, exclusive of tolls) the average charges for freight and tolls ranged from less than seven mills up to a little over one cent, and averaging about nine mills, of which nearly one-half were tolls; which the principal lines of transportation were enabled to charge in the absence of anything like competition, by railroad or otherwise.

If this comparison had been between these principal roads and the Erie Canal, it must have been still more favorable to the canal, and when the heavy rates of tolls are reduced, as they will be compelled to by sufficient competition, the whole charge will not exceed six mills, or about one-fourth the railroad charges; even as it is, the charges on the Erie Canal are only about one-third the amount by railroad.

But it is to be borne in mind that the water communication is not all by canal; the river and lake portion is much cheaper, the one less than half as high, and the other about one-third.

Practical experience has demonstrated that freight can be carried over the lakes, long voyage, at a fair profit, for two and a half mills per ton per mile; while the river transportation in barges, in a fair stage of water, which the river improvements should always furnish, will pay at three mills. Now of the distance from St. Paul of eighteen hundred and ten miles to New York, only six hundred and ten miles, or about one-third, will be, by canal or river improvement, paying tolls. And of the distance from Dubuque on the Mississippi, or Leavenworth or Kansas City on the Missouri to Hampton Roads, a distance from either point approximating nineteen hundred and fifty miles, only about four hundred and eighty miles, or about one-fourth will be, either by canal or river improvement, paying tolls. The balance over both routes will be over lines less than half the cost of canal transportation, and consequently less than one-sixth the cost of railroad transportation.

Assuming then the above data, and including canal charges at seven mills, the cost of transportation from the Atlantic ports to Liverpool at one and one-quarter mills per ton per mile, and from New Orleans by Gulf and Ocean at one and one-half mills, (both of which rates have the highest authority) and the following tables will show the cost of transportation from the different points named on the Mississippi by the one or the other of the proposed routes, and when in a condition to be competed for, by the competing routes, to New York or Hampton Roads, and to Liverpool.

ROUTE No. 1.—WISCONSIN AND FOX RIVER ROUTE.

| Table No. 1. { *From St. Paul to New York, and thence to Liverpool.* | No. of Miles. | Rate Per Ton per Mile. | Cost Per Ton. | Cost per 100 lbs. | Cost per Bushel Wheat. |
|---|---|---|---|---|---|
| | | Mills. | | Cents. | Cents. |
| St. Paul to mouth of Wisconsin River, | 250 | 3 | $ .75 | – | – |
| Mouth of Wisconsin River to Green Bay, by Canal and River Improvements, | 260 | 7 | 1.82 | – | – |
| Green Bay to Buffalo, by Lakes to Buffalo, | 800 | 2½ | 2.00 | – | – |
| Buffalo to Albany, by Canal, | 350 | 7 | 2.45 | – | – |
| Albany to New York, by Hudson River, | 150 | 3 | .45 | – | – |
| Add for two transfers, | – | – | .20 | – | – |
| To New York, | 1810 | – | 7.67 | – | – |
| Cost of 1 ton, $7.67—1-20 of that sum gives cost of 100 lbs., | – | – | – | 38$^{35-100}$ | – |
| Cost of bushel of Wheat, 60 lbs. 3-5 of 100 lbs. | – | – | – | – | 23 |
| Distance from New York to Liverpool, | 3150 | 1¼ | 3.94 | 19$^{7-10}$ | 11$^{8-10}$ |
| For whole distance from St. Paul to Liverpool, | 4960 | – | 11.61 | 58$^{1-20}$ | 34$^{4-5}$ |

| Table No. 2. { *From Dubuque to New York and Liverpool.* | | | | | |
|---|---|---|---|---|---|
| Dubuque to mouth of Wisconsin River, | 70 | 3 | .21 | – | – |
| Mouth of Wisconsin to New York, as per Table No. 1, | 1560 | – | 6.92 | – | – |
| To New York, | 1630 | – | 7.13 | 35¼ | 21 |
| New York to Liverpool, | 3150 | 1¼ | 3.94 | 19$^{7-10}$ | 11$^{4-5}$ |
| For whole distance from Dubuque to Liverpool, | 4780 | – | 11.07 | 55 | 33 |

| Table No. 3. { *From Keokuk to New York and Liverpool.* | | | | | |
|---|---|---|---|---|---|
| Keokuk to mouth of Wisconsin River, | 310 | 3 | .93 | – | – |
| Mouth of Wisconsin to New York, as per Table No. 1, | 1560 | – | 6.92 | – | – |
| To New York, | 1870 | – | 7.85 | 39¼ | 23$^{2-5}$ |
| New York to Liverpool, per Table No. 1, | 3150 | 1¼ | 3.94 | 19$^{7-10}$ | 11$^{8-10}$ |
| For whole distance from Keokuk to Liverpool, | 5020 | – | 11.79 | 59 | 35$^{1-5}$ |

ROUTE NO. 2.—VIRGINIA CENTRAL WATER LINE ROUTE.

| Table No. 1. *From St. Paul to Hampton Roads and Liverpool.* | No. of Miles. | Rate Per Ton per Mile. | Cost Per Ton. | Cost per 100 lbs. | Cost per Bushel Wheat. |
|---|---|---|---|---|---|
| | | Mills. | | Cents. | Cents. |
| St. Paul to mouth of Kanawha River, . . | 1600 | 3 | $4.80 | – | – |
| Mouth of Kanawha to Richmond, by Kanawha Improvement and James River and Kanawha Canal, . . . . . | 480 | 7 | 3.36 | – | – |
| Richmond to Hampton Roads, by James River, | 125 | 3 | $.37\frac{1}{2}$ | – | – |
| Add for one transfer, . . . . . . | – | – | .10 | – | – |
| To Hampton Roads, . . . . . . | 2205 | – | $8.63\frac{1}{2}$ | 48 | $25^{4-5}$ |
| Hampton Roads to Liverpool, . . . . | 3270 | $1\frac{1}{4}$ | $4.08\frac{3}{4}$ | $20^{48-100}$ | $12^{8-10}$ |
| For whole distance from St. Paul to Liverpool, | 5475 | – | $12.72\frac{1}{4}$ | $63^{48-100}$ | $38^{1-5}$ |
| **Table No. 2.** *From Dubuque to Hampton Roads and Liverpool.* | | | | | |
| Dubuque to mouth of Kanawha River, . . | 1335 | 3 | $4.00\frac{1}{2}$ | – | – |
| Mouth of Kanawha to Hampton Roads, as per Table No. 1, . . . . . | 605 | – | $3.83\frac{1}{2}$ | 39 | $23^{2-5}$ |
| To Hampton Roads, . . . . . . | 1940 | – | 7.84 | – | – |
| Hampton Roads to Liverpool, . . . . | 3270 | $1\frac{1}{4}$ | $4.08\frac{3}{4}$ | $20^{48-100}$ | $12\frac{1}{4}$ |
| For whole distance from Dubuque to Liverpool, | 5210 | – | $11.92\frac{3}{4}$ | $59^{48-100}$ | $35^{18-20}$ |
| **Table No. 3.** *From Keokuk to Hampton Roads and Liverpool.* | | | | | |
| Keokuk to mouth of Kanawha River, . . | 995 | 3 | $2.98\frac{1}{2}$ | – | – |
| Mouth of Kanawha to Hampton Roads, as per Table No. 1, . . . . . | 605 | – | $3.83\frac{1}{2}$ | – | – |
| To Hampton Roads, as per Table No. 1, . | 1600 | – | 6.82 | 34 | 21 |
| Hampton Roads to Liverpool, . . . . | 3270 | $1\frac{1}{4}$ | $4.08\frac{3}{4}$ | $20^{8-10}$ | $12\frac{1}{2}$ |
| For whole distance from Keokuk to Liverpool, | 4870 | – | $10.90\frac{3}{4}$ | $54^{8-10}$ | $33\frac{1}{2}$ |
| **Table No. 4.** *From St. Louis to Hampton Roads and Liverpool.* | | | | | |
| St. Louis to mouth of Kanawha River, . . | 807 | 3 | 2.42 | – | – |
| Mouth of Kanawha to Hampton Roads, as per Table No. 1, . . . . . | 605 | – | $3.83\frac{1}{2}$ | – | – |
| To Hampton Roads, . . . . . . | 1412 | – | $6.25\frac{1}{2}$ | $31^{1-5}$ | $18\frac{1}{2}$ |
| Hampton Roads to Liverpool, . . . . | 3270 | $1\frac{1}{4}$ | $4.08\frac{3}{4}$ | $20\frac{1}{2}$ | 12 |
| For whole distance from St. Louis to Liverpool, | 4682 | – | $10.34\frac{1}{4}$ | $51^{7-10}$ | $30\frac{1}{2}$ |

ROUTE No. 2.—*Continued.*

| Table No. 4.—*Continued.* | No. of Miles. | Rate Per Ton per Mile. | Cost Per Ton. | Cost per 100 lbs. | Cost per Bushel Wheat. |
|---|---|---|---|---|---|
| | | Mills. | | Cents. | Cents. |
| Distance from St. Louis to New York, *via* Wisconsin and Fox River, | 2052 | — | — | — | — |
| Distance to Liverpool, | 3150 | — | — | — | — |
| *Via* Wis. and Fox River—Whole distance from St. Louis to Liverpool, | 5202 | — | — | — | — |
| *Via* Va. Central Water Line—Whole distance from St. Louis to Liverpool, | 4682 | — | — | — | — |
| Difference from St. Louis to Liverpool, in favor of Va. Central Water Line, | 520 | — | — | — | — |
| Table No. 5. { *From Cairo to Hampton Roads and Liverpool.* | | | | | |
| Cairo to mouth of Kanawha River, | 735 | 3 | 2.20½ | – | – |
| Mouth of Kanawha to Hampton Roads, as per Table No. 1, | 605 | – | 3.83½ | – | – |
| To Hampton Roads, | 1340 | – | 6.04 | 30¹⁻⁵ | 18 |
| Hampton Roads to Liverpool, | 3270 | 1¼ | 4.08¼ | 20 | 12 |
| For whole distance from Cairo to Liverpool, | 4610 | – | 10.12⅜ | 50¹⁻⁵ | 30 |
| Table No. 6. { *From Cincinnati to Hampton Roads and Liverpool.* | | | | | |
| Cincinnati to mouth of Kanawha River, | 208 | 3 | .62²⁻⁵ | – | – |
| Mouth of Kanawha to Hampton Roads, as per Table No. 1, | 605 | – | 3.83¼ | – | – |
| To Hampton Roads, | 813 | – | 4.45⁹⁻¹⁰ | – | – |
| Hampton Roads to Liverpool, | 3270 | 1¼ | – | – | – |
| For whole distance from Cincinnati to Liverpool, | 4083 | – | – | – | – |

These tables show that by the completion of the system of improvements advocated, the rates of transportation between any point on the Mississippi, (from St. Paul down to Memphis,) and the Atlantic, will be reduced to about *one-third* the present charges; while the cost, even to Liverpool, will not exceed one-half the present charges to New York. The cost of transportation over either of the two great roads in New York, from Lake Erie to the city of New York, (an average distance of four hundred and fifty miles only,) is now about fifty per cent. greater than the entire cost from the Mississippi, even as far up as St. Paul, as I have already shown,—nay, the cost from Lake Erie to New York, by railroad, is now as great as it will be from the Mississippi to Liverpool. On every bushel of wheat, the saving will be at least forty cents over present modes of transportation, and on all other products in like proportion. And this saving will be added to its value in the hands of the producer, whether he sends it to market or not. If the comparison be from the Missouri River it will be still more favorable to the proposed water communications; for while the distance, by water, either through the Virginia Central Route, or by way of the Gulf, from Kansas City, Leavenworth and Omaha respectively, are less than from St. Paul and Dubuque respectively, and the costs of transportation consequently about the same; they are some three hundred miles further from the lakes and from New York. It would cost less to go from Omaha or Kansas City to the Atlantic Ocean, either at Hampton Roads or New York, than even to reach the lakes at the nearest point by railroad. The distance by railroad to the lakes is about five hundred miles, the transportation over which would be at least ten dollars per ton; while, as shown by the following tables, the cost by water will be considerably less.

No. 3.—GULF ROUTE.

| Table No. 1. | *From Cairo to Liverpool,* via *New Orleans.* | No. of Miles. | Rate Per Ton per Mile. | Cost Per Ton. | Cost per 100 lbs. | Cost per Bushel Wheat. |
|---|---|---|---|---|---|---|
| | | | Mills. | | Cents. | Cents. |
| Cairo to New Orleans, | | 1040 | 3 | $3.12 | 15¼ | 9$^{2-5}$ |
| New Orleans to Liverpool, | | 4755 | 1½ | 7.13 | 35½ | 21$^{1-5}$ |
| For whole distance, | | 5795 | – | 10.25 | 51 | 30$^{3-5}$ |
| From New Orleans to New York is | | 1850 | 1½ | 2.77½ | – | – |
| Add cost from Cairo to New Orleans, | | 1040 | – | 3.12 | – | – |
| | | 2890 | – | 5.89½ | 29½ | 17$^{7-10}$ |
| Being 12¼ cts. per ton, 1$^{1-5}$ cts. per 100 lbs., and ½ ct. per bush. less than by Hampton Roads. | | | | | | |

| Table No. 2. | *From Memphis to Liverpool,* via *New Orleans.* | | | | | |
|---|---|---|---|---|---|---|
| Memphis to New Orleans, | | 798 | 3 | 2.39½ | – | – |
| New Orleans to Liverpool, | | 4755 | 1½ | 7.13 | – | – |
| For whole distance, | | 5553 | – | 9.52½ | 47½ | 28 |

## VIRGINIA CENTRAL WATER LINE FROM MISSOURI RIVER.

| Table No. 1. *From Omaha to Hampton Roads and Liverpool.* | No. of Miles. | Rate Per Ton per Mile. | Cost Per Ton. | Cost per 100 lbs. | Cost per Bushel Wheat. |
|---|---|---|---|---|---|
| | | Mills. | | Cents. | Cents. |
| Omaha to mouth of Kanawha River, | 1492 | 3 | $4.48½ | — | — |
| Mouth of Kanawha to Hampton Roads, as per Table No. 1, Route No. 1, | 605 | — | 3.83½ | — | — |
| Omaha to Hampton Roads, | 2097 | — | 8.32 | 41$^{1-5}$ | 23$^{3-5}$ |
| Hampton Roads to Liverpool, | 3270 | — | 4.08¾ | 20¼ | 12 |
| Whole distance, | 5367 | — | 12.40¾ | 61$^{7-10}$ | 35$^{3-5}$ |

| Table No. 2. *From Kansas City to Hampton Roads and Liverpool.* | | | | | |
|---|---|---|---|---|---|
| Kansas City to mouth of Kanawha River, | 1368 | 3 | 3.56$^{2-5}$ | — | — |
| Mouth of Kanawha to Hampton Roads, as per Table No. 1, Route No. 1, | 605 | — | 3.83 | — | — |
| Kansas City to Hampton Roads, | 1973 | — | 7.39$^{2-5}$ | 37 | 22¼ |
| Hampton Roads to Liverpool, | 3270 | — | 4.08¾ | 20$^{2-5}$ | 12 |
| Whole distance, | 5243 | — | 11.48$^{18}$ | 57$^{2-5}$ | 34½ |

When it is remembered that the grain producing and stock raising States to have this benefit, now raise *one thousand millions of bushels of grain*, some conception of the magnitude of the saving to be realized may be approximated. It is to be borne in mind too, that all of this saving is part of the percentage of profit. The farmer who can raise a bushel of wheat for fifty cents, and realizes seventy cents for it at his stack yard, makes a profit of twenty cents; but if, by a reduction of the cost of carrying it to market, the value to him is increased forty cents, then his profit will be sixty cents, or an increase of three-fold, so that while the value of a bushel of wheat may be increased but twenty-five per cent., the profit of raising it will be increased two hundred per cent. The pittance of two hundred dollars profit on the raising of one thousand bushels, will be increased to six hundred dollars. It is the profit which measures the increase of wealth to the producer, and every interest trading with him shares in his increased prosperity. He will buy and use more of the products of other industries and enterprise; not only because he will have more to buy with, but because his purchases will come to him cheaper.

The stream of wealth which will find its source in the increasing quantity and increased value of the products of the fertile and almost boundless West, will flow a swelling tide of wealth through every channel of productive industry, trade and commerce. It will dig its rich treasures from the bowels of the mountain; harness the waterfall; lift the ponderous tilt-hammer; send back and forth the swift-moving shuttle; — fill the ware-houses with the products of our own manufactures, and with merchandise from abroad; and whiten the sea with our commerce. There is not an interest but will feel the benefit directly or indirectly in a greater or less degree.

If the expense of this whole system had to be paid out of the national treasury, and to be met by taxation of the people, it would be a wise economy promptly to go about it, and complete it at the very earliest moment. The benefits as shown, will more than return double an expenditure of *a hundred millions* of dollars; and it would be but a niggardly economy and a penny-wise and pound-foolish policy which would refuse the outlay. But I intend to show that all these benefits may be realized without any such draft on the Treasury of the United States.

Having thus attempted to show the general benefits of the whole system, I propose now to examine the several routes constituting, with river improvements, that system.

First the Gulf Route: Of this I need say but little. The importance of the Mississippi as an outlet to and through the Gulf is historical; the present obstructions to its free use and the heavy port charges, wharfage, towage, and other obstacles, have already been presented to this body, and considered by them. The necessity of the removal of every obstacle and cause, which *can* be obviated, in order to furnish the best possible outlet, is fully recognized.

While it is questioned whether it can ever be the outlet, to any considerable extent, of the products of a colder region, yet, even without that, it must be a great highway of trade; the products of the soil from Memphis down,— now very great in value, and to be quadrupled in the next ten years, which does not find a better market up the river, must seek this outlet. The trade too, between the Mississippi Valley, and the northern part of South America, Central America and Cuba, just beginning to be developed and appreciated, and destined to a wondrous growth in a few years, has the Mississippi River and the Gulf as its only proper highway.

The Wisconsin and Fox River improvement between the Mississippi and the Lakes, needs no advocacy from me as to its entire practicability and great importance; these have been repeatedly presented to Congress in memorials from the States of Iowa, Wisconsin and Minnesota. A survey and an estimate of costs have been made under Government authority. A recent convention called by the Governors of four States, three of whom were in attendance, have with entire unanimity presented it to the favorable consideration of Congress. It is already in good hands; and will only be considered by me, in so far, as it may be necessary, in connection with the central water line improvement; to which I now lastly proceed to call your attention.

This, though the first projected, and the first to be commenced, of all the canal enterprises in this country, having for its earliest projector and advocate, a no less distinguished person than GEORGE WASHINGTON himself, who as far back as 1784, in a letter to the then Governor of Virginia, looking with prophetic wisdom to the immense interests and population which must thereafter fill this great valley, pronounced this "the shortest, cheapest and best route for a water communication between the Atlantic and the invaluable country West." This enterprise, though of much greater magnitude, until the commencement of the late civil war, had been so entirely prosecuted on private and State account, as not to invite the particular attention of the country at large. It is only within a short period, when it became apparent that it could not be completed without the aid of the General Government, that its importance as a great national work has been but partially brought to the consideration of the general public.

Beginning at the mouth of the Kanawha, two hundred and eighty-four miles below Pittsburgh, the central water line contemplates the improvement of the Kanawha for about eighty-nine miles, so as to give a channel of sufficient width and a depth of six feet at all times for steamboats and barges;—thence for a distance of one hundred and nineteen miles further, the stream is to be made navigable with locks and dams; the locks to be two hundred feet long and forty feet wide, and the depth, both in the locks and in the channel to be seven feet at all times. This brings the improvement to the western base of the Alleghany Mountains, where the canal proper commences, which extends from thence two hundred and seventy-two miles to Richmond, where it locks down into tide water of a depth of eleven feet, and from thence a ship navigation of about one hundred and twenty-five miles reaches Hampton Roads near the mouth of the Chesapeake Bay. The canal proper is to be seventy feet wide at the water line, seven feet deep, with banks sloping two feet for one foot of descent, and consequently forty-two feet wide at the bottom; the locks to be one hundred and twenty feet long and twenty feet wide, with capacity for boats of two hundred and eighty tons burthen, or at least one-sixth greater capacity than the Erie Canal. The feeder to the canal, passing through the Alleghany Mountains, as recommended by the engineer, will be the Greenbrier on the West side, which is sufficiently elevated for the purpose, and affords an abundant supply of water.

This improvement will form a continuous water line from the Ohio River to Hampton Roads, a distance of about six hundred and five miles — where it reaches one of the best harbors on the Atlantic; both the harbor and the outlet to the ocean having a sufficient depth to float the largest ships; with easy egress and ingress, to and from the ocean, and at all times free from obstruction. It is distant from Liverpool one hundred and twenty miles more than New York, and from Havre forty miles more; while it is nearer to Havana, and of course to New Orleans, by two hundred and five miles, and to Rio Janeiro by three hundred and sixty-five miles.

With this completed, I have the authority of practical and intelligent men experienced in the business of steamboating and towing barges, for saying, that with one steam tug towing five barges, and each carrying fifteen thousand bushels of wheat or four hundred and fifty tons of freight, and drawing from three and a half to four feet of water, (which the river improvements will always give,) they can pass from St. Paul down to Cairo at the rate of ten miles an hour, and up the Ohio and Kanawha at the rate of five miles; and returning reverse that rate. Arriving in the Kanawha, the freight will be transferred to canal boats, through elevators, at a small cost — the lifting of grain up out of the barges, and pouring it down into the boats, by its airing and friction, and by reversing the order from top to bottom, will check any tendency, which grain in bulk may have to heat or mould, and thus enable it to reach market in better condition than if there were no transfer. No other transfer will be made until the seaport is reached.

The tabular statements already furnished will show the estimated cost of this route, and also a comparison from different points with the other routes. This comparison shows that from Cairo, the competing point, the cost of this to either the Atlantic or Liverpool is about the same as the Gulf route.

From the Mississippi from about fifty miles below Dubuque, the cheapest route, (when both lines are open.) will be by way of the Wisconsin and Fox River improvement.

The following, taken from the recent report of Mr. LORRAINE. Chief Engineer of James River and Kanawha Company, will show the views entertained of this enterprise by the friends of the New York route; and coming from an adverse source, is entitled to the more weight:

"Mr. McAlpine in his report of 1853, conceded that 'the dividing line of trade between the Virginia and the New York Canals, when the former and the enlargement of the Erie Canal are completed, will be one hundred and ten miles north of Portsmouth and Cincinnati.' That was before the contemplated enlargement of the Virginia Canal. If his calculations had been based on a canal through Virginia of greater capacity than the Erie Canal, he no doubt would have conceded all that is now claimed for it.

"In the annual statement of the trade and commerce of Buffalo for the year 1865, reported for the Buffalo Board of Trade, by Mr. E. H. Walker, there is an interesting review of the commerce of the lakes and Erie Canal and the competing routes, and first amongst the competing water routes, he places the James River and Kanawha Canal, of which he says:

"'Were this canal as large as the present Erie Canal, notwithstanding its numerous locks, and its nearly one thousand nine hundred feet of lockage lift, about the same as that of the Genesee Valley Canal, it would, from its being open nearly all the year, be a strong competitor for the trade of the western States. The Ohio River is as free as the lakes, with the distance from the Mississippi to Point Pleasant, about the same as from the Mississippi to Buffalo. The States west of the Mississippi, including Missouri and Iowa, and those States immediately west of the Missouri, as well as the southern portions of Illinois, Indiana and Ohio, and Kentucky, would be more immediately tributary to the James River and Kanawha Canal, than to the Erie, unless ship canals should be constructed through Ohio and Indiana.'

"The Hon. Israel D. Andrews, in his valuable report on Colonial and Lake trade, says of the James River and Kanawha Canal:

"'Could this canal be carried into the Ohio Valley with a sufficient supply of water, there can be no doubt it would become a route of an immense commerce. It would strike the Ohio at a very favorable point for through business. It would have this great advantage over the more northern works of a similar kind, that it would be navigable during the winter as well as the summer.

"'The route after crossing the Alleghany Mountains is vastly rich in coal and iron, as well as in a very productive soil. Nothing seems to be wanting to the triumphant success of the work but a continuous water line to the Ohio.'"

The qualifications suggested by Mr. Walker as to the size of the canal is removed by the present plan, and to a considerable extent the amount of leakage also, as by a change of location forty-four locks are saved. The question about supply of water is also met by this change. I do not propose to discuss the question of the practicability of the route; as it has been accurately surveyed and estimated, and its entire practicability repeatedly endorsed by the ablest engineers of the United States. I can only adopt the opinion of the present Chief Engineer, that "I do not think the crude, offhand, superficial views of unprofessional persons, ought to weaken the confidence that the opinions of these eminent Chief Engineers should impart to the public."

It will be seen that while the water lines are all open, the shortest, cheapest and best route from the Upper Mississippi for extending down the river to a point between Dubuque and Davenport, will be by the Wisconsin and Fox River route, from thence down the inclination is in favor of the Central route, or the Gulf route, with a margin of about one hundred miles in width, extending across the States of Ohio, Indiana, Illinois and Iowa, nearly one thousand miles in length, of highly productive and well cultivated country, in a condition to be competed for upon nearly equal terms, as to the charges of transportation, between the Northern route on the one hand and the Central route and the Gulf route on the other.

The competition will compel the lowest paying rate of charges on each route, and increased facilities, in order to meet the competition of the other.

Even from the mouth of the Wisconsin River, the point most favorable for transportation over the Wisconsin and Fox River and Lake route, the difference in favor of that route over the Central one, does not exceed five cents per hundred pounds, and as the Mississippi River is always open from St. Paul down, when the route by the lakes and Erie Canal can be used, any attempt to take advantage of the pressure to get through the lakes and Erie Canal by raising the charges more than five cents on the hundred pounds, will always be checked by the available competition of the Central route.

So too, when the Northern route is closed, and no longer a competitor of the Central one, any attempt on the part of the Central route to extort high rates either of tolls or transportation, will be checked by the completion of the Gulf route. So that the completion of each and every one of these improvements is necessary to enable the full benefit of the others to be realized, and thus fully to secure the primary and grand object of cheap transportation.

But the Central route, besides its material and necessary share in the general object has other advantages peculiar to it, which commend it especially to favorable consideration. Over the Northern route it has the advantage of being open free for use for at least four months of every year when transportation of heavy products is most wanted, while the former is obstructed by ice.

Over the Southern or Gulf route, it has the advantage in reaching a port convenient and easy of access to the ocean for the largest vessels, in being always free from obstructions of every kind; greatly in distance, somewhat in time, and avoiding heavy rates of insurance, port charges, towage, and last and greatest in passing through a climate more friendly to the transportation of Northern products during the warm months and especially of grain in bulk. Over both it has the advantage of constituting part of the line extending from East to West nearly two thousand miles from Kansas, wholly within the limits of our own country, and therefore free from interruption in case of war.

The Central line has one other advantage over both the others, the importance of which can hardly be overestimated. It passes through the very heart of the great Kanawha coal region which in its area, the number and thickness of the veins, the quantity and quality of the coal, the facility for mining it, and the cheapness at which it can be placed on the banks of the river ready for shipment, has the advantage over any and all other coal regions in the United States.

From two-thirds to three-fourths of the barges which will go into the Kanawha River freighted with produce for an Atlantic market, after transferring their freights into the canal boats, will be empty and wanting return freight; this the coal, the salt, and the iron of that region will furnish; and in order to have such return freights they will be both able at a profit and willing, to bring back these articles at two-thirds the rate charged for forward freight. Splint coal, a semi-cannel bituminous, free from sulphur, superior to the very best Youghiogheny coal, can be delivered on the route at from two dollars to two dollars and fifty cents per ton; while cannel coal, equal to the very best English cannel, can be delivered there at from twenty-five cents to fifty cents more per ton — while the charge for transporting it as return freight in barges even as far up the river as St. Paul, will not exceed the sum of three dollars and thirty-five cents — making the outside cost delivered there about six dollars; and this can be done for at least sixty days in every year when it cannot be transported over any line connecting with the lakes, and at a cheaper rate than over any other line when all the water communications are open. At the various points lower down the river, it can of course be carried still cheaper, and during a longer period of time when all water connection through the lakes is closed.

One of the resolutions declares both of this and of the Wisconsin and Fox River improvements, that "at a low rate of tolls they will pay the principal and interest of the cost of construction."

Is this warranted, as to the Central Water Line, and will it be a good security for a loan of the bonds of the Government, returning the advance for the payment of the interest while the work is being constructed, and thenceforth keeping down the interest and paying the principal at maturity, say within twenty years after the issuing of the bonds?

In considering this question we are not left to mere conjecture. The wonderful history of the Erie Canal, and a comparison of the circumstances connected with the operations of that great work, with those under which the enterprise will be inaugurated and accompanied, furnish sufficient data for reliable conclusions.

On page 447 of the official report of the State Engineer of New York for the year 1863, (already referred to,) there are two tables, the one showing the cost of construction of each one of the New York canals with the improvements and land damages, and also showing the amount up to the 30th of September, 1862, with interest; the other showing the gross earnings, expenditures for repairs and net gain or loss, from 1817, up to the same period. These include the twelve New York canals, aggregating a distance of eight hundred and seventy-six and three-quarter miles; the statement as to each one being separate.

From these tables it appears that the entire cost of the Erie Canal from its inception to the date given, including the cost of the original work, with the improvements, was $38,977,831.16 (nearly thirty-nine millions,) which sum with the interest up to that date amounted to the sum of $52,491,915.74; while during the same period the gross receipts were $71,783,670.65, (nearly seventy-two millions,) and after deducting expenses, ($12,518,860.03,) there remained a net profit of $59,264,810.62, not only sufficient, up to that date, to pay the entire cost of construction with interest, but leaving a surplus of nearly seven millions of dollars for the State, and to be applied in the construction of other canals. Of the gross earnings it appears that but little more than *one-sixth* were required to meet expenses, repairs, &c., while the balance, or about *five-sixths* were net gain. And this included not only the period *after* the enlargement but before, and when the canal was in an unfinished condition, and the cost of repairs much greater, and the receipts less. Since the 30th of September, 1862, the net earnings have been about *twenty millions of dollars more*. This and the previous net earnings with about one-sixth of the amount added to it from the net earnings of the other canals have built about five hundred and twenty-six miles of additional canals, and paid the repairs and operating expenses of seven of them, which did not meet their own expenses, leaving only about fifteen millions due on the whole canal system which the net earnings of five years will pay.

No other improvement, by railroad or otherwise, can make such an exhibit. The Erie Canal has not only paid for its own construction out of its tolls, but makes itself a present to the State with about twenty-seven million dollars of net profit; with which more than five hundred miles more of canals for the accommodation and development of the wealth of the whole State, have been constructed.

This work had a long, sickly and lingering struggle against adverse circumstances, for prosperous and vigorous vitality; its friends and advocates had to meet the sneers and sarcasms of men, who, in the language of the Canal Commissioners, "with too much pride to study, and too much wit to think, were ready to undervalue what they did not understand, and condemn what they could not comprehend." We now witness the triumphant vindication of their wisdom in the grand results.

The water line through Virginia will start at the point the Erie Canal has reached; the country which it is conceded must be tributary to it, even when the Northern line is available, and the immense amount of freight which must use it when that line is closed, with a capacity practically more than double that of the Erie Canal, by reason of its freedom from obstruction by ice for the period of the year when the other is closed; with the almost limitless amount of coal, iron, salt and lumber to be transported both East and West, over it from along its line; with all these advantages, (making transportation, even from Chicago while the Northern line is closed, cost less than half the rates wholly by rail to New York) must carry an amount of tonnage which will not fall short of an equivalent of through tonnage, to seven million tons per annum. The tolls on this amount, at two and a half mills per ton per mile, but little over half the average of the Erie Canal, which has been about four and one-tenth mills, and was very recently three and three-quarter mills; the tolls, I say, on this amount, for four hundred and eighty miles, will aggregate eight million four hundred thousand dollars. Deducting one-sixth of this amount for expenses, will leave seven millions of net income. Now, if a loan of bonds be made to the amount of *thirty-six millions of dollars*, the gold interest on this at six per cent., even with a premium of thirty-five per cent. will amount to two million nine hundred and sixteen thousand dollars. This the income will meet, and leave a surplus of over *four millions*. But this amount of freight will probably not be reached the first, second, or even the third year, but from the first it will pay the interest, and continue to increase from year to year, until at least the amount of tonnage named will be reached.

There have already been expended nearly twelve millions of dollars in the construction of the James River and Kanawha Canal, and the work was completed on the same scale as the Erie Canal, before the enlargement, for a distance of one hundred and ninety-seven miles from Richmond, its Eastern terminus. Of the gross income during a period of about twenty-five years, more than three-fifths were net profit, and was to the amount of more than three millions of dollars, applied principally in payment of interest on the loans, which have now been converted into stock. If an advance be made of the Government credit, a first and only lien should be taken to refund whatever advances of interest may be made, and to meet both the principal and the future interest as it falls due, carefully guarding the interest of the Government by all careful legislation.

The whole work can be completed in four years, (this statement is warranted, not only by the able Chief Engineer of the James River and Kanawha Company, but meets the endorsement of that distinguished Engineer, B. H. LATROBE, Esq.) and may be made available and profitable to the extent of one million tons in two years. By advancing the bonds as required every six months, the interest which will accumulate up to the time of completion, will not, at the very greatest, reach six millions, to be advanced during a period of four years. And this is every cent the Government will, upon every reasonable calculation, ever be called upon to advance. A still better showing can be made as to the Wisconsin and Fox River improvement; the amount required is comparatively small, and one million of dollars will more than cover any advance of interest the Government may ever be called upon to make.

With this showing, is the resolution unwarranted that the completion of these improvements, with the aid of Government credit, will not add to, but greatly lessen the burthen of taxation on the people?

Nothing is asked to be given. A loan of the credit of the Government, and a comparatively small advance of interest, to be amply secured and speedily returned, is all that is required to accomplish the grand result.

Mr. STRANAHAN: I wish to expedite business, and therefore desire to say that, although we have had a long speech, and a most interesting and instructive one, on the subject of canal transportation, the experience of the past twenty-five years is altogether against slack water navigation, and canals in mountain regions. In the passage of the Alleghany Ridge, the Pennsylvania Canal from the Oswego to the Ohio, is abandoned, and a railway has taken its place; the Chesapeake and Ohio Canal has proceeded no further than Cumberland.

Mr. PORTER: I thought I was entitled to the floor immediately after Mr. MONROE got through.

Mr. STRANAHAN: I yield the floor to Mr. PORTER, to allow him to move a reference of the matter to a Committee.

Mr. PORTER: I desire to add the following:

*Resolved,* That the report of this Committee be placed in the hands of the Secretary forty days previous to the next annual meeting, that he may transmit copies of the same to the constituent bodies.

Mr. RANDOLPH: If this paper takes the course proposed in the resolution, will it take precedence over all other questions to be submitted to the next meeting?

The PRESIDENT: No, Sir. The question is on considering this resolution.

It was agreed to.

Mr. HOW: When is this Committee to report?

Mr. HOLTON: I would like to enquire as to the expense of printing; how this is to be met.

Mr. PORTER: We propose to do our own printing.

On being submitted to vote, Mr. PORTER'S resolutions were adopted.

Mr. HAZARD: I want to bring a subject of importance before this Board, and would ask leave to read, for the information of the house, a preamble and resolutions from the Board of Trade of Buffalo, in regard to the importance of enlarging the Erie and Oswego Canal.

Permission being given, Mr. HAZARD read the following:

WHEREAS, The abundant and steadily augmenting products of the Northwestern States, and the unexampled increase of business upon all the lines of communication between the West and the East, the annual movement amounting to many millions of tons, and the rapidly increasing foreign and domestic demand for the staples of our great food producing states; and also for the forest and metalliferous regions; and

WHEREAS, The Erie Canal, since its construction, has been the great thoroughfare and channel of commerce, connecting our inland seas within the Atlantic Ocean; and being not only the cheapest mode of transport, but the main regulator in cost of transit of all other lines of transportation between the West and the East; and

WHEREAS, By the rapid development of the Western States, and by the immense annually increasing movement of the great staples of the country, the Erie Canal is frequently taxed to its utmost capacity, its tidal tonnage having increased in volume from two hundred and twenty-one thousand four hundred and forty-seven thousand tons (in 1842) to three million tons in 1868, nearly eighty per cent. of which is the product of the Northwestern States; and

WHEREAS, The enlargement of the Erie and Oswego Canals to a size sufficient to admit the passage of steamers of six hundred tons, would increase the capacity of three million tons to nearly ten million tons per annum; and would not only cheapen the price of transportation nearly fifty per cent., but lessen the time of transit in the same proportion, thereby greatly encouraging the settlement and cultivation of vast fertile regions in the far Northwest, giving cheap food to our Eastern States, and enabling us to compete successfully with European food producing countries in the markets of the world; therefore

*Resolved*, That the National Board of Trade hereby recognizes the great importance of the Erie Canal, and its truly national character as the great highway and channel of inter-communication between the Northwestern and the Eastern States; and expresses the belief that the objects set forth in the foregoing preamble, will be obtained in an eminent degree by the enlargement of the Erie and Oswego Canal locks.

*Resolved*, That this Board would view the adoption of some settled policy by the Legislature of the State of New York, having for its object the enlargement of this great water highway, thereby cheapening and facilitating the movement of the productions of the country, as an evidence of a wise, liberal and national statesmanship.

The PRESIDENT : Coming from the Buffalo Board of Trade, these resolutions can be received on a two-thirds vote.

Mr. PORTER : I should like to know if they are presented by the Board of Trade, or upon the authority of the gentleman individually.

Mr. HAZARD : We have authority from the Buffalo Board of Trade to present them at the proper time.

The Board agreed to receive them, and they were ordered to be placed at the foot of the calendar.

Mr. BRUNOT: I wish to say a word in explanation of some remarks I made yesterday. In speaking of the Ohio River improvement, I endeavored to illustrate the point by referring to the North River, and stated that if the North River could be reduced to the condition of the Ohio, no one would expect, except by an expenditure of perhaps one hundred million dollars, to bring it back to its normal condition. I was understood by many gentlemen as saying that it would take a hundred million dollars to improve the Ohio. I did not say that; and the explanation I wish to make is, that the highest estimate of the most extravagant plan proposed for the improvement of the Ohio has been, by its friends about ten million dollars, and by its enemies twenty to twenty-five million dollars.

Mr. GRANT: I wish to make an enquiry in relation to the order of business. In the proceedings of this Board at Philadelphia, page one hundred and thirty-four, a resolution respecting the navigation of the Northern Lakes, appears as having been introduced, and on page one hundred and thirty-seven, I see that it was laid over to another meeting; but in making up the programme, by some omission it was not placed there; and I should like to ask if it may not now properly come before the Board.

The PRESIDENT: I find that it was postponed generally, and therefore has lost its order upon the calendar.

Mr. RANDOLPH: I move a suspension of the order of business, to enable me to offer a resolution relative to adjournment.

Carried.

Mr. RANDOLPH: I now move that the sessions of this annual meeting of the Board close with the sitting of to-day.

Mr. WETHERILL: 'I move to amend by adding, and that we select as our next place of meeting, the city of Baltimore.

Mr. EGAN: I desire to know the recommendation of the Executive Council on that point.

The PRESIDENT: The Executive Council recommend Richmond.

Mr. STRANAHAN: I move as an amendment, that our next meeting be held at Richmond.

The question was put on closing the sessions of the Board this day, and that the next annual meeting be held in Richmond, and both propositions were agreed to.

Mr. NAZRO: I desire to offer certain resolutions of thanks.

Permission to read for information was given, and Mr. NAZRO read as follows:

*Voted,* That the thanks of the National Board of Trade be presented to his Honor the Mayor, and to the City Council of Cincinnati, for the use of this room, for the elegant banquet, and for the many other attentions received at their hands.

*Voted,* That the thanks of this Board be presented to the President, officers and members of the Cincinnati Chamber of Commerce, for the great kindness shown to us collectively, individually, and by their committees.

*Voted,* That the thanks of the Board be presented to the citizens of Cincinnati, the railroads and the various associations and art galleries, for the many acts of courtesy bestowed upon us.

The PRESIDENT: The question is on the suspension of the rules to allow the introduction of the votes read by Mr. NAZRO.

Agreed to; the votes of thanks were carried unanimously.

Mr. GUTHRIE: I desire to ask permission for Mr. BURWELL, of New Orleans, to be heard.

Carried.

Mr. BURWELL: The Chamber of Commerce of New Orleans, referred to the Executive Committee of this body, certain resolutions of a national character, relating to the establishment of reciprocal trade, and of a commercial policy throughout this continent. These resolutions have not been reported upon, and they do not appear upon the official calendar; I ask therefore, to present equivalent resolutions, as was allowed in the case of the Louisville Board. I will read the resolutions:

*Resolved,* That the attention of the Executive and Senate of the United States be respectfully called to the state of commercial treaties between the United States and all other American States, and with all European powers holding colonial dependencies upon this continent.

*Resolved,* That the agricultural, manufacturing and shipping interests of the United States would be greatly promoted by the adoption of a continental commercial policy; that for this purpose it will be important to obviate all impediments to international intercourse by conventions of reciprocal commerce, and by removing or reducing, as far as may be possible, the municipal or local charges in all ports of entry or delivery of each of these countries.

I ask that these resolutions be referred to the Executive Committee, that they may be considered by this body, and receive such attention at the ensuing session, as the magnitude of the subject deserves.

Mr. MEIER: I second the motion.

Carried.

Mr. BAGLEY: I desire this body to reconsider the vote of yesterday in reference to the report on American shipping. If the action of the Board remains as it is, it will strike a death blow at the ship-building interests of the country. I move to reconsider the vote, and propose to offer the following as an addition to the second resolution, if allowed:

And do further recommend that a bounty shall be allowed on all material of American growth or manufacture entering into the construction of vessels built in the United States, equal in amount to the duties which would have been paid upon said materials had they been imported from foreign countries.

I think it is no more than justice for our ship-builders to be put upon such a footing that they will be able to compete with foreign countries, while our merchants also shall be allowed to go abroad to buy their ships when they desire to do so.

The PRESIDENT: If the order of business be suspended for the purpose of receiving a motion to reconsider, and that should prevail, and if the gentleman from Detroit makes his motion to reconsider, and that should be agreed to, it brings up the section that was voted upon precisely as reported upon by the Committee on shipping. If the Chairman of that Committee will consent to any modification of the resolution, I think it might be carried, but unless he does so, the question will have to be upon the precise words rejected before, and in order to effect this, a vote of two-thirds of the body will be necessary to a reconsideration.

Mr. BAGLEY: I understand that the Chairman is willing to accept this. I move to suspend the rules for the purpose of reconsidering the clause in the report on American shipping, which was rejected yesterday.

Carried ; Yeas 34 ; Nays 9.

Mr. BAGLEY : I move to reconsider the vote.

Mr. WETHERILL : I second the motion.

The PRESIDENT : Both gentlemen having voted in the number controlling this question, it is now in order to reconsider it.

The motion to reconsider prevailed; Yeas 33 ; Nays 7.

Mr. BAGLEY : I ask the Chairman of the Committee on shipping if my motion is satisfactory.

Mr. HINCKEN : It is satisfactory to the Chairman, and I move its adoption.

The PRESIDENT : The question now is upon the clause proposed by Mr. BAGLEY.

On being put to vote, the motion was declared carried.

The Yeas and Nays being called for, the vote stood as follows :

Yeas : Messrs.—

| | | | |
|---|---|---|---|
| Allen, (Geo. N.,) | Davis, (Geo. W.,) | Holton, | Randolph, |
| Bagley, | Egan, | How, | Ropes, |
| Boynton, | Fraley, | Ilsley, | Stranahan, |
| Bradford, | Grant, | King, | Thurston, |
| Brunot, | Guthrie, | Kirkland, | Topp, |
| Buell, | Hand, | Loney, | Trezevant, |
| Burwell, | Harris, | Malone, | Walton, |
| Buzby, | Hazard, | McGraw, | Wetherill, |
| Carpenter, | Hincken, | Nazro, | Wilbor, |
| Carrington, | Hoffman, | Plumer, | Young—41. |
| Converse, | | | |

Nays : Messrs.—

| | | | |
|---|---|---|---|
| Biggs, | Davis,(Geo. F.,) | Meier, | Porter, |
| Branch, | Drake, | Michener, | Shryock, |
| Cobia, | Duvall, | Monroe, | Taylor, |
| Crichton, | Gano, | Parr, | Thomas—16. |

Mr. THURSTON : I desire to offer the following :

WHEREAS, Many of the subjects submitted by constituent bodies of the National Board of Trade have necessarily had but an imperfect hearing, from a disposition to limit the length of the session; therefore,

*Resolved*, That the Secretary is hereby instructed to notify all bodies, members of the National Board of Trade, that hereafter all sessions of the Board will continue two weeks, unless business be sooner concluded.

I ask for a suspension of the rules, that it may be considered.

Carried.

Mr. STRANAHAN : I move that it be referred to the Executive Council.

Mr. HINCKEN : I do not expect that this Board will in future require to remain in session so long as at this, its first session. We assembled here for the first time, and almost every member had one proposition, and some had more. Now these propositions cover nearly all the questions that will come before this Board; and I think if we limit our sessions to one week, we shall accomplish as much as if we extend them to two. We cannot expect business men, — and we only want such — to spend so much valuable time in discussion. It is too much to ask of business men to spend two weeks in the discussion of matters that ought to be disposed of in two hours. I would limit the sessions to one week.

Mr. THURSTON : I accept the amendment.

Mr. RANDOLPH : I am opposed to the resolution. It seems to me that the experience we have had at this meeting, will indicate to members that they need not expect to get away in two or three days, as many did when they left home to attend this session; but I would not hold out the idea that this Board will remain in session for one or two weeks. We need not limit the time; we should be governed by the circumstances of the occasion, without indicating anything definite as to the length of the session.

Mr. ROPES : I think the suggestion on this subject is right, and it is fortunate that it has been brought forward at this time. As the discussion will appear in our records, I think all that is necessary has been done; I support the motion of the gentleman from New York, that it be referred to the Executive Council.

Mr. HOLTON : I think it very important that this resolution shall pass without reference, with all due deference to the gentleman who has proposed this. If it is known beforehand that the business of the Board cannot be disposed of in one or two days, Boards of Trade and Chambers of Commerce will send only such delegates here as can remain till the necessary business is completed.

The PRESIDENT: The question is on referring the resolution as amended to the Executive Council.

On vote, the motion was carried.

The PRESIDENT: The next business is the further consideration of the proposition from the St. Louis Board of Trade, with reference to the navigation of the Mississippi.

Mr. SHRYOCK: I have a proposition I wish to present, endorsed by the St. Louis Board of Trade, the St. Louis Chamber of Commerce, and the Chambers of Commerce of Cincinnati, Dubuque and Quincy, Illinois. I do not wish to argue it at length, but to present it for reference, that it may come up at the next meeting:

WHEREAS, The Boards of Trade of the cities of Cincinnati, Louisville, Nashville, Dubuque and Quincy, having unanimously indorsed a memorial to Congress that originated in the St. Louis Board of Trade, praying Congress to take such action as would restore to navigation that important tributary of the Mississippi River known as Bayou Manchac, connecting the Mississippi River with the deep waters of Mobile Bay and the Gulf of Mexico; and

WHEREAS, Said memorial has also been unconditionally endorsed by hundreds of the people of the Mississippi Valley (as will appear by the accompanying documents,) therefore,

*Resolved*, That the interests of the people of the Mississippi Valley require the use of all and every water way possible between the Mississippi River and the deep sea, and we hereby most respectfully ask the Congress of the United States to grant the prayer of the memorialists, and beg leave to say that the interests of commerce demand that this work should be done as speedily as possible.

Mr. PORTER: I am opposed to this reference. I regard it as of the nature of a private enterprise, and though its friends have procured the endorsement of men of eminence, there are, as I know, many opposed to it.

Mr. SHRYOCK: I dislike much to hear this project spoken of as a private enterprise. Neither I nor any of the gentlemen advocating it have a particle of interest in it.

Mr. BURWELL: I rise to say that I do not regard it as a private enterprise. There are, however, conflicting propositions, which I was requested to present, but inasmuch as they are of a strictly local character, I was advised that I was not authorized to occupy the time of the Board in regard to them. As far as the

Manchac Canal is concerned, it might benefit New Orleans to the extent of getting cord wood and sweet potatoes at a cheaper rate; but as only a seven foot channel could be had into the Gulf, and as it would cost perhaps five million dollars to complete it, the Government, I think, would be disinclined to expend such a sum in the furtherance of such a project.

Mr. RANDOLPH : Is this a project to pass a canal by way of Lake Ponchartrain and Lake Borgne to the Gulf?

Mr. SHRYOCK : I do not, at this laté hour of the session, propose to detain the Board with the great commercial project referred to in the resolution. I only desire to file the resolution for the future consideration of the body, and present a few reasons in its favor.

This important connection between the Mississippi River and the system of Lakes to the Gulf of Mexico, once a navigable tributary of the Mississippi, has been closed since the year 1813, greatly to the detriment of the commerce of the whole country. If it can be restored by Congressional action, the benefit will be felt alike by the people of every locality.

Prior to the war of 1812, this Bayou was navigated by boats and sail vessels trading between Mobile Bay and Pensacola and the Florida coast to Baton Rouge and towns on the Mississippi River. It was found a safe passage for schooners and small craft trading with New Orleans, which did not dare to venture on the stormy waters of the Balize and take the hazard of being stranded on the bars at the mouth of the river.

Without further remark, I beg to present a memorial which has been very extensively signed by men of all classes engaged in active business:

*To the Senate and House of Representatives, in Congress assembled:*

The Board of Trade of the city of St. Louis, having been solicited by various organizations, as well as innumerable influential individuals living and doing business in the Valley of the Mississippi, to memorialize Congress to order a survey of Bayou Manchac and its connections between the Mississippi River and the Gulf of Mexico, and to make an appropriation for the clearing out of obstructions in the same, with a view to re-opening *direct* communication between the Mississippi River, *via* Lake Ponchartrain, and Mobile Bay and the Gulf of Mexico, beg leave to state that they have given the subject their serious consideration, and find it to be entirely practicable and of vast importance to the commercial interests of the country, from the fact that, by the trifling outlay of not to exceed a *quarter of a million of dollars*, a great public highway can be opened, which will place in direct communication two sections of the country, greatly in need of and daily consuming the products of the other, but which have now to reach their destination by a no less circuitous route than New Orleans, causing the unnecessary expense and delay of transhipment, which would be entirely obviated by the opening of the communication thus proposed, and which would in addition open an immense trade in lumber, rosin, iron ore, and many other commodities, but which now, from the circuitous route and the necessity of breaking bulk, thereby adding greatly to the expense of transportation, amounts to a prohibition.

But it is not in this view of the case alone that your memorialists wish to urge upon your honorable body the survey and appropriation they ask for, but it is in a national aspect, for, by the opening of the Bayou Manchac and its connections, the entire products of the West can reach Mobile, one of the finest harbors on the seaboard, by the steamers now regularly plying the Mississippi and its tributaries, discharging their cargoes of grain and other products ('without intermediately breaking bulk) on board of vessels destined for any or all of the European ports, and while your memorialists would not say ought that might be construed into a detraction of the port of New Orleans, still, it is a well understood fact, that the expense of towage of vessels to and from the port of New Orleans, together with the obstructions of the bar at the mouth of the river, adds greatly to the delay and expense of the receiving and delivering of cargoes at that port, while at the port of Mobile these delays and expenses are both obviated, as the vessels can, without assistance, run into a safe harbor, and within easy access for other crafts to come alongside and effect a mutual exchange of cargo, which would place the grain-growing States of the West in direct and economical communication with the seaboard, and thereby enable them to compete successfully with the grain-growing countries of Europe. Your memorialists feel that it is the duty of the General Government to accomplish this enterprise, if for no other reason than from the fact that prior to the war of 1812, natural and easy communication was open through this pass, from the Mississippi River, just below Baton Rouge, thence into the River Amite and Lake Maripas, and thence through Pass Manchac into Lake Ponchartrain and the gulf. But General JACKSON, fearing the British might take advantage of that communication to cut off New Orleans, placed obstructions in the way which have proved a barrier to its navigation up to the present day.

Your memorialists therefore, feel that, aside from any commercial considerations, it is the duty of the General Government to remove at least such obstructions as were placed there for the general good, and that by this course they are only doing an act of justice to the section of country through which it traverses, and to those whose business pursuits place them in contact with it; and in urging this enterprise they do not feel that they are attempting to build up one city or section at the expense of another, for while the city of New Orleans might for the time lose a portion of the trade she now has, your memorialists feel assured that the impetus that would be given to trade and commerce on the Mississippi River would throw into her lap much more than she would lose by the opening of this new and important route to the seaboard. Your memorialists, therefore, feel assured in saying that no project has ever been presented to the General Government fraught with such grand results, and at so trifling an expense, as the one now presented.

Your petitioners therefore pray, etc.

This memorial was originated and endorsed before the Board of Trade of St. Louis was aware that by order of the late Secretary of War, Mr. STANTON, a survey had been made and the entire feasibility of the work pronounced upon by a competent engineer of the United States army, whose report I now have.

The cost stated in this report I am satisfied, Mr. President, is far greater than will be required to accomplish this work. The bed of the Bayou is still intact for miles. There is to-day a sufficiency of water in the channel to allow boats drawing seven feet to approach within five miles of the Mississippi River. The Mississippi River would run a sufficiency of water through this channel its entire length for all purposes of navigation, at all seasons of the year, were it not for the levee of thirty-three feet built across the mouth of the Bayou, severing its connection with the Mississippi, and which is kept in good repair, fearing the Father of Waters will seek his old outlet to the sea through which, for probably six thousand years, he claimed an indisputable right.

Opponents to this water connection between the river and gulf have found marvellous difficulties in the way and allege them to be of such huge proportions as to render the scheme impracticable; that the Bayou has grown up with trees and roots, that it is filled with the vegetable deposit of fifty years, and that crocodiles and copperheads are so abundant that navigation can never be restored.

The only outlet for grain and western products, seeking a market on the Atlantic seaboard, in South America and in Europe, transported by the Mississippi, is through the Balize. There are not and cannot be sufficient facilities for transferring the produce from our river boats and barges to steamers and other vessels. This transfer must, of necessity, take place at the port of New Orleans, which is not a seaport, any more than Vicksburg is or Cairo, except that it is so much nearer the sea. What I mean is, that sailing vessels, which do nearly all our carrying trade, cannot run into and out of the port of New Orleans, but must needs be towed by steamers; this is done at such heavy cost, and the delays and dangers of navigation over the bar and through the passes from the river to the gulf, cause so much expense and delay, as to render shipments unprofitable if not impossible. This combination of disadvantages renders the Mississippi River almost useless as a channel of communication with the outer world.

It is a fact, which I imagine the people of New Orleans will not attempt to controvert, that such has been the cost of towing into and out of their harbor, that their tonnage has greatly decreased. With foreign ports their trade has diminished greatly beyond the naturally to be expected results of the war and the consequent ruin of the country; instead of having almost a monopoly of the coffee trade of the Mississippi Valley, New York and Baltimore, by reason of the ease by which vessels sail into those ports and land their cargoes, deliver coffee to the cities on the Upper Mississippi, at less price than can possibly be done through the port of New Orleans. At this very time vessels are anchored in Mobile Bay and in the deep waters of Lake Borgne, loading with cotton, transported by rail, from New Orleans to lighters in Lake Ponchartrain, and thence to the ship, necessarily at considerable cost, but the outward bound vessel can better afford to pay this tax than the enormous charge of towing into and out of the harbor of New Orleans and the heavy port dues while on the berth.

A sailing vessel of eight hundred tons capacity will carry twenty-six thousand bushels of wheat out of New Orleans to New York or Liverpool. The towage and port charges on a vessel of this class will fall but little below three thousand dollars, which is equal to about eleven cents per bushel on the wheat, which must, of course, come out of the shipper's pocket, and ultimately come out of the grower's. Time would fail me, Mr. President, were I to attempt to present in all its bearings the difficulties to be overcome before the shipments of Western produce can be made *via* New Orleans on such terms as will make it either profitable or desirable to use our great national highway to the markets of the world by that route. I know that shipments have been made direct from St. Louis *via* New Orleans to Liverpool, and sold at small profits, which would have paid handsomely if the transportation charges had been reasonably less.

I have given this subject much thought and can only see one way to remedy the difficulty before us, and that is to make a direct and easy connection between the Mississippi River and Mobile Bay, where vessels of the largest class can anchor in one of the best harbors of the world, and where the waters are calm enough for our Western steamers and barges to lie along side and discharge into them or into elevators erected for the purpose, and to receive in return cargoes designed for the West. This can be done, Mr. President, by opening the Bayou Manchac and by no other way, unless some artificial work can be done at some eligible point at or near New Orleans. We have no right to demand this of the State of Louisiana. But we have the right to Bayou Manchac, for it was a natural waterway, and as much a mouth of the Mississippi River, and an outlet to the sea as South Pass or Pass a Loutre, before it was closed by General JACKSON.

Another consideration of importance is, that the day is not far distant when California with its wonderful soil, and the States on the Pacific, will be large producers of wheat, barley and rye, and we shall be forced to such sharp competition, that unless we can reach New

York and Boston with our grain for at least half the present cost of transportation, we shall have to allow California, Oregon and Washington to supply those markets, and the farmers of the Mississippi Valley will have to turn their attention to other staple products, which will of course, check our progress and lessen the value of our lands. We have at our command the facilities to defy all competition if we will only wisely use the means nature has provided for us.

The cost of carrying a ton of merchandise on the ocean is only one and one-half cent a mile, on the lakes two cents, on the river two and three-fourths cents, on a canal five cents, but on a railroad twelve and a half to thirteen cents per mile. Thus you see how cheaply by river to the gulf and by the ocean to New York, grain can be moved. By the same calculation, when corn is transported by rail twelve hundred and fifty miles, its value is consumed by transportation, and wheat will be so heavily taxed that investments in it will be hazardous.

We have an Atlantic seaboard of three thousand five hundred miles, and an inland navigation counting the shores and tributaries, of thirty thousand miles. Upon these waters floats a commerce three times greater than the entire foreign commerce of the country.

You no doubt remember, Mr. President, when our foreign commerce was looked upon as much the most important interest of our country. But now, see how it is eclipsed by the trade between the States and by the handling of domestic products for our home markets. In 1860, the entire product of the United States was one billion nine hundred million dollars. Its exports were three hundred and seventy-three millions one hundred and eighty-nine thousand dollars, less than one-fifth, leaving four-fifths for exchange between the States.

The Mississippi drains one million seven hundred and eighty-five thousand square miles of territory, which contains seven hundred and sixty-eight square miles of the finest lands in the world. Here is space enough for one hundred and fifty States the size of Massachusetts, and had it now as much population, according to area, we should now have a population of nearly two hundred millions. In the fourteen States that may now be called the Middle States, the landed property is estimated at eight and a half billion dollars, fully one-half the value of all the United States.

These States claim to have more than half of all the improved lands and to have a majority of the population of the United States; and notwithstanding their wealth almost beyond computation from cereal products, not more than one-fifth of the vast domain is under cultivation. Professor WATERHOUSE estimates the annual commerce of the Mississippi River at two billion dollars, nearly half of which is derived from eight or ten Western States. The agricultural bureau basing its calculation on past results, estimates the cereal products of the West in the year 1870, at seven hundred and sixty-two million bushels, and in the year 1900, at three billion one hundred and twenty-five million bushels.

I trust I have shown the desirability and practicability of this great water-way to the deep sea, which will relieve the commerce on the Mississippi River of many heavy burdens and charges now laid upon it unnecessarily, and I ask in conclusion, that the National Board of Trade will endorse a project that so materially affects the interests of the people of the great West.

Mr. HOLTON : I believe we have already passed a resolution that Congress shall be asked to consider what is its duty in the further improvement of the navigation of the Mississippi River. I understand this to be a proposition to go through some lagoon or bayou ; but I confess my inability to sit and traverse all the schemes that have been brought up here within the last twenty-four hours. I believe, however, this is covered by the reasonable and proper action we have already taken, and therefore I move the indefinite postponement of the whole subject.

The motion prevailed by a vote of, Yeas 35 ; Nays 17. The President appointed the following gentlemen as the Committee on the subject of water communication between the Atlantic and the Mississippi Valley :

<table>
<tr><td colspan="2">Mr. PORTER, Louisville,</td></tr>
<tr><td>Mr. STANARD, St. Louis,</td><td>Mr. BROWN, Portland,</td></tr>
<tr><td>" BURWELL, New Orleans,</td><td>" CONVERSE, Boston,</td></tr>
<tr><td>" TOPP, Memphis,</td><td>" HINCKEN, New York,</td></tr>
<tr><td>" MONROE, Dubuque,</td><td>" WETHERILL, Philadelphia,</td></tr>
<tr><td>" MUNN, Chicago,</td><td>" PARR, Baltimore,</td></tr>
<tr><td>" TAYLOR, St. Paul,</td><td>" HUGHES, Norfolk,</td></tr>
<tr><td>" GANO, Cincinnati,</td><td>" CARRINGTON, Richmond.</td></tr>
</table>

Mr. TAYLOR : As I understand the scope of the enquiry now referred to this Committee, it will take the water communication between the Mississippi Valley and the Atlantic coast ; would this not be the proper time for the reference of every proposition bearing upon this subject? Mr. GRANT, of Oswego, called the attention of the Chair to a proposition in relation to the lake communication between the West and the Atlantic coast, which was referred to the next regular meeting of the National Board of Trade; without wishing to raise any question upon that proposition, I should be glad if the house would take some course by which that resolution may be brought up, in order that the whole subject be considered and reported upon.

I move the suspension of the rules, that the resolution appearing on page one hundred and thirty-four of the proceedings of the first meeting of the National Board of Trade in Philadelphia, shall be referred to the Committee which has just been named.

Mr. PORTER: The gentleman will remember that Mr. MONROE, offered as a substitute, certain resolutions which cover that very resolution.

The motion to suspend the rules was put, and carried.

Mr. TAYLOR: I move that the resolution in favor of a ship canal be referred to the Committee on water communications.

Mr. STRANAHAN: It is evident that we shall have a great many subjects referred to this Committee. Now, our Executive Council is made up of representative men, and I suggest the propriety of having all these resolutions referred to it, instead of to any Committee that may be raised in this body.

Mr. TAYLOR: I accept the proposition of the gentleman from New York, and ask that this proposition be referred to the Executive Council.

Mr. CONVERSE: As to the reference to the Executive Council, I do not think that it is a proper body to which to refer matters of investigation; it is an Executive Council, and it will occur to all that its members will not be prepared to entertain propositions of this kind, coming from all parts of our country, so that they shall receive that deliberation which may be necessary to enable us to come to such conclusions as may be proper and desirable.

Mr. HINCKEN: The Executive Council will be the only body having a legal existence until the next session of this Board. I shall not continue as a delegate after I go out of this room. The Council is the only proper reservoir for the reception of this business, and such as this.

The PRESIDENT: The question is on the modification of the proposition of the gentleman from St. Paul, so that the resolution shall be referred to the Executive Council.

Agreed to.

Mr. EGAN: I move that the regular order of business be suspended to enable the gentleman from Detroit to introduce a resolution from the Board of Trade of Detroit.

The motion was seconded, and Mr. BAGLEY read for information the following :

*Resolved*, That in the opinion of the National Board of Trade, it is the duty of Congress to inquire into the causes of the present depressed condition of the copper interests of our country, and to adopt such measures as in their judgment may be deemed best to make this great mineral wealth of the North a source of revenue to the Government.

The question of suspending the rules was agreed to.

Mr. BAGLEY : I move the adoption of the resolution which I have just read.

Mr. KIRKLAND : It seems to me that this resolution opens the whole tariff, one of the most complicated questions of a commercial nature ; and as I do not think it is within the province of this Board to instruct Congress to take action to favor any particular article, I hope the resolution will be voted down. As a Board representing all interests, we should not commit ourselves to take definite action on anything special or local.

Mr. MICHENER : I move that the resolution be referred to the Executive Council.

Mr. ROPES : I fear that all such resolutions will amount to nothing at all. As long as our standard of value is so utterly wrong, every interest will suffer. Our Western friends are finding that out by degrees. Ship-owners and builders found it out long ago ; now the copper interests and the manufacturing interests are finding it out, and there will be no end of representations to Congress, for every interest is bound to go under in consequence of this depreciated currency. I think it would be wisest to say nothing in reference to these interests until we have a standard of currency established.

Mr. BAGLEY : I hoped this resolution would not have opened a discussion. I have no wish to enter into a discussion on the depressed condition of the copper interest of this country.

I ask this Board whether the copper interest is not an important interest ; and if the money that is to pay our debt, has not to come out of the soil in the shape of minerals or grain, or the products of the cotton lands? I do not wish to bring up any question of trade or tariff; nothing of the kind; but if I were permitted time, I could show that unless some relief is offered to the copper interests of this country, they must be abandoned. The resolution merely calls the attention of Congress to the depressed condition of this interest, and ask the adoption of such measures of relief as shall in their wisdom be deemed best.

Mr. COBB: There is a bill now before Congress to reduce the duty on India cloth, thus involving the interests of the Western States on the hemp question, which I think should be considered in connection with Mr. BAGLEY's resolution. I therefore move to amend by including the hemp and flax interests of the country. I do this to facilitate business.

Mr. BAGLEY: I am willing to accept the amendment of the gentleman from Louisville, and also to include any industry, whether in the State of Kentucky or Louisiana, or anywhere else if it is in a depressed condition.

MR. THOMAS: I would like to ask if the copper interest is not now protected, and if so, to what amount?

Mr. BAGLEY: The tariff in reference to foreign copper has not been changed since 1860, or '61; the duty was fifty cents per hundred, and two and one-half cents on copper imported in ingots.

Mr. WETHERILL: When we were considering the shipping interest, the gentlemen from Boston and Baltimore were strongly in favor of adopting some measures; they could not regard that as sectional, but insisted that it was a national interest.

It seems to me that it is a special interest; and the gentlemen who so strenuously favored a movement like that, should not now rise and say that this Board should have nothing to do with special interests when they are clearly in favor of aiding the shipping interest.

If the gentleman from Detroit can show that the copper interest is of vast importance, and if the gentleman from Louisville can satisfy us of the importance of the hemp and flax interests, we should adopt such resolutions as this; I therefore hope that every gentleman will leave all questions of sectionalism, and vote for the adoption of this resolution.

Mr. BAGLEY: In the south of Michigan, there are dependent upon this interest, forty thousand people; and fifty million dollars are invested in it.

Mr. HAND: I agree with Mr. WETHERILL that it seems strange that gentlemen who were in favor of the special legislation we were discussing yesterday, should now turn round and oppose this proposition. I move the previous question.

The motion for the previous question was withdrawn at the request of Mr. ROPES, who desired to make a personal explanation in reply to the charge of inconsistency made by the gentleman from Philadelphia.

Mr. ROPES : It is unfortunate if debate cannot be carried on without personalities. I did not utter one word yesterday, on the shipping interest; I was cut off on a motion for the previous question; we were thus prevented from stating our views.

I will state that the proposition which I did vote for, was, not to foster the shipping interest by any special gift from the Government, or by levying any duties; but, on the contrary, by allowing merchants to buy their ships abroad, and pay on them such duties as the Government of the country should see fit to impose. In other words, that ships should be put on a footing with other merchandise; as it is well known that ships cannot be built in this country in the present condition of things; though the various materials that go into the building of ships, coming from abroad, do not in the least interfere with the use of domestic articles, because if they were not furnished at a lower price the ships could not be built; therefore, not a pound less of iron, hemp, or anything would be sold in this market in consequence of the proposed drawback on the foreign articles used in the manufacture of American ships. That was the ground on which this subject was presented, and not on the ground of receiving special favor from the Government; it was simply for the withdrawal of the intolerable and unreasonable restrictions that exist in connection with the ship building and ship owning interests.

The copper interests, on the contrary, are all protected. I do not deny their right to such protection; but I take it that it is not a business that especially calls for our action at this time; there are other interests which require more protection than it does.

Mr. MICHENER : I withdraw my motion to refer these matters to the Executive Committee.

Mr. KIRKLAND : What I designed to convey to the house was that this is a sectional, local matter; that particular interests are at stake; that as a National Board of Trade we are asked to attend to the copper interests of the Northwest, and that I did not think we should deliberate on any such question. It is now claimed that I advocated a sectional interest in one case, and refuse to do it in another. This copper interest, I admit, is important; entering as the article does into the construction of ships, and manufactures of every kind. The interest of ship building is to cheapen everything entering into the construction of a ship. The copper interest comes and asks us to interfere for its benefit; is the Board to go to Washington and interfere on behalf of the mining interests? I say if the mining interests cannot maintain themselves under the present circumstances, let them go down. They have protection, and they wish now to charge an additional duty to put up the price of copper, that they may make more money, especially in the mines of Lake Superior, which have perhaps made more money than any mines in this country. The ship building is not a local interest. It includes all the steamers on the lakes, on the Mississippi, and every vessel that floats on our waters, rivers, or the sea.

You are now asked, as a National Board of Trade, to lend your influence to build up this peculiar interest at the expense of all the other interests of the country; and though many of us represent interests diametrically opposed to this action, certainly no one here would oppose anything that is of general interest to the country. There are gentlemen on this floor who have copper investments that have advanced from three to five hundred per cent. within the last few years.

Can this Board, in view of the influence it is expected to exert, come forward and lend the weight of that influence for the advancement of this special interest?

I move that it be laid on the table.

The motion was seconded, and put to the vote, and declared lost.

Mr. STRANAHAN: I move that it be referred to the Executive Council.

Carried.

The Board took a recess of an hour, to partake of lunch, provided by the Cincinnati Chamber of Commerce, and to visit the new Commercial Hospital Building.

## AFTERNOON SESSION.

The Convention was duly called to order.

Mr. HOFFMAN : As the Providence Board of Trade is not here, I move that the consideration of the recommendation of that Board on Tare on Cotton, be postponed to the next meeting of the Board.

Agreed to.

The PRESIDENT : The business next in order is the resolution of the Baltimore Board of Trade.

Mr. LONEY : I have no desire to make a speech but will simply state that this is a proposition offered by our Board with a view to aid Congress in perfecting some of the laws relating to duties :

*Resolved*, That upon the presentation to Congress of any bill, to alter the duties on imports, or change the internal revenue laws, it shall be the duty of the Secretary to send printed copies of said bill or bills to each constituent body.

The Baltimore Board desire to offer a second resolution, as follows :

*Resolved*, That whenever it is contemplated to make a change in the law imposing duties on imports, or the internal revenue, it shall be the duty of the Secretary to notify the proper Committees in both Houses of Congress, of the existence of the National Board of Trade, and to offer the services of the Board, to assist the Committees in perfecting the proposed law.

Mr. DRAKE : I think, the expense that this would incur has not been properly calculated ; the printing would be a very large item. Moreover, I think it would be inexpedient to adopt this proposition, for there is no important change made in the revenue that the local papers of the country do not notice at length ; and no well-informed person, who is interested in the subject, fails to examine these questions.

Again, I doubt the propriety of this body so tendering its services to the Committees ; I think the offer would not be received in the spirit in which it is tendered. And I do not see how the Board is to render these services ; how it is to meet together, or how it can assist the Committee in their deliberations.

Mr. HINCKEN: When we met for the first time to consult about the organization of this National Board of Trade, I then understood it to be our aim to come together for the purpose of consulting what would be for the best interest of commerce, and to act, through our local representatives, on the Congress of the United States. That, I believe, is the object of our coming together. We were to act upon our individual representatives, and not upon the Congress of the United States as a whole. But all our propositions seem to have been discussed with an indirect purpose to send them to Congress. This, it seems to me, will defeat our ends. Instead of having attention called to a subject from numerous quarters, we shall have one grand petition, which will be laid aside. If the original intention of the Board is carried out, we shall have a stream, from every city represented in this body, and by that means shall augment our influence in the Legislature of the United States. If we adopt the rule of offering our services, as a sort of cabinet to advise what should be done, I think we shall be laughed at; and therefore I hope the gentleman from Baltimore, for whom I have personally great respect, will withdraw the resolution.

Mr. LONEY: The object of this resolution was to place in the hands of the constituent bodies, any original bill for a change in the tariff laws or internal revenue, in order that those bodies might suggest such alterations in the laws as agreed with their views.

I am perfectly willing, if the gentlemen wish, to strike out the second resolution, leaving only the first, so that it shall be the duty of our Secretary to furnish copies of such bills as may come before Congress to local Boards of Trade.

I withdraw the second resolution.

The PRESIDENT: The first resolution is before the body.

Mr. WETHERILL: I agree with the gentleman from New York in regard to this matter. It strikes me that this Board was organized for a different purpose. On the important matter of specie payments, this Board decided not to enter into details; and now this resolution would not only make us recommend details, but each local Board would be notified for the purpose of suggesting such alterations in the details as it might desire.

I move to lay the whole matter on the table.

Carried.

The PRESIDENT: The next business is the resolution passed by the Baltimore Board of Trade, proposing an amendment to the Constitution:

## SUBSTITUTION OF DELEGATES.

WHEREAS, There is no provision in the Constitution of the National Board of Trade, allowing the sending of substitutes for the regularly elected delegates; and, whereas, it may frequently happen that the delegates, (duly elected) may be unable to attend some meeting of said Board ; and, whereas, it might be desirable for this Board to send delegates peculiarly fitted to advocate or defend some particular interest or matter at a special or regular meeting of said Board ; be it

*Resolved*, That this Board present to the National Board of Trade, the following as an addition to the Constitution, viz :

"It shall be competent for any local organization to send substitutes for any of their regularly elected delegates, to any meeting of this Board."

Mr. LONEY : That proposition was suggested by the fact that Mr. SCHUMACHER, a member of the Executive Council in June last, found it impossible to attend this meeting; it became necessary for him to resign, and relinquish his position as a member of this body. Under these circumstances, we thought if we could send a substitute, it would be an advantage to our Board, as it might be to other local Boards, if a member should wish to resign, from sickness, or any other cause. I hope the resolution will pass.

Mr. DAVIS : It seems to me that this question is an unnecessary one. The election of delegates is entirely in the hands of the local Boards; and I would ask if after the annual election of five members by the Cincinnati Chamber of Commerce, and if by reason of disability one should resign a month before the meeting of this body, whether it would be competent for our Chamber to elect another member ?

The PRESIDENT : The Chair thinks that it would be perfectly competent to do so.

Mr. DAVIS : I move that the whole matter be laid upon the table.

Carried.

The PRESIDENT: I desire to bring a subject before you, and therefore request Mr. HAZARD to occupy the chair.

Mr. HAZARD took the chair.

Mr. FRALEY : I am about to ask for a suspension of the order of business, to enable me to have a vote taken upon a question which I understood the Committee on Finance yesterday agreed should be considered with the proposition of my friend from Cincinnati.

The proposition is this:

That the National Board of Trade recommends that Congress provide by law that on and after the first Monday of March, 1869, the legal-tender notes of the United States and the notes of the National Banks shall be receivable for duties on imports, in the following sums and proportions: For the said month of March, five per cent., and for every two months thereafter an increment of five per cent., until by such increments, fifty per cent. of the whole amount of duties on imports may be thus payable.

I ask for a suspension of the rules to state the question on this proposition.

Granted by an unanimous vote.

Mr. FRALEY: I will not trespass more than five minutes upon the attention of the house. One resolution of the Finance Committee passed upon favorably by this Board, requires the banks to retain the specie which they shall receive for the payment of interest on the public debt pledged for its circulation; this is a principle analogous to that. I am, myself, thoroughly convinced, if the Government of the United States shall provide by a simple proposition, such as I have here stated, for the gradual equalization of the paper currency with gold; that silently, steadily, and without fixing a day for the resumption of specie payments, we shall come to such resumption before the end of fifteen or eighteen months.

I do not propose to break in upon the present condition of things, so that our friends in the West and South need not fear that we shall attempt to withdraw the currency from circulation among the people; but I merely wish by this process to simplify and equalize the approximating of gold to paper.

After the first Monday in March, ninety-five per cent. of the duties would be payable in gold; at the end of two months ninety per cent.; again at the end of the next two, eighty-five per cent; and so on, until fifty per cent. of the duties would be payable in the legal-tender notes of the United States and National Bank notes. The immediate effect of the passage of such a law would unquestionably be to reduce the premium on gold, and gradually to improve the prospect of resumption until it was fully obtained.

With these remarks, I leave the subject with the house; and as when the resolutions were in order, under the motion of Mr. HOLTON, of Milwaukie, the previous question could apply to them, it would apply to this proposition as to others.

Mr. PORTER: I ask to strike out that part of the proposition relating to the National Bank notes.

Mr. FRALEY: I am opposed to three currencies; I would get back as rapidly as possible to one.

Mr. BRUNOT: How much would be the amount of paper cancelled each month?

Mr. FRALEY: There would be no cancellation of any paper.

Mr. HOLTON: I move the previous question.

Mr. TAYLOR: Is there not a pledge, by law, to the holders of the securities of the United States, that the customs shall be collected in gold for the purpose of paying the interest on them?

Mr. FRALEY: No, Sir; only that the interest shall be payable in gold.

The motion on the previous question was put and carried.

The Yeas and Nays were called on the resolution, and the proposition was lost, not receiving a vote of two-thirds.

Yeas: Messrs.—

| | | | |
|---|---|---|---|
| Allen, (Geo. N.,) | Davis, (Geo .W.,) | Hoffman, | Michener, |
| Boynton, | Fraley, | Holton, | Shryock, |
| Bradford, | Hand, | Kirkland, | Stranahan, |
| Buell, | Harris, | Loney, | Thomas, |
| Burwell, | Hazard, | Malone, | Walton, |
| Buzby, | Hincken, | Meier, | Wetherill—25. |
| Carpenter, | | | |

Nays: Messrs.—

| | | | |
|---|---|---|---|
| Bagley, | Converse, | How, | Randolph, |
| Biggs, | Davis, (Geo. F.,) | King, | Ropes, |
| Branch, | Drake, | McGraw, | Taylor, |
| Brunot, | Egan, | Nazro, | Thurston, |
| Carrington, | Gano, | Plumer, | Topp—23. |
| Cobb, | Guthrie, | Porter, | |

Mr. FRALEY having resumed the chair, announced the next business to be the amendment of Article IV of the Constitution, proposed by the Philadelphia Board of Trade.

Sec. 1. The officers of the Board shall be a President and four Vice-Presidents, who shall be elected at each annual meeting by ballot, and on a majority of all the votes cast, they shall serve until their successors are chosen.

Stated elections shall be the first business in order. The administration of the affairs of the Board shall be vested in the President and Vice-Presidents, and one delegate from each State that may be represented by delegates in attendance at any annual meeting; but no delegate shall be chosen from any State that is already represented by the President or by a Vice-President.

Such delegates shall be elected in the same manner as the President and Vice-Presidents.

The Board may, by a vote of two-thirds of the delegates present at any annual meeting, elect additional delegates to the Executive Council from such localities as it may deem of sufficient importance commercially to be entitled to such representation. The officers and delegates so chosen shall be constituted and known as the Executive Council.

Five of their number shall constitute a quorum for the transaction of business.

In the absence or disability of the President, a Vice-President to be designated by his associates shall preside; and if the President and all the Vice-Presidents be absent, then a chairman, *pro tempore*, shall be chosen by the members of the Council present at any meeting.

Mr. HAND: I move to refer the proposition to the Executive Council, to report at the next meeting.

Carried.

The PRESIDENT: The next recommendation, to amend Article X of the Constitution, is from the Boston Board of Trade:

Strike out the word "sixty" in the fourth line of Section 1, and insert the word "forty," so that notice of proposed amendments shall be required to be submitted "at least forty days previous to the meeting" at which they are to be considered.

The SECRETARY: This is suggested in order that the time of notice of amendments to the Constitution may be made to conform to the time of notice required for other subjects which are to be brought before the Board. As all will naturally be included in the same official notice to the constituent bodies, it seems proper that the same time for notification to the Secretary should be given to all.

Mr. RANDOLPH : I think the words as they now stand in our Constitution, are to be regarded as the result of a clerical error. It will be remembered that in Philadelphia there was some haste in concluding our business, and it was left to the Committee having the matter in charge, to make any verbal alterations that might be deemed desirable to render the whole harmonious and consistent. I move that the amendment be adopted.

Carried.

Mr. PORTER : I believe the next order of business is the proposition of the Louisville Board of Trade.

The long preamble and resolution which have been already read, are not exactly to the point. I therefore offer this as a substitute :

WHEREAS, The rich alluvial bottom lands of the Mississippi River subject to overflow, require protection by means of levees ; and

WHEREAS, The productions of said lands afford the great staples of export, contributing largely to make the balance of trade in our favor, and thereby increase the national credit ; therefore,

*Resolved*, That we do hereby most respectfully ask the Senate and House of Representatives, in Congress assembled, to render the necessary aid by endorsing the bonds of such States as may issue bonds for this purpose, secured by a lien upon the lands thus protected, to be used in the construction of levees to secure the bottom lands of the Mississippi River from overflow.

I reserve the right to speak, but yield the floor.

Mr. TOPP : This is a subject which is of great interest to the people of the entire Mississippi Valley. That valley is liable to an overflow of forty miles in width, subjecting twenty millions of acres to inundations, If we take out one-third for water-courses, and that which could not be restored, it will leave about thirteen million acres of land, every acre of which would produce one bale of cotton. If I were amongst strangers who did not know me, I should say that there is a great deal of it that would produce much more than a bale. In 1861 I was informed by a most respectable person, that a plantation he had in cultivation, produced more than two bales to the acre. This question is one that vitally concerns our people, and is of interest, not only to all that part of the South, but indirectly to every part of the Union. It is a country which might produce, if it were in cultivation, thirteen million bales of cotton.

I am aware that there are many gentlemen here who think that we are venturing rather deeply into the subject of internal improvements on the guarantee of the Government, and that we may perhaps, have caused a suspicion on the part of many, if not their censure, for being reckless in our recommendations. I have therefore prepared a resolution, which I think, if the Board will give it a few minutes consideration, it cannot hesitate to adopt:

*Resolved,* That this Board regards with deep solicitude the reclamation of the rich alluvial lands of the Mississippi River. It recommends to the favorable consideration of the Congress of the United States, the passage of an act, with suitable guarantees, authorizing the President of the United States to guarantee the bonds of the States of Mississippi and Louisiana for an amount not exceeding ten millions of dollars each, and of the State of Arkansas not exceeding four millions of dollars, not having more than thirty years to run to maturity, with coupons for interest at the rate of six per cent. per annum, payable semi-annually, whenever said States, or either of them, shall by law provide for leveeing the river in said States, or either of them, and shall, in said law or laws, provide to tax annually the product of cotton raised on said overflowed districts, to an amount sufficient to pay the interest on the bonds issued by said States, and guaranteed by the United States, and for an annual sinking fund sufficient to pay the principal by the time of maturity.

Mr. RANDOLPH : I move the adoption of that as a substitute for the Louisville proposition.

Mr. TOPP : If this proposition is accepted the very moment it goes into effect it will infuse new life, new spirit and new energy into all that country.

Mr. PORTER : After carefully reading the gentleman's proposition, and finding it substantially the same as my own, I accept it as a substitute for the whole matter.

Mr. DAVIS : I desire to say that when this subject was brought forward before the Cincinnati Chamber of Commerce, we gave the matter some consideration, and passed resolutions in favor of aiding those States whose levees had been injured by the war; we desired that Congress should do all that was possible. If anything can be done, I think this Board should lend its influence that it may be done.

Mr. HOLTON: This seems to me to come under the objection I before raised, that it is not within the province of Congress. It is my opinion that Arkansas, Louisiana and the other States bordering on the Mississippi, are going to have better credit than the United States Government; and that they need no endorsement of the United States Government. These States are all bravely going forward to do as other States have done; the power is already at hand to carry out these grand measures, and they need no endorsement of the Government of the United States. I believe the United States Government is a poorer endorser than those very States themselves.

Mr. GUTHRIE: I have listened with pleasure to what has been said, and I cannot but move in the direction of aiding these States. Now is the time they need help, if ever. We have been moving to help others, to extend aid to the West; and as all that these Southern States ask is a loan to aid them in their great work, I hope the resolution will be carried.

The question was put on Mr. TOPP's resolution, and carried.

The PRESIDENT: The next question in order is the resolutions from the Dubuque Board of Trade, on the Pacific Railroad:

WHEREAS, The Pacific Railroad with its several branches being a great national measure, in the successful prosecution of which, and in the faithful execution of the laws creating the same, the people of the whole country are deeply interested; and

WHEREAS, It is asserted by very many of the friends of that enterprise in all parts of the country, that it has been diverted from its original destination "westwardly" from its initial point southeastwardly, down the valley of the Missouri River, to the irreparable injury and destruction of the entire system of railroads running south-westwardly through the State of Minnesota and westwardly through the northern portion of Iowa, and through Wisconsin: therefore, be it

*Resolved,* That the National Board of Trade which meets in Cincinnati on the third day of December next, be respectfully requested to recommend to Congress such action as may be necessary and proper to secure its restoration to the original route westwardly, as provided by law.

*Resolved,* That this preamble and resolutions duly authenticated by the officers of this Board, be transmitted to the President of said

Board of Trade Convention, with a request that he lay the same before said Convention for its consideration and action.

WHEREAS, The foregoing preamble and resolutions from the Board of Trade of the city of Dubuque, in the State of Iowa, have been addressed to this Convention, for its consideration and action, therefore

*Resolved,* That Congress be respectfully requested to adopt such legislation as may be necessary to carry out and enforce the true intent, meaning and purpose of the Pacific Railroad law of Congress and amendments thereto, in relation to said North, or Sioux City Branch of said road.

Mr. THOMAS : I desire to state that we ask this Board to petition Congress on but one point, and that is to investigate the law ; and if additional legislation is necessary to carry out and enforce the law already existing, that that be adopted. We do not ask this Board to endorse the view of the Dubuque Board of Trade; we simply want the moral support of this body in requesting Congress to examine the question.

The motion was seconded and a vote taken ; the result being doubtful, the Yeas and Nays were ordered.

Yeas : Messrs.—

| Allen, (Geo. N.,) | Egan, | How, | Shryock, |
|---|---|---|---|
| Bradford, | Fraley, | Ilsley, | Taylor, |
| Branch, | Guthrie, | Kirkland, | Thomas, |
| Burwell, | Hazard, | Loney, | Topp, |
| Cobb, | Hoffman, | Monroe, | Walton—22. |
| Drake, | Holton, | | |

Nays : Messrs.—

| Biggs, | Davis, (Geo. F.,) | Malone, | Randolph, |
|---|---|---|---|
| Boynton, | Davis, (Geo. W.,) | Meier, | Ropes, |
| Buell, | Hand, | Michener, | Stranahan, |
| Buzby, | Harris, | Nazro, | Thurston, |
| Cobia, | Hincken, | Plumer, | Wetherill. |
| Converse, | King, | Porter, | 23. |

The PRESIDENT : The next question for the consideration of the Board will be the resolutions of the Buffalo Board of Trade on the enlargement of the Erie Canal.*

---

* See pp. 304 and 305.

Mr. HAZARD : I hope no gentleman will refuse to vote in favor of this preamble and the resolutions. We simply ask the endorsement of this National Board of Trade as to the character of the Erie Canal, as being the great highway between the East and West. It being the great regulator of the traffic, we wish to see the canal enlarged, so that the prices of transportation between the East and the West shall be reduced fifty per cent. I therefore move the adoption of the resolutions.

Mr. ALLEN : I second the motion. I thought at first when the Buffalo gentlemen brought this before the body, that they wanted to get their hands into the Treasury of the United States, but they only ask for the recommendation of this Board that New York shall take the proper steps for the enlargement of the canal.

The preamble and resolutions were voted on and agreed to.

The Board then took up the resolutions of the Cincinnati Chamber of Commerce, offered by Mr. GANO, as follows:

The Cincinnati Chamber of Commerce submits the propriety of an effort to secure uniformity in trade reports, trade statistics and standards of measures of commodities, so that all constituent bodies shall be able to show weekly, monthly, or yearly statistics computed for the same dates, by the same measure, and in like forms; and proposes the following:

*Resolved*, By the National Board of Trade that its constituent bodies be requested to submit propositions or suggestions in regard to this matter, to the Executive Council; which body shall, after due consideration, make recommendations and submit a plan by which trade statistics, trade customs and standards of measures may be made uniform for the entire country.

Also,

The Cincinnati Chamber of Commerce suggests the propriety of an effort to secure a reform of the irregularities in the laws of the States of the Union, referring to the organization of corporations, especially of the parts of those laws which refer to the liabilities of subscribers to the stock of joint stock associations.

Mr. TAYLOR: I desire to make a statement of facts. When the original proposition for the establishment of the National Board of Trade was made at Detroit, it was suggested that it be a Bureau or Department of the Government at Washington; and a Committee of one was appointed to wait upon the Secretary of the Treasury, and confer with him upon the expediency of establishing such a bureau.

The Secretary informed that Committee that it was in the power of the business men of the country, through their own organization, to attain the object more effectually by voluntary association, independently of and entirely disconnected with the Government; and that he should regard an effort for obtaining statistical information, under the direction of the National Board of Trade, as a most material contribution to the Government, as well as to the people generally. And I may perhaps be allowed, as having served on that Committee, and as cognizant of the facts of which I have spoken, to say that I regard this proposition as more vital to the efficiency of this organization, and more useful to the Government than almost any other proposition that can be brought before us.

The adoption of the resolutions having been moved and seconded, the first was carried unanimously.

The PRESIDENT: The question now is on the second resolution.

Mr. WETHERILL: I move to refer it to the Executive Council. Carried.

Mr. GANO: I wish to have the Secretary instructed to submit a copy of the paper on Decimal Weights and Measures, which appears in the Philadelphia proceedings, to the Chairman of the Ways and Means Committee of the House of Representatives, without asking any action of this body in regard to the decimal system; I therefore offer this resolution:

*Resolved*, That the Secretary be instructed to submit a copy of the paper on the Metric system of Weights and Measures which appears in the Philadelphia Report of the proceedings of the National Board of Trade, to the Chairman of the Ways and Means Committee of the House of Representatives at Washington.

The resolution was agreed to.

Mr. HARRIS: I have much pleasure in offering the following:

*Resolved,* That the thanks of the National Board of Trade are eminently due, and are hereby tendered to its President, the Hon. FREDERICK FRALEY, for the very faithful and impartial discharge of his laborious duties at its present protracted session.

Mr. HAZARD : I second the motion.

The question was put by Mr. PORTER, who was called to the chair, and it was unanimously carried.

Mr. PLUMER : The other day when the Civil Service Bill, now before Congress, was brought up, and Mr. WETHERILL introduced his resolution, I voted in the affirmative to lay it on the table. I did so, Sir, not because I do not most heartily approve the provision of the bill, but because I had a fear that it was not germane to the objects of which we should properly take cognizance. On further reflection I feel that this is a subject upon which we should pass ; and, therefore, as the motion was laid upon the table, I move that that vote be reconsidered.

Mr. HINCKEN : I agree with Mr. PLUMER, and repent of my action in moving to lay it upon the table ; but now I second the motion that it be taken from the table. .

The motion was agreed to.

Mr. PLUMER : I now offer this as a substitute to Mr. WETHERILL's resolution, now taken from the table.

*Resolved,* That the National Board of Trade, composed, as it is, of the representatives of the practical business men of the country, recognizes the importance of those provisions of the Hon. Mr. JENCKES's Civil Service Bill, (so called,) now before Congress, which are designed to secure increased efficiency in the administration of the revenue laws of the United States, by competitive examination, by appointment in view of merit, and by removal from office, for cause only.

Mr. HOLTON : I move that the word " practical " be stricken out.

Mr. DRAKE : I also made some remarks adverse to the subject, but I desire to say that the general principles of the bill I heartily endorse, and I think it comes within our province as business men of the country, to act upon it. One of the greatest evils from which the country suffers, is the inefficient and dishonest administration of public affairs ; and I believe that this bill is a most happy idea in the direction of reform. I am disposed to vote for the proposition.

The question was then put on Mr. PLUMER'S resolution, as amended by Mr. HOLTON, and was adopted.

Mr. ALLEN :. I now move that this Board adjourn.

The PRESIDENT : Before putting this question to your decision, I beg leave to say a single word. I am profoundly sensible of the honor which you have conferred upon me by the vote of thanks so unanimously passed.

I have endeavored in discharging the duties of this Chair, to conform as nearly as practicable under the circumstances of our organization, to the rules of the House of Representatives of the Congress of the United States ; and for this unanimous expression of approbation of my course, I feel very grateful to you all. This is a very difficult position to occupy, and it is not easy reasonably to satisfy a body of gentlemen thus brought together ; but to you, to your intelligence, to your practical and quick sense of what is right, I have been greatly indebted for the support I have received in this position and for the order and success of our deliberations.

It is painful to me, gentlemen, to say to you the word Farewell. We came here in joyfulness, with a conviction that we might do something to promote the interests of this great and beloved country of ours, now so happily united in the bonds of peace, and I think that we have done something to promote those interests.

In the midst of our deliberations we have been startled by an accident, by a dispensation of Providence, the wisdom of which we cannot understand, but in the justice of which, under our convictions that everything that is ordered by God is ordered aright, we must religiously and faithfully acquiesce. We are about to be subjected to the perils of a journey in returning to our respective homes; and therefore the parting hour with us must be, under such a dispensation as has lately taken place, one of unusual solemnity. And independently of such casualties, we have the uncertainties of ordinary existence, the inroads that must be made upon our number by age, and by disease ; and it is scarcely possible that we, as a body, comprising the same individuals now convened, may ever be permitted again to assemble upon earth. But I think, my brothers of the Board, we have by our week's work been so united in fraternity and in love, that whether we meet again in this world or not, we have the assurance that we may meet again in a better world ; and long as we may live, separated as widely as we may be, we shall always cherish in our hearts the recollections of our associations this week, for those recollections will ever be most pleasant.

My brothers of the Board, I do not know that I may ever be permitted to meet with you again. Probably I am the oldest member of this body, and my chances of life, under ordinary circumstances, will therefore be least of any among you. But I have had the good fortune to meet with a large proportion of the members of this Board during the last three years, at various places in our beloved country, and I have always received from them such expressions of their confidence, regard, and I may say love, that I am almost overwhelmed with the feeling which these indications of your regard produce upon my mind.

I have only one more word to say, gentlemen; and that is the parting Farewell! If we are permitted to meet together again, may our meeting be characterized by the same harmony which has existed here; and if we are not so permitted, may God bless us all!— Farewell!

Mr. TAYLOR: I move that the special thanks of this Board be presented to our Secretary, Mr. HILL.

The motion was seconded, and unanimously carried.

Mr. HAZARD: I move that the thanks of the Board be tendered to the reporters and gentlemen of the press, for the faithfulness with which they have reported the proceedings of this Board.

Unanimously carried.

The question was then put on the motion to adjourn, which was unanimously carried.

The PRESIDENT: This Board is adjourned *sine die*.

Three enthusiastic cheers were given for the Cincinnati Chamber of Commerce.

# APPENDIX.

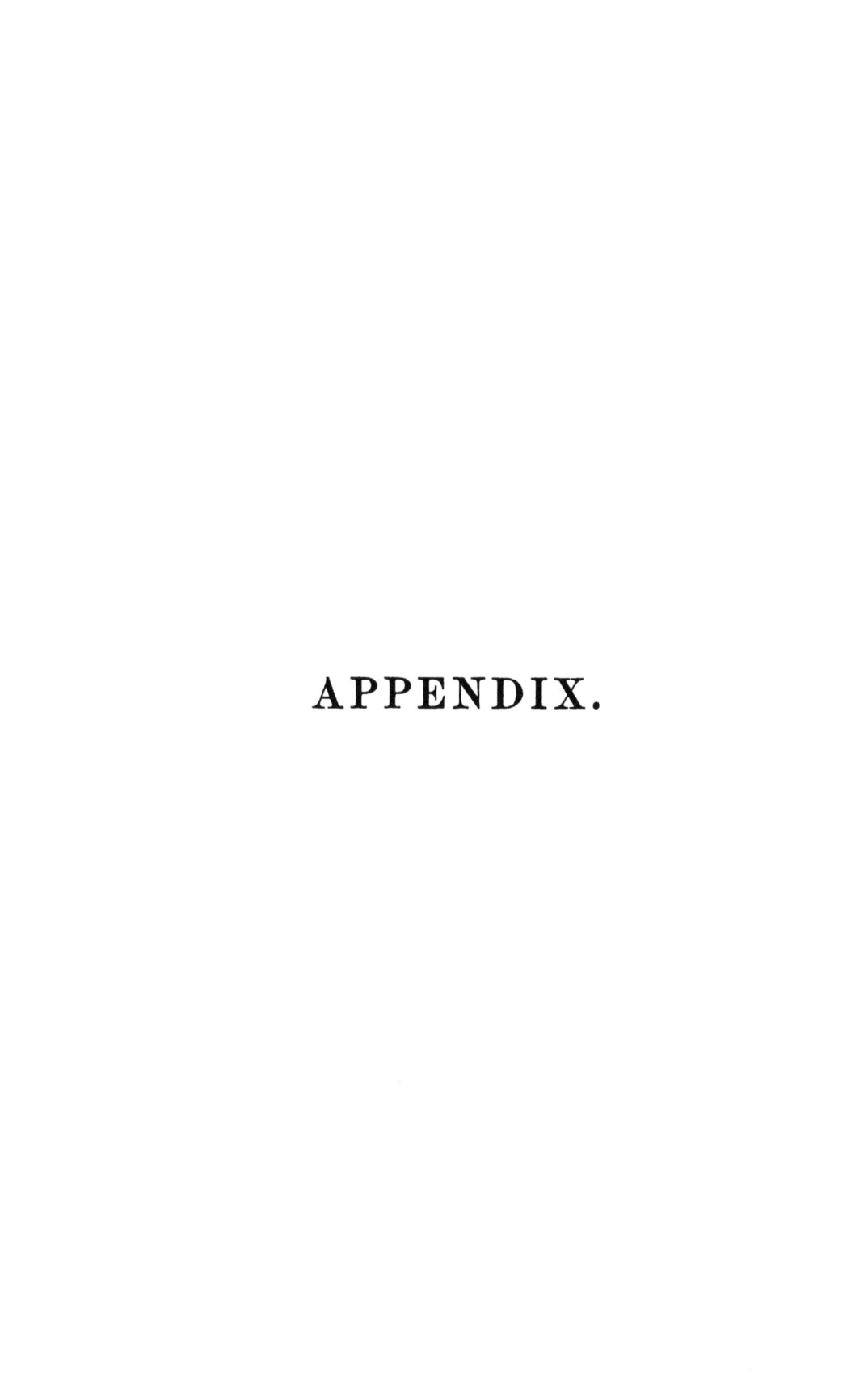

# RECEPTION OF THE NATIONAL BOARD OF TRADE.

## DECEMBER 2, 1868.

The National Board of Trade received a hearty welcome to Cincinnati on the evening of Wednesday, December 2nd, the first day of its gathering in the city. The reception was tendered by the Cincinnati Chamber of Commerce, and took place in Pike's Music Hall, which was decorated with evergreens, and ornamented with a fine display of national banners, bearing the names of all the States in the Union. A large gathering, composed of the best citizens, with their wives and daughters, filled the gallery and a considerable portion of the floor of the hall. The delegates, accompanied by their escorts, members of the Cincinnati Chamber of Commerce, many of the city authorities, and members of the City Council and School Board, filed into the hall at eight o'clock, taking their places in front of the platform, from which they were formally welcomed by Mr. JOHN A. GANO, President of the Cincinnati Chamber of Commerce, in the following address:

GENTLEMEN OF THE NATIONAL BOARD OF TRADE:

With a profound sense of the distinguished honor conferred by the event, I have the pleasure of introducing you to the business men of our city, as represented by the Cincinnati Chamber of Commerce.

The distinction given our city, by making it the place of your first regular meeting, is fully appreciated, and this occasion is provided by our Chamber, that its members may have an opportunity to make the personal acquaintance of men honored as you are by the various commercial bodies of the country as their representatives in so important an organization as the National Board of Trade.

In thus making you acquainted with the people here assembled, let me assure you that you can consider each one present, not wearing your distinctive badges, a special host to further the interests of your association, and to make your sojourn among us in every way a pleasure.

The organization of our National Board of Trade must be considered one of the progressive steps in the development and upbuilding of our commerce. When we reflect how great are the interests incident to or involved in that commerce, not merely as relates to the increase of our national wealth and power, but as relates, also, to the higher obligations imposed by its civilizing influences, the wonder is that we have only so recently provided a plan by which the commercial and industrial interests of the country can, in some measure at least, have the benefit of the associated experience, study and thought of those who are practically most interested in them.

So rapid, however, has been the enlargement of the industries and trade of the country, that, though continually familiar with the extraordinary steps in its progress, we can not but look with surprise on the comparison of what we are and what we were.

Only eighty years have elapsed since the pioneers who sought this, the Miami country, left their homes near the seaboard, with a spirit of enterprise and courage that has not since, with all the wonders of our material growth, been surpassed. When those hardy men and women, after their tedious, dangerous, toilsome journey over the Alleghany Mountains, placed that formidable obstacle between themselves and their early homes, and settled in the unknown, and, then supposed to be, boundless West, they naturally thought that commercial intercourse with the places they had left was an impossibility. They knew there was a Mississippi River, and a French city in foreign possession at its mouth, with no intervening congenial settlements. The thought of the exchange of their produce at that point was scarcely less than chimerical. The power of steam had not been known, and all the mechanical appliances for such means of transportation as they had, were of the rudest kind. There was then, however, in vigorous spring-time growth, the peculiar genius of American enterprise. Rough boats, scarcely deemed safe now for a coal barge, were soon laboriously piloted through the dangers of a wilderness down the treacherous rivers of this valley, laden with the fruits of the primal fatness of our land. Meanwhile Philadelphia, keen in her competition for so promising a trade, improvised the famous Conestoga wagons, with the noble Dutch horses, and soon established a great trade over the supposed insurmountable obstacles offered by the mountains — reigning monarch for a time over the avenues of trade to the West. The steamboat, then, came like a divinity to favor the commerce of the rivers. This was answered by the construction of canals, whose engineering seemed to exhaust itself. The railroad followed this, and has rushed all over the land, wherever a generous soil, or teeming, blossoming mineral, invited a strife for the exchange of their produce. Cities on the seaboard have all been brought into this wonderful competition, and each has become great, and in some way, to its neighbors, superior. The limits of the West have been measured. The dauntless pioneer has no more a place in the march of our commerce. He has preceded the progress of the *Star of Empire, and the world shall know him no more. We may well mourn his loss, for with him have gone many virtues that a refined civilization is now much of a stranger to.

Having bounded the West and found that its limits are on the confines of the East, or actually overlapping it, and realizing that we, in our progress, have only verified the past history of commerce, may we not wisely ask whether the sceptre of the power of this mighty mistress will, when our nation possesses it, as it doubtless will at some time in the early future, leave us and pass on in its course with the sun; and how shall we answer it? Surely in the echo of all true hearts we have the reply : we can only hold it by keeping alive a just sense of the responsibilities which our wonderfully precious heritage imposes. Commerce to be prosperous, must continually have justice as her hand-maiden, integrity as her guide, increasing, well-directed, economical industry as her support. If the National Board of Trade does not aid in furnishing these her requisites, and sustaining them, it will disappoint the hopes of its founders, and attain to no higher destiny than an instrument to feed a cupidity which will have its meanest expression in petty jealousies between centres of trade, and contemptible rivalries between sections. But your body, which we delight to honor this evening, has noble promise. Its organization was a part of our progress in the rightful path of commerce, and though its work will be arduous and exacting, we shall see its fruits in wiser legislation, and in the elevation of the sense of mercantile honor, to a point that will see no wrong done by the commerce protected by our national banner, either in our own or in any land.

Mr. FREDERICK FRALEY, President of the National Board of Trade, replied as follows:

Mr. President of the Chamber of Commerce of Cincinnati, and members of that body: Ladies and Gentlemen: It will be difficult for me to make a fitting reply to the eloquent address to which we have just listened. The topics upon which it touches are so broad, the ideas which it presents, so comprehensive, that it is almost beyond the power of an individual, situated as I am on the present occasion, not knowing beforehand exactly the topics which would be introduced, to venture upon an appropriate reply. But on the part of the delegates of the National Board of Trade now assembled in this city, I may say that we acknowledge what has thus been presented as a great tribute to the business men of our whole country.

We are here to consider great national subjects, in which the whole nation is interested. Not questions in which any particular part of our beloved country is particularly and locally concerned, but subjects which will go down to the bottom of our social, commercial and business life; and if we can arrive at sound conclusions to present to those who are to legislate upon these subjects, we may hope that our meeting as a National Board of Trade will not be in vain.

It is pleasant for us to sojourn for a few days in your beautiful city. It is particularly gratifying to the delegation from Pennsylvania to find here, almost, we may say, the harmoniousness of our own firesides. We of Philadelphia, particularly, can recognize in this beautiful city the right-angled Quakerism of our City of Brotherly Love, and as we perambulate your streets, the recollections of home are vividly brought to our hearts by the very names of your streets.

But the topics which my friend, Mr. GANO, has presented here to-night, as among the subjects that are to be considered by the National Board of Trade, carry me back personally to recollections that are identified with the rapid growth of this country; the increase of its population, the vast development of its resources, and the aids which the ingenuity, particularly of our own countrymen, have contributed for the enlargement of all those interests, which also have contributed to the advancement of civilization throughout the earth.

I recollect perfectly well those old Conestoga wagons, with their magnificent teams, standing in Market street, Philadelphia, prepared to receive the merchandise which was to be transported to the West, when the city of Philadelphia, as Mr. GANO has said, carried the sceptre of the domestic, as well as the foreign commerce of the United States. I have lived to see my native city shorn of that glory, taken from her by the rivalries of other cities of the Union, culminating, at last, in the holding of that sceptre by the city of New York. And now I see the rivalries of the cities of the West competing with that great commercial centre; and it is possible that before my career on earth may be terminated, I shall see the sceptre of commerce transferred to the city of San Francisco. (Applause.)

It is impossible, under the thoughts presented in the address of Mr. GANO, to set any limits to the enterprise of our people, to the growth of our population, to the development of our resources, and to the magnificent results that they will present to the world. The civilized world owes a great deal to the ingenuity and enterprise of the people of the United States. I can recollect very well when the first steamboat was started upon the Hudson River, and I glory in the recollection that that first steamboat was started by a citizen of Pennsylvania, ROBERT FULTON, who afterward adopted the State of New York as his place of residence. The wonders that the steamboat has wrought in the commerce of this country, are not to be told by numbers. I have seen the opening and the development of the great canal enterprises of this country, working for a while their magnificent results; and when they had accomplished their mission, I saw the iron bands arise that now knit the whole of this country together in an indissoluble union. I saw them place their first links upon the soil of the United States, and now they have spread out to such an extent that, in iron arms, we now outmeasure any single country on the globe. (Applause.)

I have seen that other wonderful work of invention, given to the world in its perfect form by the genius of an American citizen — the electric telegraph. Where it will reach, what it will perform, what may be its ultimate influence upon religion, commerce and civilization, who can tell? With a people, such as we have, with resources such as we have, it is no marvel that the intelligence of the business men of the United States has at last sought out an organization by which the representatives of the great interests of this country, shall be periodically brought together, in a common fraternity and a common brotherhood, in which consultation for the good of the whole, shall be carefully and deliberately had; upon the conclusion of these deliberations we may hope that such a stimulus will be given to the agriculture, to the commerce, to the mechanical arts, and to the manufactures of this country, that the result which my friend, Mr. GANO, has so eloquently described in their true and perfect development, may be attained.

It will be a part, an humble part, of the gentlemen who are now associated here, as the delegates of the National Board of Trade, to further this great work. It is pleasing to us that the first real meeting of this national institution is held in one of the cities of the great West — the youngest child of our American system of government — the great West, which, at the outset of our history as a nation, was a wilderness. The place upon which we are now standing witnessed the struggle between the hardy pioneers of those days, and the Indian occupants of this territory. The white man planted his foot upon the soil with the energy of Anglo Saxon influences; that foot has never moved backward. It is continually moving forward, and we see now before us, not only in this city, but in Detroit, in Chicago, in St. Louis, and as we travel farther and farther westward, the fulfilment of the prediction that "Westward the course of Empire takes its way." (Applause.)

The West will, of necessity, in a few years, if it has not now, become the shaping hand of the destiny of this great nation, and it is a matter of pure and unfeigned rejoicing with us in the East and in the South, that the lessons of our common ancestry, filled with patriotism to our country, and with honest effort to educate and civilize the people, to disseminate the blessings of a free press and free schools, upon which the security and happiness of this great country permanently rest, have been seized by the West. And now, in the institutions of learning which they are building up, in their application of science to manufactures and the useful arts, in their devotion to collegiate institutions, and in everything that is calculated to fit them to be the rulers of this great nation, they are going forward in the right direction. May God give them good speed, and may we all live to realize the influence of those powers that are now at work for the welfare of our beloved country, and for the happiness and comfort of all — for the whole and the yet uncivilized portions of the globe. (Applause.)

I thank you, Sir, on behalf of the gentlemen of the National Board of Trade, for the eloquent welcome and cordial greeting which you have given us to-night, and I have only to regret that the task of replying and of returning thanks for the preparations that have been made for our comfort while among you, has not been confided to an abler voice and to a more potent head; but you will accept the imperfect effort I have made to present to you our thanks, as the sincere expression of our true and heart-felt emotions. We shall go to our labors to-morrow and shall continue them here, cherished by the consciousness that we are to have your support in this great work; and when we are called upon to bid you a reluctant farewell, we shall carry with us this cordial welcome to the end of our lives. (Applause.)

Mr. GANO: Members of the Cincinnati Chamber of Commerce, our guests are in your hands.

After the speaking, the assembly promenaded the hall for about half an hour, when they were entertained by the evolutions of a portion of the Zouave Battalion, who went through their drill with great precision. At ten o'clock, refreshments were furnished in the arcade of the hall, the tables being bounteously spread, and presenting a most elegant appearance. From the supper table the assembly returned to the hall and spent the remainder of the evening in dancing.

# BANQUET AT PIKE'S MUSIC HALL.

## DECEMBER 4, 1868.

On Friday evening, the fourth of December, the delegates to the National Board of Trade, by invitation of the city authorities of Cincinnati, partook of a banquet at the above hall.

At the dais table sat the Mayor, the President of the National Board, and other gentlemen. Five other tables, running at right angles, accommodated the remainder of the guests.

Ample attention having been paid to the feast of good things, the assembly was called to order by His Honor Mayor WILSTACH, who spoke as follows:

Gentlemen of the National Board of Trade: It becomes my duty, as Chief Executive Officer of this city, to welcome you to its hospitalities. It is a duty I perform with pleasure, because I believe not only that meetings of this nature are calculated to benefit our own city in many ways, but that they will result in making valuable acquaintances between the merchants and business men of this and the other cities of the Union.

Interchange of ideas between those who are transacting the business of the commercial world, will result in great good to each and every part of the country. It will add to the stock of knowledge of the wants and necessities of trade, and render easy the task of providing the requisite remedies.

We have every reason to be proud of the progress of our country, in the means of transportation, facilities for extending commerce, both inland and foreign, and all the varied means by which trade and commerce are carried forward.

The vastness of our domain, however, affords opportunity for a still further increase of these facilities, and more extended means of transacting that immense commerce which will inevitably flow from the settlement and cultivation of this great and diversified country.

You have met together to devise ways and means to accomplish this purpose. I trust your deliberations to that end will be crowned with every success, and that you will each and all part with the gratifying assurance that you have done the country some service.

I am informed that you have honored our city by making it the initial place of the meeting of the National Board of Trade. For this honor you will please accept our thanks.

The interests of the great West will, I doubt not, occupy and enter largely into the deliberations of your association. They are broad and comprehensive, and require the fostering care and guidance of the practical minds of the country — of large-brained statesmanship — such as is always found among the class your association represents.

We of the West need new lines of railway — new avenues in which to direct and carry on the immense traffic soon to result from the resettlement and resumption of the industrial pursuits in the great South and Southwest.

To you, more than any other body of men, belongs this important task.

Our own city is anxiously looking forward to the day (which must come, if its prosperity is to continue) when it shall be connected by additional iron bands with the South, which of late has been so desolated by the evils of war, but which will soon "blossom as the rose," under the shrewd management and untiring industry of a class of emigration which will inevitably "occupy and possess" its fertile soil.

Others are expected to address you during the evening; and the "good cheer" before us invites consideration.

Permit me, gentlemen of the Board of Trade, to repeat, that you are cordially welcomed to the hospitalities of our city.

I propose as a sentiment:

*The National Board of Trade*: May it become the Mentor of that higher Congress holding its sessions in the National Capital.

Mr. FREDERICK FRALEY, President of the Board, responded as follows:

Mr. Mayor and Gentlemen of the Council of Cincinnati: On the part of the delegates to the National Board of Trade, I acknowledge with gratitude the cordial welcome you have extended to us this evening. If the delegates to this National Board of Trade were not men of iron heads, or iron hearts, I fear that we should be overcome entirely by your hospitalities. (Applause.) But the men of business in this country can stand pressure of all kinds, and their past history has shown that the more they are trodden upon, the more prosperous they become. (Laughter and applause.)

We feel, Mr. Mayor, that it is a good thing for us to be here; (cheers) good because we are in the lap of the great West; good because we are in proximity to the old loved South; (loud applause;) good, Mr. Mayor, because this National Board of Trade has brought together men from all quarters of our beloved land, and we are here in fraternal council to promote the interests of this country.

We have put upon our programme, business of the highest importance to the nation; we have already disposed satisfactorily of a part of it, and, Mr. Mayor, we intend to stay here patiently until we accomplish the solution of it all. (Applause.) We have inaugurated our proceedings by determining that the principles of dealing in this country shall be for cash. We have determined, so far as the influence of our opinions and wishes extends, that the laws of war upon the ocean shall be made conformable to the laws of war upon the land; that private property shall be as safe there as it is upon the fields and plains of the land. (Cheers.)

We are now busily engaged in the discussion of a problem which lies at the foundation of our national prosperity — the resumption of specie payments — and we hope that we shall present some feasible, satisfactory plan for the solution of that great problem, which will address itself to the wisdom of Congress at Washington for their adoption. (Applause.)

We mean, Mr. Mayor, to do something for the commerce of our country by restoring the flag of our nation to the ocean, and building up our tonnage to the magnificent proportions it has occupied heretofore, so that the American flag, shall again be found floating in every harbor of the world.. (Loud cheers.) We intend to demand for the cities of the West that they shall be permitted the direct entry and importation of their own goods. We mean, Mr. Mayor, if the expression of our opinion can accomplish it, to cheapen the telegraphing system, so as to place that great instrument of social intercourse and social influence on foundations as beneficent as those upon which the national postage system now rests.

But finally, Mr. Mayor, we propose to do for the great West what you have so eloquently indicated in your speech. We mean that the iron arms of the railroads shall be extended East, North, South and West, so that those divisions of the quarters of the compass shall be obliterated, and the Union be made complete and perpetual by those iron bands. (Applause.)

We rejoice, Mr. Mayor, in the prosperity of Cincinnati. We have seen her grow from nothing to number a population of nearly three hundred thousand souls, and that within a period of about seventy or eighty years. And we see in .the rapid growth of the cities all around us, that this great West will soon be filled with a population almost as teeming and industrious as we are taught to believe exists in China.

We are multiplying so rapidly that the child now toddling through the streets of Cincinnati, may live to see the United States peopled by one hundred millions of souls. We truly, Mr. Mayor, have a country in which we can glory. (Applause.) And as all quarters of the Union are now at peace, and able to devote themselves to those industrial pursuits which give prosperity to the land, we ought with heartfelt thanks to look up and glorify God for the good gifts which He has thus given to men. (Cheers.)

Mr. Mayor, allow me, in conclusion, to propose a sentiment:

*Cincinnati, the Queen of the West — Beautiful and cordial:* May her prosperity in the future be equal to her prosperity in the past.

Mr. J. L. KECK, President of the City Council, acknowledged the remarks of Mr. FRALEY, as follows:

Mr. President of the Board of Trade: We feel highly honored by the expression of your thanks for the few courtesies we have extended as a city government to your Board. You will excuse me from making any lengthy reply, for I deem it improper, as a city official, to occupy the time which belongs to our guests, and modesty forbids me to speak of ourselves. (Applause.)

Permit me, Mr. President, and you, gentlemen of the National Board of Trade, to express the hope that the results of your deliberations, the convictions you may arrive at, and the recommendations you may make, will receive the endorsement and the approval of those whom you represent, and that the result may be to the best interest of the commercial community of our great country. (Applause.)

In conclusion, Mr. Mayor, with your permission, I propose:

*The Portland Board of Trade.*

Mr. J. B. BROWN, of the Portland Board of Trade, responded.

He said that he was surprised that the far-off city of the East should be the first called upon to respond to a sentiment. He tendered the thanks of the city of Portland, and of its Board of Trade, for the generous hospitalities with which Cincinnati had received her guests here, and he would particularly thank the Queen City of the West for the wonderful consideration which Cincinnati, in common with the other cities represented by the National Board of Trade, bestowed upon that unfortunate city of Portland when one-third of the city was laid in ashes. He said we could hardly conceive the condition in which his city was on the morning of the fifth of July, 1866. But when the city was paralyzed and stood appalled at the position in which she was placed, they began to receive from the cities of the United States, first from Boston, then from New York, and then from the cities of the West, sympathies and substantial tokens of their sympathy.

The next toast was:

*South Carolina, the home of a Marion and a Routledge.*

Mr. HENRY COBIA, of Charleston, was called upon to respond, but excused himself, and gave the following sentiment:

*Agriculture, commerce and the mechanic arts:* they add wealth and material aid to any people.

The next toast given was:

*The Mother of Presidents — Old Virginia.*

Mr. CHARLES S. CARRINGTON, of Richmond, responded, acknowledging the compliment of being invited to speak to such a toast:

It is so long since we in Virginia have been present at such a feast as this, that I am embarrassed in the selection of a topic suitable to the occasion. I recollect that in old times, at such feasts, our custom was to speak spontaneously — from the heart. This feature of spontaneity is a necessary feature of whatever I may say to-night.

In speaking, Sir, from the heart, my first utterance is that Virginia is in full sympathy, in perfect accord and harmony with all of the great inspirations of this occasion — with the sentiments and purposes of this noble body of men, which this noble city is honoring here to-night, and which purposes, in the language of the distinguished gentleman who presides over this body, embraces every thing which concerns the dignity and honor, the wealth and welfare of the whole country. (Cheers.) I cannot pass, Sir, from this impulsive speaking without, in the name of Virginia, returning now her hearty thanks to Cincinnati for all of that kindly courtesy which has made us feel since we have been among them that we are one with them.

Now, Mr. Mayor, I hesitate as to what I shall say next. If, Sir, you and I were alone — if I could speak to you in confidence I would say — because the high honor has been conferred upon this city by the National Board of Trade of holding its first meeting here and you would not therefore be our rival — that in due time it is our purpose to invite this National Board to hold its next meeting even in the city of Richmond. (Applause.) We hesitated, Sir. I hope that we shall not be censured for this hesitation — we cannot spread before you such a feast as this, or extend to you such entertainments as we have enjoyed here, but we will extend to you a welcome which will make you at home with us. (Cheers.) Come gentlemen, to us — we have been divided — long years have separated us — we ought to see more of each other. It is only necessary that we see more of each other, and know each other better, in order that a spirit of harmony and fraternity may prevail. (Applause.)

Sir, I should like to say so many other things in this fraternal spirit that I would gladly continue this strain of remark; but I remember that there are others here to be heard, and I close by again thanking the city of Cincinnati for its munificent hospitality. (Applause.)

The Mayor then gave as the next toast:

*The Northern Wheat Belt.*

Responded to by Mr. JAMES W. TAYLOR, of St. Paul, Minnesota.

Mr. Mayor and Gentlemen: Our friends the President of the Cincinnati Chamber of Commerce, and the President of the National Board of Trade, the other day, in the reception in this hall, alluded appropriately to the early foundation of this city upon the emigration and the sterling qualities of the old commonwealth of Pennsylvania. But I am told, by those familiar with the growth of Cincinnati, that it was founded upon an early stratum furnished by that State upon the original settlement from Virginia and Kentucky. New York followed with her life-giving influence; the New England States were soon represented upon her streets by their sterling qualities of thrift and integrity; and then Europe sent here her representatives to crown the organization of this city and its growth with that cosmopolitan character which looks over the whole world, and pours into the granaries of America the products of every part of the globe. (Applause.) And it is that composite structure, that true representative of American character and American society, which prevails over the Western valley. (Cheers.) Cincinnati, the Queen City and the pioneer of the West, here upon the site of Fort Washington, is a development of that truly American spirit which brings the North and the South, the East and the West, into one grand, harmonious nationality. (Applause.) Then, Ohio was a Western State; now, Ohio is the Middle State of the Republic, almost the keystone, seizing from Pennsylvania her crowning glory. The sons of her soil are now seen and felt, and known all over every portion of this Mississippi Valley, and westward to the Pacific coast, and there is not a hamlet in my own State of Minnesota but is proud of the presence of the sons and the daughters of Ohio. (Cheers.) Sir, I am not so forgetful of the necessities and the proprieties of this occasion as to indulge at any length in these remarks, grateful as they are to me. But here, in acknowledgment of the hospitalities and courtesies of the citizens of Cincinnati, allow me to say a few words in anticipation of the progress of this great metropolis — to cast a horoscope of your destiny.

I remember that those early men of the city of Cincinnati showed their sagacity by throwing out a net-work of turnpikes and canals all over this valley of the Ohio, giving themselves by that far-sighted policy the rank which you hold, and now there comes a new theatre of activity and action for you. Here upon the most southern point of the Ohio River, here fronting the new South, this regenerated South, this loyal, devoted South (Cheers,) here is a new destiny for you.

Walking with one of your citizens, before the late unfortunate struggle, he pointed to the manufactures of Minnesota as her great prospect in the future, and the markets of those manufactures South of the Ohio River and the Gulf of Mexico. That is the field; and Cincinnati and Louisville and Pittsburgh and St. Louis must march forward, with all the banners of commerce flying, for a conquest of business, for a victory even more renowned than those of war. (Applause.)

Aye, Baltimore, Richmond and Washington on the East, will form the flanks, and will develop her gold fields, her coal mines, her iron mines — the sleeping wealth of that great axis of the Union. And you here, upon the banks of the Ohio, must take up the march to the Gulf of Mexico, and must occupy all the strategic points to the Gulf.

But I must not forget that I speak for the Northwest; and while thus you work out your own destiny, show that you are as broad, as national, as comprehensive in your views as your fathers were before you. Let the North and the West, all the avenues and communications between the lakes, the rivers and the gulf of the East, and that mighty Pacific coast, which is the key of the great commerce of the Orient, all share your sympathy and support in a truly fraternal and national spirit. In that trust, with that assurance, with that confidence, Minnesota returns her cordial thanks and ˙greetings for the reception which she has received at your hands. (Loud applause.)

The Mayor announced that they would next be addressed by a delegate from under the shadow of Plymouth Rock.

Mr. HAMILTON A. HILL, of Boston, said:

Mr. Mayor: I have the honor to stand here in behalf of the two delegations from the city of Boston, who are your guests to-night, to tender to you our most cordial thanks for the splendid hospitality which you have offered to us on this occasion. I am glad of this opportunity to acknowledge to the citizens of Cincinnati the appreciation we have of the kindness, of the attention, and of the favor which we have received from them during the few days which it has been our pleasure to spend in this city. We in Boston have had the honor, within less than a year, of receiving a call from distinguished citizens of your metropolis, Sir, and it gives us great pleasure upon this occasion to return the call, and to renew the friendships and revive the associations of that visit.

It is right, also, that I should say that we in Boston feel in reference to the National Board of Trade, that a great debt is owing to the city of Cincinnati for the organization which assembles us together to-day. We consider that we are indebted to the representatives of your Chamber of Commerce for coöperation and counsel at Boston, and afterward at Philadelphia, in bringing this Board to where it now is. And I desire to-night to return thanks to the delegates of Cincinnati, who at those two meetings united their deliberations and their efforts with the delegates from the other cities of the country, to the attainment of this end.

Boston rejoices in this National Board of Trade for many reasons, but chiefly because it is national. Our first meeting in Boston, which to be sure, was not a meeting of the Board of Trade, but a convention preliminary to its formation, was composed of representatives from twelve or thirteen States. The meeting at Philadelphia a few months later, comprised representatives, I think, from fifteen States. To-day we have in our membership the representatives of seventeen or eighteen States. Thus our circle is gradually widening, and now we are looking forward to the day when the whole sisterhood of States shall be represented in the Board which is entertained here to-night. (Applause.) We are glad also that under the present Constitution of this body it is our privilege to go from city to city, and from State to State. It is only by intercommunication such as this, it is only by bringing our citizens into close personal contact, that in this wide land, in this land of magnificent distances, we can hope to become thoroughly acquainted with each other, to know each other, and to love each other as the citizens of one common country ought to do and desire to do. (Cheers.) And we believe that in the movement from city to city of this National Board, and in the convening on social occasions like the present, of the representatives of the great cities, and of the whole land in its broad extent, to discuss those questions which lie at the foundation of our national prosperity, and to cement fraternal bonds, we are promoting objects which must be dear, and which are dear to every patriotic American. We rejoice further in the belief that this Board, which, with other influences, is tending to develop more and more a national feeling in this country, is also going to prepare the way for something still wider and higher even than a national feeling, I mean an international feeling; that sentiment which operates to unite country to country, and nation to nation, around the wide world. (Applause.)

It is noteworthy, Sir, that among the very first subject to which we have given our attention, and upon which we have taken definite action, has been a question wider in its scope even than our own broad land, an international question, having to do with the relations of all the civilized nations of the earth. I rejoice in this because I believe it to be a happy augury of that blessed spirit which in due time, yea, and we may believe soon, will actuate and pervade all the nations of the earth. (Applause.)

It has been said on the floor of our Board during the present week, that commerce is the handmaid of peace; and we may be sure, as the influence of commercial men shall be increasingly felt in this and in other lands, that the nations will be brought nearer and nearer together, and war, whether foreign or domestic, will become at length an impossibility. (Applause.) Commerce is truly a peacemaker; and by means of the local Chambers of Commerce here and elsewhere, the National Board of Trade of the United States, the Associated Chambers of Commerce of Great Britain, and other kindred organizations, the time is to be hastened which will bring all the nations of the earth into intimate and permanent accord. Thus the new year, the golden year, will be ushered in, of which the poet speaks, when he says, with an elevated and a felicitous conception of the beneficent influences which commerce is destined to exert among men:

> "Fly, happy, happy sails and bear the Press,
>   Fly, happy with the mission of the Cross,
> Knit land to land, and blowing havenward,
>   With fruits, and silks and spices clear of toll,
> Enrich the harvest of the golden year.
>
> But we grow old. Oh, when shall all mens' good
>   Be each man's rule; and Universal Peace,
> Lie like a shaft of light athwart the land,
>   And like a lane of beams across the sea,
> Through all the circle of the golden year." (Applause.)

The Mayor gave:
*The Cotton City of Tennessee.*

Response by Colonel TREZEVANT, of Memphis.

He began by alluding to the music played by the band. Some of the pieces were once very dear to his heart; one of them reminded him of the recent struggle in this country; but the next strain brought out the ever-merry singing notes of Yankee Doodle; and next he heard a tune that he never had ceased to love, and if he had but one desire to express, it would be:

"The star-spangled banner, O long may it wave,
O'er the land of the free and the home of the brave." (Great cheers.)

The speaker then alluded to the near relations, in a commercial point of view, between his State and city, and Cincinnati and the Northwest. But a few days ago, said he, I returned from a trip South of Tennessee, in the inland, where I went on business of internal improvement — for it has been my object in life to build up, not tear down — though I did help to tear down a little for a while. And when I was down in that sunny land of the magnolia and the jessamine, my feelings were overcome with sorrow for the present, though tinged with joy for the future, Some of your people say we are disloyal. You don't know us. We are loyal in this — loyal to the flag and the Union. We are loyal — not in worshipping all the laws that are passed, but in obeying the laws. While we may not, and can not, and will not, acquiesce in sanctioning in our hearts all that may be passed as laws, we will obey them as long as they are laws. We think some of the laws have been unkind to us, but we obey them while they remain laws. In that sunny land of the South, I saw little girls, eight and ten years old, in the fields picking cotton for their fathers. What for? To help their fathers and brothers improve their condition, and lift them above the pangs of poverty. You can form no conception of what we have suffered in this way. But, thank God, as the old song says:

"There's a good time coming."

Mr. Mayor: I need scarcely say in behalf of the Memphis delegates, that we feel flattered at this reception. It is an outpouring of liberality on the part of the people of Cincinnati that we cannot help appreciating.

St. Louis was next called upon. The toast was responded to by Mr. THOMAS ALLEN.

St. Louis, he said, was represented here by several gentlemen much abler than himself, and he might fail in returning as he desired, thanks for the hospitality and generous kindness which had been shown the members of the National Board of Trade. He trusted that St. Louis would ere long have the pride and pleasure of reciprocating the kindness.

One of the aims of the National Board of Trade was to reconstruct the commerce of this country, and in this attempt we were doing much to cement in brotherly love all the cities and States of the Union, and to infuse new blood into all the commercial arteries of this great land. The Board simply offered suggestion and recommendation; but if its legislative power were only equal to its wishes, it would cement East and West by opening a grand Union railroad from the Atlantic to the Pacific Ocean, a mile wide, if necessary, with half a dozen tracks, upon which the produce of the West might be sent to the East for a cent per ton. (Laughter and applause.) We would free the Mississippi and all its tributaries from all obstructions, and we would extend the levee down the Mississippi on both sides, and put a railroad on the top. (Laughter and cheers.) We would open a line from the James to the Ohio, that would bring into communication the great waters of the valley of the Mississippi and the Atlantic; we would improve the Ohio, and relieve it from the annoyance which has sometimes been associated with it of being dry one half of the year and frozen the other half. We would unite our friends of Chicago with the great valley of the Mississippi by a ship canal, that should reach from the Mississippi to west of Lake Michigan, and then down the lakes through to the Atlantic, by the way of the Gulf of St. Lawrence. (Cheers and laughter.) We want our friends at Portland, in the East, to be connected by rail with Portland on the Pacific coast, through the State of Minnesota; and we would further like to have a railroad from the city of Cincinnati, by way of St. Louis, spreading out through Kansas into Utah, thence to the coast, and another line through West Missouri, on the thirty-fifth parallel of latitude, and thence on to San Diego. (Laughter.)

I would extend another railroad from Louisville down by the way of Cairo or Memphis, or both, running it into Texas, and thence carry it on through the States of Mexico to the Pacific Ocean — to Northern Mexico. (Laughter.) Be assured of our good intentions if our acts fall short. (Cheers.)

Let me wind up by proposing a toast to the memory of the late Justice McLean; and as Ohio has honored us by a Chief Justice, who now sits upon the bench of the Supreme Court, let me include the name of Chief Justice Chase.

Judge Noyes was called upon to reply.

He desired to give expression to the welcome and kindly greeting which the people of Cincinnati desired to extend to the distinguished merchants and men who had honored Cincinnati with their presence. Happily, most happily, we were able to congratulate ourselves that our troubles, conflicts and trials were past, and peace restored. (Applause.)

Again the industries of the country were permitted to thrive, our resources were being developed, fraternal feeling was again in the ascendant, and sections, though geographically separated, were living in the bonds of love and unity. The eminent men who composed the Board of Trade had a great task before them; he believed them equal to the task, and he confidently believed that the consultations of the Board would ultimately result in added prosperity and happiness to the whole land. (Applause.)

The city of Milwaukie was called for, and Mr. E. D. HOLTON replied:

Milwaukie, he said, had responded with alacrity to join with those who represented the mercantile interests of the country to consult on the great question of finance and the varied interests of ever-extending commerce. There were subjects which challenged the attention of every man of thought in this and other lands. He came from a State that believed in hard work; she believed in it, loved it, and gloried in the results which came of it. Milwaukie had reasons to feel attached to Cincinnati. Many of her best citizens formerly hailed from the Queen City of the West. They were interested in her welfare, and proud of the industry, growth and enterprise of that city. Cincinnati had reason to be proud of what she had done toward erecting an altar to culture, refinement and education, not less than for what she had accomplished in directing man to that source of good from which all our blessings flow.

As he sat, with a lady, in the gallery of that hall, on Wednesday evening last, and looked at the bright and enchanting scene witnessed on that floor, he could not but be struck with the bearing of the young men, citizen soldiers, and the gentler maidens that composed the happy throng. There was an air of gallantry and refinement, which spoke of gentleness and culture, good to be witnessed.

After expressing the pleasure he felt in participating in the generous feast, he sat down amid loud applause.

In answer to loud calls, the Rev. A. D. MAYO said:

He supposed he was invited, not because he was a clergyman, nor because he was a member of the Board of Education, but because he was brought up in a store in the good old State of Massachusetts.

He paid a high compliment to the business men of the country, admitting that many of the most valuable lessons of his life were received while he was yet associated, as a youth, with the business affairs of life. Theology and literature had taught him something, but many lessons of self-sacrifice, charity, forbearance, and the performance of the stern duties of life he had learned not from books, or institutions of learning, but from those whose daily life was spent in the varied avocations of trade.

He drew a vivid picture of the important and civilizing influences of commerce, and concluded with proposing a toast to that prince of merchants and generous benefactor, GEORGE PEABODY. (Applause.)

The city of Baltimore being called upon by the Mayor, Mr. HENRY DUVALL responded:

He expressed his hearty thanks for the kind and generous greeting extended to the members of the National Board of Trade by the City Council of Cincinnati, and by the citizens generally. Baltimore, he said, felt a deep interest in the Board of Trade, and he trusted that when the central position of that city was considered, holding, as she did, one hand toward the North and East, and the other toward the South and West, Baltimore would be honored with the next sitting of the honorable body to which he was proud to belong. Baltimore had taken a new stand in industry and enterprise, and she was disposed to avail herself of all honorable aids to compete successfully with her sister cities of the Atlantic seaboard. (Cheers.)

He thanked God that peace was once more blessing the land, and that the energies of this great country were being devoted to developing her resources and raising products that materially helped in feeding and clothing the whole world. They wanted the citizens of the West to become better acquainted with Baltimore and its citizens, feeling assured that the more they knew of each other the firmer the bonds of mutual esteem and respect would be cemented. (Applause.)

Michigan being called upon, Mr. GEORGE F. BAGLEY, of Detroit, responded:

He said he felt proud to represent Detroit, as she was the city in which the National Board of Trade was first conceived. It was born in Boston, the Athens of America, betrothed in Philadelphia, that city of brotherly love, and he was happy to assist at its nuptials in Cincinnati. (Laughter and applause.) Detroit would watch with great interest the career of the National Board of Trade. In behalf of his State, he desired to hereby thank Cincinnati for the generous hospitalities which had been extended to the gentlemen of the Board who were now sojourning in this city.

Chicago being called, Mr. CHARLES RANDOLPH responded:

The members of the Board, he said, had at this convention, to-day, been talking on time, and if, on this occasion, he exceeded five minutes they had liberty to call time on him. (Laughter.) He could not consent to occupy more than sufficient time to thank the City Council of Cincinnati, and the citizens, for the splendid reception and entertainment of the evening. He thanked them on behalf of the Board of Trade, for the exceeding good taste that had been manifested in entertaining this body. They had come here for the purpose of transacting certain definite and important business. They did not come here to engage in festivities, and the citizens had acted accordingly. They had not interfered with the business of the Board, but by judicious management had entertained them well, and at the same time allowed them to proceed uninterruptedly with the business for which they had assembled in this city.

My friend, Mr. ALLEN, continued Mr. RANDOLPH, was exceedingly liberal in his ideas of what the Board of Trade would do if it had the power, and if he could control it. (Laughter.) I thank him for his liberality, in behalf of the whole country, but I can only say that I think he is a little extravagant in the matter of those six tracks to the magnificent railroad proposed to run from East to West, connecting the Atlantic and Pacific Oceans. We in Chicago have concluded that five are enough — three of them passing through St. Louis, and two of them through Chicago, and my word for it, we will beat you at that. (Loud laughter.) Some times, I know, our young city which has grown with such rapid strides, is charged with being somewhat on the high pressure principle. (Cheers and laughter.) It is some times said we are a little on the spread eagle style out there, but so far as I am concerned commend me to the Golden Eagle of Cincinnati, whose sparkling examples have been so abundantly displayed here. (Laughter.)

We produce no such products as this. In manufactures of all kinds, Cincinnati is far ahead of us, and far our superior, and, what is more, we never expect to overtake her in this direction. We say to you, go on, the field is broad; you have the country south of you, which we trust, has been regenerated and is now being reorganized, and it is a field worthy of your utmost endeavor, and we say to you, go up and occupy the land. We trust you will be successful beyond your most sanguine expectations. (Loud applause.)

Loud calls were then made for General CLINTON B. FISK. In response he said, if he spoke at all, it would be to respond for San Francisco, inasmuch as they had everything in San Francisco, including some things which we had not in Cincinnati, and among those things were genuine earthquakes. (Laughter.) In the character of their citizens there were blended the stern industry and thrift of

Boston, the wide-awake go-aheaditiveness of New York, the solid soberness of Philadelphia, the generous hospitality of Cincinnati, and the retiring modesty of Chicago (laughter,) and a good many other things. They were very grateful out there on the Pacific coast, that the people of the East and the North were stretching out their iron hands toward them. He trusted the National Board of Trade would do all in its power to induce Congress to give them, not one railroad only, but three great thoroughfares through the land. (Cheers.)

He believed that by the construction of a railroad from the northern limits of this country, across to Portland on the Pacific coast, and by the construction of another railroad by the thirty-fifth parallel, railways might be had that would run every month in the year. He had to express the gratitude of the far West to Chicago and St. Louis for stretching out their hands to them.

The General continued in an eloquent strain concluding with —

"Lord of the universe, shield us and guide us,
   Trusting thee always through shadow and sun,
Thou hast united us; who shall divide us?
   Keep us, oh keep us, many in one!
Then up with our banner bright,
Spangled with starry light,
Spread its fair emblem from mountain to shore;
   While through the sounding sky
   Loud rings the nation's cry,
Union and liberty, one evermore." (Applause.)

Mr. HENRY T. BUELL, of Albany, responded for the Board of Trade of that city.

The city of Albany, by its delegates to the National Board of Trade, merely desires to return its hearty thanks to the City Council, the Chamber of Commerce and the citizens of Cincinnati, for the kind attentions and courtesies extended to them during their visit to this beautiful Queen City of the West.

Coming, as we do, from one of the oldest, if not the very oldest city in the United States, quaintly described in the old geography as a city of eight hundred houses and four thousand inhabitants, all standing with their gables to the street, we are probably more strongly impressed than the gentlemen from the progressive cities of the West, with the wonderful development we see on every hand. The noble public edifices, the commodious business houses, the general beauty and elegance of the private residences, all bear witness to the wealth and culture of your people.

We have constant evidence of their kindness and hospitality, their liberty and public spirit. We have learned that the rapid growth of the West, illustrating Bishop Berkeley's line,

"Westward the course of Empire takes its way,"

promises to remove at no distant day the power of the country to the Great West. So we rejoice in being able to claim a distinct interest in it as part of our glorious Republic.

Mr. A. O. BRANNIN, of Louisville, who was next called upon, tendered, on behalf of Kentucky, most cordial thanks for the reception given them on this occasion. Cincinnati and Louisville were only separated by one hundred and fifty miles of water communication; shortly they would be divided by only one hundred and eight miles of railway. (Cheers.)

Mr. BRANNIN drew an interesting picture of the growth of the West, and believed that when the obstructions and barriers of trade, which it was the aim of the National Board of Trade to remove, were removed, there was one grand career of prosperity open before the country.

*The Land of Penn:*

Was responded to by Mr. GEORGE L. BUZBY, of Philadelphia:

He thought the members of the National Board of Trade could not be accused of indolence. After able and varied discussion on financial and commercial matters all day, he came here to listen to still more eloquence, precisely as if nothing had been said during the day. At this stage of proceedings he was warned that a speech would be about as welcome as a second sermon when the audience were only waiting for the benediction. He would resume his seat after thanking Cincinnati for the hospitality she had so liberally dispensed.

*The Empire State:*

Was responded to by Mr. A. P. GRANT, of Oswego:

He expressed his gratification at what he had seen in Cincinnati; its many imposing structures unmistakably indicated its wealth and progress, and most heartily did he pray for its every prosperity.

Mr. J. S. T. STRANAHAN, of New York, also made an appropriate address, after which Mr. KECK, of the Common Council, in a humorous little speech, adjourned the meeting — a gathering long to be remembered by all who participated.

The above report has been compiled from the Cincinnati papers of the following morning.

# INDEX.

# INDEX.

|  | PAGE. |
|---|---|
| Address of Welcome, | 1 |
| Adjournment, | 337 |
| Admission of Members, | 22, 69 |
| Allen, Mr. G. N., Remarks on Direct Importations, | 258 |
| Allen, Mr. T., | |
|     Remarks on Finance, | 141 |
|     Speech at Banquet, | 356 |
| Alluvial Lands of the Mississippi, | 329 |
| Amendment to Constitution, | |
|     Adopted, | 329 |
|     Proposed, | 324, 328 |
| American Shipping, | 5, 47, 177, 308 |
| Atlanta Exchange, Application for Membership, | 25 |
| Bagley, Mr. G. F., | |
|     Proposition on Finance, | 95 |
|     Remarks on the Copper Interest, | 319 |
|     Speech at Banquet, | 359 |
| Baltimore Corn Exchange admitted, | 22 |
| Banquet at Music Hall, | 347 |
| Bayou Manchac, Restoration of, | 311 |
| Bills, Tariff and Revenue, | 323 |
| Bounty on Shipbuilding, | 308 |
| Branch, Mr. J. R., | |
|     Remarks on Cash Sales, | 38 |
|         "    " Finance, | 139 |
| Brannin, Mr. A. O., Remarks on Finance, | 97 |
| Bridges across the Mississippi, | 275 |
| Brigham, Mr. W. M., Remarks on Cash Sales, | 38 |
| Brown, Mr. J. B., | |
|     Remarks on Finance, | 135 |
|     Speech at Banquet, | 350 |
| Brunot, Mr. F. R., | |
|     Remarks on Finance, | 119 |
|         "    " River Improvements, | 268 |
|         "    " the Disaster on the Ohio River, | 175 |
|         "    " " Shipping Interest, | 205 |
| Buell, Mr. H. T., Remarks on the Telegraphic Service, | 226 |
|     Speech at Banquet, | 361 |
| Burwell, Mr. W. M., | |
|     Remarks on Direct Importations, | 258 |
|         "    " Finance, | 152 |
|     Resolutions on Reciprocal Trade, | 307 |

## 366 INDEX.

PAGE.

Buzby, Mr. G. L.,
    Remarks on Cash Sales, ................................................................ 34
    " " Finance, ................................................................ 112
    Speech at Banquet, ................................................................ 359
By-laws adopted, ................................................................ 25, 173
Cairo Chamber of Commerce admitted, ................................................................ 72
Canadian Finance, ................................................................ 217
Canal Improvements, ................................................................ 304, 333
Canal, Niagara Ship, ................................................................ 318
Carpenter, Mr. G. O., Resolution thanking Telegraph Lines, ................................................................ 176
Carrington, Mr. C. S., Speech at Banquet, ................................................................ 351
Cash Sales of Produce, Debate on, ................................................................ 29
Cental Measurement of Grain, ................................................................ 5
Chalmers, Mr. J. R., Remarks on Finance, ................................................................ 100
Cincinnati Chamber of Commerce,
    Propositions from, ................................................................ 279
    Reception of, ................................................................ 341
    Thanks to, ................................................................ 307
Cincinnati, Municipal Authorities of,
    Banquet of, ................................................................ 347
    Invitation from, ................................................................ 67
    Thanks to, ................................................................ 307
Civil Service Reform, ................................................................ 6, 26, 335
Cobia, Mr. H., Toast at Banquet, ................................................................ 351
Committees,
    On Admissions, ................................................................ 19
    " American Shipping, ................................................................ 49
    " Currency and Finance, ................................................................ 163
    " Improved Water Communication, ................................................................ 317
    " Telegraphic Reform, ................................................................ 67
Congressional Action on Finance, ................................................................ 224
Constitution Amended, ................................................................ 329
Copper Tariff, The, ................................................................ 28, 319
Council Bluffs Board of Trade, Application for Membership, ................................................................ 71
Crichton, Mr. W., Remarks on Maritime Law, ................................................................ 59
Davis, Mr. G. F.,
    Remarks on Finance, ................................................................ 92
    " " Maritime Law, ................................................................ 54
    " " River Improvements, ................................................................ 268
Davis, Mr. G. W., Remarks on Finance, ................................................................ 151
Dawson, Mr. T. W., Remarks on Finance, ................................................................ 109
Debates,
    On American Ocean Commerce, ................................................................ 204
    " Cash Sales of Produce, ................................................................ 29
    " Civil Service Reform, ................................................................ 26
    " Direct Importations, ................................................................ 256
    " Finance and Currency, ................................................................ 75, 214
    " Maritime Law, ................................................................ 49
    " Pacific Railroads, ................................................................ 238
    " Telegraphic Service, ................................................................ 63, 225
    " the Copper Tariff, ................................................................ 319

# INDEX. 367

| | PAGE. |
|---|---|
| Delegates in attendance, | 2 |
| Delegates, Substitution of, | 325 |
| Direct Importations to the Interior, | 4, 256 |
| Disaster on the Ohio River, | 175, 279 |

Drake, Mr. E. F.,
 Remarks on Cash Sales, ..... 30
  " " Civil Service Reform, ..... 26, 335
  " " Finance, ..... 149
  " " Telegraphic Reform, ..... 66, 226

Duvall, Mr. H., Speech at Banquet, ..... 359
Drawback on Shipbuilding Materials, ..... 193
Dubuque Board of Trade admitted, ..... 23
Duration of Sessions, ..... 310
Election of President, ..... 10
Election of Vice-Presidents, ..... 13
Erie and Oswego Canals, ..... 304, 333
Executive Council, Annual Report of, ..... 4

Fisk, Mr. C. B.,
 Remarks on Finance, ..... 160
  " " Pacific Railroads, ..... 251
 Speech at Banquet, ..... 360

Fraley, Mr. F.,
 Address at Adjournment, ..... 336
  " " Music Hall Reception, ..... 343
  " " on Reëlection, ..... 15
 Proposition on Finance, ..... 326
 Remarks on Finance, ..... 124
 Speech at Banquet, ..... 348

Galveston Chamber of Commerce admitted, ..... 72

Gano, Mr. J. A.,
 Address at Music Hall, ..... 341
  " of Welcome, ..... 1
 Proposition for River Improvements, ..... 274
 Remarks on Finance, ..... 157

Grant, Mr. A. P., Remarks on Finance, ..... 111

Guthrie, Mr. S. S.,
 Remarks on Cash Sales, ..... 41
  " " Finance, ..... 156

Hand, Mr. J. C., Remarks on Finance, ..... 116

Hazard, Mr. G. S.,
 Remarks on Cash Sales, ..... 36, 40
  " " Finance, ..... 155
 Resolutions on Canal Improvements, ..... 304, 333

Hill, Mr. H. A.,
 Elected Secretary and Treasurer, ..... 6
 Paper on American Shipping, ..... 178
 Speech at Banquet, ..... 353

Hincken, Mr. E.,
 Remarks on American Shipping, ..... 47, 73, 177
  " " Cash Sales of Produce, ..... 33
  " " Civil Service Reform, ..... 27, 335
  " " Finance, ..... 108

# INDEX.

Hoffman, Mr. C. J.,
 Remarks on Cash Sales, ............................................. 30, 39
  "  " Finance, ..................................................... 111
Holton, Mr. E. D.,
 Remarks on Cash Sales, ............................................. 39
  "  " Finance, ........................................... 106, 159, 214
  "  " Internal Improvements, .......................... 263, 331
 Speech at Banquet, ................................................... 358
Hughes, Mr. R. W., Remarks on Finance, ................................ 110
Immunity of private property at sea, Debate on, ........................ 49
Incorporation of the Board, ............................................ 6, 28
India Cloth, Duty on, .................................................. 320
Kanawha Canal, ......................................................... 278
Keck, Mr. J. L., Speech at Banquet, .................................... 350
Kirkland, Mr. R. R.,
 Remarks on American Shipping, ..................................... 208
  "  " Cash Sales, ....................................... 37
  "  " Direct Importations, ............................ 257
  "  " Finance, ......................................... 79
  "  " Maritime Law, ................................. 50, 61
Kreikhaus, Mr. A., Remarks on Finance, ................................. 147
List of Delegates, ..................................................... 2
Loney, Mr. F. B., Remarks on Finance, .................................. 76
Manchac Bayou, Restoration of, ......................................... 311
Manson, Mr. B. T., Remarks on Finance, ................................. 137
Maritime Law, Debate on, ............................................... 49
Mayo, Rev. A. D., Speech at Banquet, ................................... 358
McGraw, Mr. T., Proposition on Finance, ................................ 95
Meier, Mr. A.,
 Remarks on Finance, ............................................ 75, 161
  "  " Pacific Railroads, .............................. 239
Members admitted, .................................................... 22, 69
Minneapolis Board of Trade, Application for Membership, ................ 90
Mississippi River,
 Alluvial lands of, ................................................ 329
 Improvement of, .............................................. 260, 311
 Navigation of, .................................................... 274
 Passes of, ........................................................ 312
Mobile Board of Trade, Application for Membership, ..................... 72
Monroe, Mr. T., Speech on Internal Improvements, ....................... 283
Munn, Mr. I. Y.,
 Remarks on Cash Sales, ............................................ 32
  "  " Finance, ......................................... 90
National Banking Law, Change recommended, .............................. 224
Nazro, Mr. C. G.,
 Remarks on American Shipping, ..................................... 204
  "  " Finance, ......................................... 83
  "  " Maritime Law, .................................... 57
Niagara Ship Canal, .................................................... 318
Nomination of Officers, ............................................. 9, 11
Norfolk Board of Trade admitted, ....................................... 70

## INDEX.

|  | PAGE. |
|---|---|
| Officers elected, | 10, 13 |
| Order of Business, | 17 |
| Pacific and Atlantic Telegraph, | 12, 176 |
| Pacific Railroads, | 6, 170, 238 |
| Parr, Mr. I. M., Remarks on Cash Sales, | 33, 40 |
| Peters, Mr. G., Remarks on Finance, | 110 |

Plumer, Mr. A.,
  Remarks on Cash Sales, .................................................. 42
    "  " Civil Service Reform, ................................... 335
    "  " Finance, .............................................. 85

Porter, Mr. J. J.,
  Remarks on Cash Sales, .................................................. 33
    "  " Direct Importations, .......................... 259
    "  " River Improvements, .......................... 278, 281
    "  " Steamboat Disaster, ........................... 176

| President, Election of, | 10 |
|---|---|
| Produce, Cash Sales of, | 29 |
| Railroad Bridges, | 276 |
| Railroad Interests, Speech on, | 164 |
| Railroad Iron, Free Admission of, | 44 |
| Railroads, Pacific, | 6, 170, 238 |

Randolph, Mr. C.,
  Remarks on Cash Sales, .................................................. 34
    " . " Finance, .............................................. 86
    "  " Pacific Railroads, ................................. 244
    "  " Railroad Bridges, ................................. 276
  Speech at Banquet, .................................................. 359

| Raum, Mr. G. B., Speech on Finance, | 129 |
|---|---|
| Reception at Music Hall, | 341 |
| Reciprocal Trade, Proposition for, | 307 |
| Reform in the Civil Service, | 6, 26, 335 |
| Reform in the Telegraph, | 63, 224 |
| Remission of Duties on Shipbuilding, | 193 |

Reports,
  Of the Executive Council, ............................................. 4
  " " Treasurer, ................................................. 7
  On American Shipping, ................................................. 177
  " Finance, ............................................................ 214
  " the Telegraphic Service, .......................................... 224

Resolutions Adopted,
  On Cash Sales of Produce, ............................................ 29
  " Civil Service Reform, ............................................. 335
  " Currency and Finance, ............................................. 214, 224
  " Direct Importations, .............................................. 259
  " Maritime Law, ..................................................... 61
  " Pacific Railroads, ................................................ 238
  " the Alluvial Lands of the Mississippi, ........................... 330
  " " Navigation of the Mississippi, ................................. 274
  " " Ohio River Disaster, ........................................... 279
  " " Shipping Interest, ............................................. 203, 308
  " " Transportation of Petroleum, ................................... 175
  " Uniformity in Trade Statistics ..................................... 333

47

# 370 INDEX.

                                                  PAGE.

Ronald, Mr. F. S. J.,
    Remarks on Cash Sales, ................................................. 41
        "    " Finance, ............................................... 95

Ropes, Mr. J. S.,
    Proposition on Finance, ................................................. 163
    Remarks on Finance, ................................................ 81, 161
        "    " Maritime Law, ......................................... 54

Sessions, Length of, ............................................................ 310
Shipping, American, ............................................. 5, 47, 177, 203, 308

Shryock, Mr. L. R.,
    Remarks on Bayou Manchac, ............................................. 312
        "    " the Navigation of the Mississippi, ... . .................. 275
        "    " " Telegraphic Service, ..................................... 225

Springfield Board of Trade, Application for Membership, ..................... 23, 70

Stanard, Mr. E. O.,
    Remarks on Cash Sales, ................................................. 31
        "    " Finance, ............................................... 145
        "    " River Improvements, ................................... 266

Statistics of Population, &c., .................................................. 262
Statistics of Tonnage, .......................................................... 178
Steamboat Disaster, ............................................................ 175
Steam Commerce, American, ................................................... 182
Steam Commerce, British, ................................................ 183, 201

Stranahan, Mr. J. S. T.,
    Proposition on Finance, ................................................. 162
    Remarks on Finance, ..................................................... 109
    Speech at Banquet, ...................................................... 362

Subsidies to Steamship Lines, ................................................. 196
Substitution of Delegates, ..................................................... 325
Tare on Cotton, .............................................................. 323
Taussig, Mr. W., Remarks on Finance, ......................................... 142
Tax on Whiskey, ................................................................ 4

Taylor, Mr. J. W.,
    Proposition on Finance, ................................................. 164
    Remarks on Finance, ..................................................... 216
        "    " Maritime Law, .......................................... 53
    Speech at Banquet, ...................................................... 352

Telegraphic Courtesies, ................................................... 12, 21
Telegraphic Reform, ...................................................... 63, 224
Thanks to citizens of Cincinnati, ............................................. 307
    " the President, ....................................................... 336
    " " Secretary and the press, ............................................ 337

Thurston, Mr. G. H.,
    Letter offering use of wires, ............................................ 12
    Speech on Telegraphic Service, .......................................... 228

Topp, Mr. R.,
    Proposition on Finance, ................................................. 106
    Remarks on Pacific Railroads, ........................................... 248

Trade Statistics, Uniformity in, .............................................. 333
Treasurer's Report, ............................................................. 7

INDEX. 371

Trezevant, Mr. J. T.,
 Remarks on American Shipping,...................................208
  " " Finance,....................................104
  " " Maritime Law,.......................52, 60
  " " the Mississippi,...................................261
 Speech at Banquet,...................................356
Turpin, Mr. V. A., Remarks on Finance,...................................87
Two-thirds vote, By-law requiring,...................................25
Uniformity in Trade Statistics,...................................333
Uniformity in laws governing Corporations,...................................333
Union Pacific Railway, Diversion of line,...................................332
Vice-Presidents elected,...................................13
Virginia Central Water Route,...................................291
Votes of Thanks,...................176, 256, 307, 335, 337
Walbridge, Mr. H.,
 Remarks on Pacific Railroads,...................................252
 Speech on Railroad Interests,...................................164
War, Effect of on American Shipping,...................................185
Water Communication, Committee on,...................................317
Weights and Measures, Metric System of,...................................334
Wetherill, Mr. J. P.,
 Remarks on American Shipping,...................................209
  " " Civil Service Reform,...................................26
  " " Finance,...................................117
  " " Improvement of the Mississippi...................................272
  " " Pacific Railroads,...................................241
  " " Telegraphic Reform,...................................64
Whiskey, Tax on,...................................4
Wilbor, Mr. S.,
 Remarks on Cash Sales,...................................42
  " " Finance,...................................157
Wilstach, Mayor, Speech at Banquet,...................................347
Winsor, Mr. H.,
 Remarks on Finance,...................................117
  " " Maritime Law,...................................58
Wisconsin and Fox River Route,...................................290
Yeas and Nays,
 On American Shipping,...................................212, 309
 " Cash Sales of Produce,...................................43
 " Civil Service Reform,...................................27
 " Currency and Finance,...................................219, 327
 " Pacific Railroads,...................................254
 " Telegraphic Reform,...................................237
 " Union Pacific Railroad,...................................332

Lightning Source UK Ltd.
Milton Keynes UK
UKHW012149201118
332686UK00007B/400/P